Leabharlanna Poiblí Chathair Bhaile Átha Cliath
Dublin City Public Libraries

Comhairle Cathrach
Bhaile Átha Cliath
Dublin City Council

Marino Branch
Brainse Marino
Tel: 8336297

73

Due Date	Due Date	Due Date

MANCHESTER
1824

Manchester University Press

Church, state and social science in Ireland

Knowledge institutions and the rebalancing
of power, 1937–73

PETER MURRAY AND MARIA FEENEY

Manchester University Press

The right of Peter Murray and Maria Feeney to be identified as the authors of this work has been asserted by them in accordance with the Copyright, Designs and Patents Act 1988.

Published by Manchester University Press
Altrincham Street, Manchester M1 7JA
www.manchesteruniversitypress.co.uk

British Library Cataloguing-in-Publication Data
A catalogue record for this book is available from the British Library

ISBN 978 1 5261 0078 8 hardback
ISBN 978 1 5261 2172 1 paperback

First published by Manchester University Press in hardback 2017
This edition first published 2019

Typeset by Out of House Publishing
Printed in Great Britain
by TJ International Ltd, Padstow

For Mary, Joan, Timmy, Cisco, Marta, Susan and Kate

Contents

Tables

Abbreviations

AOH	Ancient Order of Hibernians
ATGWU	Amalgamated Transport and General Workers' Union
CDC	Central Development Committee
CDT	County Development Team
CICA	Commission to Inquire into Child Abuse
CII	Civics Institute of Ireland
CIU	Council of Irish Unions
COFLA	Cardinal O'Fiach Memorial Library and Archive (Armagh)
CRD	Council for Research and Development
CSG	Catholic Social Guild
CSO	Central Statistics Office
CSSC	Catholic Social Service Conference
CSWB	Catholic Social Welfare Bureau
CWC	Catholic Workers' College
DATI	Department of Agriculture and Technical Instruction
DDA	Dublin Diocesan Archives
DET&E	Department of Enterprise, Trade and Employment
DF	Department of Finance
DFA	Department of Foreign Affairs
DIC	Department of Industry and Commerce
DICS	Dublin Institute of Catholic Sociology
DL	Department of Labour
DT	Department of the Taoiseach
ECA	European Cooperation Administration
EDB	Economic Development Branch (Department of Finance)
EPA	European Productivity Agency
ERI	Economic Research Institute
ERP	European Recovery Programme
ESRI	Economic and Social Research Institute
EVS	European Values Survey
FFA	Ford Foundation Archives

HSC	National Joint Committee on the Human Sciences and Their Application to Industry
ICA	Irish Countrywomen's Association
ICMC	International Catholic Migration Commission
IDA	Industrial Development Authority
IIRS	Institute of Industrial Research and Standards
IMI	Irish Management Institute
INPC	Irish National Productivity Committee
IPA	Institute of Public Administration
ITGWU	Irish Transport and General Workers' Union
ITUC	Irish Trade Union Congress
IWL	Irish Workers' League
LDA	Limerick Diocesan Archives
LRS	Limerick Rural Survey
MSRB	Medico-Social Research Board
NAI	National Archives of Ireland
NBSCCCI	National Board for Safeguarding Children in the Catholic Church in Ireland
NDS	Newman Demographic Survey
NFA	National Farmers' Association
NLI	National Library of Ireland
NLP	National Labour Party
NUI	National University of Ireland
OECD	Organisation for Economic Co-operation and Development
OEEC	Organisation for European Economic Co-operation
OSTP	Office for Scientific and Technical Personnel
QUB	Queen's University Belfast
RDS	Royal Dublin Society
RIA	Royal Irish Academy
SRC	Social Research Committee
SRDF	Special Regional Development Fund
SSISI	Statistical and Social Inquiry Society of Ireland
TA	Technical Assistance
UCC	University College Cork
UCD	University College Dublin
UCG	University College Galway
UCG SSRC	UCG Social Sciences Research Centre
VEC	Vocational Education Committee
WUI	Workers' Union of Ireland

1

Introduction

Knowledge, they say, is power. One manifestation of the power of the Catholic Church within the independent Irish state in the middle decades of the twentieth century was the virtual monopoly its clergy and the educational institutions under their control possessed over the discipline of sociology. The first university posts in this discipline were filled in 1937, the year in which the voters of the twenty-six-county state ratified a new constitution that blended Anglo-American liberal democratic norms with distinctive new provisions reflecting Catholic teaching. Verbal genuflection before the social prescriptions of papal encyclicals was to be found in this document although, as Joe Larragy (2014: 201) notes, 'Catholic social *power* rather than Catholic social *teaching* was the prevalent factor in the Irish case and for a long time the formula suited an authoritarian church in a parsimonious state dominated by the rural petit bourgeoisie.' But times, churches and states change. In 1973, when both parts of Ireland entered what was then the European Economic Community (EEC), a secular, professional association of Irish sociologists was also founded.

In this book the rebalancing of power between Church and state in the period between 1937 and 1973 is explored through a case study of the Irish knowledge institutions that engaged in social science teaching and research. Here the aspect of the Catholic Church of greatest relevance is what John Whyte (1980: 16–21) termed the 'grip on education of unique strength' it possessed within the southern Irish state. Securing this grip was a great reservoir of clerical person power and a laity hierarchically mobilised and disciplined by devotional innovation and institutional expansion (Mac Giolla Phadraig 1995; Inglis 1998). Leading a movement that constituted the most significant source of popular pressure on that educational system, Gaelic League President Douglas Hyde in 1906 wrote that 'they [the priests and the church] are always on the spot, they have the women behind them, they can do almost what they like'.[1] The critically important feature of the southern Irish state is its developmental strategy shift from the late 1950s. At this time an uncoupling of public policy from the cultural, political and religious aspirations that fuelled the nationalist struggle for Irish self-government and shaped government policies in the early decades of independence took place. Newly installed at the centre of the state's project were membership of the EEC, the attraction of export-orientated investment from transnational corporations and the gearing of education to create a labour force that met the requirements of such investors.

With the new state's activism in the education field mainly channelled into attempts to revive the Irish language (Akenson 1975), the southern Irish educational system that began to be transformed in the 1960s was up to that point very largely unchanged from the form in which it had been inherited from the now truncated United Kingdom. It is therefore with the United Kingdom of the 1801–1922 period and the manner in which its governments struggled with, and eventually settled, the Irish University Question that examination of Irish sociology's origins needs to begin.

Churches and the British state in Irish higher education

According to Boylan (1999: 1) '[T]he two most significant developments in Irish education during the course of the 19th century were the creation of a national system of primary education in the early 1830s, and the establishment of the Queen's Colleges at Belfast, Cork and Galway in the mid 1840s.' Underlying government educational reform efforts were the principles of denominationally mixed education within a hierarchically integrated national structure. Opposed to them were the denominational agendas of the Anglican, Catholic and Presbyterian Churches. In the university case, Ireland already had the University of Dublin with its single college (Trinity) and its alignment for more than two and a half centuries with the established Anglican Church. The Queen's Colleges were therefore intended to cater for Catholics and, in the Belfast case, for Presbyterians. Within both these churches opinion was divided as to the acceptability of the new creations. In the Catholic case concessions were sought from and refused by the government before Rome came down on the side of the scheme's opponents. With the Presbyterians, acceptance won the day, although a college (Magee) analogous to the Catholic national seminary, St. Patrick's College Maynooth, in the complete control that the General Assembly exercised over it, was also established in Derry. Having rejected the Queen's Colleges, the Catholic bishops founded a Catholic University in Dublin in 1854, appointing a high-profile English convert from Anglicanism, John Henry Newman, as its first Rector. Newman's *Idea of a University* lives on as a monument to his time in Dublin but, hamstrung by lack of endowments and an absence of recognition for its degrees, the university in the form in which it was founded could not flourish.

Disestablishment of the Church of Ireland in 1869 was followed by the passage in 1872 of Fawcett's Act, which removed all religious tests from Dublin University. The effect of this change was to make Trinity College even less acceptable to the Catholic hierarchy than it had previously been. In their eyes it now resembled the Queen's Colleges in its godlessness and the first version of the Irish Catholic Church's 'Trinity ban' dates from this time. As originally formulated in 1875, and reaffirmed by the Maynooth Synod in 1927, this prohibited Catholic clerics from advising or facilitating students in any way to go to Trinity College (Burke 1990).

Religion versus scientific rationalism

During the 1860s a new factor further complicated the Irish University Question – the rise in Britain of scientific rationalism or Huxleyism. An intellectual movement that increasingly became a professional network as its leading adherents acquired a growing number of academic posts throughout the British Empire (Jones 2001:190–191; O'Leary 2012: 40–41), Huxleyism promoted a reform of scientific education 'which required that the older universities move away from their original character as religious foundations for the training of clergymen and that the curriculum in "sensitive subjects", in particular those which touched on Creation and on human origins, be rid of the influence of theology' (Jones 2001: 189). In August 1874 one of Huxley's closest associates, the Irish-born John Tyndall, delivered a Presidential address to the British Association for the Advancement of Science in Belfast in which 'he exhorted his fellow scientists to "wrest from theology the entire domain of cosmological theory"' and 'envisaged "the mild light of science" as a powerful liberating influence on the youth of Ireland, and as an effective bulwark against any future "intellectual or spiritual tyranny" which might threaten the welfare of Irish society' (O'Leary 2012: 30; Brown 2005). In October the Irish hierarchy issued a pastoral letter that responded to Tyndall and presented his views as a vindication of their demands for Catholic clerical control over the environment in which Catholics received their higher education that the government had rejected when the Queen's Colleges were established. Tyndall's speech was influenced by what he perceived to be the neglect of science at the Catholic University in Dublin (O'Leary 2012: 30). The failure of the Devonshire Commission to recommend funding for the Catholic University's science faculties had in the same year prompted a Catholic periodical, *The Tablet*, to comment that 'denied endowment and legal recognition, the Catholic University, should, in the opinion of the Royal Commission found and endow chairs open to Messrs. Carpenter, Tyndall, Huxley and Herbert Spencer and all the scientific rationalists of the day' (quoted in Jones 2001: 192).

To sociologists one name stands out here – that of Herbert Spencer, who normally commands a place in any wide-ranging treatment of the classical nineteenth- and early twentieth-century age of sociological theory (e.g. Coser 1977: 88–127; Ashley and Orenstein 1990: 141–171) and is usually the only English theorist to do so. Spencer (1820–1903) was a political Liberal – later a Liberal Unionist – with a strong leaning towards the minimal role of government favoured by *laissez-faire* economists. His social background was that of provincial English Dissenting Protestantism and in his working life he was at various times a railway engineer, an inventor and a journalist. His social circle included leading British natural scientists of his day and aspects of his evolutionary theory of social development are said to have anticipated the biological theory of the evolution of animal species put forward by Charles Darwin, whose work was publicly championed and popularised by T. H. Huxley. Like Huxley, Spencer embraced the agnosticism which, despite its limited appeal in Ireland, was a recurring preoccupation among and a regular target of attack for Irish Catholic writers (O'Leary 2012: 77–80). Spencer never held an academic post but *The Tablet's* reference to the possibility that he might was, as we will see, not to be the last made to him in the course of Irish university controversies.

The Royal University and the Department of Agriculture and Technical Instruction

At the end of the 1870s new legislation ushered in a major reorganisation of Irish university education. The three Queen's Colleges were under the direction of the Dublin-based Queen's University, whose Senate 'not only had complete control over examinations leading to degrees and diplomas but prescribed the courses that students must follow in the colleges before they might present themselves for these examinations' (Moody and Beckett 1959: 225). This was now abolished and replaced in 1882 by the Royal University. Following the London model, this was an examining body whose examinations were taken by students of the Queen's Colleges, of Magee and of the now renamed Catholic University – in all of which the Royal University funded fellowships – as well by students from a variety of other colleges and individuals pursuing private study. As Moody and Beckett (1959: 289) note, 'the principle that public money must not be used to subsidise sectarian colleges was at last abandoned, though not openly or explicitly'. At the same time 'the fellowship system rescued the catholic University College [Dublin] from a situation that had become desperate and started it on a new career in which it quickly became the rival of the Queen's Colleges for the rewards of the Royal University'. The Senate of the Royal University was, like the Boards which presided over primary and secondary schooling, 'balanced' with an equal number of Protestant and Catholic members. Unloved on either side of the divide, the Royal University nonetheless survived for nearly three decades as the period of Unionist 'killing Home Rule by kindness' passed without any new university education initiative.

That period did, however, witness important changes in the organisation of Irish science, within whose development three broad historical strands have been distinguished. The first has been variously termed the Anglo-Irish or Ascendancy strand. Its practitioners were drawn from the island's Protestant social elite and its practice had predominantly the character of a cultural accomplishment rather than that of a set of activities with practical, economically relevant applications (Yearley 1989: 319–320). Here Irish prominence within nineteenth-century astronomy is cited as a case in point. Trinity College, the Royal Dublin Society (RDS) and the Royal Irish Academy (RIA) were the institutional embodiments of this scientific strand. During the nineteen century a second 'administration' strand emerged. Here a set of science and arts institutions were taken over (mainly from the RDS) or newly established by the state. Initially the institutions concerned came under the control of a London-based department but, from the creation in 1899 of a Department of Agriculture and Technical Instruction (DATI) for Ireland, they were 'now being administered as a group by the new department as instruments for the general improvement of Irish science' (N. Whyte 1999: 13). Most of this group clustered around the Leinster House headquarters of the RDS, and to their activities the DATI during its lifetime added new agricultural and fisheries research facilities. The state employees staffing these bodies were mainly English. Other functions of the DATI were to fund scientific and technical instruction in secondary schools and, working with the local authorities created or democratised by the 1898 Local Government Act, to found technical schools supported by a combination of centrally provided funds and local rates. The Technical Instruction Committees which proliferated after 1900 were, as we will see, to survive the department that stimulated their formation. A third strand in Irish science was that of Nationalist scientists, mainly drawn from the Catholics who comprised a majority of the population but a small minority of its scientific community (Finnegan and Wright 2015). The creation of the National University of Ireland in 1908 provided this strand with its major institutional base and it is to this final chapter of the story of the Irish University Question within the politics of the United Kingdom that we now turn.

The University Question settled?

After two Royal Commissions had investigated different aspects of Irish higher education in the 1900s, Liberal Chief Secretary James Bryce unveiled the government's reform proposals in January 1907. These envisaged the 'enlargement of the University of Dublin so as to include, as well as Trinity College, the Queen's Colleges of Belfast and Cork and University College, Dublin with Maynooth, Galway and Magee as "affiliated institutions"' (Moody and Beckett 1959: 381). Bryce, however, was on the point of leaving Ireland and the task of putting new legislation on the statute book fell to his successor, Augustine Birrell. The new Chief Secretary adopted a very different approach. Trinity, which had mounted a vigorous lobbying and pamphleteering campaign against the Bryce proposals, was left untouched. The Queen's Colleges in Cork and Galway were brought together with University College, Dublin (UCD) as constituent colleges of a formally non-denominational but *de facto* Catholic-orientated National University of Ireland (NUI) to which Maynooth was attached as a 'recognised college'. The Queen's College in Belfast became a third separate Irish university, again a formally non-denominational institution but generally regarded as coming under Presbyterian influence. Achieving a widely accepted settlement in an area of long-running contention, the Irish Universities Act, 1908 was a skilful exercise in the accommodation of conflicting interests but also a precursor of the island's partition.

The Trinity opposition to the Bryce proposals had been partly based on a claim to superior status – 'one of the first-fruits of the scheme is that our degree would be immediately conferred by Act of Parliament on thousands of persons who have never received our teaching nor passed our examinations. This is analogous to a debasing of the currency ... the value of the degree would be at once depreciated.'[2] But it also extended the pattern whereby 'subsequent [to 1874] inquiries into the universities in Ireland were dogged by the question of whether the Catholic bishops would allow the teaching of Darwinism and the generally hostile or evasive answers they gave to this question' (Jones 2001: 193). One Trinity statement proclaimed that 'if the University teaching is to be shared by Colleges which hold conflicting views, there must be constant occasions of strife and bitterness ... it is contrary to our best traditions that the boundaries of science should be fixed, directly or indirectly, by ecclesiastical authority, or the impulse of speculation arrested by clerical intervention'.[3]

Bryce himself had drawn a distinction between 'advanced subjects which are non-controversial' (i.e. where no Catholic/non-Catholic distinction applied) and less advanced ones – a category he elided with that of 'all subjects into which theological controversy may enter'. Mathematics, physics, modern and ancient languages he considered to be examples of the former. Into the latter category fell philosophy and history, where 'alternative graduation courses ought to be provided ... I believe that exists already in the case of the Royal University'. In this context Bryce thought the new university ought to retain the legislative provision that already prevented Queen's College teaching staff from misusing their positions.[4] Here Trinity critics charged that in Bryce's formulation the provision was to be substantially extended rather than being merely retained, and raised the position of 'a lecturer advising his class to read some passage in Herbert Spencer's works'. Because these works were on the Vatican's Index of Prohibited Books 'such advice would, from a legal point of view, certainly be "reasonably offensive" to the faith of the Roman Catholic students attending him'.[5]

Despite being yoked together by Bryce, the positions of history and philosophy were quite different. In history, whereas the Catholic University had developed a distinctive approach to the subject, the new dispensation of the 1880s took the curriculum 'out of the prelates' hands'. But this was a matter of little practical consequence as 'Catholic students simply did not attempt degrees in history from the Royal University of Ireland' (Barr 2003: 73–75). Defining the situation of philosophy was the call made in 1879 by Pope Leo XIII in one of his first encyclicals, *Aeterni Patris*, 'to reinstate, and to propagate far and wide, the golden wisdom of St. Thomas [Aquinas] – unto the greater glory of the Catholic faith, the advantage of society and the progress of all the sciences' (quoted in Magrath 1885: 3). A few years later the first Royal University examination papers attracted strong Catholic criticism, although not all Catholic commentators were convinced that abandoning a common programme, a common paper and common prizes were the best means to attain the pope's end. Fr. James B. Kavanagh, a Royal University Senator and former seminary professor of philosophy, argued that what was needed was the raising of the standard of philosophy in Irish Catholic colleges to the level attained in the Catholic countries of continental Europe. There 'the philosophical literature of France and Belgium contains many very able works on the modern developments of Mental Philosophy, and in refutation of its many errors', one example being how 'the theories of Herbert Spencer are exhaustively discussed and ably refuted by Abbé Blanc' (J. B. Kavanagh 1886: 29):

> This great Pope yearns for a highly educated Priesthood, who are able to combat error effectively and to 'give reason for the hope that is in them' ... the system of alternate papers means, if I rightly understand it, that papers in Philosophy for Catholic students should be set from Scholastic Philosophy and in Scholastic Terminology, and that the Catholic Student should not be required to understand modern

> Philosophical systems, or to know the language in which modern Philosophical errors are promulgated … How can a Catholic Priest give reason for the hope that is within him if a layman submit to him an article in the *Nineteenth Century* or the *Contemporary Review*, and ask him to explain and refute the Philosophical errors it advances, if the Priest has heard of the error for the first time, and is in utter ignorance of the whole subject or if, even though perfectly familiar with the true answer, he cannot apply his knowledge, because his training has been so limited that he knows nothing of the Philosophical language in which the article is written?
> (J. B. Kavanagh 1886: 19)

Nonetheless from 1887 a system in which candidates were examined on either scholastic or non-scholastic philosophy papers was instituted (Moody and Beckett 1959: 299). Dual arrangements survived the 1908 settlement in the case of Queen's University Belfast (QUB), where uncertainty over its ability to attract students disposed the predominantly Protestant authorities to partially accommodate representations received from the Catholic community through the establishment of a lectureship in scholastic philosophy. This controversial move was subjected to but survived both legal challenge and a degree of persistent opposition from within the university. While relatively few studied scholastic philosophy, Catholic students attended Queen's University in considerable numbers from the outset. The subject's accommodation helped foster cordial relations between that university and the Catholic diocese in which it was situated, with students for the priesthood from Down and Connor regularly graduating in Arts there as well as studying in Maynooth (Moody and Beckett 1959: 406–411; C. Daly 2009: 7–9).

The Catholic Church and an independent Irish state in Irish higher education

The institutional shape of science and higher education at the time the Irish Free State was created in 1922 is shown in Table 1.1

Alterations began when Leinster House was taken over from the RDS as the site of the new state's parliament. On security grounds, the adjacent Royal College of Science was also displaced from its premises in September 1922. In 1924 the Ministers and Secretaries Act overhauled the ramshackle Irish administrative system, replacing a large number of 'Castle Boards' with a much smaller number of government departments. In 1899 Horace Plunkett had been at pains to try to distinguish the DATI from the usual (and much reviled) Castle Board. His creation was now broken up, with most of the DATI's portfolio of cultural, educational and scientific institutions becoming the responsibility of the Department of Education. In 1926 the University Education (Agriculture

Table 1.1 Science and higher education institutions in Ireland, 1922

Science and arts institutions	Universities
Clustered around Leinster House, Dublin	National University of Ireland with
National Gallery	constituent University Colleges in
National Library	Cork (UCC) Dublin (UCD)
National Museum	Galway (UCG) and, with the status
Natural History Museum	of Recognised College, St. Patrick's
Royal College of Science	College, Maynooth
Botanic Gardens (Glasnevin, Dublin)	Dublin University/Trinity College (TCD),
Geological Survey (Hume Street, Dublin)	to which Magee College, Derry is linked
Albert Agricultural College (Ballymun,	Queen's University Belfast (QUB)
Dublin) and other DATI-administered	
agricultural and fisheries educational	
and research facilities	

and Dairy Science) Act transferred to UCD the Royal College of Science and another institution formerly attached to the DATI, Albert Agricultural College. UCD had filled a Chair of Agriculture in 1919 with a professor who retained his existing Albert Agricultural College posts. Its undergraduates had attended the specialised agriculture courses offered by the Royal College of Science after completing two years of general science study in UCD and qualified for both an associateship of the College and a degree of the university on passing their final examinations. But, as the Royal College of Science had been in the process of aligning itself with Trinity College, its merger with UCD was a shotgun marriage with the weapon being held in the hands of Cumann na Gaedheal ministers who were also UCD staff members (McCartney 1999: 112–113; N. Whyte 1999: 136–146). UCD's Engineering School occupied the old Royal College of Science buildings while UCD's acquisition of Albert Agricultural College and its north Dublin farm left agriculture students in Trinity College, which had the longest-established degree in the field, completing their studies in UCD under an ad hoc arrangement. The 1926 Act also transferred the dairy farming side of the Royal College of Science's work to University College Cork (UCC), which thereby acquired a faculty of Dairy Science.

A national framework created for adult education

It was also in 1926 that a Commission was established to review the other part of the DATI's legacy, the technical schools and the Technical Instruction

Committees under which they operated. Subsequently the Vocational Education Act, 1930 maintained and extended statewide the flexible system based on representative local government structures and supported by a mix of funding sources that had developed since 1899. A novel element was provided by the incorporation under the vocational umbrella of 'continuing' education alongside 'technical' education. The latter catered for those aged from sixteen upwards and was provided mainly on a part-time basis through night classes. The former was aimed at fourteen to sixteen year olds and consisted mainly of full-time day courses. Continuing education was thus potentially competitive with denominationally controlled primary and secondary schooling but 'having been given ministerial assurances on the limited role of the continuation education being provided under the 1930 Act, the Catholic hierarchy tolerated the system' (Coolahan 1981: 84). A strong clerical presence on local Vocational Education Committees (VECs) and departmental circulars which imparted a strong religious and cultural nationalist aura to vocational schools helped to sustain this tolerance or, at any rate, to inhibit public expressions of intolerance. During the 1940s the Department of Education itself seriously considered absorbing the continuing education side of vocational schooling into an expanded system of denominationally controlled primary education. Such an initiative did not materialise but 'pressure was maintained on the Minister and the Department during the 1950s so that the Minister was simultaneously attempting to satisfy the demands of the bishops and to reassure the threatened local authorities whose schools he was funding from public funds' (O'Buachalla 1985: 357).

The technical education provided for those aged sixteen and upwards was less contentious than continuing education but it did not escape criticism. The Technical Education Commission of the mid-1920s found it 'disquieting' that 'the large majority of the schools in the Saorstat are concerned with commerce and domestic economy and rarely with technology, art and craft work'. Two decades later the Commission on Vocational Organisation criticised the continuing preponderance of commerce and domestic economy and the absence of strong links to either the agricultural or the manufacturing sectors of the economy (Coolahan with O'Donovan 2009: 150 and 158–159). Higher technical education with a genuine technological content remained confined to Dublin and the other cities. where institutions like Dublin's Bolton Street and Kevin Street colleges 'served a national as well as a municipal role' (Coolahan 1981: 100). What VECs offered outside the cities was less strictly technical than adult education of a broadly popular type, which, around Cork and Galway but less so in the case of Dublin, was linked to NUI extra-mural initiatives from the mid-1940s. Central to the creation of such institutional linkage was the propagation of Catholic sociology.

The Catholic Church, Trinity College and the NUI

The post-independence period witnessed an intensification of the Catholic hierarchy's ban on Catholics attending Trinity College. As noted above, this originally applied only to the actions of the clergy. In 1944 Lenten Regulations promulgated in the Dublin archdiocese by Archbishop McQuaid stipulated that 'no Catholic may enter the Protestant University of Trinity College without the previous permission of the Ordinary of the Diocese', adding that 'any Catholic who disobeys this law is guilty of Mortal Sin'.[6] The next Plenary Synod, held in Maynooth in 1956, adopted the ban in this extended form nationally, specifying that only the Archbishop of Dublin was competent to give permission for attendance. The government's establishment of a Commission on Higher Education in 1960 prompted an intense anti-Trinity barrage made up of memoranda to the Commission from UCD President Michael Tierney, a series of articles in *Studies* by retired UCC President Alfred O'Rahilly and a particularly stark pastoral letter from Archbishop McQuaid.

Over time Archbishop McQuaid had moved from regarding the formally non-denominational NUI constituent colleges as providing a 'sufficiently safe' environment for Catholic students to describing UCD as the 'lawful heir' to the Catholic University that had preceded it. Facilitating this development were, first, the 'very special relationship' (McCartney 1999: 201) of the archbishop to UCD's President from 1947 to 1964, Michael Tierney, and, second, the liaison committee comprising NUI college presidents and selected bishops set up in 1950. Here the initiative had been taken by the college presidents, who had 'agreed that it was desirable to ask the help of the Hierarchy in formulating a policy on the future of the University'. The letter requesting this help specifically identified three 'matters which have become quite urgent in recent times' – the relationship between the Medical Schools of the NUI colleges and Catholic hospitals, 'the making of arrangements for the better and more thorough teaching of Philosophy and Sociology, especially for lay-students' and 'Trinity College, in particular its endowment from public funds and the possibility of an increase in this endowment'.[7] In relation to state financing of the universities, Cumann na Gaedhael in the 1920s and Fine Gael ministers in the first inter-party government (1948–51) were unabashed partisans of the NUI. Eamonn de Valera, however, was more sympathetically disposed towards Trinity College and the governments he headed more generous in the share of the small amount of funds provided to universities that it was allocated in the period after 1945. Bipartisan political support for liberal treatment of Trinity was to grow during the 1950s as a countervailing influence to the bishops' backing of NUI interests became operative.

Irish sociology has scholastic philosophy not Spencer for its founding father

In the late 1930s a chair in St. Patrick's College Maynooth and a lectureship in UCC inserted sociology into the complex of institutions and political forces just described. This insertion occurred solely on the Catholic side of a denomination-ally divided system. Spencer's name might be invoked in Trinity's Edwardian pamphleteering but that college did not make its first appointments in sociology until 1971. Outside economics its social science strengths lay in the fields of politics and public administration and Basil Chubb's representation of Trinity on the first Council of the Economic and Social Research Institute (ESRI) in 1966 reflected this. Representation on this Council for QUB was discounted as 'they teach only social Administration in Queen's'.[8] By contrast, that university's small Scholastic Philosophy Department supplied the Christus Rex Society of priest-sociologists with a long-serving first chairman (Cahal Daly) and two NUI social science professors elected to the ESRI Council in 1966 had either briefly taught scholastic philosophy in QUB (Jeremiah Newman of Maynooth) or would have done so if prior commitment to a Dublin VEC adult education social science initiative had not supervened (James Kavanagh of UCD).[9]

Papal strategy and Catholic sociology

With his first encyclical *Aeterni Patris*, Pope Leo XIII in 1879 had begun 'the radical restructuring of Catholic thought by the imposition of the philosophy and theology of St. Thomas Aquinas as the sole system of ideas mandatory on all seminaries and colleges for the training of the clergy' (McSweeney 1980: 61). His successor, Pope Pius X, reinforced this orthodoxy with his early twentieth-century onslaught on Modernism. Moreover 'the revival of Thomism by Pope Leo XIII was not a matter of peripheral interest in Church history affecting only clerics and their training … It was the centre of a political strategy intended to bring about a restoration of a Christian social order, an organic hierarchic society united by common values and common faith under the temporal king-ship of secular rulers and under the ultimate authority of the Pope' (McSweeney 1980: 68). Pursuit of this strategy accounts for 'the remarkable energy which the popes devoted to declarations not only on matters of doctrine but on a wide range of social, political and cultural issues'. Here 'no fewer than 185 papal encyclicals were issued between 1878 and 1958 as well as innumerable, messages radio broadcasts and speeches to a vast array of different audiences' (M. Conway 1996: 13). The different dimensions of a Leonine strategy that in its

Table 1.2 Elements of the Leonine papal strategy

Primary enemy	Socialism (and Communism)
Primary ally	Moderate bourgeoisie (reformist wing)
Cultural program	Philosophy of Thomas Aquinas
Political program	Christian democracy (or Catholic Action)
Economic program	Social Catholicism
Ecclesial program	Parallel structures (plus centralised ideological controls)

Source: Holland 2003: chart 2, 115

essentials remained operative into the late 1950s are encapsulated in Holland's (2003) chart (see Table 1.2).

Modifications applied to these elements within the specific Irish context, with its defining fusion of religion with ethnicity and its relegation of class to a secondary role. Irish socialism was weak and its leaders in the main proceeded not from an atheistic and/or anti-clerical hostility to the Catholic Church but rather sought (albeit in vain) to identify their project with Catholic values – socialism as 'applied Christianity' – and to stress the compatibility of their programme with the legitimate social reforms endorsed by Leo XIII in his landmark 1891 encyclical on economic and social issues, *Rerum Novarum*. On the other hand, the Free State government sought and secured the hierarchy's backing in 1931 for a 'red scare' based on a leftward shift in the stance of the clandestine Irish Republican Army (IRA). Later in the 1930s first Cumann na Gaedhael and then Fine Gael rhetoric would tar all anti-treaty republicans – Fianna Fail as well as IRA – with this brush. Violence against Catholic clerics during the Spanish Civil War, the imprisonment of central and eastern European prelates after the Second World War and the mistreatment of Irish missionaries in Communist China also became focal points for protest movements that helped to give the red menace a profile in Ireland out of all proportion to the strength of its local embodiments.

The Irish bourgeoisie was less divided into 'moderate' and 'extremist' wings than into Protestant and Catholic ones. Politically the Irish Catholic majority had accumulated power through the nineteenth century as its Penal Laws era disabilities were removed, local government institutions were reformed and enfranchisement qualifications were lowered. But, particularly in the urban context, Catholic advances in the political sphere were not accompanied by a corresponding growth in economic power. Especially in private sector manufacturing, transport, banking and insurance, the commanding heights of the economy long remained in Protestant hands and a sociologist studying the small Protestant minority south of the border could chart the continuing importance of the 'Protestant firm' until its decline set in as late as the 1960s and 1970s (Bowen 1983: 98–103).

From the beginning of the twentieth century a succession of organisations emerged to combat Catholic disadvantage – principally the Catholic Association, the Ancient Order of Hibernians (AOH) and the Knights of Saint Columbanus. *Three Railways and a Bank* was the title given to a pamphlet collecting articles published in 1901 by the weekly *Leader* alleging widespread discrimination against Catholics in the filling of coveted white-collar jobs. This prompted the formation of Catholic Shareholders Committees to demand the filling of railway clerkships by open competitive examination in tandem with the launching of a national Catholic Association which aimed to overthrow the economic and social ascendancy of Protestants and to give 'organic' expression to Catholic values in Irish life. Initial support for this wider project from the Catholic hierarchy gave way to a condemnation by Archbishop Walsh of Dublin, who accused the Catholic Association of being responsible for 'enormous injury' to Catholic interests after the aggressive tone adopted in its 1903 *Handbook* prompted a strong Protestant backlash. The archbishop's action left a movement which had adopted a non-political stance – 'the Catholic Unionist is as welcome to become a member of the Catholic Association as anyone else' (Catholic Association 1903: 18) – fatally wounded.

The next home to be offered to Catholic employment discrimination and professional subordination resentments was the 'faith and fatherland' politics of the AOH. In effect a counter-Orangeism, the AOH shared with its Protestant enemy a common northern heartland and an affinity to the European artisan-Masonic family of brotherhoods with its characteristic use of symbols, signs, passwords and rituals (Beames 1982). In 1902 a new constitution stimulated membership growth by giving the Order greater unity and increased respectability. A political struggle for mastery of the AOH ensued in which, led by Joseph Devlin, the Home Rule parliamentarians comprehensively triumphed over their Sinn Fein rivals (Foy 1976). The administrative arrangements of the 1911 National Insurance Act then provided the means by which the AOH achieved national penetration and massive membership growth. By the spring of 1913 the insurance section of the Board of Erin had recruited 150,000 members or one in five of Ireland's insured population and by 1915 its Dublin head office employed 200 clerical staff. Among the bishops attitudes to the AOH ranged from the supportive to the hostile, with the latter in some instances prompting the sponsorship of rival diocesan insurance societies. Inextricably tied to the cause of Home Rule, the AOH as a major political force perished alongside the Parliamentary Party as it was swept aside by Sinn Fein during the later Great War years. Partly, perhaps, out of filial piety, the only nationally significant post-independence southern politician to link himself with the Order was James Dillon.

The Irish organisation most durably associated with combating Catholic economic subordination is the Knights of St. Columbanus. If the AOH in its brief heyday countered the Orange Order by replicating its emphasis on public shows of strength, the Knights countered Freemasonry by adopting its secretive modus operandi. The order's own historian argues that 'a policy of discretion and privacy' was 'the only reasonable precaution for an infant society finding itself pitted against the entrenched power and influence of old established and not infrequently hostile interests' and admits that 'the rituals of the order were borrowed from the American Knights of Columbus who, lacking any established precedent, had derived that ritual in modified form from the Freemasons' (Bolster 1979: 33).

The Knights were founded in Belfast in 1915 and established a Dublin headquarters in the early 1920s as its birthplace was being ravaged by sectarian violence. South of the border, particularly in the late 1920s and early 1930s, claims of a red threat emanating from the pro-treaty side of the political divide had their counterpart in 'Republican, and later Fianna Fail, suggestions that Cosgrave's government enjoyed the support of Freemasons, and even that it depended for its survival on such support' (Patrick Murray 2000: 274). As with Communism, a ready supply of papal denunciations of Freemasonry could be pressed into Irish service. Public actions of the usually private Knights reflected the order's relatively educated and wealthy business and professional profile. One of the Order's Belfast founding members, the barrister James P. Kerr, wrote the first Irish book on Catholic social principles and, after the move southwards, the Knights were the source of the endowment of the Maynooth Chair of Catholic Sociology and Catholic Action first filled in 1937.

The insistence on Thomist orthodoxy is generally held to have gravely damaged Catholic scholarship while at the same time imparting 'a tone of confident certainly' to the wider papal project (McSweeney 1980: 73; M. Conway 1996: 14; O'Leary 2012: 100). In Ireland the elevation of Thomism and the condemnation of Modernism were not, as elsewhere, accompanied by academic purges. O'Leary (2012: 101–102) comments that 'the dominant tendency was to regard modernist ideas as a threat to very foundations of the faith' and refers only to one Maynooth professor, Fr. Walter McDonald, 'who was censured and carefully watched by his clerical colleagues' in the pre-independence period. Certainly on one, and possibly more, occasions McDonald's removal from his chair was a course of action opened up to, and possibly pressed upon, the Irish hierarchy by Rome (W. McDonald 1925: 156 and 325–326; Privilege 2009: 64 and 75). But, while he denounced McDonald vehemently to other bishops in his correspondence, Cardinal Logue 'was supremely conscious of the fact that this was a controversy over a "scientific subject"' and that, in the context of its efforts to secure its higher education objectives, 'the Irish Church could ill-afford accusations that it was engaged in a witch hunt' (Privilege 2009: 62). Lesser sanctions were applied and the fact that McDonald's book *Motion* had been proscribed by the Sacred Congregation of the Index was not published. Nonetheless during these years an Irish Catholic institutional culture of pronounced intellectual caution and hierarchical control was strongly reinforced. This would have serious consequences for some advocates of economic and social policy change from a Catholic viewpoint after 1922.

In politics a distinction applies between the 'closed' continental European Catholicism to which papal strategy was primarily applicable and the 'open' Catholicism prevailing in the Anglo-American group of countries towards which the Irish pattern gravitates (J. H. Whyte 1981). In the former an exclusively Catholic political party was interlinked with purely Catholic organisations for employers, farmers, waged workers, youth, etc., operating amid a Catholic population under strong clerical guidance. In the latter there was no Catholic party (although there was often a distinctive skew in Catholic party preferences), key social organisations like trade unions were constituted on a non-confessional basis and the Catholic clergy did not (or at some stage ceased to[10]) take part in politics. However, Ireland, with its Catholic majority, was not a typical member of the Anglo-American group and, once southern statehood had been achieved, a movement to break with institutions inherited from an era of Protestant dominance and to refashion Irish institutions along properly Catholic lines soon emerged.

The ongoing flow of papal encyclicals provided the inspiration for a Catholic social movement with an institutional reconstruction agenda. In *Rerum Novarum*, the foundational document of Social Catholicism, Leo XIII sought 'to find a religious solution to the social question which for nearly a century had been posed in anti-religious terms' (McSweeney 1980: 61). The problem was unrestrained individualistic capitalism, to which socialism, by denying the right to private property, was proffering a false solution. The source of a real solution lay within a church that could teach justice to the warring, but in reality interdependent, forces of capital and labour. Justice laid duties upon both the worker and the employer. The former were entitled to organise themselves to secure their rights through trade unions; the latter were obliged to pay a just, as distinct from a market, wage. The state should be limited in its role but that role properly encompassed the protection of the worker's dignity and the prevention of abuses such as excessive labour. Here then was a third way that, whatever its limitations might be, situated social questions primarily on the terrain of justice rather than

that of charity. The great Dublin lockout of 1913–14 prompted the Irish hierarchy to issue a joint pastoral letter in which they urged that:

> Employers and men should not be content with such fragments of that noble Christian
> philosophy of industrial and social life as seem to suit them at the moment. They should
> read the Encyclical over and over again. And the boys and girls of the industrial classes, as
> they grow up, should be thoroughly schooled in a teaching that is so appropriate to their
> condition of life, if they are to be trained aright for the duties of Christian citizenship.
>
> Irish Labour Troubles. "Pronouncement by Roman Catholic Hierarchy"
> *Irish Times* 23/2/1914

The lockout did not, however, result in substantial and sustained attention being
given to industrial or related social issues (such as slum housing) by the clergy or by
Catholic lay activists (McMahon 1981). In February 1914 the bishops had asserted
that 'had the healing influence of native rule been felt for even a few years, we cannot believe that the bitter privation, the enormous waste, the loss, the shame, the
sin of this insensate conflict would have been entailed on a city where commerce
and manufacture need to be fostered with tender care instead of being recklessly
endangered in a senseless war between workers and employers'. But native rule
when it eventually came in a form that faithfully imitated British party politics,
parliamentary procedures and civil service practices left some unsatisfied as to
its Catholicity. The 1931 papal encyclical *Quadragesimo Anno* – whose updating
of *Rerum Novarum* 'unequivocally condemned "economic liberalism", offered still
stronger support to workers, directly challenged the new national concentrations
of capital, highlighted the principle of subsidiarity, and proposed a corporativist
alternative to both liberal and socialist models of society' (Holland 2003: 206) –
has been seen as the rallying point for radicals. Yet in the year it appeared W. T.
Cosgrave was already complaining to Cardinal MacRory about:

> The attitude of certain periodicals which, by their titles, lead the general public
> to believe that they are authorised exponents of Catholic doctrine. Though we
> are aware that these papers have no official sanction, we are also aware that many
> pious Catholics are misled by the titles of these publications whose comments
> on Government policy and on Government departments often inaccurate and at
> times so intemperate as to be violently abusive, have done considerable damage not
> merely to the political party associated with the Government, but to the State as a
> whole, and have resulted in the weakening of respect for authority. Other papers,
> while their comments are more temperate, purport to lay down Catholic principles
> and their application to various aspects of governmental activity and notwithstand-
> ing the absence of any authoritative pronouncements by the Hierarchy, criticise
> Government for failing to follow the interpretation of those journals in these mat-
> ters. The danger and injustice of these comments and criticisms come from the fact

that the general public sees only that a charge is made against the Government of acting contrary to Catholic principles. The result is a weakening of the authority of the Civil Government in a country where such a weakening is so undesirable. (quoted in Keogh 1996: 207)

Sociology and the Irish Catholic social movement

The story of how the Catholic social movement became a force in independent Ireland is told in John Whyte's (1971 and 1980) standard work on Church–state relations. By comparison with continental European countries – or even the neighbouring island, where the Catholic Social Guild had existed since 1909 – Irish Social Catholicism is judged to have been weak in the first quarter of the twentieth century. Before partition Belfast had been to the fore in this field thanks to the efforts of Fr. James O'Neill (Bolster 1979: 16–27), while south of the border the Jesuit Fr. Edward Cahill had taken the initiative in 1926 by founding An Rioghacht. *Quadragesimo Anno* was the catalyst for a strong upsurge in Irish Social Catholicism. In relation to the movement's subsequent growth the first Irish university appointments of sociologists are linked by Whyte to the creation of new organisations (particularly Muintir na Tire), the proliferation of social study weeks (especially those held at the Jesuit Clongowes Wood College), the rise of press advocates (notably the weekly *Standard*, to which UCC's Alfred O'Rahilly was a prolific contributor), the emergence of episcopal champions (bishops Dignan of Clonfert and Browne of Galway as well as Archbishop McQuaid of Dublin) and a current of extreme radicalism represented by the writings of Archbishop McQuaid's fellow member of the Holy Ghost order, Fr. Denis Fahey.

Whatever their party composition, Irish governments had from the outset enshrined Catholic moral values in state law through censorship of books and films, prohibition of the sale of contraceptives and (from 1937) a constitutional prohibition on divorce. Applying Catholic social principles that called for radical institutional reconfiguration within the state was a different matter. Here Whyte chronicles how a clash between vocationalism and bureaucracy took shape in the 1940s with battles being fought over the Dignan plan for social security, the Report of the Commission on Vocational Organisation and the Mother and Child Scheme. From this contest bureaucracy emerged victorious in terms of institutional architecture, although in policy fields like health arguments based on the Catholic principle of subsidiarity were effectively deployed to shape the form and limit the extent of state intervention.

Whyte's study is essentially one of relations between the Irish national hierarchy and the southern Irish state. It does not explore the relationship of either with the Vatican. Yet 'by the end of the nineteenth century Rome was the centre of Catholicism' in everyday practice as well as in theory (McSweeney 1980: 50). Liturgical regulation, journal publishing and high-level appointment control were key features of this centrality. They were reinforced by a range of other binding ties such as national seminaries established in Rome 'to instil that Roman bias in attitude and theology in the more promising clergy selected for Roman training by their national hierarchies' and the 'lines of authority centred on Rome' systematically implanted within the religious congregations (McSweeney 1980: 50–51).

Later studies of Church and state relations in independent Ireland (particularly Keogh 1995) have gone beyond Whyte to explore these Roman dimensions. In politics they have highlighted the Luzio mission undertaken during the Irish Civil War of 1922–23, the establishment of diplomatic relations between the Irish state and the Holy See at the end of the 1920s, the visit to Rome of the Secretary of the Department of External Affairs to forestall papal opposition to de Valera's constitution in 1937 and the channelling of Irish funds to opponents of the Communist Party in Italy in the run-up to the crucial general election of 1948. In relation to the social sciences, two Roman initiatives stand out. The first of these came in June 1938 when the Vatican's newly established Central Office for Catholic Action informed Cardinal MacRory of 'the programme it intends to carry out in accordance with the sovereign wish of the Holy Father'. This required the Irish hierarchy 'to ensure the coordination and thereby the greater efficiency of the apostolate of the laity'.[11] The second was communicated to the cardinal in June 1939 by the papal nuncio, who wrote that 'In order that a start may be made towards ensuring some practical provision for a deeper study of Catholic Sociology in the Seminaries of Ireland, I have been instructed by the Cardinal Secretary of State to beg Your Eminence, in the name of the Holy See, to include this important question among the matters which are to be taken up by the Irish Bishops at their coming annual meeting.'[12]

Irish catechisms of sociology

How the growth of an Irish Catholic social movement within the broader framework of papal engagement with modernity's political and social complexities surrounded Irish Catholic Sociology's emergence can be illustrated by examining its staple non-periodical literary product: the manual, primer or textbook of social science. In 1916 the December issue of *Studies* reviewed three books under the heading 'Social Science'. One emanated from the Catholic Social Guild in England: the other two were Irish. Alfred O'Rahilly's *A Guide to Books for Social Students and Workers* was the first title in the University and Labour series and reflected a sustained interest in adult education and sociology on the part of a mathematical physicist that would fully flower while he held the UCC posts of (unpaid) sociology lecturer (1937–48) and president (1943–54). Two further titles were to be published in this series – one a study of poverty in Cork (MacSweeney 1917) and the other a discussion of Marxian socialism (Larkin 1917) – before it lapsed into an inactivity from which it would be revived twenty years later. The other Irish book was James P. Kerr's *A Catechism of Catholic Social Principles: For Employers, Workmen, Social Workers, Study Circles, etc.* In its Preface, Kerr traces its origins to a call by Bishop Tohill of Down and Connor for members of the St. Anthony's University Graduates' Conference of the Society of St. Vincent de Paul in Belfast to undertake the task of disseminating these principles. The spiritual director of that conference, Fr. James O'Neill, was the founder of the Knights of St. Columbanus, a project with which Kerr was closely associated (Bolster 1979: 18–28). The book's two later editions – in 1924 and 1927 – are dedicated to Fr. O'Neill's memory.

A university lecturer and a barrister, both O'Rahilly and Kerr were laymen. Admittedly O'Rahilly had spent about a decade in various Jesuit houses of formation and was all but ordained when he changed career path. His wife having died before he retired from the presidency of UCC – the couple had two children – O'Rahilly then proceeded to ordination as a member of the Holy Ghost order, spending the last years of his life in Dublin as a member of the Blackrock College community. Apart from later publications by O'Rahilly while he remained a layman or associated with his UCC initiatives, this early burst of lay activity was followed by a period in which all the authors of Irish Catholic sociology books were priests.

The third (1927) edition of Kerr's catechism was not only revised and enlarged but also adapted for use in schools. 'Boys and girls attending Intermediate schools' were also the target audience of Monsignor Michael Cronin's *Primer of the Principles of Social Science* first published in 1924 and of which new editions continued to appear into the mid-1950s, more than a decade after the author's death. Thorough schooling of 'the boys and girls of the industrial classes … in a teaching that is so appropriate to their condition of life' was, as we have seen, advocated by the hierarchy in the light of the great Dublin lockout, although the proportion of such southern Irish children receiving secondary schooling during the period of the primer's succession of editions was not high. Publication of the primer came at a point in Cronin's life where he left the academy for a parish (Rathgar) and a range of other archdiocesan responsibilities. After studies in Ireland, Germany and Rome he had been a seminary (Clonliffe) professor of ethics, a Fellow of the Royal University and, from 1909 to 1924, Professor of

Ethics and Politics in UCD. After 1924 he was to exert considerable influence over publications by Irish clerics dealing with economic and social issues in his role as the Dublin ecclesiastical censor, upon whom Archbishop Byrne placed the greatest reliance. On his death an appreciation in the *Irish Independent* described him as 'one of Dublin's most cultured and versatile priests'.[13]

In 1932 a work of much greater length than anything hitherto published in Ireland on the subject appeared – Fr. Edward Cahill's *The Framework of a Christian State: An Introduction to Social Science*. Its preface described its contents as 'originally prepared in connection with the writer's duties as Professor of Social Science in Milltown Park, Dublin' and his lectures to the Central Branch of An Rioghacht (Cahill 1932: xiii). Its close to 700-page length was the result of joining with the usual Catholic social principles exposition of an extended historical sketch. This began in the time of the Roman Empire, dwelt in detail on medieval Christendom before proceeding to deal with the succession of evils made up by Protestantism, liberalism, individualistic capitalism, socialism, Bolshevism and Freemasonry. The Jews feature under the last two of these subject heads. The Bolshevik overthrow of Kerensky's Russian government in 1917 is said to have been aided by Jewish finance. Jewish interests are said to control the press and the cinema in Europe and America and to exercise this control in a manner which is 'definitely anti-Catholic and Masonic'.

When the UCC governing body approved the establishment of a lectureship in sociology in 1937 the college found that it did not have the funds to pay a lecturer. Alfred O'Rahilly – then UCC's Registrar, Professor of Mathematical Physics and much else besides (Gaughan 1986, 1989, 1992 and 1993) – was to take on the additional role of unpaid sociology lecturer for nearly a decade until Fr. Jerome O'Leary was appointed. A revival of the University and Labour series followed, with ten titles appearing between 1938 and 1951 (see Table 1.3).

Four of these were contributed by O'Rahilly himself. Of the seven authors published in the series, only two were clerics. O'Rahilly's own contributions varied from short booklets with an unfinished quality (*Aquinas versus Marx, Social Principles*) to the much longer work on *Money*, whose second edition (1942) ran to 642 pages. This tome O'Rahilly described as 'a development of some of my lectures on Sociology, a University Extension course and some articles in *The Standard*'. Originally conceived as 'merely a popular pamphlet ... the matter grew to such an extent that only half of it is contained' in the 436-page first edition. The second edition was half as long again because 'the two final chapters – on *Purchasing Power* and on *State Intervention* – may be regarded as a very condensed summary of the projected and mostly written second volume ... which is unlikely to be published during this unpropitious period' (O'Rahilly 1942: vii and xxiii).

Table 1.3 Titles in the Cork University Press University and Labour series, 1938–51

Author	Title	Year published
O'Mahony, James E.	*Reform or Revolution?*	1938
Hogan, James	*Modern Democracy*	1938
Larkin, Rev. W. Paschal	*Economics and the Worker*	1938
O'Rahilly, Alfred	*Money*	1941
Bastible, Rev. James	*Radio Talks on Politics*	1944
McCarthy, Bridget G.	*Some Problems of Child Welfare*	1945
O'Rahilly, Alfred	*Aquinas versus Marx*	1948
O'Rahilly, Alfred	*Moral Principles*	1948
O'Rahilly, Alfred	*Social Principles*	1948
Geary, R. C.	*The Official Cost of Living Index Number and Its Critics*	1951

Source: library catalogues

If endowment by the Knights of Saint Columbanus meant that paying a sociologist's salary was not a problem at Maynooth, the qualifications required in the person filling the chair were, with the Faculty of Philosophy unanimously passing in October 1937 a resolution declaring 'that according to our conception of the duties attaching to this professorship (of Catholic Sociology and Catholic Action) none of the applicants is at present adequately qualified either academically, or from the point of view of published work, or from the point of view of practical experience in social organisation'. The successful appointee, a priest of the Armagh province, Fr. Peter McKevitt, was dispatched first to Louvain and then to Rome for further study before he began teaching in Maynooth in the 1939–40 academic year. In 1944 he published *The Plan of Society*: 'this work which forms the basis of the course in Catholic Sociology in St. Patrick's College, Maynooth, is offered to a wider public in the hope that it may prove useful to the increasing number of students of social science'. The book features the rarity of a mention for a nowadays acknowledged founder of the discipline other than the routinely denounced Marx – there are disapproving references to Durkheim – but remains on a well-trodden path with its proclamation that 'the social teaching of the Church is then the only foundation of a complete study of society' (McKevitt 1944: iii–ix).

The next impetus for Irish sociology textbook writing came from 'another indication of His Grace's "up-to-date" solicitude for the members of his flock' (J. Kavanagh 1954: vi) – the foundation by Archbishop McQuaid of the Dublin

Institute of Catholic Sociology (DICS) in the early 1950s. The *Manual of Social Ethics* that its first director, Fr. James Kavanagh, published in 1954 was intended 'primarily to meet the needs of the many adults' attending DICS courses. A new and revised edition appeared in 1964, the year in which Fr. Kavanagh was appointed a Lecturer in Social Science in UCD. His elevation to Professor of Social Science followed two years later.

Between the two editions of Kavanagh's manual the DICS spawned an alternative introductory treatment, *Catholic Sociology: A Beginner's Textbook* by Fr. Ambrose Crofts, which appeared in 1960. The Dominican author was by this time a veteran worker in the fields of Catholic Action and Catholic sociology. Ordained in 1920, he had studied in Ireland, Rome and Louvain, 'where he took a special course in social studies'. Based in Dublin, he took a leading role in reorganising and revitalising the Catholic Young Men's Society movement in the 1920s. Moving to Waterford as prior, he was the directing influence of that city's Aquinas Study Circle for much of the 1930s.[14] During this period the Circle focused its attention on the Labour Party and the trade unions, seeking to combat leftist tendencies and foster Catholic influence within these bodies (Crofts 1935). It was with specific reference to the activities of this Circle that one speaker at the 1937 Irish Trade Union Congress observed that 'practically all actions of labour leaders, trade union officials and unions had been under a semi-theological microscope'.[15] Appointment as his order's vicar-provincial took Crofts to Australia in 1938. Attached to the Dublin office of the *Irish Rosary* on his return to Ireland, he was one of an increasing number of priests (and later of lay people) drawn into teaching adult classes by the expanding activities of the DICS.

From 1916 to 1960 Irish Catholic writers constructed sociology as the social branch of ethics. A staple set of topics – marriage, family, Church, state, private property, relations between capital and labour – was dealt with in terms of very general principles. Variation in treatment was primarily due to the level of sophistication of the audiences addressed, which principally consisted of adult learners, school pupils and seminarians, with a nod towards a more general readership of conscientious Catholic lay people. In so far as this literature had any developmental impetus, this was introduced by the ongoing flow of papal encyclicals. Providing an overarching framework for these social ethics expositions was the Thomistic concept of natural law. Taking *Rerum Novarum* as an example, Curran (2002: 25) underlines how 'the encyclical heavily depends on neoscholasticism and its natural law approach' by pointing out that 'nine of the thirty-nine footnotes refer to Thomas Aquinas; all but two of the others refer to scripture (the exceptions are two references to Gregory the Great and Tertullian from the era of the early church)'. There is, he notes, 'no dialogue with contemporary thinkers'.

Several of the Irish Catholic sociology books just discussed begin with an outline of natural law and it is regularly invoked in all of them. Thus Fr. McKevitt
(1944: 8) argues that, while the natural law does not lay down rigidly the type of
social institution that men must adopt, history also shows that 'man has a limited
range and that he cannot comfortably fit into any type of society'. Referring to
English industrial capitalism he observes that 'violation of the natural law brings
its retribution, though the evil may not be apparent for a long time'. In common
with many other Catholic scholars of the period, Fr. Crofts (1960: 51) idealises
the 'organic medieval type of society' and associates with it 'certain principles
of social co-responsibility which are valid for all time and for all conditions of
human society'. First among these is 'the acceptance of a social code founded on
the divine and natural law'. A more contemporary and inclusive role for natural
law was envisaged by Fr. Kavanagh (1954: vi), who hoped that it 'will have a message for the many outside the Church, to whom Pope Pius XI extended a warm
invitation to join in the battle against the powers of darkness'.

In 1950 Pope Pius XII reaffirmed the status of Thomism in the encyclical
Humani Generis. With his death in 1958 the Leonine era, and with it the Catholic
philosophical monopoly of Thomism, drew towards a close. In January 1959, the
holding of a new Church Council was announced by his successor, Pope John
XXIII. It is tempting to attribute change in the practice of Irish Catholic sociology to a late 1950s confluence of this new Church departure and the gathering
momentum of a southern Irish state developmental strategy shift. But the empirical turn in Irish Catholic sociology was by this time well under way. Fr. Jeremiah
Newman, who succeeded McKevitt in Maynooth in 1953, was its main public
standard bearer. While steeped in Thomist philosophy by his clerical education,
Newman nonetheless conceived sociology in distinctly different terms from
those hitherto prevailing in Ireland. To a Muintir na Tire audience in 1959 he
criticised over-concentration on the exposition of social principles: 'Sociology
was a science ... one aspect of this science had been largely neglected in Ireland
and that was the careful collation and study of social facts':

> This aspect of sociology is the one that has made most progress outside Ireland. In
> Europe and America – either through the financial help of the State or of big business
> foundations – social survey work and research have made huge strides over the past
> half century. Failure to take adequate cognisance of facts is an insuperable obstacle to
> efficient organisation and good planning. It entails a basic carelessness as regards the
> adequacy of policies, which are bereft of an important criterion of their suitability ...
> Only factual surveys will show with certainty what should be concentrated on, where
> this or that industry should be located and what are the root causes of migration and
> emigration. Indeed in every sphere we have need of a greater consciousness of more
> efficient organisation and the adequate use of material and human resources.[16]

One version of the salient facts of the Irish economic and social situation was set out in November 1959 for an officer of the Ford Foundation in New York by an English economist:

> Ireland's economy is indissolubly linked with the UK by the force of emigration (40–60,000 a year), a common banking and currency system, exports and imports (about 80% either way), capital ownership. It is therefore analogous to a poor part of the UK. It is based upon an inefficient and declining industry – agriculture. There is little future in expanding agriculture, and in any case the expansion is certain to *reduce* the number of people employed … Extreme protection had led to a few small and highly-inefficient locally based industries. This has raised the price level and (by depressing real wages) adds to the emigration probably more than the employment it gives retards emigration. Indeed without emigration the Irish would starve. Recurrent crises plus the development of the Common Market have led to a reversal of the protectionist policy; and the only alternative appears to be complete free-trade and laissez-faire. (Already with hardly any defence expenditures Irish taxation is as heavy as the UK's!) (John Vaizey to Stanley Gordon, 1/11/1959: reproduced in Peter Murray 2012a: 74)

The author, John Vaizey, had acquired his familiarity with Irish conditions through his visits to Dublin to carry out archival research for the portion of a bicentenary history of Guinness's brewery he would co-author (Lynch and Vaizey 1960). For the southern state he prescribed a change of outlook which he claimed was already starting to occur within the national elite:

> First, clearly get rid of their illusions. Above all, nationalism and Irish mysticism. Next that all the world loves them and hates the English, and that Northern Ireland is languishing under oppression … Then that agriculture plus protection equal a rising standard of living. Lastly, and above all, that emigration is a 'Bad Thing'. Already Lemass, the Prime Minister, Dillon, the Leader of the Opposition, and a few others are feeling their way towards this point of view. They are handicapped by a lack of informed public support. (The press is still uniformly nationalist), but the top civil servant – T. H. Whitaker, Dept. of Finance – their head economist, McCarthy at the Dept. of Statistics – their adviser, Patrick Lynch, chairman of Aer Lingus – and people like Senator (Professor) George O'Brien of U.C.D., say all these things in private. (Peter Murray 2012a: 74)

Whether this was an entirely accurate representation of the views of the people named may be questioned, but, in its own breezily brutal way, Vaizey's letter does vividly register a sense of the crisis with which they were confronted. Recurring balance of payments difficulties had been addressed by restrictive policies that had depressed economic activity and sent emigration soaring to ever greater heights. There had been little or no engagement with the movement towards greater European integration until this had become inevitable. Then the Irish position was to seek, alongside Greece and Turkey, special concessions as a country 'in the process of economic development'. Greater integration with the UK economy was pursued but no progress was made as a result of the absence of British interest in the Irish proposals. A British U-turn in relation to the EEC provided a route out of this becalmed situation in 1961. Ireland joined its neighbour as an applicant for full membership, performing its own policy U-turn by claiming to be capable of coping with the free-trade conditions it had sought a few years earlier to stave off into the indefinite future.

A positive economic growth performance over a number of years was by now available to back this claim, but even the official Irish position was premised on a major programme of adaptation in Irish industry being successfully carried through. Serious examination of the Irish application had yet to begin when the French veto on British entry ended the negotiations for EEC enlargement. Full EEC membership remained the state's objective and the conclusion of an Anglo-Irish Free Trade Agreement in 1965 marked the decisive defeat of the protectionism whose advocates had been fighting a losing battle since the late 1950s (Whitaker 2006). From this point Ireland's future industrial growth lay not with indigenous industries adapted to face free trade but with an industrial base newly created by an inflow of foreign direct investment. Successful adaptation of most of the existing base may or may not have been a feasible objective but it was never pursued by the Irish state in a manner that could have held out a prospect of successful attainment. Instead a revamped and much better-resourced Industrial Development Authority (IDA) sought to attract US investors who had hitherto shown little inclination to locate plants south of the Irish border. Alongside the key low taxes and generous grants elements in the package offered to such investors was a suitably skilled workforce, the product of an education system whose radical transformation had begun in the early 1960s.

The transformation of Irish education had two key aspects. First, participation in its second and third levels was dramatically expanded from what had been in international terms a very low level. Second, the overriding priority hitherto given to religious formation and language revival was altered by a new emphasis on mathematics, science and business or business-relevant subjects like modern languages. Initially the combined thrust of expansion and reorientation had its greatest impact on second-level secondary and vocational schools and through new regional technical colleges offering sub-degree courses. But for the universities the shape of things to come was revealed when in 1967 the Minister for Education set aside the recommendations the Commission on Higher Education had produced after extremely lengthy deliberations and announced the merger of Trinity College and UCD. Ultimately this merger did not proceed, but in the upheaval its proposal caused the hierarchy's Trinity ban – the cornerstone of denominationalism in Irish higher education – was fatally undermined (O'Flynn 2012; Walsh 2014).

With courses that were more applied in content and governance that was less autonomous in relation to the state than that of the universities, two National Institutes of Higher Education offering degree-level qualifications were established in Dublin and Limerick. Both were later reconstituted as universities, by which time the formal autonomy of the institutions that already had this status had long been eroded by their incorporation into the state's manpower planning. This exercise geared graduate output to the demand projected to arise from new investments by the US high-technology companies being targeted by IDA promotional activity (Murray and Wickham 1982; White 2002: 184–188). By this means the lion's share of funding was channelled into engineering and computer science, although such was the scale of increase in student numbers feeding through from lower levels that all disciplines experienced a degree of expansion in the late 1960s and 1970s. Arts and social science subjects began to expand again at the end of the 1980s after the dramatically cheaper cost of production of their graduates was rediscovered within the twin contexts of very high levels of technical graduate emigration and of general unemployment (see Sheehan 1987).

Growth in the size of university departments as a result of broader educational expansion was one of two major changes affecting Irish sociology. The second was the creation, from the late 1950s, of a new sector of research institutes. These owed their existence in most cases to an injection of resources that either came from a source external to Ireland (usually the USA) or whose use was subject to agreement between external (again usually US) and Irish decision-makers. Sociological input featured alongside that from a range of other, usually 'harder', scientific disciplines in institutes concerned with agriculture, physical planning and social medicine. A fully-fledged specifically social scientific institute was created in 1965 when the existing Economic Research Institute was converted into an Economic and Social Research Institute. Integration of education into economic plans had formed the context in which its expansion gathered pace and a further widening of the scope of planning to encompass social development as well as economic growth lay behind the creation of the ESRI.

Before the ESRI was created a succession of proposals emanating from the Catholic social movement for state funding to assist the creation of research centres or institutes had been turned down. The empirical turn in Catholic sociology could not therefore be translated into the generation – as distinct from the consumption – of social research on any significant scale, as all Catholic social movement actors without a university base were denied the resources needed to become involved in the production process. By the early 1970s non-university embodiments of Catholic sociology were disbanding (the Christus Rex Society) or seeking to reinvent themselves in ways that would effectively sever their social science connections (Muintir na Tire). While university chairs of sociology were still almost exclusively in the hands of clerics who had been directed into the field by their ecclesiastical superiors (J. H. Whyte 1980: 332), the supply of qualified clerical candidates was drying up at a time when a state policy of third-level expansion was creating additional teaching positions. The laicisation of the discipline was well under way. The state rather than the Church now shaped its structures. Ironically the government programming approach that had provided the context of educational transformation and research institute creation that produced this shift in control had itself fallen into disarray just as the state's goal of full EEC membership was attained.

Plan of this book

A key reason why the Irish Catholic social movement failed to realise its project of reconstruction was because a conservative hierarchy baulked at the radicalism of some of its proposals. Critiques of banking and finance capital formulated within the movement were particularly divisive and, as Chapter 2 shows, on these issues ecclesiastical disciplinary mechanisms were invoked to silence some of its radical voices. During the Second World War/Emergency period Communist influence became the movement's overriding concern and Catholic adult education initiatives were launched to counter this threat. To provide such education a number of new institutions with a social science focus – the Catholic Workers' College and the Dublin Institute of Catholic Sociology – were created alongside the colleges of the National University of Ireland.

Chapter 3 examines the changing face of Catholic sociology in Ireland during the 1950s and 1960s. It has four principal strands. First, the collaboration of Maynooth's professor with Muintir na Tire in seeking European and North American help to foster rural sociology. Second, the use made by Archbishop McQuaid of his power within UCD to establish social science teaching in the state's largest university. Third, the tension between useful and critical social science that emerged as the growing number of Irish Catholic immigrants in an increasingly secular Britain became a focal point for research proposals. Finally, the manner in which Ireland's initially abundant, but later faltering, supply of religious vocations and the maximisation of its clergy's contribution to worldwide Catholic missionary efforts was studied. All of these strands are tied together by a common turning away from a predominant preoccupation with ethical principles and towards increasing involvement in empirical social investigations.

Chapter 4 broadens out the focus from Irish sociology to examine Irish scientific research. Its central theme is the way in which resources provided or jointly controlled by US actors underpinned the development of a modern scientific research infrastructure within the state in the period after the Second World War. The scientific fields principally affected by these financial injections were applied research related to agriculture, industry and economics. Money flowed into these fields from two major sources: the Grant Counterpart Fund, which was a legacy of Ireland's participation in the Marshall Plan, and private US foundations. In other fields, such as management and 'human sciences', significant resource transfers took place in kind as much as in cash through productivity and technical assistance programmes. The infrastructure developments that clustered in the late 1950s and the early 1960s interacted with older scientific institutional configurations laid down under the union with Britain and subjected to emaciating neglect after the advent of political independence.

Chapter 5 returns the focus to the social sciences. The injection of resources into Ireland's scientific research infrastructure at the end of the 1950s created two new social science research producers – the Rural Economy Division of An Foras Taluntais and the Economic Research Institute. In the former rural sociology took a recognised place alongside a variety of other agriculture-relevant disciplines. In the latter the distinction between the economic and the social was a blurred and indistinct one. During the first half of the 1960s the unenclosed field of social research was to be the subject of a series of proposals from actors located within the Catholic social movement to a variety of government departments for the creation of research centres or institutes. This chapter details these proposals and the fate of consistent refusal with which they met. Empirical social research in Ireland was funded and organised in a manner that effectively excluded the participation of any Catholic social movement actor without a university base when the government approved the transformation of the Economic Research Institute into the Economic and Social Research Institute. This approval for a central social research organisation was crucially linked to the project of extending the scope of government programming to encompass social development as well as economic expansion.

Chapter 6 examines the relationship between the programming state and social research. Initial crisis conditions had enabled increased social spending to be left off the government programmers' agenda. The changed politics of increasing prosperity, as well as the expanding ambitions of the programme framers, meant that this could no longer be sustained during the 1960s. Ireland's social security provision became an object of both political debate and social scientific analysis in this period. The official response to this ferment was a Social Development Programme to which the ESRI was initially seen as a vital provider of inputs.

During the 1960s a Save the West movement challenged both programmers and governing politicians. The official response to this challenge involved new structures for rural development with which the social sciences interacted, as well as expanded social welfare provision to a class of smallholders whose resilience would later become an object of significant sociological study.

Chapter 7 concludes the study by first noting how ambivalently clerical sociologists responded to the changes wrought by state planning practice in the 1960s. Demands from champions of such planning that the discipline should begin to play a different societal role are next examined. During the 1970s the hierarchy combined failure to plan for a continuation of a significant clerical presence among practitioners of sociology with the casting of itself as the conscience of Irish society. The warding off of abortion, contraception and divorce was thereby entrusted to a highly selective but this-worldly 'sociological' empiricism rather than to theological dogmatism. Initially successful, this strategy has become progressively less effective as popular confidence in Church leaders has declined dramatically. Detached from the institution that framed the working lives of their disciplinary predecessors, today's sociologists debate the respective contributions that factors such as higher education levels, economic marginalisation of the poorly educated and the uncovering of hidden histories of the abuse of clerical power have made to this decline.

Notes

1   TCD Library, Manuscripts Department, J. O. Hannay Papers, Ms. 3,455, D. Hyde, President, Gaelic League, to Rev. J. O. Hannay, Gaelic League Executive member, 11/7/1906.

2   Dublin University Defence Committee, Pamphlets Bearing on Mr. Bryce's Proposed University Legislation for Ireland, 1907, 'Trinity College Dublin and the Proposed University Legislation for Ireland', p. 6.

3   Dublin University Defence Committee, Pamphlets Bearing on Mr. Bryce's Proposed University Legislation for Ireland, 1907, 'Trinity College Dublin and the Proposed University Legislation for Ireland', pp. 4–5.

4   Dublin University Defence Committee, Pamphlets Bearing on Mr. Bryce's Proposed University Legislation for Ireland, 1907, 'Mr. Bryce's Speech on the Proposed Reconstruction of the University of Dublin. Annotated Edition issue by the Dublin University Defence Committee', pp. 27–31.

5   Dublin University Defence Committee, Pamphlets Bearing on Mr. Bryce's Proposed University Legislation for Ireland, 1907, 'Mr. Bryce's Speech on the Proposed Reconstruction of the University of Dublin. Annotated Edition issue by the Dublin University Defence Committee', annotation on pp. 31–32.

6   Dublin Lenten Regulations, *Irish Independent*, 21/2/1944

7   COFLA, D'Alton Papers, ARCH 12/4/3/6–8, box Education -2 Universities, folder 'The National University', correspondence dealing with meeting of Episcop. Comm. with Presidents, M. Tierney, President, UCD, to Archbishop D'Alton, Armagh, 18/9/1950.

8   ESRI, box 1, History of ERI/ESRI, file 'No. 1 Closed', M. D. McCarthy, director, Central Statistics Office, to T. K. Whitaker, Finance, 14/10/1966.

9   DDA, McQuaid Papers, AB/8/B/XV/C/392–3992, D. Mageean, Bishop of Down and Connor, to J. C. McQuaid, Archbishop of Dublin, 10/9/1948, J. C. McQuaid to D. Mageean, 13/9/1948.

10 In the Irish case, according to Patrick Murray (2000: 417) by 1937 'the Church had disengaged itself from active participation in the electoral process in the South: priests featured only to a minimal extent as platform speakers or public supporters of candidates'.

11 COFLA, MacRory Papers, ARCH/11/1/3, Actio Catholica, Cardinal Pizzardo, Vatican Central Office for Catholic Action, to Cardinal MacRory, Armagh, 29/6/1938.

12 COFLA, MacRory Papers, ARCH 11/1/4, Apostolic Nunciature, Archbishop P. Robinson, papal nuncio, to Cardinal MacRory, Armagh, 10/6/1939.

13 'Right Rev. Mgr. Cronin: An Appreciation', *Irish Independent*, 25/8/1943.

14 'Obituary: Very Rev. Ambrose Crofts O.P.', *Irish Press*, 30/9/1963.

15 'Trades Congress and Mr. Larkin', *Irish Times*, 7/8/1937.

16 'For Success in Life We Must Face Facts', *The Landmark*, September 1959.

2

Sociology and the Catholic social movement in an independent Irish state

Introduction

This chapter examines the emergence of sociology as a subject taught in southern Irish universities and adult education courses in the 1930s and 1940s. It also takes in the wider context of this development – the growth of a Catholic social movement with ambitions to reshape the state's institution and policies in line with the principles expounded by papal encyclicals. Negatively influential in blocking state intervention projects in fields such as health, this movement failed in its positive goal of bringing a vocationalist Irish social infrastructure into being. Moreover the Irish Catholic Church was divided during the early decades of Irish independent statehood by critiques of banking and finance capital formulated within this movement and ecclesiastical disciplinary mechanisms were invoked to hierarchically silence some of its radical voices. During the Second World War/Emergency changes in the wider world and developments within Irish politics provided Ireland's Catholic social movement with an alternative focus around which it could more successfully unite. The rise of the atheistic Soviet Union to superpower status, fears regarding the spread of Communism across Europe and divisions which had opened up within the Irish labour movement prompted a wave of Catholic adult education initiatives with trade unionists as their primary initial target audience. To provide such education new institutions with a social science focus – the Catholic Workers' College and the Dublin Institute of Catholic Sociology – were created alongside the colleges of the National University of Ireland.

The failure of Catholic radicalism

Why in a state with an overwhelmingly Catholic population did the advocacy of Catholic social principles make so little positive headway? Vigorous defence of the institutional status quo by governing politicians and civil servants together with weaknesses inherent in the vocationalist alternative proposed to it form a large part of the explanation. On these points Whyte's interpretation has been supported and amplified by later studies. Those studies have broken new ground by exploring the lack of united commitment on the part of the Catholic Church itself to the movement for change that invoked Catholic principles and papal authority. Of the bishops Don O'Leary (2000: 188) concludes that from the foundation of the state 'their main emphasis was on moral codes of conduct and the social teaching of the Church was neglected'. Taking the case of attempts made to establish a Council of Education constructed along vocationalist lines, he shows how one of the Church leaders Whyte particularly identifies with the Catholic social movement, John Charles McQuaid, was actively involved in frustrating the project, believing that that the Church's educational interests were better served by leaving the existing arrangements undisturbed (O'Leary 2000: 49–53). Wider prevalence of Church leadership satisfaction with the status quo is emphasised by Finin O'Driscoll (2000: 140): '[T]he Catholic Church itself had arrived by 1937 at a satisfactory relationship with the state and complemented this by firmly ensuring that internal radicalism – political and economic – did not disrupt the new consensus.' O'Driscoll focuses on a set of issues that Whyte does not consider, although 'the concentration on credit, currency and fiscal reform by Irish [Catholic social] commentators was unique among their European counterparts' (O'Driscoll 2000: 139). Examination of the experiences of writers critically addressing these financial issues illustrates both the extent of division within the Catholic Church on social questions and the operation of the mechanisms by which potentially disruptive radicalism was curbed by that Church's leadership.

Ecclesiastical censorship and Maynooth professors

As early as October 1922 a Maynooth professor of philosophy, Peter Coffey, had written to W. T. Cosgrave arguing for a radical departure in credit control policy by the new state. Coffey's arguments were dismissed by Cosgrave and his advisers. Coffey found himself prevented from publishing his work by a combination of his college's statutes and diocesan ecclesiastical censors, while one of the main outlets for discussion of a 'Distributist Solution' to Irish social problems by Coffey and other Maynooth academics – the *Irish Theological Quarterly* – was discontinued (O'Driscoll 2000:124–128). Coffey – with little success – fought to get his work into print through successive appeals to the Maynooth College Visitors, to the Irish bishops as a body and to Rome. In 1929 he was passed over for promotion to Maynooth's Chair of Ethics, a position which went instead to Cornelius Lucey, subsequently the Bishop of Cork and Ross. Coffey's own prospects of becoming a bishop were irretrievably blighted. He might on a number of occasions have become a parish priest – as Peter McKevitt was to do in the early 1950s – but he chose instead to remain at Maynooth, where he died in 1943 (Jennings 2009).[1]

The principal mechanism employed to silence Coffey was embedded in his Church's hierarchical authority structure by canon law – the ecclesiastical censor's *nihil obstat* (nothing obstructs) and the bishop's *imprimatur*. Censorship had to take place in the diocese where the author lived, in the one where the work was published or the one where the book was printed. Certain dioceses had a greater role to play in the process than others – as Coffey himself noted on one occasion, 'Dublin being the main publication centre for Ireland, the Dublin theological censors can wield a very deterrent influence.'

Coffey's difficulties with censors began following a sharp turn on his part – which occurred around 1917 – away from mainstream scholastic philosophy concerns and towards social questions (Jennings 2009: 236–238). The obstacles to publication he encountered in his new field were similar to those experienced earlier by Coffey's Maynooth colleague, Walter McDonald. McDonald's censorship travails began after he had addressed the relationship between theology and modern physics in his 1898 book *Motion*. This was referred to Rome, where it was condemned and ordered to be withdrawn from sale. Thereafter McDonald was a marked man – not dismissed, as he might have been, but periodically admonished or reprimanded and continuously stifled (W. McDonald 1925; Privilege 2009: 60–76). The first page of McDonald's *Reminiscences of a Maynooth Professor* records that 'it is February 1913; and not very many days since I was told that a MS volume of *Notes and Queries in Sacramental Theology*, which I submitted to one of the authorised censors of the diocese of Dublin, had not the least chance of getting a Nihil Obstat as, in case it was published, it would be delated to Rome almost immediately, and as surely would almost as quickly be condemned there'.

This was the fifth volume McDonald had written over a ten-year period to have ended up in this literary limbo. He did succeed in publishing two works in the year before his death in 1920 – but in London and with a Westminster *imprimatur*. After his death his literary executor had McDonald's reminiscences undergo censorship in Westminster. Theologically the work required only very minor changes to surmount the *nihil obstat* barrier but the *imprimatur* was refused 'on the ground that no book which criticized the ecclesiastical system of the Irish Church so strongly could receive the appearance of official approval from an English diocese'. With the censor's changes incorporated, McDonald's reminiscences were published by the non-Catholic Jonathan Cape in 1925 (Gwynn 1967: 52–53).

McDonald and Coffey were both frustrated by hobbling limitations placed upon the development of their subjects by the priority that the bishops who controlled Maynooth accorded to the supply of pastors for parishes and teachers for diocesan colleges. Both had supported Dr. Michael O'Hickey, Professor of Irish in Maynooth, whose criticism of a hierarchy that at first opposed, but later accommodated to, the demand that Irish be an essential subject for matriculation in the NUI led to his dismissal in 1909 (McDiarmid 2000). McDonald was O'Hickey's adviser as he pursued a fruitless appeal in Rome over the succeeding years before returning to Ireland in 1916, where he died shortly afterwards. McDonald himself had in 1899 appealed aspects of the condemnation of *Motion* to Rome but the result had only been to draw further sanctions upon himself. This previously trodden path to Rome was taken by Coffey in relation to his social and economic writings in the early 1930s but the outcome was no more favourable for him than it had been for his forerunners.

Ecclesiastical censorship and social thought

The attachment to economic and financial orthodoxy expressed by Cosgrave in his correspondence with Coffey in 1922 was subsequently reinforced by a series of expert commissions – the Fiscal Inquiry Committee (1923), the Commission on Agriculture (1924) and the Banking Commission (1927): 'Ireland would maintain parity and financial links with sterling, produce food for Britain and retain a free-trade industrial sector' (M. Daly 1992: 16). When Fianna Fail came into office in 1932, the banking and financial sector of the economy were left largely untouched by its early iconoclasm. In 1934 a Commission on Banking, Currency and Credit was established. Safe hands predominated within a large and somewhat diverse group of commissioners, while heterodox ideas claiming Catholic legitimacy featured significantly in the evidence the commission received (Lee 1989: 199–200; M. Daly 1992: 153–153; O'Driscoll 2000: 132–137). At its conclusion two minority reports dissented on Catholic social grounds from the majority's recommendations for policies of even greater orthodoxy than those already in place. One of these minority reports was written by UCC's Alfred O'Rahilly and the other, signed by Peadar O'Loghlen, a backbench Fianna Fail TD, was the work of a group associated with An Rioghacht. Catholic criticism of the financial system continued to be voiced into the 1940s through press and periodical contributions as well as by the publication of O'Rahilly's *Money* (1941) and Fr. Denis Fahey's *Money, Manipulation and Social Order* (1944). However, the member of the Catholic hierarchy who served on the commission – Bishop McNeely of Raphoe – was a co-author of an Appendix to the Majority Report which denied that existing banking and financial arrangements were unjust and that they constituted an impediment to the institution of a soundly Catholic social policy.

As his associates mounted an assault on the Department of Finance and the banking establishment, An Rioghacht's founder Fr. Edward Cahill was being subjected up to surveillance and restriction by his own Jesuit order that lasted up until his death in 1941. Cahill was forbidden by his Provincial to present evidence to the Banking Commission and, after his offer to Eamonn de Valera of assistance in the drafting of a new constitution had been accepted, a committee of five Jesuits was formed to take over the task of providing the advice (Faughnan 1988; O'Driscoll 2000: 133; Curtis 2010: 147). When Cahill criticised the Banking Commission majority report in August 1938 he was told to submit to the Jesuit censors anything he proposed to say in public on the subject and advised that his remarks were 'likely to be offensive to many good Catholics' (Curtis 2010: 147–149). The Holy Ghost order does not seem to have imposed curbs on Fr. Denis Fahey, although – as will be seen below – he was to experience difficulties with diocesan ecclesiastical censors. As a layman, O'Rahilly was not subject to clerical control processes, although in 1942 the Department of Finance complained to the state's Emergency press censor about the 'violent campaign' to which it was being subjected by O'Rahilly's sounding board, the *Standard* (O'Drisceoil 1996: 230). O'Rahilly's actions as a Banking Commission dissident had previously prompted that Department to try and block his appointment as a member of the Commission on Vocational Organisation (O'Leary 2000: 76). Earlier, while the Banking Commission was at work, the Minister for Finance, Sean McEntee, had had groups campaigning for financial policy changes investigated by the Gardai (O'Driscoll 2000: 135).

Archbishop McQuaid, Father Denis Fahey and Maria Duce

In relation to the most prominent social Catholic critics of the financial system a distinction can be drawn between those for whom the baleful influence of Masonic and/or Jewish power loomed large (Fr. Edward Cahill and Fr. Denis Fahey) and those for whom it did not (Fr. Peter Coffey and Alfred O'Rahilly). John Whyte (1980: 73) observes that many of Fr. Fahey's ideas were derived from Fr. Cahill, 'in particular his belief in a conspiracy of Freemasons and Jews against the Church'. In Whyte's view Fahey is 'of most interest as marking the extreme wing of Irish Catholic thought … the man whose vision of a truly

Christian social order entailed the most thoroughgoing changes in the conditions actually existing in his day'. He was not a representative figure, but neither was he an entirely isolated one since 'one influential member of his own order certainly sympathised with him – his very first book contains a warmly commendatory introduction from the Reverend J. C. McQuaid, then Superior of Blackrock College' (J. H. Whyte 1980: 72–73).

McQuaid's elevation to the rank of archbishop was at this point more than a decade in the future and, as a professor in the Kimmage Manor seminary of his Holy Ghost order, Fr. Fahey dealt for the present with the Dublin censors appointed by Archbishop Byrne. In January 1936 one of these, Dr. John Kelly of Clonliffe College, informed the archbishop's Secretary that he proposed to authorise the publication of Fr. Fahey's *The Mystical Body of Christ in the Modern World*. But written in pencil on the letter are the words 'Held up. Proofs sent to Abp's House'. These proofs found their way to another censor, Monsignor Michael Cronin, author of *A Primer of the Principles of Social Science* and a highly influential figure in Dublin diocesan administration (Morrissey 2010: 148–149). Dr. Kelly was subsequently told not to attach the diocesan licence to Fr. Fahey's book.

Monsignor Cronin had had a shorter version of the book submitted to him personally by Fr. Fahey a year earlier and had responded with a rejection. He now wrote that 'I should not care to see His Grace's name on this book. Fr. Fahey quotes extensively from hysterical American newspapers, and I am not sure that some of the statements are not libellous. At all events they might make things very difficult for the Archbishop.' Specific illustrations from the book relating to Jewish power and Masonic practice are cited, as is the charge that its constitution made the Irish Free State a place where 'a Mason can be at home while a Catholic cannot'. This, Cronin wrote, 'speaks for itself' – as it undoubtedly would for as staunch a supporter of pro-Treaty politicians as the archbishop. Turning finally to religious matters, the manner in which Fr. Fahey constantly invoked the Mystical Body of Christ is deprecated. Cronin ends with a reference to a lecture by Fahey on the subject that he had attended: 'I didn't understand half what he said, and I know that the other listeners, for they told me, understood practically nothing. We don't need this book.'

This damning dismissal was not, however, to be the end of the matter. Some six weeks later the publisher Browne and Nolan contacted Dr. Kelly 'as their usual Censor' and informed him that Fr. Fahey had obtained the *imprimatur* of the Bishop of Waterford. The author wanted the printing of his book to proceed without delay. The publisher wished 'to make sure that whatever they do as a Dublin firm will not be against Canon Law or without the permission of the Dublin ecclesiastical authorities'. Sharing their misgivings about the propriety of the *imprimatur* obtained, although he noted that 'Messrs. Browne and Nolan have some sort of office in Waterford', Dr. Kelly sought advice from Archbishop's House, which was not inclined to take the matter further. Written on Fr. Kelly's letter is: 'Reply – book may be printed with Waterford nihil obstat & address. Browne and Nolan Dublin and Waterford. No exact Dublin address.'[2] As Fr. Walter McDonald at the end of his life had done before him, Fr. Fahey was to circumvent Dublin censorship from this time onwards by having his work printed and published outside the capital. His writings were one way in which Fr. Fahey made his mark on Irish Social Catholicism: his role as guide and mentor to the activists of Maria Duce was the other. John Whyte (1980: 165) justified devoting attention to this group by the argument that 'one can learn something of the tendencies in society by observing on which particular fringe of it the lunatics break out'. Here the manner in which hierarchical control was brought to bear on Maria Duce is the main focal point.

Maria Duce was formed in 1942 by members of the Legion of Mary whose proposal 'to form, in the Legion, special praesidia to strive for supernaturalism's supremacy in public life'[3] had been turned down by that movement's leadership. In its early years it operated as a study group under the guidance of Fr. Fahey, in whose writings the distinction between (evil) naturalism and (good) supernaturalism played a central role. From 1945 until the early 1960s the new group disseminated an irregularly published newspaper, *Fiat*, and at the end of the 1940s its public profile was raised by a number of campaigns. Under its own name it agitated to have Article 44 of the 1937 Constitution amended to acknowledge the Catholic Church as the one true Church. Under the banner of the Catholic Cinema and Theatre Patrons Association it engaged in what one critic dubbed 'holy hooliganism' by picketing venues where the work of politically objectionable authors or performers featured.[4]

While Maria Duce had a presence in Belfast, Cork and Limerick, it was largely a Dublin-based phenomenon. Archbishop McQuaid's relationship with the group has therefore been the subject of much discussion. By his own account the archbishop's initial general approach was to try and dilute Fr. Fahey's influence over the Ducists: '[A]t least twice I summoned the chief men in the group and requested them to make a three year course of study of Catholic Social Teaching on an approved programme, in order to utilize their undoubted goodwill to better purpose ... It has been my purpose to deal very gently with the group, for the members are good Catholics, and to assist in guiding their efforts into channels of useful social work.' The particular direction in which the archbishop pointed Maria Duce was the Oxford-based Catholic Social Guild's Certificate and Diploma programme, which the Dublin Guilds of Regnum Christi were already following. Over fifty Ducists enrolled in the course and proved themselves to be apt students: '[T]he general standard maintained was of a high level, particularly clear in setting forth the Church's teaching and the proof from Natural Law against Divorce.'[5] But, possibly because they were following this course in tandem with studies under Fr. Fahey of Fr. Fahey's writings, the effect desired by the archbishop – whereby Ducist energy would be tempered by qualities such as discretion and restraint – did not material-ise. Increasingly, therefore, the archbishop looked to the disintegration of the group once Fr. Fahey's death (which occurred in January 1954) had deprived it of its main guiding light and to the subsequent absorption of former members into 'well-controlled associations'.[6] Indeed he hastened the disintegration by, among other things, insisting in late 1954 that the group change its name.

As noted above, Dr. McQuaid had, at a younger age, praised Fr. Fahey's work in print. But when he became an archbishop, he adopted the viewpoint expressed by Monsignor Cronin in 1936. Responding to a query relating to Fr. Fahey from Cardinal McRory in 1943, Dr. McQuaid apologized for a delay in dealing with the matter that had been caused by the monsignor's serious (and, as it was to prove, terminal) illness. With his letter he enclosed 'the report of Mgr. Cronin from our files on the first book: The Mystical Body of Christ and the Modern World' and referred to a second book by Fr. Fahey that had been rejected by the Dublin censorship the previous year. Here 'the Censor's illness prevents my sending the circumstantial report' but the book was described as 'bearing on finance'.[7] Cronin's views on this subject were of such soundness that Sean McEntee had written to him in March 1940 praising a paper he had presented to a Social Study Congress and continuing that:

> I was hoping that it would be printed in full in some of those weekly journals, which are holding themselves out as Catholic but which, I fear, are playing a most dangerous part by creating a rather wrong impression in the minds of our people as to the true significance of the Holy Father's great pronouncements and as to the circumstances to which they are applicable. When I was Minister for Finance I regarded this as a very alarming development, because theories which are dangerous, not merely from the economic point of view but in their moral and social aspects, were being popularized by these specious tactics.[8]

Of one populariser of the theories McEntee deprecated – Fr. Fahey – Archbishop McQuaid had in 1943 offered Cardinal McRory an assessment that strongly ech-oed Monsignor Cronin's earlier critique:

> It is fair to say, in general, of all Fr. Fahey's work that: 1) he will never err in doc-trine; 2) but, he will frequently err in good judgement, and this error will take the

shape of excerpts from newspapers as proof of serious statements, unwise generali-
sations and, where the Jews are concerned, remarks capable of rousing the ignorant
or malevolent. In his own Congregation, Father Fahey is not regarded as a man of
balanced judgement. He is a wretched professor, obscure and laborious. My fear in
his regard is that he will incur legal action sooner or later and will fail, for want of
solid proof that a Court can accept. When all that is said, one willingly admits that
in Father Fahey one has a most exemplary priest, of deep sanctity, and a man who
will very generously sacrifice his time and health to help anyone: not a small sign of
genuine holiness.[9]

The context for this observation was an application by Fr. Fahey to the cardinal
seeking an Armagh *imprimatur* for a work entitled *The Kingship of Christ and the
Conversion of the Jewish Nation*. This work had not been presented for imprimatur in Dublin, where Fr. Fahey resided, because, he told the cardinal, 'it has
been impossible for me for years past to present any book in the Archdiocese
of Dublin with any hope of its being passed'. The death of Archbishop Byrne
and his succession by an archbishop who had once commended Fr. Fahey's work
had not brought about an easing of his Dublin censorship problems. Thereafter
he sought, and usually obtained, clearance for the works that made up what he
termed the Maria Regina series in three other dioceses – Cashel and Emly, Cork
and Ferns.

The first title – *The Kingship of Christ and the Conversion of the Jewish Nation* – was
to be last in the series to secure an *imprimatur*, bringing to an end a search that
stretched over a decade. This began in Ferns in the early 1940s, when Fr. Fahey
secured the agreement of Bishop James Staunton to provide an *imprimatur* provided the work was by passed the diocesan censor. Bishop Staunton subsequently
changed his mind on the matter. Fr. Fahey next 'tried in Cork but, though the
Rev. Censor was delighted with the book, the refusal of the Imprimatur by the
Bishop of Ferns was an insuperable obstacle'. Armagh was the next port of call,
prompting Cardinal McRory's contact with Archbishop McQuaid, seeking 'to
know "how the land lies"' and the response from Dublin quoted above. The cardinal ultimately 'thought it my duty in all the circumstances to refuse the imprimatur; but I'm very sorry for poor Dr. Fahey, whom I don't know personally, but
who seems a very pious and earnest soul'.[10]

More than four years then elapsed before Fr. Fahey wrote to Archbishop
McQuaid in November 1947. Having rehearsed the book's unhappy history to
date, he revealed that 'I want to add on two or three chapters to the book and
to offer it to a friendly publisher in England' without having to reveal the fact
that it had previously been refused an *imprimatur*. The reply advised that canon
law required the disclosure of the previous refusal: 'I see no other way out of

Table 2.1 Diocesan *imprimaturs* for books in Fr. Fahey's Maria Regina series

No.	Title	Date	Diocese
1	The Kingship of Christ and the Conversion of the Jewish Nation	1953	Ferns
2	The Workingmen's Guilds of the Middle Ages	1943	Cork
3	The Mystical Body of Christ and the Reorganisation of Society	1945	Cork
4	The Kingship of Christ and Organised Naturalism	1943	Cork
5	Money, Manipulation and Social Order	1944	Cork
6	The Tragedy of James Connolly	1947	Cork
7	The Rulers of Russia and the Russian Farmers	1948	Cashel
8	The Church and Farming	1953	Cork

the impasse, I am very sorry to say.'[11] Finally, after a further lapse of five years, the book appeared in the year before Fr. Fahey died, carrying the *imprimatur* of the bishop who had refused to provide his authorisation a decade earlier, James Staunton of Ferns. Whether or not this *imprimatur* is genuine has been the subject of some speculation (Athans 1991: 71; see also Gaughan 1993: 199–200; Delaney 2001: 496–497).

Shortly after Fr. Fahey had finally succeeded in getting *The Kingship of Christ and the Conversion of the Jewish Nation* published, an opportunity to breathe new life into Maria Duce's becalmed campaign to change Article 44 arose. In March 1953 Cardinal Ottaviani, Pro-Secretary of the Supreme Congregation of the Holy Office in the Vatican, delivered a lecture on the duties of the Catholic state in regard to religion whose uncompromising terms appeared to endorse the Ducist position. Fr. Fahey produced an English translation of the lecture which Archbishop McQuaid's staff in late 1953 intervened to stop *Fiat* publishing (Delaney 2001: 508–509). Fr. Fahey may already have died by the time the translated lecture appeared in pamphlet form (Ottaviani 1954) with a Cashel *imprimatur* in 1954. By then an address in which the pope – who had been under pressure from US churchmen on the issue – distanced himself from Ottaviani's views and buttressed the position of defenders of the existing Irish constitutional position had been made in December. This papal trump card was played by Monsignor Arthur Ryan of QUB's Scholastic Philosophy Department when he spoke at a March 1954 Magnificat Society meeting in UCD on toleration. Giving permission to the monsignor to speak at this meeting in his diocese, Archbishop McQuaid observed:

What a subject these young people choose! The position could have been more difficult if anyone had taken serious note of the publication – outside Dublin – of Cardinal
Ottaviani's conference by the group formerly known as *Maria Duce*.[12]

At this stage the archbishop had not yet insisted on the group changing its name,
as he was to do in November of that year, although he had communicated his
'emphatic disagreement with use of the name of the Blessed Virgin Mary in your
activities' in November 1952.[13] The group began life as Firinne by approaching
Cardinal Ottaviani with complaints about its treatment and about the state of
Catholic life in Ireland. On 13 May 1955 the papal nuncio wrote to Archbishop
McQuaid enclosing a letter he had received from Ottaviani. Addressing the
wider issues raised, the archbishop responded that:

It is very incorrect to say that one finds 'apathy, ignorance and incapacity among the
vast majority of Irish Catholics'. I can answer only for the Catholics of my own diocese
but they comprise from one quarter to one fifth of the whole Catholic population of
the Republic. It is correct to say, on the evidence that I hold, that there is a very great
interest now being shown in Catholic social teaching. In the years before and during
the war, it was not possible to sustain interest in study circles. The circumstances have
completely changed in the last five to seven years. Further, I have now, at length, been
able to take measures in the University to have Catholic philosophy permeate all the
Faculties, and I can hope that our educated lay-folk in the near future will no longer
show themselves to be infected by the Protestant English Liberalism that had caused,
and is still causing, so much confusion in our country.[14]

Vatican oversight and Social Catholicism in Ireland

A repressive Vatican certainly made the Irish hierarchy more censorious. A discussion of Dublin diocesan censorship practice argues that, after the papal condemnation of Modernism in 1907, the Irish Church 'had become cabined and
confined within a very traditional theology, and prized "orthodoxy" above all'
producing a 'prevailing episcopal ethos of control and caution in matters relating
to theology, social philosophy and morals' (Morrissey 2010: 146–147). Given
the bishops' desire to buttress the pro-Treaty position after 1922, politics might
be added to this list and the overall ethos had indigenous as well as exotic roots.
It is questionable therefore whether the fact that 'the bishops had to answer to
the Holy See' provides a full explanation for the determination on their part
'to keep an original mind, like that of [Peter] Coffey's away from the teaching
of [sociology]' (Keogh 1997: 75). But, as noted above, Irish answers to Vatican
questions relating to sociology were required twice at the end of 1930s.

The first of the two inquiries came in June 1938 from the Vatican's Central Office for Catholic Action, with which Peter McKevitt established close contact after his arrival in Rome from Louvain in the autumn of that year.[15] It was to McKevitt that the Irish hierarchy in the first instance referred the preparation of a response and at its June 1939 meeting it had before it his proposals. For any bishop made uneasy by any of the radical interpretations of Catholic social teaching in the preceding years, this document made for reassuring reading. It envisaged Catholic Action as the co-ordination under clerical control at national and parochial levels of the efforts of existing and newly created lay organisations to address the 'existing or threatened dangers' faced by the Church in Ireland. As specified, these dangers were identical with the moral themes the bishops' pastoral letters addressed year on year:

> The primary difficulty is with the young of both sexes ... The Christian family is threatened by the frequentation of dancehalls and by late hours which have become usual. Amongst the youth there is less strength of character and less enterprise, and a tendency to drift. The absence of discipline and self-denial is shown in the craze for amusements. It is in large measure also the cause of late marriages as there is an unwillingness to make the required sacrifices to establish a home. The falling away is also a partial cause of the flight from the land. The dependence on State aid is also a symptom, while the absence of legitimate ambition, or of the strength to work perseveringly to attain such an ambition, is a reason why no state-aid can solve the problems. For the country as for the church, the perquisite of development is the soundness of the people and especially of the youth ... It is necessary then to arouse a general sense of responsibility but in particular it is necessary to train the young men and women so that having become conscious of the existing dangers they may set a new standard. It is only such a trained group of the population that can ensure effective obedience to pastoral directions in the face of established customs.[16]

The only political observation in the proposals occurs immediately after this passage when it is noted that 'incidentally, it would be easier to purify the trade unions of their communistic leanings, if we had the means of giving a more Catholic formation to the young men and women of the towns'.[17] In his September 1937 application for the Catholic sociology and Catholic Action chair, McKevitt had emphasised how working in Dundalk – by southern Irish standards a sizeable and vibrant manufacturing centre where 'in addition to the ordinary missionary work, I conducted study clubs and periodical debates on the social question' – had 'given me a practical knowledge of industrial conditions'. Earlier writing to the president of Maynooth College regarding two lectures he would be giving to seminarians on the work of priests with employers and trade unions, he also referred to the relevance of his pastoral experience before concluding that 'neither [lecture] would be controversial but would rather tend to combat the impatience of the young with conditions falling short of the ideal'.[18]

In its conclusion his 1939 document states that 'the proposals finally adopted by Your Lordships would be the basis of the teaching of Catholic Action in Maynooth', an alignment that would ensure a supply of young priests capable of directing the new initiatives in the parishes. Fitting the Maynooth lectures on Catholic social science into the same framework would, McKevitt adds, 'ensure sane and fruitful development'. Writing from Rome in January 1939 to the president of Maynooth College, McKevitt observed that the draft scheme he was preparing for the hierarchy's June meeting 'will involve a certain amount of preliminary discussion and some sort of general approval here'. In June his proposals appear to have been dealt with by the Irish hierarchy's Standing Committee meeting the day before the general meeting of all the bishops. Here, to judge by a handwritten note on the meeting by Cardinal MacRory, there seems to have been little enthusiasm for launching a new national initiative: 'Dr McKevitt not to be expected to do anything at present in the country.'[19]

Joining McKevitt's proposals in the business dealt with by the Irish hierarchy at their June 1939 meetings was a second inquiry from the pope's Secretary of State, Cardinal Maglione. This concerned the education being received by the Irish clergy in social science, and a sub-committee of three bishops was set up to prepare a response. The sub-committee's report described, and stressed the satisfactory nature of, the arrangements in place in the diocesan colleges and in the national seminary, with the creation of the chair McKevitt had been appointed to fill featuring prominently. It then offered the following general observations:

> The three signatories have spent many years on missionary work amongst the Irish people and may therefore be allowed to state their opinion that there is very little danger of Socialism or Communism obtaining a footing amongst them. Except for two or three cities the population of Ireland is rural and agricultural and for all Ireland is 75% Catholic. The Catholics are all practising and most regular in receiving the Sacraments. The rural workers are not organized in Unions. In the Cities and large Towns the Catholic workers are nearly all good practicing Catholics. Certainly over 90% are. They are of course in Trade Unions. Close contact between the Priests and the workers has always existed. Priests all over the country are active members of various educational and social bodies, such as Vocational Education Committees, Old Age Pension Committees etc. A Bishop is Chairman of the National Health Insurance Committee (Eire) in which every manual worker (man and woman) is insured against sickness and disability. Another Bishop is Chairman of the Vocational Commission (Eire), at present sitting. Recently closer contact has been made between the Bishops and the Labour Leaders. A gratifying fact which may be claimed as a beneficent result of this contact is that a few months ago the Trades Council by an overwhelming majority vote decided to revise their Constitution immediately so as to bring it into harmony with Catholic teaching in all Social questions.[20]

The 'Trades Council' referred to here was in fact the Labour Party, which had in 1936 adopted a constitution that defined its objective as the setting up a 'Workers' Republic' and included a commitment to bringing about public ownership of 'all essential sources of wealth'. The compatibility of this constitution with Catholic social teaching was raised with the hierarchy by one of the party's trade union affiliates, the Irish National Teachers Organisation. The issue was referred to a committee of experts for detailed consideration. To these experts a workers' republic had objectionable class-war overtones, while the scope of public owner-ship envisaged conflicted with rights to private property upheld by the Church. The Labour Party subsequently revised the offending matter along acceptable lines (J. H. Whyte 1980: 82–84; McGarry 2000). Before the Second World War concerns about Labour's leftist leanings expressed by Fr. Ambrose Crofts and his Waterford Aquinas Study Circle associates were not evident at Church leader-ship level. By its end, however, 'the danger of Socialism or Communism obtain-ing a footing' was a much more serious cause of concern within the Church and a bone of significant contention within a divided Labour movement.

Communism and the Irish Labour movement

The Irish Trade Union Congress had assumed the role of a Labour Party in 1912 in anticipation of a Home Rule parliament coming into existence. South of the border this structure continued until 1930, when congress and party were sep-arated with provision for constituent unions to affiliate themselves to a party based on individual membership. A decade of turmoil and violence had passed before Labour contested the post-Treaty election of 1922. In the 1920s, as anti-Treaty republicans clung to abstentionism, Labour politicians assumed the role of the Opposition in the Free State's parliament while the Free State's army turned from waging civil war to crushing rural trade union militancy. By the late 1920s, when de Valera's Fianna Fail ceased to practice abstentionism, Labour was relegated to living in its shadow and to playing the role of the most durable – if not always the largest – of the state's minor parties. At the local level it endured as a set of 'highly personalised constituency machines, led by politicians for whom ideology meant looking after the forgotten people of Ireland's property-obsessed society: urban and rural labourers, public housing tenants and social welfare recipients. Socialism, in so far as they considered it, was a threat to their election prospects' (O'Connor 2005: 37–38).

The Irish Trade Union Congress (ITUC), established in 1894, continued to operate on an all-Ireland basis. But, with its affiliated unions organised on divergent local, Irish or British Isles lines, it experienced growing internal tensions. While the strongly nationalist Irish Transport and General Workers' Union (ITGWU) was the main beneficiary of explosive membership growth during and after the First World War, a significant British Isles general workers' union presence was also established around this time in the shape of the Amalgamated Transport and General Workers' Union (ATGWU). The situation regarding large general unions was further complicated when, after a decade in the USA, James Larkin, the ITGWU leader in its early years, returned to Ireland in 1923 and clashed with the new leadership dominated by William O'Brien and formed the breakaway Workers' Union of Ireland (WUI). Among the smaller and/or more specialised unions the struggle for political independence was accompanied by a wave of Irish breakaways from amalgamated unions with British headquarters. The proportion of the membership breaking away varied, but in most cases the breakaway and the original organisation were to be found coexisting in a less than amicable fashion, although the investment in enmity appears to have been considerably greater among union officials than among the rank and file (Hannigan 1981).

After plummeting during the 1920s, union membership recovered against the backdrop of industrialisation behind high tariff walls in the 1930s. As it did so, the Fianna Fail government signalled to the ITUC its intent to legislate if internal reform measures to tackle a perceived state of irrational fragmentation and internecine conflict were not forthcoming. An ITUC commission of inquiry was set up but no agreed basis for proceeding was found. Stalemate on the issue of reorganisation left the ITUC on the brink of a split in 1939, when an 'advisory' Council of Irish Unions was formed with the ITGWU at its core. The first year of neutral Ireland's Emergency was marked by an upsurge in industrial disputes. Proposals to severely restrict the right to strike formed the initial government response but, with a growing closeness between ITGWU leaders and Fianna Fail Ministers for Industry and Commerce as its context, the focus moved towards trade union rationalisation. Here the emphasis was initially on tackling the multiplicity of unions by eliminating smaller ones, but over time this shifted to excluding unions with British headquarters. In its final form the Act passed in 1941 discriminated against such unions in a number of ways, the most crucial of which related to a tribunal given power to award the sole right to organise a particular class of workers to a specific union (C. McCarthy 1977: 202–206).

Splits in the Labour Party and Irish Trade Union Congress

Internal division and behind-the-scenes collusion by some of their number with the government prevented the trade unions becoming an effective vehicle for popular protest in the early years of neutral Ireland's Emergency. Within ITUC pre-existing strains were exacerbated by the strong union membership growth that wartime conditions stimulated north of the border and the active involvement in the congress that the mainly British-based union beneficiaries of this growth exhibited. By 1944 these British-based unions had a majority on the ITUC Executive and early in 1945 the Congress finally divided over attendance at a world trade union conference being hosted in London by the British TUC. For the ITGWU and a number of smaller Irish unions attendance was incompatible with Ireland's neutrality and they withdrew to form the Council of Irish Unions (CIU) when the sending of a delegation was approved. The Fianna Fail government's reaction to the split in congress was that 'generally speaking, it will be our policy to build up the prestige of the Council of Irish Unions and to treat it as the more representative organ of Trade Union opinion'.[21]

Southern Ireland's tiny Communist Party membership had found itself in tune with mainstream sentiment favouring Irish neutrality in the 1939–41 period of the Molotov–Ribbentrop Pact. Then the Soviet Union was invaded by Nazi Germany. The party's sole southern branch (Dublin) was dissolved and, as a memorandum sent to the Minister for Defence by the Head of G2 (Army Intelligence) in February 1944 noted:

> About the middle of 1942 it was observed that individuals who had hitherto been associated with the Communist Party, and in that capacity had severely criticised the members of the Irish Labour Party, were advocating support for the Labour Party. The Communist Party of Ireland as such appears to have been pushed into the background but contacts with the Communist Party in Belfast remained. There is no evidence to show that the gradual infiltration of the communist element into the Labour Party was preceded by any discussions and arrangements and it can only be inferred that the Labour Party tacitly accepted support from persons who were formerly extremely hostile to them.[22]

Active campaigning against the hardship and inequity of Fianna Fail's Emergency regime (O'Drisceoil 2005: 264–267) revitalised and radicalised the Labour Party. Communist entryism in Dublin occurred in the context and formed a minor part of a massive and rapid expansion which saw a statewide increase in branches from 174 in 1941 to 750 in 1943 (Girvin 2006: 243), with many created in places where Labour (let alone Communism) had previously had no presence. Striking electoral gains were made at the June 1943 general election, when Labour and a new farmers' party, Clann na Talmhan, advanced at the expense of both Fianna Fail and Fine Gael. The 'red scare' was up to this a point a weapon that had been deployed against radical Republican elements rather than Labour. When Sean MacEntee first targeted Labour in this fashion in the 1943 election campaign, it proved ineffective, if not counter-productive, and a number of his ministerial colleagues asked him to desist (Puirseil 2007: 99–100). But the red scare was to prove more than effective on a second outing in 1944 after the Labour Party had been split.

The Labour Party, like the ITUC, experienced a major shift in its internal balance of forces during the Emergency years. Rapid expansion and a new activism had loosened the grip on the party's structures long held by the largest general workers' union in the state, the ITGWU. This enabled both James Larkin senior and James Larkin junior to join the party and stand successfully as Dail candidates in 1943. Industrially Larkin senior had been the bitterly detested enemy of the ITGWU leadership for the two decades since the power struggle that ended in the WUI breakaway. Politically both Larkins had – albeit in somewhat different ways – been identified with Communism and its hostility to the Labour Party over the same period, although both now claimed to have severed their Communist connections and professed a willingness to work amicably with former enemies within the Labour Party fold. Labour's leader William Norton seems to have calculated that the ITGWU would not act on its threats and that a party with a broadened base could be sustained despite the bitterness of trade union rivalries. However, as noted above, the industrial politics of the Emergency period had seen an alliance forged behind the scenes between Fianna Fail ministers and ITGWU leaders. A new party political niche had been carved out.

In January 1944 the ITGWU, having failed to secure action against the Larkins, disaffiliated from the Labour Party. Most of the Labour TDs linked to that union then formed a breakaway National Labour Party (NLP).

While longstanding hatred of the Larkins may have been the main reason for the ITGWU's disaffiliation, a newly minted concern about Communist penetration of the Labour Party quickly came to dominate the war of words it sparked off. In part this was due to a tactical shift on William O'Brien's part to shore up support within his union for the disaffiliation move. It also reflected the recruitment of new allies from outside the Labour movement for the National Labour cause – the *Standard* and its most prominent contributor, Alfred O'Rahilly. Between January and May 1944 (when another general election was held) Communist penetration of the Labour Party was featured in almost every issue of the *Standard*. Of some twenty pieces published, three carried O'Rahilly's name. The NLP reproduced at least five (two of which were identifiably O'Rahilly's) in leaflet form.[23] *Standard* contributors apparently had access to intelligence material collected by state security agencies, as many of their articles contained minutely detailed accounts of Communist machinations within the Labour Party. A committee of inquiry set up by the Labour Party leadership to investigate the ITGWU allegations espoused natural justice as its guiding principle and refused to give decisive weight to the kind of evidence that the *Standard* was proffering:

Evidently this data has been collected through the activities of '*agents provocateurs*' planted at the head of the so-called Communist organisation. Material of such a character, collected in such a manner, must be viewed with the gravest suspicion. A singular feature of the whole matter is the freedom with which such information is made available indiscriminately to Mr. McEntee, to the officers of the ITGWU, to the features writer in the Standard for use against the Labour Party.[24]

For Labour's leaders destructive factionalist action within the party principally emanated not from Communists but from the ITGWU – since 1940 'a distinct section within the party acting in concert to further aims of their own and determined ultimately to dictate the policy of the party or to wreck it'.[25] Loyalty to the Labour Party, not past membership of another organisation (be it the Fianna Fail, Fine Gael or Communist parties or the Irish Republican Army) was to be the test for assessing a member's *bona fides*.[26] The half a dozen expulsions that followed the inquiry were mostly of members held to have breached this loyalty obligation by their attendance at functions held in connection with the October 1943 Communist Party Congress in Belfast.

The split left Labour in disarray when a snap general election was called in May 1944. Here the Fianna Fail government was also able to capitalise on a number of other issues – the 'American Note' episode, the introduction of children's allowance payment – to successfully restore the overall Dail majority it had lost in the previous year's election. The Labour vote fell sharply. Eight Labour and four National Labour TDs were returned compared with the seventeen seats the united party had held after the 1943 election. In the aftermath the road to rehabilitation for Labour pointed out by the *Standard* was to make its personnel acceptable to Catholics in the way that its programme was.

A third battlefront: adult education in social science

Entering the fray on the National Labour side, O'Rahilly had written to Cork ITGWU official P. J. O'Brien in February that it was 'a pity' that 'this split will do awful damage to Labour' but that it was 'better now than when a crowd of communised emigrants return' at the end of the war. To ITGWU General Secretary William O'Brien in Dublin P. J. O'Brien wrote later the same month that Dean Sexton – a diocesan censor whose *Nihil Obstat* is to be found on a number of Fr. Fahey's Maria Regina works – 'preached twice last Sunday, in strong terms about C.P. and praising the action of those who broke' and that a number of parish priests in other parts of the county were also beginning to speak out.[27] Elsewhere, John D'Alton – president of Maynooth College at the time of Peter

McKevitt's appointment and now Bishop of Meath – kept a press cuttings file on the split.[28] In Dublin, where John Charles McQuaid had displayed a high level of social activism since his appointment in 1940, a Jesuit correspondent of the archbishop's observed that:

> I imagine that communistic labour can only be effectively fought by Christian labour & hence your two ideas seem to call for translation into action as soon as possible. Firstly the [Catholic Workers' Institute] now in your mind quite a time & second an extension & intensification of the retreat movement for Workers & Middle class such as we have here.[29]

Alongside warring political parties and trade union congresses, the Irish Labour movement was soon to acquire a new battleground – adult trade unionist education in social science subjects – over which Catholic social activism and a secular conception of labourism would fight an unequal battle (Peter Murray 2009: 101–106). By the early 1950s one wing of a divided Labour movement had sponsored the People's College, which modeled its approached on that of the British Workers' Educational Association (WEA), while a Catholic alternative was being proffered by extended or newly created extra-mural programmes at UCC, UCD and UCG, by the Catholic Workers' College (CWC) and by the Dublin Institute of Catholic Sociology (DICS). According to the *Standard* the approaches differed because:

> The activities of the adult education movement in Britain have been largely directed towards propagating Marxism. This is a position which we here in Ireland cannot support. We believe that the social and economic structure of society must be based on the moral law, and that most of our economic ills have sprung from violation of the Ten Commandments and that these ideas must be the root of all our activities in the field of adult education. (quoted in Gaughan 1992: 168 and 170, n. 11)

The creation of the People's College derived from an initiative taken when Labour was on the crest of a wave of electoral success in 1943. Despite the disruption caused by the party and congress splits, an experimental course in economics and social science taught by UCD academics was launched in 1945. This apparently began well but then suffered a slump in attendance which led to its abandonment. By the time Labour's educational initiatives were revived in 1948, courses for workers based on Catholic teaching had been launched in Cork and Dublin.

O'Rahilly was the prime mover in Cork, where he had been involved in adult education initiatives for more than three decades (O'Murchu 1989). Prior to his role in the 1944 party split he could also claim a long involvement in labour issues through his role as arbitrator in industrial disputes and membership of Irish delegations to International Labour Organisation conferences (Gaughan 1992: 36–125). His Banking Commission minority report had been signed by the two of his fellow commissioners who were drawn from the Labour movement. By his own account he had been approached to stand for Labour in Cork at the 1943 general election, while in the following year P. J. O'Brien placed his intervention in the party split within a longer-term context in which O'Rahilly 'has at all times been a very good friend of ours here, and in no uncertain way has stood openly with us when strong forces ranged against us, and when he could easily have kept out of issues'.[30] The course UCC launched in October 1946 'was very highly regarded by trade union leaders in Cork, whether they supported the ITUC or the CIU' (C. McCarthy 1977: 389).

In Dublin the discussion under way between Archbishop McQuaid and members of the Jesuit order at the time of the Labour Party split had led to a Dublin diocesan priest, Fr. James Kavanagh, spending two years at Campion Hall in Oxford studying social and economic theory. On his return the archbishop made Fr. Kavanagh available to teach at Rathmines High School of Commerce a workers' course modeled on the one O'Rahilly had launched in Cork. In line with post-war international developments in their order's work, Dublin Jesuits took a leading role in giving adult social science education for workers a wider and more permanent form than that of the Rathmines course. As a counter-mobilisation to the launching of the People's College took off, Fr. Edward Coyne was appointed as director of a new programme of extra-mural studies launched by UCD in January 1949 with a two-year diploma in social and economic science aimed at trade unionists as its flagship. A Jesuit-run Catholic Workers' College (CWC) operating independently of UCD was established under Fr. Edmond Kent's direction in 1951, 'when worker-students who had successfully completed the first diploma course at U.C.D. indicated their desire to continue the study of economic and social questions' (Gaughan 1992: 184). Meanwhile Fr. Kavanagh, following his Rathmines debut, had become director of a newly established Dublin Diocesan Study Centre which was later renamed the Dublin Institute of Catholic Sociology.

After the party split, Labour Party TDs outnumbered the National Labour contingent and south of the border the rival congresses were of roughly equal affiliated membership strength but Church-backed adult education proved overwhelmingly stronger than its secular rival. The People's College was unable to forge university links and struggled to attract financial backing even from trade unions affiliated to the ITUC. When a motion from the ITUC Executive in 1954 urged more support for the People's College from affiliates, the debate was peppered with contributions – one from a Labour TD, another from a

Senator – praising the course O'Rahilly had launched in UCC. One such speaker concluded: 'I am afraid that the Irish worker is frightened of the trade union movement's educational schemes unless they are assured beforehand that the education has Christian as well as trade union principles.'[31]

'The training of well-informed propagandists for the movement' had been the aim of the initiative that launched the People's College, but the college could only survive by taking a cultural turn – moving away from the initial emphasis on economics and social science to offer courses on literature, music and the visual arts. Turning away from either socio-economic course content or from a trade union student body was also to be a feature of the development over time of the People's College's Catholic rivals (Peter Murray 2009: 101–106). In the case of the CWC the original focus – education of Catholic members of trade unions – almost immediately began to widen, with courses being provided over its first decade for employers and managers, civil servants, primary school teachers and nurses. The college also ran pre-marriage courses and a course in 'political and social science for young politicians'.

Occurring during a period when the international Cold War was at its height, these shifts in focus reflect a distinctive pattern of Irish anti-Communism. The 1944 Labour Party split shows how Irish neutrality denied Communism the period of wartime popularity and respectability it enjoyed elsewhere while the Soviet Union fought with Britain and the USA under a United Nations banner. The huge demonstrations that protested against the persecution of the Catholic Church in Communist-controlled Central and Eastern Europe in the late 1940s (Cody 1979: 78) effectively took up where Irish Christian Front rallies of the Spanish Civil War period (McGarry 1999: 109–134) had left off. Domestically, however, the threat of Communist subversion within the Labour movement had insufficient substance to sustain focused Catholic educational counter-mobilisation over the long term. The reunification of the Labour Party by 1950 illustrates this point.

While ministerial powers of nomination were used to appoint CIU adherents and exclude ITUC ones when the opportunity arose, a Supreme Court decision that the key tribunal provisions of the 1941 Trade Union Act were unconstitutional denied the ITGWU and its satellites the real benefits they might have expected to derive from alignment with Fianna Fail. When the governing party lost its overall majority in the 1948 general election, National Labour TDs defied CIU instructions and opted to join four other opposition parties in forming a new government rather than backing a continuation of the outgoing one (Puirseil 2007: 130–131). One of these other opposition parties was Labour. It had been the target of further Fianna Fail red-baiting in the general election campaign, although the party that now channelled the popular discontent that had flowed towards Labour five years earlier – Clann na Poblachta – drew most of the fire from this quarter. Communists in the Labour Party might have escaped an extensive purge in 1944 – according to a 1947 G2 memorandum 'it can be accepted that they exercise at least as much influence in it now as they did then'[32] – but the price they paid was enduring the stifling caution with which William Norton led the party after the split. Finally in October 1948, with Labour ensconced in the first inter-party government, entryism was terminated and Communists launched a new party. Inaugurating it, Michael O'Riordan declared:

> The politicians are talking about the country entering into military alliances if a deal can be done about partition. Already we have been committed to the Marshall Plan and are witnessing the humiliation of having a commission in our midst from a foreign country with power to interfere in our internal economic affairs. Ireland is being lined up in the Anglo-U.S. Imperialistic camp in opposition to those countries which have ended the privileges and power of their wealthy classes, but the Irish people must make it clear to the politicians that they want no part of the Imperialist war plans and have no quarrel with these countries which are building a social system along the Socialist lines James Connolly envisaged for Ireland.[33]

The Irish Workers' League (IWL) did not use the term Communist in its title but the hope a G2 memorandum attributed to its founders that this might lessen the hostility it encountered was not to be fulfilled. Archbishop McQuaid's clergy and lay Catholic groups relentlessly harried the IWL wherever it was discovered, most notably in the case of the breaking-up of a consumer co-operative society serving the Inchicore and Ballyfermot areas of Dublin (Kilmurray 1988). In 1953 a G2 'Memorandum on Communism in the State' estimated that IWL membership 'does not exceed 150' and concluded that its organisation was effectively confined to Dublin.[34]

The Congress split was less easily repaired but a Provisional United Trade Union Organisation was in place from 1955 with full reunification in the Irish Congress of Trade Unions (ICTU) being achieved in 1959. Only in the adult education field did the mid-century convulsions of Irish Labour leave an enduring legacy of institutional fragmentation, with the People's College and direct descendants of CWC and DICS maintaining separate existences down to the present day. This might not have been the case had Archbishop McQuaid accepted proposals for reorganising of Dublin-centred adult education provision in the mid-1950s.

These proposals emerged from intra-clerical discussion in Dublin over the 1954–56 period in which two of the archbishop's secretaries – Fr. Christopher

Mangan and Fr. Liam Martin – appear to have taken the initiative along with Fr. Feichin O'Doherty, Professor of Logic and Psychology at UCD and a member of its Board of Extra-Mural Studies (BEMS). Now retired from UCC, ordained a member of the Holy Ghost order and living in Blackrock College, O'Rahilly was also drawn into the exchanges. The focal point of the discussions was the contrast between how adult education provision operated out of Cork and the Dublin arrangements. A key feature of the Cork model was the partnership between UCC and the vocational education system at both local and national levels. Correspondence between O'Rahilly and the Department of Education in 1952 set out the agreed principles underlying this co-operation:

> (1) The Courses are prescribed and the examinations are conducted by us [UCC]. As examiners we have appointed some inspectors of the Department of Education and one or two vocational teachers.

> (2) The teachers are appointed in the usual way by the Vocational Education Committees. It has been agreed that the teacher of Sociology should be nominated by the Catholic Bishop of the diocese. Furthermore all the other teachers must be accepted by us as competent. This arrangement does not of course invalidate the strictly legal position that all the teachers are appointed and paid by the Vocational Education Committees.

> (3) From a strictly legal point of view the teaching is on the same level as the teaching of other subjects in the Vocational Schools. But we have an understanding that the classes conducted for our diplomas will not be inspected except with our concurrence. Otherwise, these adult students would not regard our classes as being of a new type and the teachers would also not be able to carry out with full independence the courses we have prescribed.

As expressed from the Department of Education side, the context for spelling out these principles was that 'relations are not the very best elsewhere, and if some member of a Vocational Committee elsewhere wanted to be difficult he might choose to misinterpret the understanding about inspection'.[35] Here 'elsewhere' mainly meant Dublin and its hinterland. A memorandum for Archbishop McQuaid highlighted the shortcomings. UCD had few extra-mural centres in operation, it had failed to get the Leinster VECs involved, while, within the capital, 'Dr. Tierney's attitude to the Dublin VEC has always been aloof, and his relations with the CEO are non-existent. So far as they have been expressed at all, it seems to be that he regards their claims in the field of the teaching of technology with suspicion and hostility.'[36]

Whereas in Cork 'every opportunity was taken to publicly proclaim the position occupied by the V.E.C. Teachers and Officers in the movement and to emphasise the indebtedness of the movement to them',[37] in Dublin this was far from being the case:

The course wherever given is the UCD course. The sponsoring body, e.g. the local Vocational Education Committee, are the hosts, they provide the room, light, heating etc. but they do not run the course. For the purposes of running the course, timetable, payment of lecturer etc. a special ad hoc committee is set up. This committee may consist of the same people as the V.E.C. but it acts as a special ad hoc committee in regard to the extra-mural course.

Lecturers on the UCD course had to be approved individually by the BEMS before they could begin teaching which, according to O'Doherty, in practice meant that UCD graduates vouched for by members of the BEMS were recruited and that for 'Sociology, Social Ethics, philosophy and theology generally, almost any priest would be automatically approved'. O'Doherty considered the fees charged to UCD extra-mural students to be too high and the payments to lecturers to be over-generous. None of the expenses incurred by host bodies were reimbursed.[38] O'Rahilly was quoted as considering that, compared to those of Cork, the BEMS courses were 'too abstract and lack any adaptation to the mentalities of the categories of the people whom they are supposed to cater for'.[39] Dublin admirers of his Cork system were told by O'Rahilly that 'close relations with the V.E. people are not only religiously desirable but quite indispensable',[40] while he continued to insist on the central position that sociology must occupy across the spectrum of adult courses, as 'nowadays, even for a trade unionist or a tradesman, merely technical instruction is not enough to fit him for life':

So Sociology should be part of every full-time course & should be developed & made available for practically all students. If we do the job properly & have men trained, the Sociology course could be the most popular and stimulating. Experto crede![41]

The expected succession of Fr. Coyne as director of the UCD BEMS by a layman 'who has not received a proper training in Catholic philosophy'[42] provided another argument for changing the current arrangements. As discussion proceeded, what took shape was a plan whereby the UCD BEMS would step back into an advisory and examining role, with a combination of the DICS and the CWC stepping in to assume the intermediate organising roles currently played by ad hoc committees, while the vocational education system diffused 'a sociology scheme' in which, as in Cork, its staff enjoyed the status of 'full cooperators and colleagues'. To this, it was proposed to add a further layer – a Council of Adult Education. Initially this would be 'a self-created body' with educational and trade union representation, 'whose function at first would be simply to find out what is available in the country'. Later this council 'could express its interest, set up fund-raising machinery, eventually give small grants and in any case assume a supervisory and advisory character'. By this means 'gradually it would gain in prestige, by doing its job, and one hopes that the gain would be of such magnitude as to entice the Workers' [i.e. People's] College to seek affiliation'. In a notable shift away from the polemical caricature of the WEA purveyed by the *Standard* at the time the People's College was launched, formulations of this council proposal drew explicitly on the role that movement had played within the development of British adult education.[43]

In framing proposals for change O'Doherty had noted that, while financing a scheme through the vocational education system would be 'a great easement of the burden in practice, I am not sure that it would leave sufficient freedom of movement to the sponsoring bodies (BEMS, DICS, CWC)'.[44] The flow of documents on adult education in and out of Archbishop's House came to a halt as, at the archbishop's direction, a status quo criticised for duplication, fragmentation and limited outreach was preserved.[45] How the archbishop's creation, the only Irish institution of the period with sociology inscribed in its title, was to develop over the subsequent two decades is now sketched (for a similar CWC sketch, see Peter Murray 2009: 101–117 and 133–141).

The Dublin Institute of Catholic Sociology

At its initiation the Dublin Diocesan Study Centre provided meeting facilities for a number of existing study groups and in its early days DICS classes consisted, as Table 2.2 shows, mostly of groups whose members shared a common employer, be it a civil service department, a semi-state company or a private firm. Some convent schools' past pupils' unions and miscellaneous religious groupings provided the base of almost all the groups where a common employer did not feature. By the beginning of the 1960s these groups had gradually given way to a subject-centred set of courses that included social ethics, social encyclicals, economics, political science and industrial relations. By the late 1960s the Institute had adopted a departmental structure with social studies, industrial relations, religious studies, cultural studies and youth leadership units.

As external and rural centres were added to the central city base (where student numbers approached 1,500 by the late 1960s), more priests from religious orders as well as an increasing number of lay people were recruited as teachers. For 1956–57 a solitary lay lecturer (in economics) is listed: by December 1958 seven out of twenty-eight lecturers teaching courses in Gardiner Place were laymen. Early in 1958 Dr. McQuaid established a Board of Studies: 'we have reached such a point of expansion that we must look to our standards'. As chairman he appointed Fr. James Kavanagh, who had been replaced by Fr. Thomas Fehilly as DICS director in October 1954 when he went to Cambridge to undertake further studies and was now back in Dublin teaching in UCD. In

November 1958 the archbishop returned to the issue of academic quality, asking Fr. Kavanagh and two clerical colleagues from UCD on the Board (professors Feichin O'Doherty and Conor Martin) 'to take in hand the outline of courses in the Institute' – courses which he went on to characterise as 'haphazard, dependent on the notions of lecturers, and passing lecturers at that'.[46]

The following year brought educational quality into collision with hierarchical control within DICS. In a letter concerning arrangements for the presentation of certificates to teaching sisters who had completed a DICS course, Fr. Fehilly referred to a committee set up by these students to consider a new programme in social studies for secondary schools: 'as you know the programme such as it is at the moment is most unsatisfactory. They have now produced a tentative programme which has been sent out to all the schools and we are awaiting their views on same.' An infuriated archbishop declined to attend the presentation ceremony, writing to Fr. Fehilly that 'it has escaped the notice of all concerned that the existing programme was prepared in understanding with, and sanctioned by the Hierarchy. The matter would be less grave if the Archbishop of Dublin – who is Patron of the Institute – were not also Chairman of the Episcopal Committee on University and Secondary Education.' A profusion of apologies and an undertaking by Fr. Kavanagh that, as Board chairman, 'I will see the nuns concerned, and explain to them their lack of competence in this matter' were required before the archbishop was sufficiently placated to write: 'Grateful. Let us hope no notice is taken of attempt to reform syllabus. At least I shall be able to explain the good spirit in which it was undertaken.'[47]

Expansion of DICS was accompanied by much discussion of the need for additional staff but few additional resources materialised. A memorandum from Fr. Fehilly in October 1960 received the response that 'it reads like a thesis on an ideal Institute' and that the archbishop, who had the find the extra staff it called for, was 'gravely straitened for want of priests'.[48] In 1962 four laymen were brought onto what had previously been an entirely clerical Board. Two were businessmen, one – James Dunne of the Marine Port and General Workers' Union – a trade union general secretary and one a former leading member of Maria Duce who had been the editor of *Fiat*. The case of Tomas Roseingrave was one in which the archbishop's policy of promoting Maria Duce's disintegration and looking to absorb its former members into 'well-controlled associations' could claim success. Having left Maria Duce in 1955, Roseingrave studied social science in UCD and thereafter embarked on a career in social research and community development. In 1964 two laywomen joined the Board, to one of whom the archbishop wrote that 'we have been, first of all, too clerical'.[49] DICS launched Planned Study Courses in 1962 in a context where 'we simply have not got sufficient priests to cater for all the numbers who would like to take

Table 2.2 Dublin Institute of Catholic Sociology groups, December 1952

Night	Group	Priest in charge	Number attending[a]
Monday	St. Louis PPU	Fr. Kavanagh	11
	Dept. of Social Welfare	Fr. Crean	10
	Legion of Mary Group	Fr. Hegarty	12
	Catholic Workers' Group	Fr. Corbett	14
Tuesday	Dept. of Agriculture	Fr. Bourke	17
	Boland's Bakery	Fr. O'Kane (Ballyfermot)	25
	Dept. of Industry and Commerce	Fr. Shouldice	30
Wednesday	Dept. of Education	Fr. Fitzsimons	28
	Land Commission (No. 1)	Fr. Con Lee	25
	Holy Child Hostel	Fr. McDowell	25
	Ex-U.C.D. Diplomatists	Fr. M. Nolan	11
Thursday	Woodworkers' Group	Fr. Keating	25
	E.S.B. (Pigeon House)	Fr. Neenan	9
	Abrasive Workers	Fr. O'Connell (Cabra)	11
	Sacred Heart P.P.	Fr. Neenan	8
	Dept. of Special Employment	Fr. Fehilly	23
Friday	Gas Co.	Fr. Kavanagh	14
	Land Commission (No. 2)	Fr. Kenny (Fairview)	23
	Jacob's	Fr. Sweeney	10
	E.S.B. (Central Stores)	Fr. McGeahen	21
Sunday (11.30)	C.I.E. etc.	Fr. Kent S.J.	14

Note: [a] The numbers given are those attending classes up to the close of the Christmas Term (total number: 366)

Source: DDA, McQuaid Papers, AB8/B/XXXV, folder Dublin Institute of Catholic Sociology 1953–1955, 'Dublin Institute of Catholic Sociology Report at End of Christmas Term 1952', enclosure with Fr. J. Kavanagh to Archbishop J. C. McQuaid, 6/1/1953

courses, outside the Institute, but we have now plenty of qualified lay people who could act as Group Leaders'.[50] Shortly afterwards the Institute developed an Industrial Relations Diploma which was to be taught at its Eccles Street base by four priests and five lay people. By the late 1960s Roseingrave was chairman of the Department of Industrial Relations.

Industrial relations was an area of overlap between DICS and CWC. Shortly after Fr. Liam Carey became the DICS director in 1963 he was asked by the archbishop to consider 'our apostolate among apprentices ... in the hope of remedying what I have always felt to be my most signal failure in the Institute; penetration of the Trade Unions by Catholic sociology'. In the following year, when Fr. Carey reported on recent contacts made and sought the archbishop's permission to accept invitations to speak to members of the boot and shoe industry, Dr. McQuaid noted: 'doing very well. Link up with all Trade Unions. You know I always wanted this.'[51] The links established between CWC and the trade unions during the 1950s were extensive. With members drawn from twelve 'of the more important' unions, a Trade Union Advisory Committee was set up by CWC in January 1954. A quadrupling of trade union student numbers was attributed to its advice and efforts, which encompassed drawing up the syllabus for trade union courses, recruiting students and winning the goodwill of union officials for the college. In 1957 eight trade union leaders were invited to form a Trade Union Board of Sponsors (a Management Board of Sponsors was formed at the same time) while a Trade Union General Purposes Committee was set up to engage in fundraising. The CWC Jesuits also cultivated more personal contacts: 'yearly visits are made to Trade Union Offices, Trade Union Officials are invited to College functions; factories are visited, etc.'. The effect of this on DICS was noted by Fr. James Kavanagh in October 1965:

> Unfortunately the Workers College got one over on us some years ago by their 'Sponsors' scheme. It seems unfair that they should try to have a monopoly of trade union financial support. We shall have to break this but it involves diplomacy of a high order to succeed especially at this stage. But we *must* do something about it.[52]

Despite, as noted above, some drift into eclecticism, among the Dublin adult education providers, CWC, with its institutionalised trade union and management links, had retained from the early 1950s the strongest emphasis on social and economic content in its courses. A 1966 survey of students attending DICS courses in Eccles Street found that participants tended to have had a relatively large number of years of formal education. Beyond a tendency for students to be drawn from areas to which the centre was most accessible, what was also noteworthy was 'the large and significant percentage of the students [who] come from those parishes which have a large number of flats and lodging houses' – such as Phibsborough and Rathmines – and 'a positive and significant correlation between the large percentage of single female students and the percentage of students who are clerical workers'.[53] Given the links with government departments evident in the mainly workplace-based groups of its early years, the Institute may well have attracted particularly strong enrolment from the lower civil service grades whose living and working conditions were to be the subject of a substantial 1970s piece of social research (O'Broin and Farren 1978).

In relation to raising finance, the DICS did – for a time – have the strong asset of its annual Social Study Congress with the profits realised on ticket sales boosting its revenue. Featuring prominent Irish and international speakers, this Congress enjoyed its heyday while Fr. Fehilly was DICS director. In 1966 Archbishop McQuaid firmly rebuffed the suggestion from Fr. Kavanagh that the Congress be held in a seminary location rather than in its usual boxing stadium one:

> Academic is written all over your suggestion of Clonliffe Aula for the Congress. Hitherto the Congress popularised for thousands Social Teaching. You would restrict the meeting to a few hundreds with discussion groups. Are you not trying to combine a Seminar for the learned with a Congress for the unlearned? My preference is altogether for the unlearned – and the Stadium.

By this date, however, the popularity of the Congress was already in decline. In June 1963 Congress attendance (and profitability) was adversely affected by 'the visit of President Kennedy during that week, and the broadcast of the Pope's Coronation on the concluding Sunday evening'. In 1964 a bus strike produced a similar effect.[54] Contingent as these factors might appear, the Congress never recovered its pulling power. To deal with its recurrent deficits, the Institute cast its eyes in the direction of the annual collection in aid of the diocesan Catholic Social Service Conference (CSSC) and made suggestions that it might receive an allocation of the proceeds. To this the constituents of the CSSC were strongly opposed with one its leading lights, Monsignor Cecil Barrett, criticising Fr. Kavanagh to the archbishop in June 1968:

> Once more he asks that Your Grace meets the Board 'to *talk* over the whole position'. He is so careful to omit committing himself to *anything* except more talk! My impression is that he would regard it as infra dig for the Board to have to raise funds. He argues that education at all levels must be subsidised – and heavily ... I'm afraid that the attendances at this year's [Social Study] Congresses have been small. Father Breen told that me there was scarcely 300 people present for the first few nights.[55]

Periodic payments were made during the 1960s by the archbishop to deal with the Institute's recurrent bank overdraft problems but no structural solution for its funding difficulties was devised. Both CWC and DICS got some state aid during this decade. A government grant was first sought by CWC in the mid-1950s and finally secured in 1961. In September 1963 Fr. Kavanagh sought the

Archbishop's permission for the DICS to seek a similar grant, assuring him that 'we would be careful not to accept Department "interference".' Agreeing to the application, Dr. McQuaid commented that 'we deserve it every bit as much as the prospering Catholic Workers College'.[56] The Department of Education was a niggardly supporter, however, and as soon as a Department of Labour was created in 1966, the Jesuit college pursued a transfer to its Vote – something its finally achieved in the late 1970s (see Peter Murray 2009: table 6.4).

Conclusion

1966 saw both CWC and DICS adopt new names from which the word 'Catholic' was absent. The primacy of a Cold War context had been eclipsed by state policy shift towards attracting foreign investment and becoming a member of the European Economic Community, which necessitated the 'adaptation' of a protected industrial base to free-trade conditions. CWC perceived itself not as prospering but as being threatened by the growth of the Irish Management Institute and the ICTU's education and advisory services, both of which benefited from the increased availability of state Technical Assistance funding in the EEC adaptation context. Both Boards of Sponsors unanimously supported a change in CWC's name, while 'objection to the designation Catholic has been voiced by no less than the Taoiseach, Mr. Sean Lemass, in conversation with one of the community'. In March 1966 CWC became the College of Industrial Relations (CIR), a change publicly presented as affording an opportunity 'for putting content into the spirit of ecumenism'.

Discussions preceding CWC's name change are well documented, but the Dublin diocesan archives contain little or nothing on the background to the renaming of DICS as the Dublin Institute of Adult Education (DIAE) announced in October 1966. This change was publicly stated to have been made at the archbishop's direction because 'the new name describes more aptly the Institute as it has developed'. The new name was the one proposed for the Institute by O'Rahilly thirteen years earlier when he advised against including 'Catholic' because 'many good layfolk (e.g. Catholic trade-unionists) fight shy of what they consider a "clerical" movement'.[57] In putting forward his suggestion for a Council of Adult Education during the early to mid-1950s discussions O'Doherty had immediately added 'before the Dept. get around to thinking of it'.[58] Returning in 1966 from a year of study at Columbia University, Fr. Liam Carey actively pursued the idea of an umbrella grouping and various providers came together in 1969 to form Aontas, the National Association of Adult Education. The Department of Education simultaneously entered the field when, at the national conference that

launched Aontas, Minister Brian Lenihan announced the setting up of a committee chaired by Con Murphy to examine adult education needs and structures.

Completing an interim report in 1970 and a final report in 1973, the Murphy
Committee placed adult education needs within a context of social disadvantage
and marginalisation, highlighting hitherto overlooked issues such as functional
illiteracy among a significant part of the adult population. In the post-McQuaid
era the development trajectory of the Institute the archbishop had created was
to increasingly involve its personnel in the area of literacy-centred 'basic' education. Adult education of this emerging type did not cease to be related to sociology in the new era but the nature of the relationship between the two that had
existed up to 1970s was radically transformed.

Offering an appreciation of Fr. Liam Carey's contribution to adult education,
his colleague Ted Fleming characterises the earlier period as one in which 'the
church was afraid of sex and communism ... sex was controlled through the
confessional and the fight against communism was fought mostly through adult
education'. He also notes that a changing pattern of postgraduate clerical education in the 1960s facilitated adult education's subsequent transformation. While
the early priest-sociologists sent abroad to study went to Catholic institutions,
the three priests who obtained the first southern Irish Adult Education PhDs
went to secular universities in Manchester, New York and Toronto. Exposure to
the theory and practice of the discipline in these overseas contexts – he studied
at both Columbia and Manchester – enabled Fr. Carey in particular to play a
key bridging role in the subsequent reshaping of Irish adult education (Fleming
2012). But postgraduate study by priests was only pursued with the permission,
if not at the direction, of ecclesiastical superiors. Archbishop McQuaid can thus
be regarded as having contributed to the shaping of both of Irish adult education's eras. How he came to be a facilitator of change can best be understood by
charting the empirical turn taken by Irish Catholic sociology in the 1950s.

Notes

1   Jennings (2009) draws on the Russell Library Maynooth, Library Collection 10/1, 'The
     Social Question in its relation to official ecclesiastical censorship and authority in Ireland
     Report Submitted to the Holy See 1930'; Part II adds events 1930–40; items 10/2
     to 10/6 contain additional information and appendices to these reports: further mate-
     rial dealing with Coffey's censorship difficulties is to be found in COFLA, MacRory
     Papers, ARCH/11/5/16, Rev. P. Coffey, PhD, St. Patrick's College Maynooth (imprima-
     tur refused), and DDA, A. B. Ryan, box 556, Mgr. Cronin's Papers, especially envelope
     marked 'Re Dr. Coffey's Book Gen Arch' and copy of P. Coffey to Bishop Morrisroe,
     Achonry, 11/12/1929, with handwritten note at bottom: 'Committee of Bishops

reported that, having examined the writings of Dr. Coffey, it was inadvisable to appoint Dr. Coffey to the Chair of Ethics. The Committee of Bishops consisted of the Bishop of Cork, the Bishop of Clogher Bp. of Killaloe.'

2   DDA, A. B. Ryan, box 556, Mgr. Cronin's Papers, Rev. Dr. J. Kelly, Clonliffe College, to Fr. Dunne, Archbishop's House, 2/1/1935, Mgr. M. Cronin, Rathgar, to Fr. P. Dunne, 6/1/1935, Rev. Dr. Kelly to Fr. Dunne, 22/2/1935.

3   DDA, McQuaid Papers, Lay Organisations, Maria Duce, AB8/B/XXI/80/29/2, 'Outline of the origin and history of Firinne, formerly Maria Duce' enclosed with T. Agar, Firinne, to Fr. C. Mangan, Archbishop's House, 17/6/1955.

4   DDA, McQuaid Papers, Lay Organisations, Maria Duce, AB8/B/XXI/80/79/1, J. Ryan, Secretary, Catholic Cinema & Theatre Patrons Association, to Archbishop McQuaid, 19/7/1949 – submitting the Association's Constitution Ryan refers to it as 'an arm of "Maria Duce"'.

5   DDA, McQuaid Papers, Lay Organisations, Maria Duce, AB8/B/XXI/80/32/2, 'The Organisation formerly called Maria Duce', statement enclosed with Archbishop McQuaid to papal nuncio, 22/12/1955; AB8/B/XXI/80/7/3, T. Agar, Maria Duce, to Fr. C. Mangan, Archbishop's House, 21/1/1950; AB8/B/XXI/80/12/1 and 2, T. Agar, Maria Duce, to Archbishop McQuaid, 20/1/51, enclosing copy Fr. C. Pridgeon SJ, Catholic Social Guild, Oxford, to Mr. Ryan, 8/1/1951.

6   DDA, McQuaid Papers, Maria Duce, AB8/B/XXI/80/6A/6, Archbishop McQuaid to Mgr. A. Ryan, Belfast, 26/3/1954.

7   DDA, McQuaid Papers, AB8/B/XV/C/12, Hierarchy Correspondence, Archbishop McQuaid to Cardinal McRory, Armagh, 3/3/1943.

8   DDA, AB Ryan, box 556, Mgr. Cronin's Papers, S. McEntee, Minister for Industry and Commerce, to Mgr. Cronin, 7/3/1940.

9   DDA, McQuaid Papers, AB8/B/XV/C/12 Hierarchy Correspondence, Archbishop McQuaid, Dublin, to Cardinal McRory, Armagh, 3/3/1943.

10 DDA, McQuaid Papers, AB8/B/XV/C/12, Hierarchy Correspondence, copy Archbishop McQuaid, Dublin, to Cardinal McRory, Armagh, 26/3/1943; COFLA, MacRory Papers, ARCH/11/5/16, Rev. Denis Fahey, C.S.Sp., Kimmage, Dublin, Re. Publication of his books – censorship problem – imprimatur refused, Fr. D. Fahey, Kimmage Manor, to Cardinal MacRory, 16/2/1943; DDA, McQuaid Papers, AB8/B/XV/C/9 and 13, Hierarchy Correspondence, Cardinal McRory to Archbishop McQuaid, 1/3/1943 and 29/3/1943.

11 DDA, McQuaid Papers, Lay Organisations, Maria Duce, AB8/B/XXI/80/48/54 and 55, Fr. D. Fahey, Kimmage Manor, to Archbishop McQuaid, 11/11/1947, Archbishop McQuaid to Fr. D. Fahey, 21/11/1947.

12 DDA, McQuaid Papers, Maria Duce, AB8/B XXI/80/6A/2, Archbishop McQuaid to Mgr. A. Ryan, Belfast, 19/3/1954.

13 DDA, McQuaid Papers, Lay Organisations, Maria Duce, AB8/B/XXI/80/27/1, archbishop's handwritten note to Secretary, 8/11/1954: 'Please send for Sec. and say that AB has already expressed disapproval of title Maria Duce and now insists on its being discontinued', copy Archbishop's Secretary to J. Duggan, Maria Duce, 8/12/1952.

14   DDA, McQuaid Papers, Lay Organisations, Maria Duce, AB8/B/XXI/80/32/2, 'The Organisation formerly called Maria Duce', statement enclosed with Archbishop McQuaid to papal nuncio, 22/12/1955.

15   Russell Library Maynooth, MCA 32/22/32, Rev. Prof. P. McKevitt, Rome, to Dr. J. D'Alton, President, St. Patrick's College Maynooth, 18/12/1938; MCA 32/22/34, P. McKevitt to J. D'Alton, 10/4/1939.

16   Russell Library Maynooth, MCA 32/22/35, 'Proposals for the Initiation of a Scheme of Catholic Action for Ireland', pp. 1–2.

17   Russell Library Maynooth, MCA 32/22/33, Rev. Prof. P. McKevitt, Rome, to Dr. J. D'Alton, President, St. Patrick's College Maynooth, 19/1/1939; MCA 32/22/35, 'Proposals for the Initiation of a Scheme of Catholic Action for Ireland'.

18   Russell Library Maynooth, MCA 32/22/24, Fr. P. McKevitt's application for Maynooth Catholic Sociology and Catholic Action Chair, 29/9/1937; MCA 32/22/21, Fr. P. McKevitt, Dundalk, to Dr. J. D'Alton, President, St. Patrick's College Maynooth, 7/10/1936.

19   Russell Library Maynooth, MCA 32/22/35, 'Proposals for the Initiation of a Scheme of Catholic Action for Ireland'; COFLA, MacRory Papers ARCH/11/2, Hierarchy, Meetings (folders 1–3), handwritten note on Standing Committee meeting, 19 June 1939.

20   DDA, Archbishop Byrne Papers, box Irish Bishops, folder Province of Tuam, sub-folder Clonfert, 'Report on Education of Clergy in Social Science'.

21   NAI, DL W63, Formation of Council of Irish Trade Unions in lieu of the Irish Trade Union Congress, S. Lemass, Minister for Industry and Commerce, to Secretary, Department of Industry and Commerce, 23/5/1945; see also NAI, DT S13,700, Congress of Irish Unions: Uniformity of State Action following Recognition of.

22   NAI, DFA A55, Communist Activities in Ireland, 'Communist Party of Ireland', G2/X/0248, 28 January 1944, enclosed with Col. D. Bryan, G2, to Minister, 2/2/1944.

23   NLI, LO P93, five leaflets containing articles including two by Prof. Alfred O'Rahilly, reprinted from the *Standard*, February–May 1944, on Communism in Irish labour.

24   COFLA, D'Alton Papers, ARCH 12/12 box 33, Political, Labour Party 1944 file, 'Committee of Inquiry, Report of the Committee Prepared for the Administrative Council and the Parliamentary Labour Party'.

25   NLI, LO P93, The Labour Party, Official Statement relating to the disaffiliation from the Labour Party of the Irish Transport and General Workers Union prepared by the Administrative Council for the information of Party Branches, Divisional and Constituency Councils and Affiliated Corporate Bodies, 5/2/1944.

26   COFLA, D'Alton Papers, ARCH 12/12, box 33, Political, Labour Party 1944 file, 'Committee of Inquiry, Report of the Committee Prepared for the Administrative Council and the Parliamentary Labour Party', enclosed with L. J. Duffy, Labour Party, to Dr. J. D'Alton, Bishop of Meath, 29/4/1944: Duffy's letter describes the subject of the inquiry as 'certain allegations featured for some time in "The Standard" newspaper'.

27   NLI, William O'Brien Papers, Ms. 13, 960, A. O'Rahilly, UCC, to P. J. O'Brien, ITGWU, Cork, 14/2/1944, P. J. O'Brien to W. O'Brien, ITGWU, Dublin, 16/2/1944.

28   COFLA, D'Alton Papers, ARCH 12/12, box 33, Political, Labour Party 1944 file.

29   DDA, McQuaid Papers, XXII/24/3, Catholic Workers' Institute 1943–45, T. Counihan SJ, Rathfarnham Castle, to Archbishop McQuaid, 12/4/1944.

30   NLI, William O'Brien Papers, Ms. 13,960, P. J. O'Brien, ITGWU, Cork, to W. O'Brien, ITGWU, Dublin, 21/2/1944.

31   Irish Trade Union Congress, *Annual Report 1954*, Dublin: Irish Trade Union Congress, pp. 141–144.

32   NAI, DFA A55, Communist Activities in Ireland, memorandum, 'Communist Group since 1945', 23/6/1947, enclosed with Col. D. Bryan, G2, to F. Boland, External Affairs, 23/6/1947.

33   NAI, DFA A55, Communist Activities in Ireland, 'To the Editor', handwritten note on two-page document states: 'Report supplied Daily Papers but not published except brief note in Mail herewith' (attached is clipping from *Evening Mail*, 'Workers League', 22/10/1948).

34   NAI, DFA A55, Communist Activities in Ireland, 'Memorandum on Communism in the State', June 1953.

35   DDA, McQuaid Papers, AB/8/B/XXXV (10–15), Adult Education, Dublin Institute of Catholic Sociology, copy of 'University College Cork Memo from the President Adult Education', 1/2/1952, copy of T. O'Raifeartaigh, Leas Runai, Education, to A. O'Rahilly, President, UCC, 22/2/1952, copy of A. O'Rahilly to T. O'Raifeartaigh, 25/2/1952, copy of T. O'Raifeartaigh to A. O'Rahilly, 28/2/1952.

36   DDA, McQuaid Papers, AB/8/B/XXXV (10–15), Adult Education, Dublin Institute of Catholic Sociology, memorandum 'Notes on the Proposed for the Introduction of Catholic Social Teaching into the Night Classes of the Technical Schools', undated.

37   DDA, McQuaid Papers, AB/8/B/XXXV (10–15), Adult Education, Dublin Institute of Catholic Sociology, 'Notes on Relations with V.E. Teachers, C.E.O.s and Committees', undated.

38   DDA, McQuaid Papers, AB/8/B/XXXV (10–15), Adult Education, Dublin Institute of Catholic Sociology, 'Memorandum on social science in technical schools', enclosed with Rev. Prof. E. F. O'Doherty, UCD, to Fr. L. Martin, Archbishop's House, 2/11/1955.

39   DDA, McQuaid Papers, AB/8/B/XXXV (10–15), Adult Education, Dublin Institute of Catholic Sociology, memorandum 'Notes on the Proposed for the Introduction of Catholic Social Teaching into the Night Classes of the Technical Schools', undated.

40   DDA, McQuaid Papers, AB/8/B/XXXV (10–15), Adult Education, Dublin Institute of Catholic Sociology, A. O'Rahilly, Blackrock College, to Fr. L. Martin, Archbishop's House, 25/1/1955.

41   DDA, McQuaid Papers, AB/8/B/XXXV (10–15), Adult Education, Dublin Institute of Catholic Sociology, notes attached to A. O'Rahilly, Blackrock College, to Fr. L. Martin, Archbishop's House, 2/2/1955.

42   This was Brian Farrell, who would later become a professor of politics in UCD and a very well-known broadcaster.

43 DDA, McQuaid Papers, AB/8/B/XXXV (10–15), Adult Education, Dublin Institute of Catholic Sociology, memorandum 'Notes on the Proposed for the Introduction of Catholic Social Teaching into the Night Classes of the Technical Schools', undated.

44 DDA, McQuaid Papers, AB/8/B/XXXV (10–15), Adult Education, Dublin Institute of Catholic Sociology, Rev. Prof. E. F. O'Doherty, UCD, to Fr. L. Martin, Archbishop's House, 19/3/1956.

45 DDA, McQuaid Papers, AB/8/B/XXXV (10–15), Adult Education, Dublin Institute of Catholic Sociology, handwritten note, undated.

46 DDA, McQuaid Papers, AB/8/B/XXXV (10–15), Adult Education, Dublin Institute of Catholic Sociology, handwritten note by Archbishop McQuaid, 15/1/1958, Archbishop McQuaid to Fr. J. Kavanagh, UCD, 27/11/1958.

47 DDA, McQuaid Papers, AB/8/B/XXXV (10–15), Adult Education, Dublin Institute of Catholic Sociology, Fr. T. Fehilly, DICS, to Fr. J. A. McMahon, Archbishop's House, June 1959, Archbishop McQuaid to Fr. Fehilly, 11/6/1959, Fr. J. Kavanagh, chairman DICS Board, to Archbishop McQuaid, 18/6/1959.

48 DDA, McQuaid Papers, AB/8/B/XXXV (10–15), Adult Education, Dublin Institute of Catholic Sociology, Archbishop McQuaid to Fr. T. Fehilly, DICS, 9/10/1960.

49 DDA, McQuaid Papers, AB/8/B/XXXV (10–15), Adult Education, Dublin Institute of Catholic Sociology, Archbishop McQuaid to Lady Wicklow, 31/12/1963.

50 DDA, McQuaid Papers, AB/8/B/XXXV (10–15), Adult Education, Dublin Institute of Catholic Sociology, Fr. J. Kavanagh, chairman DICS Board, to Archbishop McQuaid, 26/9/1962.

51 DDA, McQuaid Papers, AB/8/B/XXXV (10–15), Adult Education, Dublin Institute of Catholic Sociology, Archbishop McQuaid to Fr. L. Carey, DICS, 2/5/1963, handwritten note on Fr. L. Carey to Archbishop McQuaid, 12/10/1964.

52 DDA, McQuaid Papers, AB/8/B/XXXV (10–15), Adult Education, Dublin Institute of Catholic Sociology, Fr. J. Kavanagh, chairman DICS Board, to Archbishop McQuaid, 10/1/1965.

53 DDA, McQuaid Papers, AB/8/B/XXXV (10–15), Adult Education, Dublin Institute of Catholic Sociology, 'Some Comments on This Survey', enclosed with Fr. L. Carey, DICS, to Archbishop McQuaid, 5/12/1966.

54 DDA, McQuaid Papers, AB/8/B/XXXV (10–15), Adult Education, Dublin Institute of Catholic Sociology, Fr. J. Kavanagh, chairman DICS Board, to Archbishop McQuaid, 20/1/1966, Archbishop McQuaid to Fr. J. Kavanagh, 22/1/1966, Memorandum for the Archbishop on the Financial Position of the Institute, 13/8/1963, eight DICS Board members to Archbishop McQuaid, 15/6/1965.

55 DDA, McQuaid Papers, AB8/B/XXXII/A (iii)/12 (a) XXXII, Universities A: University College Dublin iii, Faculty of Philosophy and Sociology 11, Department of Sociology (a), Rev. Prof. James Kavanagh, Mgr. C. Barrett, Booterstown, to Archbishop McQuaid, 22/6/1968.

56 DDA, McQuaid Papers, AB/8/B/XXXV (10–15), Adult Education, Dublin Institute of Catholic Sociology, Fr. J. Kavanagh, chairman, DICS Board to Archbishop McQuaid, 11/9/63, Archbishop McQuaid to Fr. J. Kavanagh, 12/9/1963.

57 DDA, McQuaid Papers, AB/8/B/XXXV (1–5), Adult Education, Adult Education Committee, 1952–58, handwritten memorandum 'The General Problem of Adult Education', enclosed with A. O'Rahilly, Blackrock College, to Fr. L. Martin, Archbishop's House, 11/1/1955.

58 DDA, McQuaid Papers, AB/8/B/XXXV (10–15), Adult Education, Dublin Institute of Catholic Sociology, 'Memorandum on social science in technical schools', enclosed with Rev. Prof. E. F. O'Doherty, UCD, to Fr. L. Martin, Archbishop's House, 2/11/1955.

3

Facing facts: the empirical turn of Irish Catholic sociology in the 1950s

Introduction

This chapter examines the changing face of Catholic sociology in Ireland during the 1950s and 1960s. It has four principal strands. First, the joint action of the Maynooth professor and Muintir na Tire to secure European and US help in fostering rural sociology. Second, the use made by Archbishop McQuaid of his power within UCD to establish social science teaching in the state's largest university. Third, the tension between useful and critical social science that emerged as the growing number of Irish Catholic immigrants in an increasingly secular Britain became a focal point for research proposals. Finally, the manner in which Ireland's initially abundant, but later faltering, supply of religious vocations and the maximisation of its clergy's contribution to worldwide Catholic missionary efforts was studied. All of these strands are tied together by a broad turn away from exclusive preoccupation with ethical principles and towards increasing involvement in empirical social investigations.

A new professor in Maynooth

In June 1953 Peter McKevitt resigned from his post in Maynooth to become parish priest of Termonfeckin. While the bishops had decided to shelve his 1939 proposals for the initiation of a Scheme of Catholic Action for Ireland, McKevitt on his return from Rome 'threw himself into the activities of the Christus Rex Society as well as teaching the social encyclicals of the church to students preparing to become priests' (B. Conway 2011: 42). Created in 1941, and formally approved by the hierarchy in 1945, the Christus Rex Society restricted its membership to diocesan clergy and included among its chief activities the organisation of an annual social study congress and the publication of an eponymous quarterly journal (C. Daly 1967; L'Estrange 2007b). During and after his time as a Maynooth professor, McKevitt contributed articles and reviews to *Christus Rex* and to Irish theological journals. In 1944 he published a sociology textbook based on his Maynooth lecture course – *The Plan of Society*. A quarter of century later he wrote the epilogue chapter, sub-titled 'Modern Ireland', of the multi-volume *History of Irish Catholicism* edited by Patrick Corish (B. Conway 2011: 43–45).

In October 1953 Jeremiah Newman was appointed to succeed McKevitt at Maynooth. Like McKevitt, Newman had a doctorate in philosophy from Louvain and, like James Kavanagh, he had spent a period in Oxford devoted to social studies. Brian Conway (2011) argues that the Maynooth changeover represents a shift from one distinct phase of Irish Catholic sociology to another. While McKevitt held the chair, the discipline was 'confessional in orientation and for this reason tended to be reluctant to engage in scientific or empirical studies of everyday social life, preferring instead to take the papal encyclicals as its guide to Irish social life'. Newman inaugurated 'the second phase of Irish Catholic sociology [which] involved bringing theology into dialogue with mainstream sociology ... he reflected continuity with his predecessor by emphasising the need to promote Catholic sociology but, more than McKevitt, sought to utilise the standard sociological methods of social surveys in gathering data to confront the idealistic claims of Catholic theology' (B. Conway 2011: 51).

This outlook led Newman to criticise the existence in Ireland of 'a rather one-sided Sociology which pays reverence to principles and only lip-service to facts' and to discern, in the context of a prevailing approach to sociology that was 'far too general', the existence of 'a crying need' for special sociology: 'at the very least for Rural Sociology and Urban Sociology. There is need too for the Sociology of Religion' (Newman 1957: 76). This line of argument was concretely applied in the rural field through commentary on and critique of the 1954 Report of the Commission on Emigration. According to Newman, the Commission had failed to properly analyse Irish emigration's social context and had treated rural depopulation as a problem peculiar to Ireland. Drawing on British and Dutch research, he argued that it was possible to tackle rural decline by policies that underpinned a process of 'rurbanization'. This would involve creating a series of 'fairly large centres in which people who continue to live in the surrounding rural areas can find employment as well as opportunities for a satisfactory social and cultural life' thanks to 'modern methods of transport (bus, motor-cycle, etc.)' through which 'commuting is made easy between the large centre and its immediate hinterland' (Newman 1958a: 400).

Building up centres needed to be based on 'careful economic development surveys' and Newman argued that 'organizations like Muintir na Tire (Muintir) should take a leading part in all this work'. Among Muintir's national leadership his views were to find a highly receptive audience. Founded in 1937 by a Tipperary priest, Canon John Hayes, Muintir proclaimed itself to be 'a Movement for the promotion of the true welfare, spiritual, cultural and material of Ireland and, in particular, of its rural people, through the application of Christian social principles'. John Whyte (1980: 69–70) views it as 'one of the most important channels through which the new precision in Catholic social teaching became known in Ireland', while Sean L'Estrange (2007a: 568–569) characterises it as 'a "bottom-up" experiment in organising competing social interests into local communities constituted on micro-corporatist lines'. Muintir's parish guilds quickly came to the fore in the local organisation of the Emergency period's drives to try to make up shortfalls in food and fuel supplies. During the Emergency the Department of Agriculture recommended that Muintir should receive an annual grant through its Vote, but de Valera's reaction was that this 'would constitute nothing short of a disservice to the Association, because it would deprive it of the spirit of self-reliance and self-help so sorely needed in this country as a whole and among the farmers in particular' (quoted in M. Daly 2002: 258). With the advent of the Marshall Plan US aid providers were also favourably impressed by Muintir, ear-marking it along with the Irish Countrywomen's Association (ICA) and Macra na Feirme (Macra) for Grant Counterpart Fund allocations to strengthen their organisational capacities.

However, divergences between Muintir's project of an all-embracing community movement and what it perceived as the sectional interest projects of its fellow funding beneficiaries were arguably as significant as the aims these movements shared in common (see Rynne 1960: 195–97). During the 1950s these divergences were to be brought into the open by conflict over the Parish Plan for the organisation of agricultural advisory services. Originally devised by members of Muintir's National Executive, the Parish Plan was partially implemented in an adapted form by James Dillon during his stints as Minister for Agriculture in the first (1948–51) and second (1954–57) inter-party governments (M. Daly 2002: 403–406). Muintir was ultimately to distance itself from Dillon's initiatives in order to avoid damaging defections from its own ranks but not before it became embroiled in a dispute with Macra and its offshoot, the National Farmers' Association (NFA). In what Canon Hayes referred to as 'the hounding of the Plan', Muintir found itself under sustained attack from these quarters for lacking the requisite farming expertise, as 'many of the officials are national teachers and curates' (Tierney 2004: 101–102; Rynne 1960: 261–262).

The canon's death in January 1957 preceded by a few months a return to office of Fianna Fail. That party had never regarded the Parish Plan with much enthusiasm and would gradually wind it down after notice of its impending death appeared in the pages of *Economic Development*. Reflecting on the conflict over the Plan that had dogged the last years of Canon Hayes's life and embroiled the movement he had founded in a morass of recrimination, one of Muintir's leading figures, Dr. Thomas Morris, then vice-president of a major seminary, St. Patrick's College in Thurles, wrote to Newman that:

> Muintir must move over to make room for the farmers' organisations ... its function must be educational more than the 'brightening up' or recreational idea. Sociology is bound to reach Ireland some time and it is well to have the Papists equipped for the time when it comes.

Morris was not prominently associated with the public face of the discipline through bodies like the Christus Rex Society but his private letters to Newman reveal his interest in sociology and his desire to see it develop in the direction of empirical studies. In the same letter, written just after Newman had delivered the first Canon Hayes Memorial Lecture in February 1958, Morris states that '"rurbanisation" is a bit startling to me – not that that is a final condemnation! The reception in Limerick was very consoling: I really was nervous of an emotional and unfavourable reaction.'[1]

Another member of Muintir's National Executive with links to sociology was P. J. Meghen, who in the late 1950s was County Manager of Limerick. An earlier stage of Meghen's career in local government had included an extended period as a commissioner administering the town of Ennis in place of its dissolved Urban District Council (Robins 1993: 109–111). While he was discharging this role, he assisted Lloyd Warner and other members of the Harvard Irish Study team, becoming particularly friendly with Conrad Arensberg, who in 1937 dedicated *The Irish Countryman* to both Meghen and Warner (Byrne, Edmondson and Varley 2001: xli). An engineer by profession, Meghen was familiar with the sociological community studies tradition that linked 1930s Clare with Middletown and Yankee City and, more broadly, with a variety of accounts of Ireland written from a social scientific perspective (Meghen 1961 and 1963).

In the years immediately following Canon Hayes's death Meghen, Morris and Newman were to fore in seizing opportunities to turn Muintir towards involvement in sociology. During 1958, after an allocation for Technical Assistance from the Marshall Aid Grant Counterpart Fund became available to it, the Department of Agriculture invited rural organisations to submit applications for project funding. In response, Muintir successfully proposed the Limerick

Table 3.1 LRS reports: dates of publication, topics and authors

1960	Migration (Patrick McNabb)
1961	Physical Geography and Geology (P. J. Meghen and others)
1962	Social Structure (Patrick McNabb)
1963	Social Provision and Rural Centrality (Jeremiah Newman)
1964	Social History (P. J. Meghen)
1964	Volume collecting interim reports edited by Jeremiah Newman

Source: library catalogues

Rural Survey (LRS). Also in 1958 Muintir affiliated to the European Society for Rural Sociology and invited the Society's President, Professor E. W. Hofstee of Wageningen University in Holland, to address its annual Rural Week. Contrary to Muintir's intentions, Hofstee, when he came to Ireland, argued against reliance on foreign experts to carry out the fieldwork for the LRS. Instead he urged the employment of an Irish graduate for whom he offered to provide specialised training in Holland before the survey commenced. Recruited as LRS researcher, Patrick McNabb – a UCD protégé of Professor Feichin O'Doherty – spent a training period in Wageningen in late 1958 while the Dutch sociologist with whom he had worked most closely, Jelle Lijfering, subsequently visited Limerick twice to support the fieldwork initiated there at the start of 1959. Table 3.1 sets out the sequence in which Muintir published a series of interim reports on the LRS. A book collecting these (unrevised) interim reports, edited by Newman and published by Muintir, marked the completion of the survey.

Newman's contribution further developed the ideas he had put forward in his February 1958 lecture, applying what he now termed rural centrality to the specific case of county Limerick. McNabb in his social structure report produced a strikingly bold and radical analysis that emphasised the importance of class division within the rural community. From 'being a stable and closed community, having a rigid class structure assented to by all its members' Limerick had moved to a currently 'unstable and open' situation characterised by a debilitating stand-off between classes. Based on the farm family, 'the traditional class system remains intact, but the workers no longer accept it'. The farm workers had 'opted out of the rural community'. They now shunned farm work where they could and chose to steer their children towards emigration in order for them to enter other kinds of employment. Among farmers, 'the family is increasingly becoming the unit of economic production ... since the war, more and more of the larger farmers are dispensing with hired labour'. As a result 'the farmer has more or less successfully resisted the direct attacks of the workers, but only at

the price of losing them altogether'. However, a successful turning inward of
the farm family was undermined by the contrast between the situation of the
remaining children and the members of the same generation (whether farmers' or labourers' offspring) who have emigrated but return home on holidays.
This contrast 'goads the farmer's children to revolt, so that indirectly the social
conflict between farmer and worker has been carried into the heart of the farm
family and has initiated the decay of family loyalty'.

To McNabb the 'various government agencies working for the improvement
of agriculture' were 'paternalistic': 'they weaken the society by taking on too
many of its functions, as the father weakens the family by refusing to delegate
responsibility'. The forces for social change were not these agencies but movements like Muintir, Macra na Feirme, the Irish Countrywomen's Association,
the National Farmers' Association and the Irish Creamery Milk Suppliers'
Association. But these were all community-centred organisations, whereas the
society they sought to regenerate was family-centred. Muintir's ideal was a co-
operative one but this 'can be realised only by a change in the role of the father
and a complete reorganisation of the society' (McNabb 1964: 193–247).

Running in parallel with the initiation of the LRS was a Muintir scheme to
provide Irish postgraduate students of sociology with scholarships to study at US
universities (Peter Murray 2012b). In July and August 1958 Newman traveled
extensively in the United States on Muintir's behalf. His later references to this
tour, both published and unpublished, were to place it in the context of the preparations being made to undertake the LRS now that funding had been agreed.
But – while Newman obtained advice for and recruited some high-profile names
as consultants to the LRS during his US visit – the primary purpose of his tour
was distinct from, and much more ambitious in scope than, the project to be
carried out in Limerick. Stated publicly as well as privately at the time, this was
'to investigate the courses in Sociology (Rural Sociology, Social Research) which
would be suitable for post-graduate studies by Irish students and the possibility
of obtaining scholarships for such Irish students'.[2] The initiative for this investigation again came from Morris, who wrote to Newman on 28 February 1958
enclosing the draft of a memorandum 'to be sent by Fr. Morrissey [successor to
Canon Hayes as National Chairman of Muintir na Tire] to Archbishop Cushing
[of Boston] as soon as possible':

> We will, of course, write a covering letter also, telling the Archbishop that you hope
> to travel to America. The purpose of this Memorandum is to enable the Archbishop
> to pass it on to somebody with university connections, or to some possible sponsors,
> saying 'This is their idea, fix up something'. Hence some preamble and a straight
> appeal for help.[3]

The nub of 'their idea' was that 'a number of students, say ten at least, might be trained over a number of years' in sociology at US universities. Muintir's function 'must be basically educational', therefore 'social research and adult education must occupy an important place in our programme'. Ireland should have a distinctive contribution to make to the development of rural sociology in Europe but 'much leeway needs to be made up in our equipment' and 'we are painfully aware that social research in Ireland must remain in a backward state until native sociologists are available' (Peter Murray 2012b: 76–77). Fr. Morrissey's covering letter elaborated on this point:

> The lack of trained personnel in the various branches of Sociology hinders us from even preparing a proper programme of social surveys for submission to a Foundation. We are about to submit a request to the Irish Department of Agriculture for assistance financed from the Grant Counterpart Fund towards a pilot survey of the rural areas in Co. Limerick as a beginning. We cannot tell how this request will be received as social surveys are practically an unknown quantity here. Through Dr. Newman we hope to get in touch with a Dutch rural sociologist, Professor Hofstee of Wageningen, to bring him to lecture here during Rural Week (August 1958) and perhaps to obtain advice or direction from him. There is no substitute for native personnel, hence our interest in post-graduate studies. (Peter Murray 2012b: 79)

A clerical/lay mix among the scholarship holders was envisaged, although neither the memorandum not its covering letter had anything positive to say on behalf of laymen (or laywomen), while priests are considered more likely to return to work in Ireland after their studies are completed and, when they do so, to contribute to Muintir's work. Another letter from Fr. Morrissey – to the US ambassador on 12 March – suggests that 'perhaps a proportion of half lay and half clerical may be best'.[4]

Jeremiah Newman in the USA

Archbishop Cushing's initial response was neither optimistic nor enthusiastic. He predicted that 'you are going to have a very hard time in getting scholarships in this country for Irish students interested in postgraduate work in the field of social service'. He added that 'I will welcome anyone you send here and help him in any way I can but I think that it would be a wonderful thing if the Irish Societies in this country would sponsor some students'. With the archbishop making plain in subsequent correspondence that 'there is nothing I can do about arranging interviews with Universities and Colleges', Muintir eventually turned to the Washington-based National Catholic Welfare Conference for assistance in making academic contacts and organising a coast-to-coast itinerary. Arriving in New York in July, Newman made his way first to Boston.[5] There, face-to-face with Muintir's representative, the archbishop offered to take personal responsibility for the provision of five scholarships for Irish priests, 'thus providing us with as many as we would be in a position to use in the foreseeable future':

> The Cardinal's offer included financing the transportation of the students to America, and the locating of them in presbyteries in the American centres in which they would be studying (their pastoral work to be confined to weekend work). He thought that there would be no difficulty in getting pastors to keep them, even in dioceses not his own. As regards the Scholarships proper, for two years each, he said that he should have no difficulty in getting these directly himself from any of the many Jesuit universities and the Catholic University of America, when the time arose.

While in the USA Newman visited eighteen universities, identifying five to which 'for our purposes the choice can be narrowed down': Fordham in New York, the Catholic University of America in Washington, DC, the University of St. Louis, Notre Dame (Indiana) and Loyola (Chicago): 'Notre Dame may be out as regards Dr. Cushing getting a scholarship there; of that I am not sure. But the others, apart from CU, are Jesuit and he says he can also get one at CU, of which he is a trustee.'

Newman and the US academics with whom he discussed the matter were in agreement that 'it is desirable that our students get a degree (M.A.) so as to have status in the subject on return home and for psychological reasons to give them a feeling of being able to do something on their return'. Although the Irish priest-students would have very little or no grounding in 'modern' sociology at undergraduate level, Newman recorded that 'the Professors I met in the universities to which I have given special mention were agreed that our students could, with special arrangements, be enabled to get an MA in two years or at most two years plus a preliminary Summer period'. With scholarships available and university credentials apparently obtainable, only one problem was encountered. Rural sociology – the specialised branch of the discipline Muintir was most keen to develop in Ireland – might, as the memorandum to Archbishop Cushing stated, be more developed in the USA than in Europe but Newman recorded that it was not taught in any of the US Catholic universities, 'largely because most Catholics in the U.S. live in urban areas'.

Warming to the scholarship scheme, Archbishop Cushing had 'expected that we would have five men ready to go out in the Autumn of 1958' and 'thought that one of them should be made a kind of "superior" to keep in touch with the others'. Newman did not consider arrangements to send a group of this size at the one time to be feasible and in the long memorandum he wrote in April

1959, he concluded that 'the main thing is to get one man at least now ... if too long a time is allowed to lapse, people over there are liable to forget about my visit'.[6] One man's studies is all that can be documented to date as being linked to Newman's visit, though not to the wider Muintir-originated scheme of scholarships for sociology students that led to its being undertaken. In a very detailed account of the LRS that was compiled sometime after he became Bishop of Limerick in 1974, Newman wrote of his US visit that:

> As Cardinal Cushing was a good friend of Ireland and Canon Hayes, it was also decided that my first stop should be in Boston. There the Cardinal – although deeply engaged at the time in the launching of the Missionary Society of St. James – supplied me with whatever funds were needed for my visits within the States ... The way things ultimately turned out, my journey did have many results. I visited around twenty Departments of Sociology, and lectured in a number of them, such as the Catholic University of America in Washington and the University of St. Louis, making many contacts which were to be of much value for Sociology in Ireland. It was because of one of them that Professor Liam Ryan, later my successor as Professor of Sociology at Maynooth, went to St. Louis to do his degree in Sociology there.[7]

Why, with support on offer, did the scheme not proceed?

As the memorandum sent to Archbishop Cushing indicates, the co-operation of bishops 'willing to nominate priests belonging to their diocese as students of Sociology after their ordination' was essential to the operation of the pro-posed scholarship scheme. However, none of those promoting the scheme were bishops. Moreover, Muintir was a regionally confined movement – present in perhaps one third of Irish parishes, strong in central Munster but weakly repre-sented in the religiously divided north and in the poor, small-farm west of the country, where bishops were unlikely to be responsive. Added to limitations on Muintir's spread deriving from the social structure were others stemming from specifically ecclesiastical factors. As Canon Hayes's biographer notes, 'from the beginning there was opposition to Muintir na Tire and cool views of its founder' within the clergy of his Church and 'a few bishops adopted a negative attitude'. Here he specifically refers to Kerry, where 'the introduction of guilds ... was for a time tolerated rather than blessed', to Dublin, which since 1940 'has been closed to Muintir na Tire' and to Killaloe, which 'was forbidden territory while Bishop Fogarty reigned' (Rynne 1960: 170–171).

In ecclesiastical terms this meant that Muintir was a movement of the Cashel and Emly province with a much less extensive presence in the Armagh, Dublin and Tuam provinces. The closure of Dublin was particularly significant since its instigator, Archbishop McQuaid, was, by virtue of both his position and his personality, a dominant presence within the Church hierarchy for more than three decades (J. H. Whyte 1980: 75–80). He was also the member of that hierarchy 'whose deep interest in social questions led him to pioneer the contemporary approach by sending priests of his own diocese for post-graduate training in the social sciences, and by incessantly urging the pastoral importance of such training' (Ward 1964: 26). Suggested reasons for the archbishop's negative attitude to Muintir include a perception of it as a rival to the Catholic Social Service Conference he had set up in Dublin as well as distaste for the mixing of the sexes in its membership and for its Christian rather than specifically Catholic character (Cooney 1999: 157–158). The third of these reasons receives confirmation from a 1959 exchange between the archbishop and Fr. James Kavanagh, who was then teaching in UCD after his return from Cambridge. On this occasion, Fr. Kavanagh wrote seeking advice on:

> The possibility of having some Catholic body to represent Irish farmers & rural people in a proposed Catholic International Rural Body (about which the present Holy Father is said to be keenly interested). This is something like the problem which arose some years ago re the affiliation of our Trade Unions to the Christian International Federation. Conditions here are different from the continent. If, however, as Your Grace seemed to suggest, some rural members of the Dublin Adult Education courses & who are also members of Muintir na Tire, Young Farmers & N.F.A. were to form a committee to make a liaison body, that might meet the situation. I think this might be feasible. Is that what Your Grace had in mind?

To this query the archbishop responded that 'the Farmer Body does not simply exist in our circumstances. I thought of the [Dublin] Institute [of Catholic Sociology], as being the only *Catholic* body. Muintir na Tire is interdenominational. Your plan is good: try it out.'[8]

Between Newman's summer 1958 visit to the USA and his spring 1959 composition of the memorandum on its results, the death of Jeremiah Kinane left vacant the position of Archbishop of Cashel and Emly. By the end of that year Morris had been chosen as his successor. In that position he quickly joined Archbishop McQuaid as an active promoter of socio-religious research in Ireland (Ward 1964: 26). The Cashel and Emly province had an arrangement in place whereby newly ordained priests for whom no immediate vacancies existed were temporarily assigned to work in Dublin. Within months of becoming archbishop, Morris was arranging for one newly ordained priest heading for Dublin, Fr. James Holway, to study for an MA in sociology at UCD, writing to Archbishop

McQuaid on 17 July 1960 that 'I had the pleasure of meeting Dr. Conor Ward last week and was very impressed by him as a scholar and as a priest. If Father Holway can serve an apprenticeship to social research, in addition to his university studies, our diocese in turn will benefit greatly.' On 29 September, with the arrangements now in place, Morris wrote again to McQuaid that 'I am deeply grateful to you and Fr. [Conor] Martin for the trouble you have taken to arrange a course at the University for Father Holway. I am satisfied that he will have the best possible direction in his studies in sociology and the purpose which I have in mind is to have him well trained in this subject.'[9]

With Archbishop McQuaid's longstanding negative attitude to Muintir creating a stumbling block to securing the necessary episcopal backing for a US scholarship scheme operating under its auspices, the precedent-setting case of Fr. Holway shows Morris, having himself become an archbishop, looking closer to home at an Irish university in his promotion of the study of sociology by Irish priests. This was possible because of the strengthening of social science at UCD which Archbishop McQuaid's accumulation of extensive power within that institution (Garvin 1998; Cooney 1999: 295–296) had been used to support. It is to a detailed examination of this process that this chapter now turns.

Archbishop McQuaid and social science in UCD

Responding to the papal nuncio in relation to Maria Duce/Firinne in December 1955 Archbishop McQuaid had, as we saw in Chapter 2, written that 'I have now, at length, been able to take measures in the University to have Catholic philosophy permeate all the Faculties, and I can hope that our educated lay-folk in the near future will no longer show themselves to be infected by the Protestant English Liberalism that had caused, and is still causing, so much confusion in our country.' Below he will be encountered in 1962 referring to UCD's Faculty of Philosophy and Sociology as 'the Faculty for which I am particularly responsible' – as indeed it was. For the greater part of the archbishop's period in office (1940–72) the Faculty's three foundation chairs were occupied by three of his priests – Monsignor John Horgan (metaphysics, 1942–71), the Rev. Feichin O'Doherty (logic and psychology, 1949–83) and the Rev. Conor Martin (ethics and politics, 1952–80). In relation to the NUI as a whole there was also, as outlined in Chapter 1, the 1950 appeal of the college presidents for the hierarchy's help in 'formulating a policy on the future of the University', which had referred specifically to 'the making of arrangements for the better and more thorough teaching of Philosophy and Sociology, especially for lay-students', and the liaison committee of presidents and bishops whose creation this had prompted. Beyond the NUI there was, for the Dublin archdiocese from 1944 and nationally from 1956, the policing of the 'Trinity ban'. Here, having promulgated an extended version of the ban, the archbishop and his staff found that its enforcement in practice depended on alternatives to Trinity's courses being available in UCD. In the context of preparations for a liaison committee meeting in December 1951, Dr. McQuaid complained to the Archbishop of Armagh:

> Dr. Tierney has no mention in his letter of the complete failure of University College Dublin to provide for the Commerce degrees and evening lectures in Public Administration. This year again at least 100 students had to be given permission to enter Trinity, and every year that passes gives me stronger evidence of the undesirability of our Catholic boys and girls entering Trinity. Trinity College is not competing with University College, for Trinity has seized the initiative years ago and holds it unchallenged. Most of our future administrators will have been trained in Trinity.[10]

During 1952 the archbishop actively pursued this issue with UCD's president, registrar and the dean of its Faculty of Philosophy and Sociology, identifying a number of specific UCD deficits by comparison with Trinity – the length of time required to complete a degree or diploma, the opportunity to begin a degree in every year rather than in every third year, more convenient lecture times and lower fees. By October he was circulating to his fellow members of the hierarchy a statement giving details of 'the very favourable facilities for the Diploma in Public Administration, the B.A. and the B.Comm.' now on offer in the evening at UCD.[11] In the following academic year, 1953–54, another UCD evening degree, the Bachelor of Social Science (B.Soc.Sc.), was introduced. Here again the archbishop was actively involved, with, on 9 January 1953, 'Dr. Tierney, President, telephoning to request an interview with Your Grace for himself and Mgr Horgan, in regard to the establishment of a Degree in Sociology … as three meetings of the Governing Body in U.C.D. must be held before the Regulations establishing such a degree could be brought into force'. Before the liaison committee met in June 1953 Alfred O'Rahilly circulated a memorandum that 'had only one criticism to make' of this 'excellent scheme':

> I think this degree should not be available independently but should always be conjoined with another degree – B.A, B.Sc., B.Comm, M.B., B.E. – and therefore available only to those pursuing a full course for another degree. (The new Degree is really much easier as regards extent than any existing Degree) Also the title B.Soc.Sc. is rather a misnomer, it should really be something like B.Ph. … the course …is really Philosophy, Sociology being only a part.

A UCD response justified the title on the grounds that the B.Soc.Sc. emphasised the practical side of philosophy (psychology, ethics and sociology) rather than the speculative side (metaphysics) and pointed to practical difficulties impeding the implementation of a unified UCD/UCC approach to diffusing the study of Catholic philosophy across all university faculties that O'Rahilly advocated. At its meeting the liaison committee unanimously passed the motion that 'We, as a body, formally approve of the introduction of a Course in General Philosophy, leading to a special degree, for non-clerical students of the University and of the ultimate objective of having all, or at least as many as possible, undergraduates take this Course.'[12] Although both Archbishop McQuaid and Dr. Tierney supported this motion, UCD's B.Soc.Sc. subsequently retained its independent availability and over time its title became progressively less of a misnomer.

Conferring degrees on the first students to complete the B.Soc.Sc. in July 1956 UCD's president 'said that up to the present, due to shortage of staff, the Degree in Social Science has suffered certain defects, but he expressed the hope that ultimately the Degree would be one of the best the College could offer'. As the first cycle of the B.Soc.Sc. concluded, the clerical professors in the Faculty of Philosophy and Sociology reviewed its progress, lobbied for new staff and debated how new assistants ought to be deployed, addressing themselves as much to an Archbishop's House audience as to a university one. For Feichin O'Doherty 'the degree in Social Science was better than one could have expected' but 'it still requires strengthening at many points, particularly in the field of empirical sociology and in economics'. To Conor Martin 'the really pressing need of Social Science is for the inclusion of courses in empirical studies ... [T]he lack of such courses has meant that the Degree in Social Science so far has been merely the equivalent of a Pass Degree in Philosophy.'[13]

Fr. James Kavanagh's move from DICS to further study in Cambridge in 1954 appears to have been made with a future role at UCD in mind: 'two years ago Fr. Kavanagh's name was mentioned to the President in connection with Sociology for the students of Social Science' and 'the President was entirely favourable'. By the time he returned to begin teaching in UCD in the autumn of 1956 the idea of handing over responsibility for the development of the B.Soc.Sc. to him had been temporarily shelved – the archbishop considered it 'premature until we receive further help' – and Conor Martin succeeded in directing him towards what he considered to be the more important BA degree in economics and politics: '[It] has much higher standards; it is well established over the years and is taken by students as a preparation for occupations of influence and significance in Ireland.'[14] An important step towards obtaining further help had been taken in 1955, when Fr. Conor Ward went to study at one of the major centres of British social science, Liverpool University. Before he returned to

Dublin to teach at UCD, Conor Martin in July 1959 wrote to the archbishop seeking 'Your Grace's view and directive' on his suggestion that Dr. Ward be encouraged to begin a research collaboration with the diocesan Catholic Social Welfare Bureau (CSWB). Thanking the archbishop for approving 'the project of research proposed for Dr. Ward', Martin anticipated the positive effect on teaching and research his arrival would have on the department and proposed a further strengthening of its empirical research capacity in the Politics field: '[T]o have an expert, specially trained in this branch, is a necessity for the ultimate setting up of a degree in Political Science; and it would be a new inducement for the young lawyer or the young economist to take up postgraduate political studies.'[15]

By March 1960 the archbishop had proposed bringing a Jesuit lecturer from Fordham or one of that order's other American colleges 'until we can have one of our nationals trained'. The matter was brought by Monsignor Horgan to President Tierney, who was initially receptive to the idea of seeing whether Counterpart Fund money might be got to fund the appointment. But becoming engulfed by a wider crisis shortly afterwards prompted Dr. Tierney to reverse this position, as a memorandum written by Martin on 9 May describes:

> The Monsignor told me that the President was most antagonistic to the proposal of having an American Jesuit to teach the empirical side of political science. He said that the President had heard the criticism that the college was being turned into a seminary, and that the priests in it 'were falling over one another'. The Monsignor did not wish to discuss the source of this criticism. Also the President saw politics as meaning only one thing, that which priests should stay out of. If the proposal were brought before the governing body, there would be questions and controversy on the grounds that this was the meaning of 'politics', and all this would be repeated in Dail debate. I said that it was strange that the President could not see that what was intended was simply a development of one aspect of the sciences which I had been appointed to teach, and that the subject 'politics' had always been taught in the College. 'Politics' in this context did not mean political activity or taking part in political life or taking sides in Irish political controversies. The aim of the proposal was the development of the academic subject to bring it into line with the standards of about eighteen British universities. The Monsignor said that the President had brushed aside my own position – my position was that of a man teaching ethics and politics and this was quite different; he, the President, knew what politics meant if anyone did.[16]

The events which had unsettled Tierney arose from a dispute over the manner in which appointments were being made in UCD. The legislation conferred the power of making certain (more senior) appointments on the Senate of the federal National University rather than on the Governing Body of the individual college. Under Tierney the practice grew up of appointing 'College' lecturers and assistant lecturers while leaving vacant statutory positions that could only be filled by the NUI Senate. A petition to appoint a Board of Visitors to investigate the matter was eventually sent to the government, who appointed a Board consisting of three judges. When the report of this Board found the procedure being followed illegal, the government introduced a bill indemnifying UCD and allowing it to continue making appointments for a limited time period. This continuation was justified on the grounds that the Commission on Higher Education would be considering and reporting on university appointment procedures during the limited period and that specific appointments had to be made urgently if recognition of UCD's veterinary degrees in Britain was not to be jeopardised. Apart from issues of legality, the UCD practice was assailed for filling positions without advertisement or competition and making short-term, insecure appointments. As Jack McQuillan TD observed in a Dail debate on the bill: 'I know a lot of lecturers in Dublin and elsewhere: I have a great admiration for them; but I find they are frequently afraid of their lives to express the views they hold because human nature is such that they must consider their posts.'[17]

The bill enjoyed the support of both Fianna Fail and Fine Gael. The latter's speakers in the Oireachtas debates spent most of their time attacking the Visitors' report and defending the Tierney regime. Given the extent to which UCD was identified with the Fine Gael Party, Fianna Fail might have been tempted to make mischief at their opponents' expense on this issue but the manner in which Fine Gael interests interlocked with those of the Catholic hierarchy in this institution would have helped it to resist such temptation. The senior Fianna Fail figure most critical of the UCD establishment was the one it has been suggested (Cooney 1999: 332) that some leading bishops considered as the most disposed to uphold the interests of the Catholic Church and therefore the most suitable successor to de Valera, Sean MacEntee. De Valera's actual successor, Sean Lemass, had conveyed to Tierney in the middle of April 1960 his opinion 'that the Government's decision to introduce the legislation in itself implies that they do not regard the procedure as being of such a character that it should be stopped at once'. MacEntee a few days earlier had sent Lemass a letter he had received from John Kenny, the barrister and law lecturer who had petitioned for the Board of Visitors to be set up, directing the Taoiseach's attention to marked passages of Kenny's letter which 'put forward very weighty arguments in favour of keeping to the absolute minimum the period during which the Governing Body of U.C.D. is to be empowered to make appointments without reference to the [NUI] Senate'.[18] Some months later MacEntee wrote to the Minister for Education, Patrick Hillery, in relation to the composition of the Commission on Higher Education in terms quite similar to those quoted to Monsignor Horgan by President Tierney and recorded by Conor Martin:

If we are to make any progress as a nation, it is essential that greater importance be attached to scientific studies and a much more liberal provision made for their pursuit on every plane, whether theoretical or applied. In short the bias which now exists against them should be reversed. They are studies which particularly concern the laity, and as the National University was established to serve the laity mainly, they should be given pride of place. At the moment the bias is the other way and the colleges, staff and students of the National are being conditioned to the requirements of a super-seminary.

Hillery's reply presented McQuaid as an active promoter of science teaching in Catholic secondary schools, but the archbishop's UCD priorities did not lie in this direction. Congratulating Monsignor Horgan on securing new staff appointments in October 1955, he had written 'your Faculty is lamentably understaffed in contrast with other Faculties of much less fundamental value for the Faith and for scholarship', adding that 'History, Commerce and Technology are striving to over-ride the world'.[19] While the Tierney regime came in for criticism on the twin grounds of illegal appointment practice and of excessive clerical presence, the two seem not to have overlapped. The additional philosophy and sociology staff members of the later 1950s were assistants, a grade where appointment fell within the legal powers of the College.

Derailed in the middle of 1960, the project of strengthening the empirical side of politics at UCD was revived the following year and John Whyte arrived in the department at the beginning of 1962. By 1965 he had moved to Queen's University Belfast in circumstances that have been interpreted as outright dismissal (H. Kearney 2007:11) or constructive dismissal as a result of being forbidden to pursue (Garvin 1998: 312) or strongly advised against continuing (McCartney 1999: 218) his research on Irish Church–state relations. Direction to this effect came from Martin and has been attributed to possibly unnecessary fear on his part of the archbishop's attitude. What the McQuaid papers show is that UCD's first lay politics lecturer made an unhappy start to his relationship with the archbishop. On 22 September 1962 McQuaid wrote to Martin enclosing a letter he had received from Whyte and stating that in the circumstances where an applicant is unknown, a letter of recommendation is necessary. On 25 September Martin apologised, saying that 'had I thought that Your Grace would find Mr. John Whyte was quite unknown to you, I would indeed have advised him of the necessity of a recommendation'. The letter continues:

Mr. Whyte is the lecturer in political institutions in my department, about whose suitability Your Grace saw me in April last year, whose appointment you kindly urged, whose acceptance by the College I wrote to you about, in the following June, and about whose research I wrote to Your Grace last October ... His research is concerned with the Irish political tradition underlying the contemporary structure. His interest in the Independent Irish Party of the mid-nineteenth century and the political attitudes which it engendered is concerned with that research; and his interest in that research is the reason for his present request to Your Grace.

On this occasion Martin appears supportive of Whyte, although his description of Whyte's research interests is rather vague and suggests a focus that is as much historical as contemporary. The letter concludes by reiterating that Whyte 'is an exemplary Catholic trustworthy in every respect'. On the letter the archbishop has noted: '[Y]ou will now see advantage of introducing to me persons who are called on to teach in the Faculty for which I am particularly responsible.'[20] In March 1965, having been informed by Whyte of his intention to leave the College by the autumn of that year – although he had not yet secured another post – Martin wrote a memorandum proposing the stop-gap appointment of a 'fully trained Catholic American' for one year with one of the department's own graduates, Maurice Manning, identified as a suitable long-term successor once his MA thesis had been completed. The memorandum makes no reference to Whyte's research but states that his wide-ranging teaching responsibilities have been carried out 'with distinction because of his talent, training and energy'.[21] In February 1967 Martin, plainly anxious to avoid a repetition of what had happened in Whyte's case, asked if the archbishop 'would wish him to introduce to him Fr. John Chisholm, Mr. Brian Farrell and Mr. Maurice Manning who, last term, began teaching in my department'. A note on the letter reads 'please wait for less oppressively busy time'.[22]

Within months of his September 1962 exchange with Martin in relation to Whyte McQuaid can be found actively exercising the faculty responsibility to which he laid claim by initiating the separation of social science from ethics and politics. In January 1963 he asked James Kavanagh and Conor Ward to 'prepare for me a set of suggestions concerning the whole Social Studies side of your Department, such that you would in future be responsible for the Social Studies'. After receiving what he noted to be 'a very good report', he informed Conor Martin on 7 March that 'I have been examining the position of Sociology and have concluded that it should be a separate Department within the Faculty.' Martin was asked to 'kindly call on the President to discuss this proposal which I wish to promote' prior to its coming before the Governing Body. The President's agreement with the proposal was reported back by Martin on 13 March.[23]

This change was instituted during the first year in which the B.Soc.Sc. was run as a daytime honours degree. In November 1959 the English economist John Vaizey, a regular visitor to Dublin because of his research on the history of Guinness's Brewery, described UCD as 'big, poor and overwhelmed with evening students', adding that 'the clerical element is extremely strong' (Peter Murray 2012a: 74). Submissions to the Commission on Higher Education in 1961 indicated a general trend away from evening courses. Trinity planned to discontinue its evening Bachelor of Commerce and Diploma in Public Administration and anticipated the introduction of four-year daytime business studies and social studies degrees. UCD at that point still maintained its BA, B.Comm. and B.Soc. Sc. evening courses, but evening teaching was now done only by junior staff, whereas at one stage both junior and senior staff were involved. UCC had only an evening B.Comm. degree, while UCG has no evening degrees at all.[24] Developing the UCD B.Soc.Sc. had long been recognised to involve moving from evening pass to daytime honours teaching. The archbishop had written 'Yes' in the margin next to the statement in a July 1956 memorandum from O'Doherty that 'for satisfactory work in a degree of this kind, it seems desirable to have it in the daytime if possible'. A memorandum of the same date by Martin argued that:

> The ultimate expansion of Social Science into an Honours School, together with development of a full School of Political Science would provide the best centre from which to start influencing technological studies in College, and also B. Comm. studies (which are beginning to produce 'managers'). If these Schools are properly organised with highly qualified staff, and carefully planned courses, Philosophy and Sociology will be respected and their claims will win attention.[25]

From a study of the college's records McCartney (1999: 223–224) concludes that intervention rather than interference best characterises the relationship that existed between Archbishop McQuaid and UCD. In relation to the Faculty of Philosophy and Sociology, however, the archbishop did not admit the existence of the separation between diocesan ordinary and higher education institution required to make either term meaningful. In November 1955 he wrote that 'I should have at least six more priests to help me in the Faculty of Philosophy, and only when we have at least that number of Assistants, clerical or lay, can we say that we are in a position to face the task of educating the professional and governing classes of the future.'[26] Such budding lay leaders shared UCD with a large number of distinctively dressed clerical students, religious sisters and religious brothers – 12 per cent of the student body in the mid-1960s – in addition to which many lay students lived in hostels run by the religious orders (McCartney 1999: 161–162). The gradual emergence of empirical social science teaching alongside the established staple fare of Thomist philosophy was not a wholly laicising change because of the manner in which the second Vatican Council of the early 1960s altered the emphasis in clerical students' education. In May 1966 Archbishop McQuaid ordained eleven Clonliffe College students whom he described as the 'first fruits' of the new approach. This involved clerical students' initiation into pastoral work during the course of their studies: DICS and the Social Science Faculty in UCD featured in a list of agencies with whose work the new model ordinands had 'been made familiar'.[27]

The Vatican Council was a one of a number of forces of religious and social change that had by the end of the 1960s significantly altered the certainties prevailing at the start of that decade (F. X. Carty 2007 and 2010). In higher education a more activist government had proposed merging Trinity and UCD, enforcement of the ban on Catholics attending Trinity was faltering badly before it was finally abandoned and the international wave of student protest had even reached Ireland. Some things remained unchanged, however, as an August 1969 note headed 'Procedure regarding the appointment in the Diocese of a Priest on the Staff of U.C.D.' demonstrates. This was written by the archbishop's Secretary in the context of the appointment of Fr. Donal O'Donohue, an assistant in the UCD Social Science Department, to take over from Fr. Liam Carey as director of DICS. On 'the question of a successor' to Fr. O'Donohue at UCD, Monsignor Horgan advised that 'should Your Grace wish to nominate one Fr. Kavanagh would be informed' and that 'it would be for Fr. Kavanagh to refer the appointment of a Successor to the President'.[28]

Proposing empirical research on Irish emigrants

If a more empirical emphasis in the teaching of politics and sociology – together with a greater differentiation between these disciplines – was gradually emerging in the state's largest university, to what extent was empirical social research being proposed or undertaken there? The first documented initiative in this area occurs around the time of Fr. Conor Ward's 1955 move to Liverpool in the form of a proposal for the study of Irish emigration to be jointly undertaken by UCD academics and the Liverpool University sociology professor, T. S. (Tom) Simey.

Although its role has tended to be overlooked in histories of British sociology, Liverpool was, along with Leicester and the London School of Economics, one of the three universities in which the discipline was most developed during the 1950s (Wilks-Heeg 2005). As a School of Training for Social Work, Liverpool's department could trace its history back to 1905. In 1923 it acquired a chair in sociology endowed by Charles Booth, scion of a wealthy Unitarian business family in the city and author of the monumental *Life and Labour of the People in London*. In 1939, aged 33, Simey became the chair's second holder, a position he held until his death in 1969. A politics, philosophy and economics graduate of Balliol College, Oxford, Simey worked in local government before becoming a lecturer in public administration at Liverpool University. Best remembered for the biography of Booth he co-authored with his wife Margaret (Simey and Simey 1960) and for work on family structure in the West Indies that is still frequently cited, Simey seems to have been ill at ease with British and wider international trends within sociology and to have felt a considerable affinity with UCD's Faculty of Philosophy and Sociology. In August 1955 Conor Martin wrote a note on a conversation with Simey regarding the studies Conor Ward was about to begin:

> Professor Simey is an Anglican who finds no difficulty with Catholic social teaching and Catholic philosophy in general. There is more than one Catholic on his staff and there is a considerable number of Catholic students ... He values very highly Father Ward's philosophical and theological training ... One of the tragedies of the English universities, he said, had been the failure of their faculties of Philosophy to meet the real needs of students. He could get no help in Liverpool from the philosophers and had had to institute his own courses in Ethics and Politics under various disguises.

Replying to a letter from Archbishop McQuaid thanking him for the support he had given Conor Ward in the course of his studies, Simey himself wrote in June 1959 that 'I am most deeply grateful to you for saying what you do, as it gives one added courage and confidence to go on struggling with daily difficulties in the very difficult times in which we live when I find my work as a teacher is appreciated by yourself and your Church.' In 1966 James Kavanagh's application for the newly created professorship in social science in UCD included a testimonial from Simey, which McQuaid considered 'significant', stating that '[I]t is, of course, most important that the holder of this chair in an Irish University should be aware of the extent to which the branch of knowledge connected with it has fallen victim to meretricious theorising in general, and mistaken views held by those who are adherents of modern scientism and positivism in particular.'[29]

The proposed joint research on Irish emigration was described in a memorandum sent to Archbishop's House on 1 September 1955 by Feichin O'Doherty. Simey's interest in the topic was attributed to the contrast between research in Liverpool, where 'his investigators have come upon the conditions of living of some of our emigrants', and a recent visit to the west of Ireland, where 'he observed something of the conditions of life of our people before emigrating'. In the former milieu the problem of the emigrants' loss of faith 'gravely disturbed' him, in the latter the importance of people's religion in their daily lives 'struck him forcibly'. Because much work had already been carried out on the economic and statistical aspects of emigration, the topic was 'ripe for sociological-psychological investigation' to be undertaken in both Ireland and Britain. Questions to be addressed by Irish fieldwork were:

What are the social relations in which the individual lives at home in Ireland? What are the important group structures (sodalities, the football club, the pub, the gang etc.) in his life at home? What is the nature of his social grouping and standing? What are the facts about family structure? Dominant father? Or Dominant mother? What are the status objects in his environment? What is his role in his own society? What in general is the role-structure of his society? What is the place of religion in his life? In his scale of values? What is its efficacy in affecting his behaviour? What happens if conflicts develop within the family structure? How is the family structure maintained?

In Britain the questions the research would address were:

What are the answers to these and allied questions in the environment of Birmingham, Wolverhampton, Liverpool etc. when these people emigrate? What do they assimilate of the English way of life and what do they repudiate? What social (and individual) changes can be observed? Why do their patterns of behaviour change, if in fact they do? And what are the significant directions of such change? What are the significant and effective social pressures to which the individual is subject (a) at home and (b) in England? Etc. Etc.

A three-year, jointly sponsored research project was envisaged. UCD would nominate a project director who would receive initial training in Liverpool, while the planning of the project took place:

It is suggested that the director should be a layman, because of the nature of the work he will be doing e.g. he will have to sit in the local pub for hours at a time, work on a farm, join in the recreation and games of the community studied etc. etc. He should also be fully trained in Catholic Philosophy and social principles, be a good mixer with a gift of leadership and a high intelligence.

On the question of funding, the memorandum states that the Ford Foundation had made an offer to support the kind of empirical research being carried out at Liverpool but also records that 'while Professor Simey would be only too willing to make contact with the Ford Foundation in this matter he suggested that perhaps His Grace the Archbishop of Dublin might like to take up the matter directly with the Foundation'. To this Dr. McQuaid responded that 'I am willing to give any help open to me, but the Professor is already so well-known to the Foundation that he seems to be quite the best person to handle the affair.' Overall, though, his response was a very positive one:

The survey will be, I think, of great practical value. I think I understand its import, for I am acquainted with the work of Professor Gabriel Le Bras, a friend of mine for some years. May I suggest that there is ground for a comparison between the Bretons and our own people in the facts and the results of emigration. At least, I venture to suggest the comparison from my own knowledge of French conditions.[30]

This project did not get off the ground but some five years later answers to some of the research questions indicatively posed in O'Doherty's memorandum were to be proposed in another context where John Henry Newman provided inspiration and the Ford Foundation a potential source of research funding. Founded in 1942, the Newman Association brought together British Catholic university graduates and professional people. In 1953 the Association was the seed-bed of the Newman Demographic Survey (NDS), 'a voluntary organisation devoted to statistical and social research about the Catholic community in Britain, its laity, clergy and religious, its problems and its opportunities' (Spencer 1964: 32). Early work underpinned applications for more state resources to support Catholic schools and teacher training provision. By the end of the 1950s NDS was seeking to expand the scope of its work and full-time staff had begun to be appointed. In August 1958 NDS director A. E. C. W. Spencer contributed an article on Irish immigration statistics to *The Tablet* which noted in conclusion that:

> The Newman Demographic Survey has recently been commissioned through the agency of the International Federation of Catholic Institutes of social research at Geneva, to prepare two studies which should serve as a foundation for further work. The first, for the German committee organizing the International Eucharistic Congress, to be held next year in Munich, is a study of the … extent and causes of Irish migration to England and Wales, the concentration of Irish in large towns and the pastoral problems to which they give rise. The second, for International Catholic Migration Commission, is a survey of the arrangements made for the reception and integration of Irish immigrants to this country.[31]

The International Catholic Migration Commission (ICMC) was established by Pope Pius XII in 1951 'to coordinate services for emigrants, with a particular emphasis on creating links between the countries of emigration and immigration' (M. Daly 2006: 300). Until the end of the 1950s, ICMC focused its attention mainly on movement from continental European countries to non-European destinations. Some input into its conferences and publications was made by the Emigrants Section of the Dublin Catholic Social Welfare Bureau but English and Welsh involvement was virtually non-existent until the NDS was commissioned to prepare a study for the triennial conference of the Commission to be held on Ottawa in August 1960. Reflecting after the demise of the NDS on the extent to which studies of the Church and of religion by the social sciences enjoyed acceptance among Catholic Church leaders, Spencer (1964: 34–35) distinguished a succession of distinct stages, illustrated in Table 3.2.

Table 3.2 Spencer's stages of Church acceptance of the social sciences

Stage one	The social sciences are used as a means of getting the consent of an external agency to a plan or proposal that already reflects the policy established within the Church's structure
Stage two	The social sciences are used to make a better plan to implement the policy already established within the Church's structure
Stage three	The social sciences are used to study the policy itself, which has already been established within the Church's structure
Stage four	The social sciences are applied to the study of the Church's structure
Stage five	The social sciences are used to study the Church's ideology [doctrine], its acceptance and the extent of its development in the face of new situations

Source: Spencer 1964: 34–35

In the case of the work of the NDS in England and Wales only stage two had been reached when 'in 1960 an attempt was made to move into stages three and four with a study commissioned by an international organisation'. Then 'the first confidential draft created such a furore that the writer [Spencer] was denounced from abroad three times within a week to the English ecclesiastical authorities; the study had to be abandoned before it reached its final draft and its publication and private circulation is forbidden' (Spencer 1964: 35–36). More than half a century would pass before this suppressed study was at last published (Spencer 2012).

The furore began at a meeting held in London on 2 June 1960 'to facilitate the elimination of factual inaccuracies and to promote active discussion of its recommendations' before the report was 'put in final shape'. There Monsignor Cecil Barrett of the Dublin Catholic Social Welfare Bureau – one of a number of Church and state officials Spencer had met during a visit to Ireland in October 1959[32] – led an onslaught on the circulated partial draft. Particular exception was taken to a section dealing with 'The Attitude of the Immigrant'. Here drawing on Arensberg and Kimball at second hand – a *Christus Rex* article by an American Jesuit (Humphreys 1955) who had taken their depiction of Irish rural society as the baseline for a study of the effects of urbanisation on the Irish family was the section's key source – the nature of the socialisation undergone in Ireland was seen as the chief cause of the degree to which the integration of Irish Catholics into British society was being frustrated. Specifically seen as problematical was the distorting effect on character development of the strength of Irish parental and priestly authority:

The foregoing account of the potential emigrant's environment, especially its social and religious aspects, give us the key to those elements in the situation of the migrant in Britain which impede delay or prevent integration into *Catholic* society there: a lack of *self*-discipline, and *self*-control, an undeveloped sense of responsibility towards workmates, employers and non-Catholics, a social inferiority complex, a lack of articulateness about religion, a sense of ignorance about sex, and a view of clergy-laity relationships that polarises at either complete acceptance of priestly authority in *all* matters, or equally complete rejection of *any* priestly authority.

For Monsignor Barrett the principal villain of the piece was not Spencer but the London meeting's chairman, Michael Fogarty, a professor of industrial relations at University College Cardiff. A past president of the Newman Society, he was prominently involved in a Catholic Social Guild (CSG) that had become bitterly divided by post-war British welfare state development, where – holding up the work of the NDS as a positive example – 'he argued as a representative of the social sciences that the frequently amateurish nature of much previous CSG effort was inappropriate in an increasingly complex world, and that there should be a greater emphasis on rigorous social analysis and research' (Aspden 2002: 281–282). According to Monsignor Barrett, calls for the offending section's deletion at the 2 June meeting were resisted by the chairman until 'at last Professor Fogarty showed his hand and explained why he was so anxious that the objectionable section be retained – he stated that he was hopeful that he might get £100,000 grant from the Ford Foundation if he could show that there was no accurate, comprehensive, relevant information available on the Attitude of the Immigrant'. Sending Archbishop McQuaid a report on the meeting, Monsignor Barrett was 'most anxious that Fogarty, who is really Spencer's boss, should go behind our backs and send to Geneva just what suits him'. Urging Cardinal Godfrey 'to intervene to prevent … an impending disaster' on 5 June, the archbishop repeated this allegation about Fogarty's motives, adding that 'I can only express to Your Eminence my profound sorrow that the Newman Demographic Survey is being prepared under that Chairmanship.'[33]

In the wake of the 2 June meeting NDS decided to scrap virtually all of the section on 'The Attitude of the Immigrant' 'and insert a statement of the importance of a study of the cultural background and attitudes when considering the work of any institution, regretting the absence of any such study of the Irish cultural background and urging that research be set afoot in this field without delay'. Back in Dublin, however, Monsignor Barrett and Archbishop McQuaid had agreed that this offending section should be replaced by an alternative one that Barrett drafted and sent to London. Apparently out to appease Dublin at any cost, Cardinal Godfrey's Secretary, Monsignor Worlock, had, according to

Barrett, 'accepted [Barrett's] comments in toto and had instructed Spencer to re-draft his report embodying these comments and to forward a copy when completed to Father Barrett for further examination'. The report, whose presentation had been listed in the published programme for the Ottawa conference, was not delivered in time to the ICMC. Amidst the ensuing recriminations, NDS apparently preferred accepting the blame for its non-appearance to having its name attached to a document incorporating Barrett's 'eulogy on the spiritual and moral values of the Irish people' (M. Daly 2006: 305–306). According to Spencer 'the second draft included many reluctant deletions and additions, agreed at a succession of meetings with Mgr. Worlock and was eventually sent to the ICMC, the work unfinished, to be locked in its safe in Geneva and "never to be published or publicised"'. [34]

While Spencer wrote to Fr. Conor Ward in the wake of the London meeting that 'I do not envy you the task of prosecuting any sociological work in Ireland', [35] Irish Catholicism arguably turned out to provide a more congenial environment for such work than its English counterpart in the 1960s. While the tendency of Irish Church leaders to believe that 'any comments about the inadequacy of religious preparation were a slur on the reputation of the Church in Ireland' (Delaney 2007: 165) meant that prospects for an NDS move into Spencer's stages three and four while producing a report on Irish immigration to Britain were never bright, specific coincidental features of Vatican interaction with the Irish hierarchy doomed the attempt. Addressing a congress in Madrid in September 1959, Cardinal Mimmi, the member of the curia responsible for migration, stated that 'had all the Irish people who emigrated to England throughout the centuries kept their faith, perhaps the number of Catholics in the latter country would be twelve millions rather than the three millions they now number'. For McQuaid this massive 'lapsing' claim brought to a head the issue of misrepresentation at the Vatican of the Irish clergy's record which he believed to have been ongoing for more than a decade. He took the matter up with the papal nuncio, sending Mimmi through him a copy of the analysis of the CSWB Emigrants' Bureau records which Fr. Conor Ward had carried out. At the Irish hierarchy's meeting on 21 June 1960 the archbishop ended a briefing on 'what we have to contend with' in relation to NDS reports with 'one item of consolation' – Mimmi had now written to him 'greatly praising the work of the Hierarchy for emigrants'. [36]

For NDS a subsequent attempt to move into stages three and four while working on Catholic educational issues in England also produced a strongly negative response. When financial difficulties left the organisation dependent for its survival on the goodwill of a newly appointed head of the English and Welsh hierarchy at the end of 1963, its fate was dismemberment. Reflecting on this end to more than a decade's work, Spencer (1964: 37) concluded that 'to move on

Table 3.3 UCD social science research, December 1970

Completed and published	Manpower in a Developing Community (The Drogheda Manpower Survey) (1967)
	Family and School (1968)
	New Homes For Old (1969)
	Teaching in the City (1970)
Completed but not yet published	Industrial Relations in a Large Production Department
	Youth in an Irish Town
	Unmarried Mothers
	Intermediate Certificate Manpower
	Residential Care of Children in Dublin
	Training and Career Aspirations of Nurses
	Subjective Elements in Social Class
	Religious Commitment among University Students
Currently being researched	Families in Tenement Homes
	Poverty and Itinerancy
	Social Change in Contemporary Ireland
	Young Manpower in Drogheda (1970)
	Two Studies in Industrial Sociology
	Young People in an Urban Community
	Community Cooperation and Social Need
'Research carried out under the supervision of the Department'	Home Assistance (published as 'A Law for the Poor', 1970)
	Drinking Patterns of Young People
	Readmission to Psychiatric Hospital Care

Source: The Rev. Prof. J. Kavanagh, 'Social Science at U.C.D.', letter to the editor, *Irish Times*, 21/12/1970

to stages three and four one has to work within the framework of an institution of higher education, or create an independent institution'. In Ireland sociological research was located within such institutions and, while these were sites of very strong clerical influence, there were countervailing forces to such influence which – as will be discussed in later chapters – were growing stronger within the context of a state developmental strategy shift.

In December 1970 Fr. James Kavanagh responded to aspersions cast in the Dail on UCD's social science research record with a listing of projects that is reproduced in Table 3.3.[37] With funding secured from agencies such as the

Department of Labour, Foras Forbartha and the Irish National Productivity Committee, labour market, workplace, housing, community and educational research feature prominently in a broadly based mix of subject areas not unlike that being addressed in the same period by Liverpool University's social scientists. A start had been made when 'in Summer 1960 six graduates of the evening degree in Social Science of that year volunteered to join in an effort to show that a survey using personal interviews was viable', the chosen locale being a new local authority housing estate where the researchers 'had three bicycles stored for us by one of the local priests for the more distant roads'.[38]

Socio-religious research does not loom large in Kavanagh's 1970 list, but here work had been carried out by UCD-based priests as a diocesan rather than a university activity. Financed by the archbishop, young people's religious practice in three parishes – City Quay, Pro-Cathedral and Westland Row – was surveyed in the late 1960s. At the same time a number parish surveys were also being carried out in Clare and Tipperary under Muintir's auspices.

While these focused on 'the attitudes and aspirations of the people of the parishes to their social economic development' rather than on religious practice, the interviews were carried out by seminarians provided by Archbishop Morris and the exercise was characterised as 'pastoral research'. The Muintir Tipperary parish survey results were published (Muintir na Tire 1975). Correspondence concerning the Dublin surveys reveals Dr. McQuaid's doubts regarding the efficacy of having university students carry out interviews ('young people may be antagonistic to them'), his anxiety that the survey should not be publicly quoted ('parents and children just would not understand') and his refusal to disclose any of the results to a group of priests and lay people studying changing attitudes since the introduction of television ('it was a private matter'). Yet, cautious and doubtful as this outlook may have been, it still compared favourably with the situation Fr. Conor Ward encountered in 1967 when he was 'invited by some Catholic English sociologists to sit in on a meeting' where 'there was continuous expression of regret that social research relating to religious practice was not being carried out and that there were no signs that the Hierarchy of England and Wales intended that it should be'.[39]

Religious vocations and sociological research

Alongside the migratory movement of its laity, a key international concern of the Catholic Church in the post-war period was the numbers entering the priesthood and other forms of religious life. Amidst widespread anxiety about a shortfall of vocations, Ireland – which supplied not only its own needs but had several

substantial seminaries educating priests for other parts of the English-speaking
world and a number of missionary societies and religious orders supplying manpower for missions in 'pagan' countries – was a spectacularly bright spot. Its
position therefore tended to be discussed in terms of the societal features that
rendered it so productive of vocations or of its potential capacity to contribute even more to the Church's worldwide missionary efforts. Addressing the
First International Conference on Priestly Vocations in Europe held in Vienna in
October 1958, Jeremiah Newman addressed both of these topics.

In Ireland, he argued, vocations were fostered by 'very healthy Catholic family life' and 'an education system permeated by a Catholic outlook'. Historically
associated with patriotic movements and independent of the state, the clergy
held a respected position within Irish life. The priest was popularly respected
as an educated man of culture but was not cut off from the mass of the people
by cultural snobbery. He tended to be 'prized … as a manly friend and fellow
citizen rather than a scholar'. Diocesan colleges were of particular importance
as they operated as feeders for the National Seminary in Maynooth while also
functioning as general-purpose male secondary boarding schools where friend-
ships between future priests and future lay leaders were formed. Some potential
threats to the strong flow of vocations were identified. Political independence
weakened the link between patriotism and religion. Economic development,
such as it was, opened up new career and employment opportunities. Potentially
most threatening was urbanisation coupled with neglect of the rural areas: 'at
the moment roughly 50 per cent of students at the National Seminary are sons
of farmers, while nearly 70 per cent come from rural areas'. With regard to
further scope for Irish priests to work abroad, Newman concluded that 'Ireland
could lend a very substantial number of her present domestic clerical personnel', pointing to the large increase in the number of regular (religious order)
clergy that had taken place since 1920 and commenting that 'at worst this has led
in some places to duplication of effort and "competitive religion"; at best it has
meant that some priests have not enough work to do'. To this he added that 'it
should also be remembered that it is possible for a brand of anti-clericalism to
appear, based on nothing more than the fact that the clergy appear too numerous' (Newman 1958b: 718).

In 1961 a request from Pope John XXIII that more Irish priests should volun-
teer for work in Latin America led to Newman being commissioned by the hierarchy to carry out a survey of how Irish priests were deployed. More detailed
in its statistical information, and more circumspect in its commentary, this
(Newman 1962a) reached a similar conclusion about the scope for redeploying
Irish priests to work abroad. In 1961 Irish religious vocations peaked (Fuller
2002: 167) and in the same year some rare data relating such vocations to their

wider context of occupational choice was provided by a sociological survey. This survey was carried out in three parishes close to Shannon Airport – which was then being promoted as 'the first Air-Age Industrial Development Zone in the World' – by a team of staff and students from Leiden University in Holland. Broadly concerned with issues relating to education, the operation of the local labour market and migration, the survey's interim report included a table comparing the 'white collar' occupational preferences of parents in the parishes studied with the preferences of a sample of school pupils in Ennis (Vercruissje n.d.: table 4). Here 'pupils show a much higher leaning towards teaching than parents do, whereas the religious calling so important in the preferences of the parents is very low with the pupils' (Vercruissje n.d.: 15). While fragmentary evidence of this kind has to be treated with caution, it does suggest that some of the potential threats to the flow of vocations acknowledged by Newman were materialising to an increasing extent.

In September 1967 Newman and two other priest-sociologists – Conor Ward of UCD and Liam Ryan of UCC – were commissioned by the hierarchy to carry out a survey of trends in religious vocations which was stated to be 'required in view of the large number of requests for help being received for priests, brothers and nuns to serve abroad'. The report submitted to the hierarchy in June 1971 drew on three distinct surveys – one of all Irish seminaries, novitiates and houses of formation; another of all Catholic secondary schools; and a third of a sample of 1,200 Leaving Certificate students. Numerical decline was identified as being the product of a recent drop in numbers entering combined with a dropout rate among entrants that had begun to rise in the mid-1950s and now stood at around 65 per cent. It was concluded, however, that 'while there has been a decrease, it has not existed for long enough to decide that a pattern for the future is established'. Religious belief and commitment remained strong among young people. The vocations decline reflected an Irish societal context in which loss of momentum by a great religious revival coincided with the achievement of a higher rate of economic growth that produced greater affluence for the middle class. Vocations no longer flowed so plentifully from the diocesan colleges that catered for important segments of this class. But a rising tide might, it was speculated, be raising other boats, so that 'students of Brothers schools may now be moving onto the level occupied by diocesan colleges, with a consequent increase in vocations' (Newman, Ward and Ryan 1971: 48–50).

Continuity with Newman's earlier work on the topic is clearly apparent here but his views on the subject did not go entirely unchallenged. Dubbed for his work during the 1960s 'almost a one-man department of sociology' (Ferriter 2004: 6), *Irish Times* journalist Michael Viney in April 1968 wrote a series of articles entitled 'The People's Priests'. The first of these discussed vocations, noting the drop in the number of entrants and the rising dropout rate before commenting on how 'Dr. Newman's surveys of vocational patterns give arresting incidental insights into the Irish Church's view of social class'. Here he pointed out that 'nowhere does Dr. Newman suggest that the Church's pastoral renewal through service to the handicapped and underprivileged might be helped by a proletarian background or that the people's priests might find "pastoral advantage" in ability to speak the same language as the bus driver or the farm labourer'.[40]

Conclusion

A noteworthy organisational feature of the Newman, Ryan and Ward set of vocations surveys was the fact that it was carried out 'in conjunction with the Research and Development Unit' which initially comprised a division of the Catholic Communications Institute. In 1973 this Unit became a separate Episcopal Commission and was renamed the Council for Research and Development (CRD). Before and after its move from a Dublin base to Maynooth, the unit/ council 'provided a steady output of data on religious practice, vocations, seminary education, parish missions and many other aspects of Catholic life, which has provided the Episcopal Conference and the commissions with a solid basis for decision-making and future planning and development' (Fuller 2002: 142). CRD was never the exclusive source of Irish socio-religious research but its institutionalisation of ongoing work in this field within revamped post-conciliar Catholic Church structures represented a significant shift in control and initiative from the diocesan to the national level.

Before the Second Vatican Council bishops 'were absolute rulers over their subjects' and 'the nomenclature reflected this – they were referred to as "princes" of the Church, they lived in "palaces" and they "ruled" over their dioceses' (Fuller 2002: 139). The ways in which both the role of the Church and the role of the bishop were defined changed radically at the Council. Subsequently episcopal collegiality reduced diocesan independence, with the bishops tending 'to act and react collectively, by issuing joint pastorals and press releases, and holding joint press conferences' (Fuller 2002: 140). Up to this time diocesan decision-making in relation to Catholic social movements and to social science had been paramount with the hierarchy being usually unwilling to act as a body and one key individual prelate – Archbishop McQuaid – actively pursuing his own individual Dublin initiatives. Such a long-established pattern was not easily altered when the wider Church context changed. In 1967, when the study team of Newman, Ward and Ryan was established by the hierarchy to undertake the vocations study, Dr. McQuaid noted in a letter to Fr. Conor Ward: 'For vocations: Dr. Newman is Chairman. But I am quite fixed that only you may handle investigations in my diocese. You may do it in your own way.' But, by setting in motion a process that would lead to the establishment of a collegially overseen CRD, the vocations study foreshadowed the ending of a period in which an individual episcopal champion held sway. The full force of the change was brought home to Archbishop McQuaid by the manner in which the hierarchy ended the Trinity ban in 1970. A majority vote to lift the ban was then accompanied by a resolution that a chaplain be appointed to the college. Dr. McQuaid, who viewed this move as 'badly-timed', noted that 'such a resolution passed by this assembly in effect forces the Archbishop of Dublin to take a certain step within his own Diocese. It will be the first occasion on which the Episcopal Conference will have forced a measure on an individual bishop' (quoted in F. X. Carty 2007: 107).

Within the NUI the new collegiality was accompanied by a rapid decline in the high proportion of priests within 'the small band of trained sociologists in Ireland' at the end of the 1960s which John Whyte (1980: 332) had noted. As a seminary opening itself up to lay students, Maynooth most dramatically experienced the influx of an almost entirely lay complement of new staff across a broad range of disciplines within which there had historically been a significant clerical presence. Its bicentenary historian commented that 'it might perhaps be regretted that so little effort was made to prepare priest-candidates ... there was in retrospect what must be seen as inadequate planning ... yet the priesthood continued to attract talent in a way that more could have been made of' (Corish 1995: 433). But such planning, had it been attempted by the Church leadership, would have struggled to check a laicisation of social science teachers that was linked to the supersession of the solo professor or lecturer by the multi-member department.

Up to 1970 this development was effectively confined to the two Dublin universities and was linked to their involvement in preparing students for careers in professional social work. The pioneering body in this educational field had been the Civics Institute of Ireland (CII), whose activities also included the promotion of town planning (McManus 2002), housing management (Delap and Kelleher 2005) and playground provision (Kernan 2005). By the late 1930s it was providing practical placements for students on social studies/social science diploma courses that both Trinity and UCD had initiated at its prompting. But Dr. McQuaid had already put on record his suspicion of it and similar non-denominational organisations (Earner-Byrne 2007: 90) and, after he became archbishop, his new CSWB challenged or displaced the CII in a number of its spheres of activity. Alignment between CSWB and UCD accompanied this and was cemented by the 1944 move of the CII's director of studies, Agnes McGuire, to take up a similar role in UCD. This development prompted Trinity to end its relationship with CII and directly organise placements for its diploma course students (N. Kearney 2005:21–27; Earner-Byrne 2007: 93–94).

In the early 1960s Trinity upgraded its diploma to a degree, 'which will bring Dublin University more closely into line with universities in Britain, many of which already offer degrees in the subject. This will ensure that Social Science students in Trinity College will not suffer from an unfavourable comparison with those in Britain.'[41] A six-strong Department of Social Studies had developed by the middle of the decade, one of whose members – social administration lecturer Anthony Coughlan – was a cause of concern to Archbishop McQuaid because of his involvement in left-wing politics.[42] The archbishop's role in parallel UCD developments centred on the creation of an Honours B.Soc.Sc. and involving the departmental separation of social science from politics and ethics has been described above. In the 1970/71 academic year the Department of Social Science had a staff of nine – two priests (Frs. Kavanagh and Ward), two lay male sociologists (Desmond McCluskey and Cyril White) and five lay women, most of whom had social work qualifications. The 1970 Health Act created regional Health Boards with Community Care Programmes that greatly increased Irish employment opportunities for social workers: a decade earlier Agnes McGuire had rather defensively observed that 'those who are not prepared to emigrate, though they may have enjoyed the basic Social Science course while it lasted, spread the criticism that there is no future in it, forgetting that the same can be said of most other university courses so far as the home market is concerned'.[43]

Outside Dublin, the solo priest-sociologist was still more or less the norm at the end of the 1960s. By 1969/70 Fr. Edmond Dougan had been joined in UCG by two lay junior lecturers, one of whom was the Republic's future president, Michael D. Higgins. At UCC the veteran Fr. Jerome O'Leary was joined for a time by Fr. Liam Ryan until the latter succeeded Jeremiah Newman as professor at Maynooth in 1968. In 1971 UCC's president referred in a newspaper article to the fact that 'it has recently become necessary to cease temporarily to offer sociology as a course for the B.A. degree' – apparently a consequence of Fr. O'Leary's ill-health.[44] The appointment later that year of the south's first lay professor, Damian Hannan, would make a revival of the subject and the creation of a growing department possible. 1970/71 was the academic year in which sociology aligned with the expanding teaching of lay students rather than long-term seminary contraction at Maynooth when Fr. Liam Ryan 'up to this a member of the Faculty of Theology, headed a department in Arts, with service teaching only in theology' (Corish 1995: 433). A Jesuit author of landmark attitude surveys, a trade union activist and an inveterate champion of the west of Ireland causes discussed in Chapter 6 below, Fr. Micheál Mac Gréil, was an early recruit to this department but not a new one to social science teaching as he had previously taught at his order's National College of Industrial Relations (MacGreil 2014). As 'free education' at second level fed into a growing student population in higher education and priestly vocations dwindled, academic social science became a numbers game the clerical Church could not hope to win even if the active interest displayed by Archbishop McQuaid had been sustained after his departure. What the virtually complete absence of any new priests entering the profession after 1970 did was to turn an inevitable retreat that might have occurred gradually into a much more rapid transformation.

Notes

1 LDA, Newman Papers, Correspondence, Dr. T. Morris, Thurles, to Rev. Prof. J. Newman, Maynooth, 28/2/1958.
2 'In a Difficult Period the Movement Has Gained Ground – Reports Honorary National Secretary', *Landmark*, August 1958; American Catholic History Research Center and University Archives, Catholic University of America, Washington, DC, George Gilmary Higgins Papers, box 46, folder 7, Newman, Jeremiah, St. Patrick's College, Ireland, 1956–58, Biographical Data, Rev. Jeremiah Newman, M.A., D.Ph.
3 LDA, Newman Papers, Correspondence, Dr. T. Morris, Thurles, to Rev. Prof. J. Newman, Maynooth, 8/2/1958.
4 LDA, Newman Papers, Correspondence, copy Fr. M. Morrissey, President, Muintir na Tire, to S. McLeod, US ambassador to Ireland, 12/3/1958.
5 LDA, Newman Papers, Correspondence, copy Archbishop Cushing, Boston, to Fr. M. Morrissey, President, Muintir na Tire, 11/4/1958, Archbishop Cushing to Rev. Prof. J. Newman, Maynooth, 26/6/1958; American Catholic History Research Center and University Archives, Catholic University of America, Washington, DC, George Gilmary Higgins Papers, box 46, folder 7, Newman, Jeremiah, St. Patrick's College, Ireland, 1956–58.
6 LDA, Newman Papers, Correspondence, Memorandum on Visit to America – 1958 Rev. J. Newman, April, 1959.
7 LDA, Newman Papers, box 201, folder Limerick Rural Survey.
8 DDA, McQuaid Papers, AB8/XXI/126/4, Christus Rex, Fr. J. Kavanagh, UCD, to Archbishop McQuaid, 30/11/1959, Archbishop McQuaid to Fr. Kavanagh, 2/12/1959.
9 DDA, McQuaid Papers, AB8/B/XV/C/194–264, Hierarchy Correspondence Cashel and Emly, Morris, Cashel and Emly, to Archbishop McQuaid, Dublin, 17/7/1960 [238] and 29/9/1960 [241].
10 COFLA, D'Alton Papers, ARCH 12/4/3/6–8, box Education -2, Universities, folder The National University, Meeting of Epis. Committee and Presidents of the Colleges, 23 January 1952, Archbishop McQuaid, Dublin, to Archbishop D'Alton, Armagh, 29/12/1951.

11   DDA, McQuaid Papers, as yet uncatalogued box UCD/UCC/NUI, memorandum 'The Position in University College Dublin in regard to Evening Lectures, 1952', specimen covering letter, Archbishop of Dublin to 'My Lord Bishop', 21/10/1952.

12   DDA, McQuaid Papers, as yet uncatalogued box UCD/UCC/NUI, folder UCD, note of President Tierney's telephoned request for interview about establishment of degree in sociology, 9/1/1953; COFLA, D'Alton Papers, ARCH 12/4/3/6–8, box Education -2, Universities, folder The National University Memos. Corresp. leading up to meeting on 25 June 1953, note Alfred O'Rahilly, 'Philosophy for Lay Students', 12/6/1953, UCD memorandum on philosophy courses for lay students, 20/6/1953, folder The National University Liaison Meetings 1954–58, Minutes of Liaison Committee Meeting, 25/6/1953.

13   DDA, McQuaid Papers, AB8/B/XXXII/A (iii)/12 (a) XXXII, Universities A: University College Dublin iii, Faculty of Philosophy and Sociology 12, Department of Ethics and Politics (a) Rev. Prof. Conor Martin, 'Philosophy 1955–56' and 'Department of Ethics and Politics Report on Progress', enclosures with Rev. Prof. C. Martin, UCD, to Fr. C. Mangan, Archbishop's House, 25/7/1956.

14   DDA, McQuaid Papers, AB8/B/XXXII/A (iii)/12 (a) XXXII: Universities A: University College Dublin iii, Faculty of Philosophy and Sociology 12, Department of Ethics and Politics (a) Rev. Prof. Conor Martin, untitled and undated memorandum on UCD headed paper.

15   DDA, McQuaid Papers, AB8/B/XXXII/A (iii)/12 (a) XXXII: Universities A: University College Dublin iii, Faculty of Philosophy and Sociology 12, Department of Ethics and Politics (a) Rev. Prof. Conor Martin, Rev. Prof. C. Martin, UCD, to Archbishop McQuaid, 6/7/1959.

16   DDA, McQuaid Papers, AB8/B/XXXII/A (iii)/12 (a) XXXII: Universities A: University College Dublin iii, Faculty of Philosophy and Sociology 12, Department of Ethics and Politics (a) Rev. Prof. Conor Martin, Rev. Prof. C. Martin, UCD, to Archbishop McQuaid, 25/3/1960, 'A note of my meeting with Monsignor Horgan on Saturday, May 9th, 1960'.

17   NAI, DT S16840, A University College, Dublin, Act, 1960, Department of Education, Memorandum for the Government, Proposed legislation in connection with certain appointments in University College, Dublin, 1/4/1960; Dail Eireann, Parliamentary Debates, vol. 181, col. 411, 28/4/1960.

18   NAI, DT S16840, A University College, Dublin, Act, 1960, O'Muineachain, Taoiseach, to MacGearailt, Education, 19/4/1960, S. McEntee, Minister for Health, to S. Lemass, Taoiseach, 16/4/19 60, enclosing J. Kenny, UCD, to S. McEntee, 9/4/1960.

19   NAI, DT S16,803, Higher Education (1) Commission of Inquiry, 1960, (2) Commission on Higher Education Membership, S. McEntee, Minister for Health, to P. Hillery, Minister for Education, 26/8/1960, P. Hillery to S. McEntee, 1/9/1960; DDA McQuaid Papers as yet uncatalogued box UCD/UCC/NUI, Archbishop McQuaid to Rev. Professor J. Horgan, UCD, 22/10/1955.

20   DDA, McQuaid Papers, AB8/B/XXXII/A (iii)/12 (a) XXXII: Universities A: University College Dublin iii, Faculty of Philosophy and Sociology 12, Department

of Ethics and Politics (a) Rev. Prof. Conor Martin, Rev. Prof. C. Martin, UCD, to Archbishop McQuaid, 25/9/1962, with archbishop's handwritten note dated 26/9/1962.

21   DDA, McQuaid Papers, as yet uncatalogued box UCD/UCC/NUI, memorandum on the teaching of political institutions in University College, 21/3/1965.

22   DDA, McQuaid Papers, AB8/B/XXXII/A (iii)/12 (a) XXXII: Universities A: University College Dublin iii, Faculty of Philosophy and Sociology 12, Department of Ethics and Politics (a) Rev. Prof. Conor Martin, Rev. Prof. C. Martin, UCD, to Archbishop McQuaid, 18/2/1967, with archbishop's handwritten note dated 25/2/1967.

23   DDA, McQuaid Papers, AB8/B/XXXII/A (iii)/12 (a) XXXII, Universities A: University College Dublin iii, Faculty of Philosophy and Sociology 11, Department of Sociology (a) Rev. Prof. James Kavanagh, Archbishop McQuaid to Fr. J. Kavanagh, UCD, 14/1/1963, Fr. Kavanagh to Archbishop McQuaid, 23/1/1963, with handwritten note by archbishop; DDA, McQuaid Papers, AB8/B/XXXII/A (iii)/12 (a) XXXII, Universities A: University College Dublin iii, Faculty of Philosophy and Sociology 12, Department of Ethics and Politics (a) Rev. Prof. Conor Martin, Archbishop McQuaid to Rev. Prof. C. Martin, UCD, 7/3/1963, C. Martin to Archbishop McQuaid, 8/3/1963 and 13/3/1963.

24   TCD, Library, Manuscripts Department, T. W. Moody Papers, Ms. 7121, Commission on Higher Education, Minutes of Plenary Meetings, vol. 1, Fifth Meeting, 24 March 1961.

25   DDA, McQuaid Papers, AB8/B/XXXII/A (iii)/12 (a) XXXII, Universities A: University College Dublin iii, Faculty of Philosophy and Sociology 12, Department of Ethics and Politics (a) Rev. Prof. Conor Martin, 'Philosophy 1955–56' and 'Department of Ethics and Politics Report on Progress', enclosures with Rev. Prof. C. Martin, UCD, to Fr. C. Mangan, Archbishop's House, 25/7/1956.

26   DDA, McQuaid Papers, as yet uncatalogued box UCD/UCC/NUI, Archbishop McQuaid to Rev. Professor J. Horgan, UCD, 28/11/1955.

27   'Students ordained are first fruits of new training plan – Archbishop of Dublin', Irish Independent, 23/5/1966.

28   DDA, McQuaid Papers, AB8/B/XXXII/A (iii)/12 (a) XXXII, Universities A: University College Dublin iii, Faculty of Philosophy and Sociology 11, Department of Sociology (a) Rev. Prof. James Kavanagh, note to 'Your Grace' headed 'Procedure regarding the appointment in the Diocese of a Priest on the Staff of U.C.D.', 18/8/1969.

29   DDA, McQuaid Papers, as yet uncatalogued box UCD/UCC/NUI, note made after talk with Professor Simey enclosed with Prof. C. Martin, UCD, to Fr. C. Mangan, Archbishop's House, 31/8/1955; DDA, McQuaid Papers, AB8/B/XXXII/A (iii)/12 (a) XXXII, Universities A: University College Dublin iii, Faculty of Philosophy and Sociology 11, Department of Sociology (b) Letters and Memoranda from Rev. Dr. Conor Ward, lecturer, Professor T. S. Simey, Liverpool University, to Archbishop

McQuaid, 25/6/1959; DDA, McQuaid Papers, AB8/B/XXXII/A (iii)/12 (a) XXXII, Universities A: University College Dublin iii. Faculty of Philosophy and Sociology 11, Department of Sociology (a) Rev. Prof. James Kavanagh, Fr. J. Kavanagh, UCD, to Archbishop McQuaid, 10/6/1966, attaching copy of printed application for the UCD professorship in social science, handwritten note by Archbishop McQuaid.

30   DDA, McQuaid Papers, as yet uncatalogued box UCD/UCC/NUI, Rev. Prof. E. F. O'Doherty, UCD, to Fr. C. Mangan, Archbishop's House, 30/8/1955, enclosing memorandum on research project 'Emigration', Archbishop McQuaid to E. F. O'Doherty, 1/9/55.

31   A. E. C. W. Spencer, 'Irish Catholics in England', The Tablet, 22/8/1959.

32   NAI, DFA 412/20, Newman Demographic Survey, London.

33   DDA, McQuaid Papers, AB/8/B/XIX/15g/9–12, Catholic Social Welfare Bureau.

34   DDA, McQuaid Papers, AB/8/B/XIX/15g/13–54, Catholic Social Welfare Bureau; DDA, Correspondence from A. E. C. W. Spencer, Newman Demographic Survey, copy of A. E. C. W. Spencer to Dr. Kelly, editor, Analecta Hibernica, 23/8/2006.

35   DDA, McQuaid Papers, AB/8/B/XIX/15g/13, Catholic Social Welfare Bureau, A. E. C. W. Spencer, Newman Demographic Survey, to Rev. Dr. C. Ward, UCD, 6/6/ 1960.

36   DDA, McQuaid Papers, AB/8/B/XIX/15g/34, Catholic Social Welfare Bureau, handwritten 'Report on Emigrants' given to bishops' meeting, 21/6/1960, by Archbishop McQuaid; COFLA, D'Alton Papers, ARCH/12/3/4, Hierarchy General Meeting Minutes, June 1960, Emigrant Surveys.

37   Rev. Prof. J. Kavanagh, 'Social Science at U.C.D.', letter to the editor, Irish Times, 21/ 12/1970.

38   Conor Ward, speaking notes for lecture, 'The Social Science Research Centre and Ireland's Participation in the International Social Survey Programme', delivered at 'Counting, Measuring, Valuing: Four Decades of Social Science Research at UCD' conference, Dublin, April 2005. We are indebted to Professor Ward for providing us with a copy of these notes.

39   DDA, McQuaid Papers, AB8/B/XXXII/A (iii)/ 11, Department of Sociology (b) Letters and Memoranda from Rev. Dr. Conor Ward, lecturer, handwritten notes of archbishop on letters to him from Rev. Dr. C. Ward, 22/4/1968 and 15/7/1969, copy of Archbishop McQuaid to Fr. D. Forristal, 19/2/69, Rev. Dr. C. Ward, UCD, to Archbishop McQuaid, 30/9/1967. In his biography of the archbishop, John Cooney (1999: 398) attributes the removal of Reality editor Fr. Michael O'Connor both from his post and from Ireland by his Redemptorist order superiors to Dr. McQuaid's adverse reaction to the publication in the magazine of the findings of a survey (Power 1969) of UCD students. But Fr. O'Connor ceased to be editor of Reality early in 1968, while the magazine only began to publish the survey findings in instalments in mid-1969.

40   Michael Viney, 'What Class of Vocation?', Irish Times, 16/4/1968.

41   'Social Science to be Trinity College Degree Course', Irish Times, 23/2/1962.

42   DDA, AB8/B/XXIII/329/1, Archbishop J. C. McQuaid, Dublin, to Bishop C. Lucey,
     Cork, 1/11/1961; DDA, AB8/B/XXIII/330/1, Bishop Lucey to Archbishop McQuaid,
     14/11/1961; and DDA, AB8/B/XXIII/320/1, report enclosed by Bishop Lucey.
43   Agnes McGuire, 'What is Social Science? A Career in Humanity', *Irish Times*, 6/10/
     1960.
44   Donal McCarthy, 'Cork and its University', *Irish Times*', 18/5/1971.

4

US aid and the creation of an Irish scientific research infrastructure

Introduction

This chapter broadens out the focus from Irish sociology to examine Irish scientific research. Its central theme is the way in which resources provided or jointly controlled by US actors underpinned the development of a modern scientific research infrastructure within the state in the period after the Second World War. The scientific fields principally affected by these financial injections were applied research related to agriculture, industry and economics. Money flowed into these fields from two major sources: the Grant Counterpart Fund, which was a legacy of Ireland's participation in the Marshall Plan, and the Ford Foundation. In other fields, such as management and 'human sciences', significant resource transfers took place in kind as much as in cash through productivity and technical assistance programmes largely funded from US sources but delivered through the Organisation for European Economic Co-operation (OEEC) and its specialist agencies, the European Productivity Agency and the Office for Scientific and Technical Personnel. The chapter begins with an account of the relationship between the US and Irish states during and after the Second World War – the broader context in which the specific developments of the period relating to Irish science infrastructure took shape. It concludes by relating the Irish scientific infrastructure changes that clustered in the late 1950s and the early 1960s to older scientific institutional configurations laid down under the union with Britain and modified by the advent of political independence.

Ireland's relations with the USA during the Second World War

Throughout the Second World War southern Ireland pursued a policy of neutrality that enjoyed broad popular support but exposed a small state to intense pressure from Great Power belligerents. Its economy was severely disrupted during these years by an inability to import fuel, agricultural inputs and industrial raw materials. This situation was exacerbated by Britain's 'fitful efforts to use control of supplies as a lever to secure Irish concessions on strategic questions' (O'Halpin 2002: 300) – a pressure to which the Irish state was vulnerable because it had little or no shipping capacity under its control. In these circumstances Ireland turned to the USA in the spring of 1941 to try and secure ships and also munitions for the army it had expanded from its small and ill-equipped peacetime state. The diplomatically disastrous mission undertaken by Frank Aiken (Rosenberg 1980) underlined the hostility of the pro-British Roosevelt administration to Ireland's neutral stance and yielded very little in the way of supplies from one state not at war to another in the same situation.

US entry into the war at the end of 1941 closed off the option of trying to mobilise Irish-American opinion in order to bring pressure for a change in stance on the Roosevelt administration and was followed shortly afterwards by the arrival of US troops in Northern Ireland. During the war's later years, as the threat of Germany invading the British Isles receded and the prospect of an Allied victory hardened from likelihood into certainty, practical co-operation on militarily sensitive issues between the Irish and Allied authorities coexisted with high-level political and diplomatic acrimony. In February 1944 rejection of an American diplomatic note seeking the closure of the Axis legations in Dublin on the grounds that they facilitated espionage that might compromise Allied plans to invade Europe was accompanied by the placing on alert of the Irish army and the calling of the Cabinet into emergency session. Later in 1944 the same pattern of demand and rebuff was repeated in relation to asylum after the war for those the Allies regarded as war criminals (Kochavi 1995).

Hitler's death in April 1945 was followed by a formal visit to the German legation by the Taoiseach to express his condolences. In mid-May a victory broadcast by Churchill that referred to 'the restraint and poise' with which Britain had refrained from interfering with Irish neutrality, leaving 'the de Valera government to frolic with the German and later with the Japanese representatives to their hearts' content' drew a broadcast reply in which de Valera contrasted the dictates of international morality with those of Great Power expediency and portrayed Ireland as an indomitable small nation 'that could never be got to accept defeat and has never surrendered her soul'. Internationally isolated, the admission of Ireland to membership of the United Nations was blocked in 1945 and the state was to remain outside the organisation for its first decade.

After the war

Political estrangement from Britain and the USA coexisted with ongoing economic dependence. While trade with Britain remained overwhelmingly predominant, the relationship with the USA was much more important than it had been before the war. Twenty-five per cent of Irish imports came from the USA in 1947 compared with 10 per cent in 1938, a growth that mirrored the general European pattern. With its mainland undamaged by wartime destruction, the US had the productive capacity to export goods of all kinds – provided payment was made in dollars. From the establishment of the Free State Ireland had, as noted in Chapter 2 above, forgone having an independent currency by maintaining the Irish pound's parity with sterling. Ireland thus formed part of the Sterling Area, whose policy decisions were made in London. After the war the convertibility into dollars of sterling, in which substantial Irish assets were held externally in London, was suspended but Ireland was initially able to draw on the sterling area dollar pool – a fund centralising the British Empire's dollar earnings from products like Malayan rubber or west African cocoa under London Treasury control – to acquire the wherewithal for its imports from the USA.

The launching of a European Recovery Programme (ERP) in 1947 against the background of the emerging Cold War with its erstwhile Soviet Union ally brought together the economic and political dimensions of the USA's relations with Ireland. Here 'the U.S wish to isolate Ireland in retaliation for her wartime neutrality was counterbalanced by a perceived need, for security reasons, to incorporate Ireland into some American-sponsored organisation'. Ireland was seen by US policy-makers as being capable of aiding broader European recovery through increased food production: its involvement in a US-orchestrated programme could ease British financial difficulties by easing pressure on the sterling area dollar pool. Irish hostility to Communism was overwhelming but dangerous destabilisation might, it was feared, occur in the future as a result of deteriorating economic and social conditions, while the exclusion of Ireland from a European programme might prompt a revival of agitation in the USA on the issue of partition (Whelan 1992).

Irish acceptance of an invitation to attend the inaugural Paris meeting followed exchanges in which the departments of Agriculture, External Affairs and Industry and Commerce favoured participation but Finance expressed strong reservations. The first inter-party government had replaced Fianna Fail by the time an offer of US aid within the framework of the ERP was made to Ireland in mid-1948. Non-repayable grant aid had been sought: only repayable loan aid was offered. The Irish government was initially inclined to turn this offer down but accepted it when it was informed by Britain that Ireland's already restricted access to the sterling area dollar pool was to be entirely cut off with almost immediate effect. Although grant aid of $18 million was later forthcoming, close to 90 per cent of the ERP dollar allocations to Ireland between 1948 and 1951 ($128.2 million) were made in loan form.

The Counterpart Funds

In the course of Chapter 3 a number of references were made to the Grant Counterpart Fund. A state receiving US dollar aid under the ERP was obliged to deposit in a special account a local currency sum equivalent to the value of the dollars it had been given. These local currency funds were known as counterpart funds. Five per cent of the total was reserved for US government usage while the remaining 95 per cent was spent on developing the aid recipient's productive capacity. The way in which the specific developmental uses to be made of the local currency funds was decided varied according to whether the dollars to which they formed the counterpart were loaned or granted. If loaned, then the recipient country's government decided how the counterpart funds should be spent. If granted, the expenditure of counterpart funds had to be agreed between the recipient government and the US authorities. One consequence of this was that loan counterpart was quickly spent – mainly on a land reclamation scheme – by the Irish government between 1948 and 1952, while protracted negotiation of agreements between Irish and US governments held up the spending of grant counterpart until the late 1950s (Whelan 2000: 286–314). The list of grant counterpart projects eventually agreed between the USA and Ireland is set out in Table 4.1.

Two of the uses to which Grant Counterpart funding was put – the support of movements for rural regeneration and technical assistance – have already been referred to. Table 4.1 understates the amount of money actually received by the Irish Countrywomen's Association, Muintir na Tire and Macra na Feirme as a reserve fund was also initially set aside to cover contingencies and from this source an additional £4,000 was subsequently allocated to each of the three organisations. It was from the Technical Assistance allocation that Muintir secured funding from the Department of Agriculture to carry out the LRS. Aside from this very modestly scaled study in rural sociology, Irish scientific research infrastructure was a major beneficiary of Grant Counterpart Fund spending, with laboratories and equipment for the Institute of Industrial Research and Standards (IIRS) and the establishment of the Agricultural Institute accounting for a third of the total. This was a noteworthy development as 'the three and a half decades up to 1958, in which the post-partition state (from 1949

Table 4.1 Grant Counterpart projects agreed between Ireland and the USA

Project	Grant (amounts in £s)
The Subsidisation of the Delivery of Ground Limestone	1,750,000
The Eradication of Bovine Tuberculosis	700,000
The Purchase of Equipment for the Pasteurisation of Milk and the Sterilisation of Equipment	500,000
Grants to the Irish Countrywomen's Association, Muintir na Tire and Macra na Feirme	30,000
The Establishment of the Agricultural Institute	1,840,000
The Establishment of an Educational Exchange Programme between Ireland and the USA	500,000
Defraying in Whole or in Part the Costs of Technical Assistance Projects	350,000
The Provision of Additional Laboratories and Equipment for the Institute of Industrial Research and Standards	130,000
TOTAL	5,800,000

Source: Whelan 2000: table 7.2

the Republic) was following most conspicuously an internal model of development, were a period in which there was little development in science policy and only a negligible role for innovative research in relation to industry' (Yearley 1995: 180). As a result, Irish science – including the social sciences – was the subject of strong Americanising influence during the 1950s and 1960s. Nor was the Grant Counterpart Fund the only source of this influence. Agencies within the OEEC and private US foundations also played an important role.

Industrial research

The IIRS grew out of an Industrial Research Committee set up in 1933 and supported by a modest amount of piecemeal government funding. By the end of the 1930s the Committee was providing about £6,000 annually to the three National University colleges for research that was mostly concerned with trying to identify industrial uses for Ireland's abundance of peat and seaweed. Moves to place the Committee on a more secure footing were under way in the Department of Industry and Commerce by the early 1940s when these were put to one side to create the Emergency Scientific Research Bureau, whose staff sought to improvise solutions to the problems thrown up by the wartime interruption of the flow of vital imports. With the end of the war, the project of a permanent industrial research institute was revived and an Industrial Research and Standards Act was passed in 1946. A change in status left access to resources largely unchanged, however, with Sean Lemass stating at an Industry and Commerce departmental conference in September 1952 'that he was of opinion that expenditure on industrial research on the present limited scale was unproductive and wasteful because the research was too confined to be effective' (Peter Murray 2009: 75). By the early 1960s the new laboratories and equipment financed by the Grant Counterpart Fund were redressing this defect. Policies that opened up the Irish economy and emphasised export growth fostered a greater awareness of the importance of industrial research. In 1966, with an Anglo-Irish Free Trade Agreement negotiated, and the achievement of EEC entry as a central state policy objective, the US consultants Arthur D. Little Inc. were brought in to advise on changes at the IIRS[1] at the same time as they were working on what would prove to be a crucially significant reorganisation of the IDA (Peter Murray 2009: 90–92).

An Agricultural Institute

The shortcomings of the Irish economy's major sector, agriculture, dominated the list of agreed projects for the Grant Counterpart Fund. Agricultural education, agricultural research and advisory services to working farmers were all comparatively underdeveloped and were not effectively integrated with one another (Rouse 2000: 144–145). Under the first inter-party government (1948–51) and its Fianna Fail successor (1951–54) discussion of an Agricultural Institute with the Dublin mission of the European Cooperation Administration (ECA) – the US government agency created to administer the Marshall Plan – began by envisaging a body located on a central campus and covering the trinity of functions. However, the advisory component was soon removed from the institute's scope and a decision was made on cost grounds to utilise existing facility locations rather than to construct a new campus. This left an institute that would be responsible for research and teaching in conjunction with the universities. As outlined in Chapter 1, since the 1920s UCD had had a Faculty of Agriculture and UCC a Faculty of Dairy Science, while agriculture students in Trinity, which had the longest-established degree in the field, had to complete their studies in UCD under an ad hoc arrangement. With the creation of an agricultural institute it was envisaged that the UCC and UCD faculties along with a number of research stations operated by the Department of Agriculture would be transferred to it. Undergraduate agriculture students would henceforth spend their first two years studying basic science at an NUI college or in

Trinity and their final two years mastering an applied speciality within the institute. Both NUI and Trinity would 'recognise' the institute and confer degrees on those completing there the studies they had begun in a university.

Up to the signing by the two governments in June 1954 of a framework agreement for the Grant Counterpart Fund that allocated specified amounts of money to a finalised list of projects, the devil had relatively little opportunity to emerge from the detail. Thereafter, despite a broad bipartisan political support base, substantial opposition emerged to an Agricultural Institute on the lines envisaged by successive governments. Two years later all of the universities were seeking their own Faculties of Agriculture. UCD sought to hold on to what it had, UCC to broaden its existing dairy science base, UCG to create a new faculty focused on west of Ireland farming issues and Trinity to offer the full course it had been stripped of without consultation in the 1920s by government action. To this end it acquired early in 1957 an estate near Drogheda that included land that it designated the Kells Ingram farm. To the funding alongside a new Agricultural Institute of any or all of these plans – which were on occasion woven into a set of complementary regional and/or sectoral specialisations – the Department of Finance was adamantly opposed. Against this backdrop, the Catholic bishops entered the fray, championing NUI interests and deploring the level of funding being given to Trinity and the extent to which that university was to be represented on the agricultural institute's governing body. The unacceptable degree to which the institute would be state-controlled was also under fire – again from the bishops but also from farming organisations, with Macra na Feirme and its NFA offshoot in the van. The bishops affirmed the principle of subsidiarity: the negative stance of the farming organisations reflected a history of poor relations between the Department of Agriculture and agricultural producer groups (Smith and Healy 1996).

In the government's proposals 'hard' science was almost totally predominant, with the only social science input envisaged in the Department of Agriculture's lengthy list of research areas the Institute would encompass being an Agricultural Economics Research Unit. This proposal responded to comments that had been made by the OEEC on 'the inadequacy of the training in agricultural economics provided at University level' in Ireland.[2] Sociology was, however, pressed into service by O'Rahilly, to criticise the government's approach:

> After spending my life in the National University, as professor and as president of U.C.C., I am naturally concerned with preserving the workable though not ideal settlement which after a prolonged struggle Irish Catholics obtained in 1908. In 1926 this scheme was extended by the endowment of Faculties of Agriculture and Dairy Science. Now it so happens that these two faculties are those for which religious and social training are most necessary. For the holders of degrees and diplomas are not being trained for export as are so many of our medical students. They are destined to

work throughout the country as agricultural advisers, rural science teachers, creamery managers, food processing experts and so on. Clearly they should not be mere
technicians but should have a training in social principles and be equipped to be local
leaders.[3]

The Catholic hierarchy made its first intervention at a hastily arranged meeting of the bishops of Cork (Lucey) and Galway (Browne) with Taoiseach John
A. Costello on 19 January 1955. The Standing Committee of the Bishops had
met the previous day and the day before that 'proposed institute of agriculture'
had been an item on the agenda of the meeting of the 'Hierarchy/University
Liaison Committee'. Trinity's role was the main concern the two bishops conveyed to Costello. The meeting concluded with the Taoiseach stating that 'it was
necessary in dealing with the place of Trinity University in the scheme not to do
anything that would give unfriendly persons material to make charges against us
of intolerance or unfairness towards the Protestant minority, particularly in the
circumstances of the grant deriving from American sources and the problem of
partition'. Their Lordships were also told that 'they would be supplied with the
fullest information when available and that every opportunity of conferring on
difficulties would be given'.[4]

As his government fleshed out its Institute proposals over the following
months, Costello actively sought to secure the goodwill of the bishops. When the
Institute was the subject of the address to be delivered to Muintir na Tire's Rural
Week in August, one aspect 'suggested as worth considering for inclusion in the
speech but which the Taoiseach is doubtful about ... is the question of anticipating any possible objection on that the ground that there may not be sufficient
provision for the religious and moral welfare of the students of the Institute'. On
this occasion Costello's doubts were overcome and the speech, having noted that
during their initial two years students would be university-based and 'catered
for from the religious and moral aspects in the same way as students of other
Faculties', went on to give 'the most definite assurance that every facility will be
afforded for, and due precautions will be taken to ensure, the provision of equal
care for students while they are in the Institute'.[5]

After the hierarchy met in October, however, a highly critical set of views on
the Institute proposals was sent to Costello. These proposals were characterised
as 'another incursion of the State into the sphere of higher education' from which
'the essential qualities of academic freedom' were absent. Grave injury would
be inflicted on the NUI by a situation whereby 'our students of Agriculture,
who are 98 per cent Catholics, are to be withdrawn from the university atmosphere which they have hitherto enjoyed, and from the opportunity of receiving
that wide formation in Ethics, Sociology, History and other subjects which is

so necessary for true education, and are to be transferred to a purely secularist institution'. A slippery slope whereby, on the grounds of avoiding resource dissipation, Institutes of Medicine and Engineering might subsequently remove these subjects from the NUI was also discerned. Having defended 'Catholic University Education', the bishops then turned to attacking Trinity's place in the Institute scheme and what they saw as its disproportionate share of state funding for the universities.[6]

Faced with this challenge, his biographer comments that 'given his performance in the earlier [Mother and Child Scheme] controversy, Costello might have been expected to buckle; he didn't' (McCullagh 2010: 310). The lengthy reply Costello made with his Cabinet's agreement continued to offer consultation and discussion but conceded little or no ground to the criticisms the bishops had levelled at the Institute proposals. In relation to the withdrawal of students from the university atmosphere objection, it was stated that 'the Government feels that ... there has been a regrettable disregard of the relevant public declarations by the Taoiseach'. The section of the August Rural Week speech promising 'equal care' for Institute students was then quoted and the response on this point concluded that 'since, as stated by the Taoiseach, the students will pass the first two years of their training in the Universities of their choice, their opportunity of receiving formation in such subjects as Ethics, Sociology and History will not be less than that enjoyed by students of Agriculture or Dairy Science under the existing arrangements'.[7] As the 'existing arrangements' involved spending a period longer than two years at a university in order to obtain a degree, this was hardly accurate. O'Rahilly had earlier noted in relation to the Taoiseach's student welfare assurance that 'there is not a single word to this effect' in a 'White Paper' concerned 'from beginning to end with technical subjects divorced from both pure science and humanistic studies', with the latter 'assumed to be completely extraneous to the "higher education" provided in the Institute'.[8]

The recipient of Costello's reply, the hierarchy's Secretary, Bishop Fergus of Achonry, commented to Archbishop McQuaid that 'the long and the short of it is that we let ourselves in for it, and we have got it with a vengeance'. The response made after the Bishops' Standing Committee met in January 1956 expressed 'deep regret at the tone and contents of the document the Government thought well to address to us', adding that 'none of the main objections put forward by the Bishops have been answered'.[9]

However, the government needed to advance rather than merely hold its ground. While James Dillon had told a US embassy official in August 1955 that the 'vested interests will eventually be beaten down', the political reality was stated by the US ambassador in a letter to Costello in the same month: 'my

Government, almost as much as yours, would not care to launch an Institute here which contradicts substantial, informed public opinion' (quoted in Loftus 2010: 113 and 114). By May 1956 Dillon was writing to Costello arguing for the establishment of 'an independent Agricultural University', which, he suggested, could have a Faculty of Philosophy and Sociology under clerical control. This he regarded as preferable to 'a milk and water kind of research institute established at great cost ... which will add little or nothing to the resources of which we dispose already' (McCullagh 2010: 316). It was, however, to an institute concerned with research only that the second inter-party government reluctantly turned, only to lose office before the passage of its bill was completed. The incoming Fianna Fail government sought to revive the educational dimension of the project before it too fell back in the face of continuing opposition on a research-only institute which was duly established as Foras Taluntais in 1958.[10] This was initially organised into five Divisions – Animal Production; Soils; Plant Sciences and Crop Husbandry; Rural Economy; Horticulture and Forestry. The Rural Economy Division encompassed the subject matter of farm management, agricultural economics, agricultural marketing, agricultural engineering, home economics and rural sociology. While work in rural sociology formed only a small part of the overall research output of Foras Taluntais over the next three decades, this was to account for a significant proportion of the total volume of Irish sociological research in this period.

Secular American involvement in social science studies of Ireland also increased as a result of the Institute's existence. Alongside the 1950s and 1960s research of the US Jesuits Alexander Humphreys (1966) and Bruce Biever (1976) could be placed that of Joseph Bohlen of Iowa State University and Gordon Streib of Cornell. Although US agricultural extension services provided the template for the Irish proposals made during the 1950s, the insights provided by US rural sociology – such as the huge innovation diffusion literature that originated in 1940s studies of seed choice by Iowa farmers (Rogers 2003: 31–35 and 54–60) – went unnoticed while the Institute prescription for Irish agricultural catch-up was being written. But once an institute was operational, collaboration between the Rural Economy Division of An Foras Taluntais and the Iowa Agricultural and Home Economics Experiment Station brought Bohlen to Ireland as a research consultant (Bohlen and Breathnach 1968 and 1970). Foras Taluntais was also the base for Gordon Streib when he came to Ireland as a Fulbright scholar in 1966– 67. While in Ireland he collected data comparing rural and urban attitudes to family and kinship obligations (Streib 1970a and 1970b) and on Irish attitudes towards changes in the Catholic Church (Streib 1973a). Articles on old age in Ireland – Streib was a distinguished social gerontologist in his home country – on Ireland's social stratification pattern and on the restoration of the Irish language also flowed from a relatively short but highly productive stay (Streib 1968, 1973b and 1974).

The growth of higher institutes

Costello's November 1955 response to the bishops observed that 'in stating that "the proposals involve another incursion of the State into the sphere of higher education" the Bishops presumably have in mind some previous action by the state involving an incursion, or incursions, of the nature indicated. Since, however, no example of such previous action is mentioned, the Government are unable to offer any comment in this regard.' Speaking in Cork in September, Bishop Lucey had been more explicit in his criticism when he stated that 'the State has made no frontal attack on the autonomy of the Universities but it has begun to supersede them a little by the creation of the higher Institutes. There are two already, and now there is to be a third.' Quoting this speech at length, John Whyte (1980: 310) notes that 'Dr. Lucey was presumably referring to the Dublin Institute for Advanced Studies (DIAS) and the Institute for Industrial Research and Standards.' The IIRS has been discussed above. Consisting of a School of Cosmic Physics, a School of Theoretical Physics and a School of Celtic Studies, the DIAS was established in 1940 and was initially most noteworthy for its accommodation of the Anschluss-displaced Nobel laureate Erwin Schrödinger. An incongruity between this oasis of advanced activity and its host society's dearth of basic scientific infrastructure was occasionally discerned, while its status as a pet project of de Valera – a teacher of mathematics and a Gaelic League activist before he became a political leader – also prompted negative comments. As incursions of the state into the sphere of higher education, both institutes were slight in stature and even an observer as suspicious of the state as Bishop Lucey presented the universities as being superseded by them only 'a little'.

    While Bishop Lucey correctly perceived that a significant increase in the population of Irish higher institutes was under way by the mid-1950s, not all of the emergent entities were statute-created bodies like the DIAS, IIRS and Foras Taluntais. The most significant examples of the non-statutory higher institute were the Irish Management Institute (IMI) and the Institute of Public Administration (IPA). Both bodies aimed at raising existing standards of professionalism – IMI in private companies, IPA in the civil service and local government and both in semi-state organisations. Founded in December 1952, IMI launched a journal, *Irish Management*, in 1954. In the previous year *Administration* 'began life as a forum for publishing papers read to a discussion group formed by some higher civil servants'. Secrecy initially surrounded these proceedings, because as Bryan Fanning (2008: 193) observes, 'civil servants no less than priests had to negotiate gingerly institutional controls, questions of doctrine and expectations of surrender to authority'. By the end of the decade the journal was out in the open and linked to the IPA, which was founded in November 1957. A proposal for the integration of the two institutes was made by IMI in 1959. The report of a joint committee which supported integration was accepted by the Executives of the two bodies but rejected by the IMI's Council.[11] As they continued on their separate ways, both benefited from the state policy shift towards attracting foreign investment and becoming a member of the EEC. Earlier, in the austerity of the 1950s, IMI was a beneficiary of Grant Counterpart funding albeit to a more modest extent than Muintir, Macra and the ICA. A portion of the cost of setting up a Management Development Unit within IMI to run short, full-time courses with 'the task of broadening the vision of future top managers' was provided from the Department of Industry and Commerce's share of the allocation for Technical Assistance. Another feature of IMI's early years was links with productivity promotion initiatives in Europe that originated with and continued to be sustained by US aid provision. Among the fields of activity failing within the ambit of this productivity movement was social research.

The social sciences and the gospel of productivity

Along with dollar grants or loans for commodity purchases, Marshall Aid encompassed a Technical Assistance and Productivity Programme (USTAP). Technical Assistance (TA) primarily took the forms of individuals or teams visiting the USA to study the state of their particular art in a US context (Type A TA) or of US consultants visiting Europe to carry out analysis and dispense advice (Type B TA). Aid recipient states were also urged by ECA to set up national productivity centres in which government, business and trade unions would collaborate to promote the dissemination of changes that would assist in bridging the performance gap between the European and the US economies. The first Irish TA projects got under way in 1949 and in June 1950 the Irish government approved the setting up of a national productivity centre. An ambitious TA programme with a manufacturing industry focus was aborted when US aid to Ireland was suspended in January 1952 and proposals drawn up by Marshall Plan administrators for an Irish productivity centre were judged to be too elaborate and too expensive to implement. Ireland would not acquire a productivity centre until 1959. TA would not move beyond plans on paper to begin making a significant impact in workplaces until the Irish state began to fund the adaptation of its protected industrial base to free-trade conditions in the 1960s.

US aid to Ireland was suspended after the context of aid provision was changed by the 1951 Mutual Security Act from European economic recovery to 'strengthening the mutual security and individual and collective defences of the free world'. Retrospective treaty changes sought by the US government were deemed to be incompatible with Ireland's declared foreign policy and a Memorandum to the Government advised that should refusal to adhere 'entail the discontinuance of all further American aid to this country after the 31st December, 1951, the Minister for External Affairs considers there is no alternative but to accept the loss involved'. Ireland remained a member of the OEEC, which it had joined in 1948 as a condition of receiving Marshall Aid, and through this retained a formal connection with the greatly expanded productivity drive mounted in 1950s Europe (Peter Murray 2009: 19–45).

This expansion came about because the 1951 Mutual Security Act contained the Benton Amendment, which specified three US policy aims. First, to increase the role played in developing the economies of foreign countries by 'free private enterprises'. Second, to discourage production-restricting business cartels and monopolies while encouraging competition and productivity in those countries. Third, 'to encourage where suitable the development of the free labor union movements as the collective bargaining agencies of labor within such countries'. A year later the Moody Amendment earmarked $100 million in aid funding for carrying out programmes 'in furtherance of the objectives of [the Benton Amendment] with a view to stimulating free enterprise and the expansion of the economies of those countries with equitable sharing of the benefits of increased production and productivity between consumers, workers and owners'. The same amendment authorised the transfer of $2.5 million to OEEC – which by this time was divided into a majority of members who were in good Mutual Security Act standing with the USA and a minority (including Ireland, Sweden and Switzerland) who were not – for the promotion of these objectives. The larger of the Moody Amendment's earmarked sums was doled out through a series of bilateral agreements between the USA and states that were in almost all cases its military allies. The smaller earmarked sum prompted the 1953 creation within the OEEC of an autonomous European Productivity Agency (EPA) of which all OEEC members, whether US military allies or not, were members (Boel 2003: 21–60).

Ireland's connection to the productivity drive remained largely formal during the EPA's first five years in existence because its contact point – in the absence of an Irish national productivity centre – was an uninterested Department of Industry and Commerce. During this period EPA made connections with non-state actors in Ireland that included trade union leaders, the IMI and the Retail, Grocery, Dairy and Allied Trades Association (RGDATA). An active non-governmental constituency for positive Irish engagement with EPA had coalesced before *Economic Development* signaled a shift in this direction within the higher echelons of the civil service. Alongside provision of productivity education for management and trade unionists, EPA was noteworthy for 'its sponsorship of academic research in the social sciences, a new departure in many European countries. Beginning with a few research projects on the "human aspects of productivity involving human sciences", the EPA went on to develop a long-term action programme, the objective of which was to promote scientific knowledge of the problems of work' (Carew 1987: 192–193). In Britain a feature of the bilateral agreement for spending its allocation of Benton–Moody funds was 'a substantial academic component' whereby a Joint Committee on Human Relations in Industry dispensed funding to universities that stimulated a large output of publications in the area of industrial and organisational studies. This came about because 'Washington officials believed the British lacked understanding of competition, human relations and management issues, and accordingly insisted that a proportion of Benton–Moody money be spent on projects which would deal with more theoretical aspects of these questions' (Tiratsoo and Tomlinson 1998: 41–42).

Within this broader context EPA's director, Roger Gregoire, made 'a personal request' to the head of the Irish delegation to OEEC on 3 May 1957 'for your co-operation in putting into operation as quickly and efficiently as possible the Agency's programme for the human sciences and their application in industry', Project 405. The letter specifically requested 'your appropriate national authorities to constitute a joint committee in your country composed of management, trade union and government representatives as well as social scientists'. In Dublin the Minister for Industry and Commerce, Sean Lemass, 'indicated that he favoured the idea of the establishment of such a Committee'. He 'considered that the I.M.I. would probably be best qualified to examine and appraise the E.P.A. suggestion' and 'he directed that the matter be discussed informally with Mr. Hegarty, Vice Chairman of the Institute'. This decision set in train a process of consultation and discussion from which a National Joint Committee on the Human Sciences and Their Application to Industry (HSC) and an Irish National Productivity Committee (INPC) were to emerge eighteen months later (Peter Murray 2009: 80–81).

The Human Sciences Committee, 1958–63

The composition of HSC, as agreed in July 1958, is set out in Table 4.2. In the case of the university representatives, it had been agreed 'that University

Table 4.2 Constitution of Committee to operate Project 405 as agreed at the Fourth Preliminary Meeting to Consider the Establishment of a Joint Committee to Implement EPA Project 405 (1 July 1958)

Organisation	Number of representatives
Federated Union of Employers	1
Federation of Irish Industries	1
Irish Management Institute	1
State-Sponsored Companies	1
Provisional United Trade Union Organisation	4
Universities	2
City of Dublin Vocational Education Committee	1
Catholic Workers' College	1

Source: Government and Irish Congress of Trade Unions files in the National Archives of Ireland

College Dublin might be asked to nominate a representative skilled in psychology and Trinity College a representative skilled in medicine'. The first meeting of HSC was held in November, when it elected as its chairman Professor Feichin O'Doherty of UCD. Arrangements for liaison between HSC and INPC were agreed between the bodies at a 16 April 1959 meeting. Both committees would communicate directly with Industry and Commerce in relation to financial support. The department provided both committees with secretarial support but neither had a budget: TA grants provided the potential source of national support for their activities. All requests for EPA funding were to be routed through the INPC and the HSC was to make regular progress reports to the INPC.

During the lifetime of the EPA, HSC concentrated on trying to create an Irish human sciences research infrastructure, starting more or less from scratch. Here it utilised EPA projects that offered opportunities for researchers to study abroad and proposed the establishment of an Institute of Occupational Psychology (a proposal further discussed in Chapter 5 below). It also held conferences and seminars promoting ergonomic awareness and discussing adaptation to change in industry and society. Shannon – the 'first Air-Age Industrial Development Zone in the world' – provided a site for HSC collaboration with INPC, EPA and the EPA-backed Dutch researchers whose survey findings on occupational preferences were quoted in Chapter 3 above (Peter Murray 2009: 165–172).

This phase of its existence lasted until 1962. With the strength of Europe's economic recovery, the OEEC had lost much of its original rationale by the end of the 1950s. Through its own successes in technical areas like currency convertibility mechanisms it had partly worked itself out of a job. Europe's big integration and liberalisation issues had been taken over by two rival blocs within the OEEC membership – the six-strong European Economic Community (EEC) and the seven-strong European Free Trade Area (EFTA). In December 1959 it was decided to begin negotiations on a reorganisation that would enable the USA and Canada to become members. Without US money and advocacy an EPA would never have come into existence, but the US view of how a Western or 'free world' economic co-operation and development body of which it would itself be a member should be structured had no place for the productivity agency. Thus, as OEEC was transformed into the Organisation for Economic Co-operation and Development (OECD), EPA was disbanded. It ceased to exist at the end of September 1961, although some programmes and projects ongoing at that date had until June 1962 to wind up. With EPA killed off, OECD emerged as an organisation orientated towards analytical studies rather than the provision of support services. Ireland pressed for management development support to be retained but this was done only for areas in the process of economic development, a status Ireland was unwilling to embrace as it was by then seeking full membership of, rather than association with, the EEC (Peter Murray 2009: 67–69).

Adaptation of industry to EEC free-trade conditions provided the context in which technical assistance and productivity promotion continued with domestic instead of external support. In 1963 agreement was reached to reconstitute HSC as a sub-committee of an INPC that was now to be funded through an annual grant-in-aid from the Industry and Commerce Vote. The agreement provided for INPC to appoint five labour and five management members to its HSC and for these members to co-opt 'not more than eight people qualified in the Human Sciences field'. Over time the numbers co-opted greatly exceeded this limit. O'Doherty stepped down as chairman at the time of the HSC's reconstitution and was succeeded by a trade union nominee, Charles McCarthy, who was to hold the position for more than a decade. During this time HSC provided grants to support research projects, with the amount devoted to this purpose running at approximately 10 per cent of the INPC's grant-in-aid in the late 1960s. Apart from J. A. Jackson, the author of a major study of the Irish in Britain, and the London-based Tavistock Institute of Human Relations, grant recipients were based in all of the three NUI constituent colleges, in Trinity College and in the IMI. Into the early 1970s HSC played an important capacity-building role in Irish social science but a restructuring of INPC around this time created a much colder organisational climate for the funding of research, which after two decades ceased to be linked with productivity promotion in 1979. Authors whose research was funded and published by the HSC of INPC include Conor Ward, Michael D. Higgins, Tomas Roseingrave, Brian Hillery and Liam Gorman (Peter Murray 2009: 172–175).

The Ford Foundation and Irish institutions

A significant feature of post-war US aid to Europe was the dovetailing of projects financed by large private foundations with activities funded from US government sources. The foundation which stands out in this context is the Ford Foundation. Endowed on an 'unprecedented' scale following the deaths of Henry Ford and his son Edsel, 'the Ford Foundation was indeed immense' after it was restructured at the end of the 1940s (Sutton 1987: 52). The link that coincidental timing provided between this restructuring and US government European reconstruction initiatives was reinforced by common perspectives and personnel – as Carew (1987: 194–195) puts it 'the Ford Foundation was rooted in the values of the Marshall programme ... [and] became a second home for senior Marshall Plan staff'.

Just as US government money funded productivity-related social science research in Britain and elsewhere under the Benton–Moody mandate, the Ford Foundation financed for more than twenty years the 'mammoth' Inter-university Study of Labour Problems in Economic Development in which 'no fewer than ninety academic researchers in the United States and abroad were involved at one stage or another'. Its major publication, *Industrialism and Industrial Man*, was co-authored by its US-based principal researchers – John Dunlop, Clark Kerr, Frederick Harbinson and Charles Myers (Carew 1987: 196–197). In the area of European management education the Ford Foundation began by financing an EPA Pool of American Professors of Business Administration programme upon which the IMI in its early years drew heavily to staff its Irish teaching programme (Peter Murray 2009: 128–131). After EPA's demise the Foundation became directly and intensively involved in the field. Giuliana Gemelli (1998: 57) notes that 'the reports written by the professors engaged in EPA's programme were of great value to the Ford Foundation. They both defined the Foundation's policy of investments in each country with respect to the level of acceptance of management education at university, and assisted it to select those projects which were to have priority within its general policy.'

Gemelli also credits Shepard Stone, head of the International Affairs Division from 1953 to 1967, with elaborating for the Foundation 'a grander vision of Europe which foresaw three goals: the strengthening of the Atlantic Community; the reinforcing of democratic institutions; and the widening of European perspectives, towards not only the Mediterranean countries, but also those in the East'. She goes on to locate this project 'within the very complex scenario in which the Cold War, at the end of its aggressive phase, moulded higher learning into a strategic factor in political warfare' (Gemelli 1998: 45). In a sub-title Stone's biographer (Berghahn 2001) places his subject 'between philanthropy, academy and diplomacy'. Operating within the field of diplomacy were state intelligence agencies and their Cold War covert funding activities. These provided a key context of Stone's career both prior to and during his Ford Foundation years. The earliest post-war covert funding adventures involved appropriation of part of the US government's 5 per cent share of Marshall Aid counterpart moneys. Later, as covert funding acquired a routinised large-scale character, foundations were to be found delivering or supplementing payments that originated in the Central Intelligence Agency (Dorril 2000; Saunders 2000).

Some US state funds covertly channelled into movements promoting European unification did find their way into 1950s Ireland (McKenzie 2015), but, out on Europe's western extremity, this small state seemed peripheral to the grand concerns of a foundation based on the fortune amassed by the grandson of a mid-nineteenth-century Irish emigrant. Henry Ford visited his ancestral home in 1912, and in 1919 manufacture of Fordson tractors began at a large Cork city plant. Sentimentality is hardly the quality social commentators had in mind when they attached an 'ism' to his surname, yet 'it was clearly Ford's awareness of, and sentimental attraction to the area that was the first factor in making Ireland – and indeed Cork – a possible centre of production' (Jacobson 1978: 39). For the manufacture of tractors, unlike cars, an Irish base was, as Jacobson points out, not incompatible with other business considerations influencing locational choice. After a collapse in the European market for tractors in the 1920s, the Cork plant switched to manufacturing car parts. In the early 1930s Dagenham near London became Ford's European car production centre. Many Cork workers emigrated to England to continue working for Ford as the Irish plant was drastically scaled down to perform the final assembly of cars sold on the highly protected Irish market. Ford remained nonetheless a major industrial employer in Cork (Nyhan 2007) and the plant's closure in the early 1980s was experienced as a hammer blow to the local economy.

The circumstances in which this large modern manufacturing operation was originally inserted into the almost wholly agricultural area that was about to become the Irish Free State were such that 'Ford was regarded by many Irish nationalists as unique and was viewed, very unrealistically, as a quasi-Irish concern' (M. Daly 1984: 247). In the mid-1950s the Ford Foundation was characterised 'as a large body of money completely surrounded by people who want some' (D. McDonald 1989: 1). Both emaciated by domestic austerity policies and cut off from the US governmental civil and military aid flowing into Europe from 1952 on, it is hardly surprising to find Irish institutions among the throng beating a path to the Foundation's door. How these applicants fared is the subject matter of the remaining part of this chapter. Two letters written by Irish diplomats based in New York during April 1959 provide the discussion's starting point.

Irish applicants and Ford Foundation funding

On 8 April 1959 Ireland's Consul General in New York, Jack Conway, wrote to the Secretary of the Department of External Affairs regarding 'matters never before handled by the Consular Service' that 'effect a cumulative strain on our resources'. He was referring to requests his office had received within the previous year to assist approaches to the Ford and other US foundations from IMI, UCC and the unnamed promoters of 'an institute for research and studies in the Irish language and civilisation'. The consulate should not, in his view, be drawn into acting as an agent of any Irish applicant. It might be put under pressure to follow any precedent set even when the succeeding applications were 'less worthy'. Moreover 'the Foundations are private organizations in original concept and quite determinedly non-governmental in structure and tone. I am doubtful if they are desirous of governmental approaches, especially if frequent and as varied in quality as the three current matters.' Conway went on to develop his point about quality in relation to the potential Irish language and civilisation institute:

> The project at present is so much a pipe-dream (even the assumption of a 5% income on a permanent £2,000,000 endowment seems amateur) as not to warrant serious consideration beyond raising this question – why should an American Foundation rather than the Irish themselves contribute $5,600,000 to the study of the Irish language and civilization both past and present? As soon as the organizers provide a convincing answer to this question they can regard themselves as having begun their quest for funds here.[12]

Less than a week earlier the head of Ireland's Permanent Mission to the United Nations, Frederick Boland, had written a letter to the Secretary of the Department of the Taoiseach in which he began by quoting from a letter he himself had received from Lord Rosse, 'who has been over here trying to raise money for the proposed extension of the Trinity College Library':

> The Ford Foundation appears to be giving thought to the possibility of giving aid to Ireland on a very big scale indeed. Under certain conditions they seem willing to consider economic aid to the nation as a whole, quite apart from the needs of Trinity, especially if it could somehow be tied to the easing of tension between North and South ... McDaniel would like to combine meetings with some members of the Government with his visit to Trinity in the Autumn.

Noting that McDaniel was 'one of the top executives of the Ford Foundation', Boland raised the question of which 'official people' he might meet when in

Dublin, adding that 'I think the matter *may* be of some importance. I have heard before that, partly because the great Henry Ford was of Cork descent, the Ford Foundation was anxious to do something in Ireland.'[13] By late 1959 four Irish bodies which had something specific to propose to the Foundation were Trinity College, whose library required extension, UCC, which hoped to develop a Food Technology Department, IMI, which sought a general expansion of its services, and the Statistical and Social Inquiry Society of Ireland (SSISI), the sponsor of a proposal to establish an economic research body devised by a group of government department secretaries after Boland's letter had alerted them to the possibility of funding support.

With the addition of Education, the departments represented – Agriculture, Industry and Commerce, External Affairs and Finance – were the ones whose secretaries had been brought together to advise the Taoiseach at the time of abortive 1956–58 discussions on turning the OEEC into a free-trade area. Within this forum Finance advanced a proposal for 'an Economic Research Institute (or Centre)' which might be 'within or outside the Dublin Institute of Advanced Studies'. Boland's presence in Dublin during August enabled this proposal to take definite shape. Echoing Conway's earlier observations, he advocated that the Ford Foundation be approached by a non-governmental body. This criterion SSISI formally satisfied, even though most of its officers were actually senior civil servants. At the key 6 August meeting the prospects of the other applications – in relation to which the departments represented had earlier pooled their available documentation – were also assessed. Boland stated that he 'understood that the Foundation were not keen on projects involving large expenditure on buildings', which was what both Trinity and UCC were proposing. But, 'in view of Ford's associations with Cork', he assessed the UCC application – which was favourably regarded by the Department of Agriculture – to have the better prospects. He considered that its success and that of an economic research institute to be housed by the Irish government and staffed at the Ford Foundation's expense were not mutually exclusive.

On the following day Lemass was reported to have endorsed holding informal discussions with professors of economics – in his view 'the project should not be allowed to fall through by reason, solely, of failure to secure co-operation from any particular University institution', while 'the thought occurred to the Taoiseach that the Institute or Centre might possibly be located elsewhere than in Dublin – for example in Cork', although 'he did not put forward the ... idea as one to be pressed'. On 1 September the government, having discussed a memorandum from the Minister for Agriculture, agreed in principle to provide assurances of ongoing support for a UCC Food Technology facility initiated with Ford Foundation money. By 13 November, when a similar undertaking was successfully sought by the Minister for Finance in relation to an economic research institute, the UCC application had been turned down.[14]

The expectation that Ford Foundation Secretary Joseph M. McDaniel — whose earlier career had included periods as dean of the business school at Northwestern University and as a special adviser at the European headquarters of Marshall Aid administration in Paris — would be visiting Ireland had prompted the development of the economic research institute proposal but the meeting that discussed it took place in New York on 7 October. Present on the Irish side were the Minister for External Affairs, the Secretary of the Department of Finance, the governor of the Central Bank as well as Frederick Boland and Jack Conway. McDaniel was accompanied by four other Foundation officers and by Daniel Shanley, a New York businessman who was a personal friend of his and a political friend of Ireland.

The accuracy of the report of McDaniel's positive disposition, and of his all-Ireland orientation, are confirmed by a memorandum on preparations for the meeting written by one of his colleagues: 'from what Mac said I believe he is beginning to become interested in the idea of a commission representing dif-ferent universities and institutions of both parts of Ireland sponsoring an eco-nomic assessment including recommendations for the future of the country as a whole.' The Irish representatives came away from the 7 October meeting in an optimistic mood, while McDaniel recorded that 'personally I left with the feeling that there are great opportunities in Ireland for the Foundation and that we could anticipate getting a large return on a minimum expenditure'. However, the priorities of the Foundation's International Affairs department lay elsewhere in Europe and there was reluctance on its part to add another country to those it was already involved with. Supporting documentation sent from Dublin in November was seen as leaving key questions unanswered:

> The papers submitted do not speak to important points such as a) the general readi-ness of intellectual, business and political leaders to accept and use objective eco-nomic studies as a basis for practical action; b) the active interest, the competence and influence of the prospective board of directors and c) the breadth of view, quality and acceptability of the director and leading staff members. It would be unfortunate to request information of this type in writing if the Foundation were unlikely to give positive consideration. It may be that your [McDaniel's] conversation gives you a basis for judgment on these scores. In brief, is there evidence that the institute, rather than being mediocre, would be high powered and influential in a fresh way?[15]

Tilting the balance in the direction of a positive response was the intervention of a credible independent figure who could address these points and answer the concluding question in the affirmative. After graduating from Cambridge, John

Vaizey had begun his career as an economist with a study of the British brewing industry. Connections made in the course of this early work led to his being commissioned to write one of the volumes of the history of Guinness's brewery that were to mark its Dublin bicentenary. The co-author of this book (Lynch and Vaizey 1960) was Patrick Lynch, a UCD economist and friend of Vaizey's from a mid-1950s period when the two had been together in Cambridge. The time Vaizey subsequently spent 'working with uncatalogued and unsorted archives' in Dublin meant that 'through the Irish book I got to know Ireland well'. His influential work on the economics of education was developing simultaneously, with the result that 'I became an Expert on that somewhat esoteric but increasingly fashionable subject ... [and] was drawn increasingly to Paris to work with international organisations' (Vaizey 1986: 123–124). This inserted him into the personal and professional network that had developed around the close working links between leading US private foundations and the OEEC.

An Office for Scientific and Technical Personnel (OSTP) established within OEEC in the wake of the October 1957 launch of the first Sputnik satellite by the Soviet Union had become the driving force behind a push not only to increase the supply of scientists and technologists but also to secure recognition among policy-makers for the role of education as a key factor in promoting economic growth (Papadopoulos 1994: 21–33). Personal experience of Irish conditions and strategic location within transatlantic economics of education networks made Vaizey both a key advocate of Ford Foundation support for an Irish economic research institute and an attended-to informant on that institute's progress in its early years. Vaizey's intervention provided a narrative – an inward-looking country beginning to move towards engagement with the Atlantic Community under guidance from an enlightened group that was struggling to overcome entrenched resistance to necessary change – around which subsequent recommendations that the Foundation support the SSISI application were framed by its staff. Another key point of reference was OSTP, with whom Vaizey was working and from whom the Foundation obtained all the reports written in the course of a review of mathematical and scientific education in Ireland carried out by external assessors from France and the USA during 1959. To OEEC Foundation officers attributed the conclusions that 'the time is now propitious to get at Ireland's problem through education' and 'the improvement of economic and social research and training programs would establish the best base on which further educational steps could be taken' (Peter Murray 2009: 176–179; Peter Murray 2012a).

Shepard Stone visited Dublin in February 1960 and a $280,000 grant over five years to support the creation of the Economic Research Institute (ERI) was confirmed in July. ERI involvement in educational research was urged by the Foundation up to the mid-1962 initiation of the study jointly supported by the Irish government and OECD that would produce the seminal *Investment in Education* report. Monitoring progress, Foundation officer Matthew Cullen observed after an April 1962 visit that the 'Institute has only been in operation for about eight months as it experienced major difficulties in recruiting staff'. Apart from the director, R. C. Geary, none were Irish. Cullen's broadly positive report noted the closeness of the relationship between the ERI and the Department of Finance: 'it would probably be too much to say that Whitaker "runs" the Institute but such an assessment would not be too far from the truth'. This increased the potential impact on public policy of the Institute's work but, he noted, 'more difficult to assess is the question of what this relationship does to the Institute as a center of free scholarly research'.[16]

Within weeks of Cullen's visit tension arose around such freedom while preparations were being made for an interview with Lemass by the US magazine *Business Week*. Emphasising Ireland's capacity to become a full EEC member in a Brussels speech in January 1962, Lemass had said that '[T]here is good ground for the belief that a total increase in production of 50 per cent by 1970 is within the capacity of the Irish economy; in other words, that Ireland can match the collective target recently set by the members of the Organisation for Economic Cooperation and Development.' But growth rate forecasts supplied by the ERI in May were too low to be compatible with this. The IDA, which was preparing material for the interview, ignored the ERI forecasts. Whitaker observed approvingly that 'it is one thing to obtain the views of individual experts on what may happen but it would be quite another for an official organisation to quote expectations of what will happen which are not in line with government intentions'. For Lemass his own department's minute on the matter concluded by drawing his attention to 'the pessimistic nature of the contributions of the personnel of the Economic Research Institute; if forecasts such as those now received find their way to potential investors in Irish industry, the prospects of securing industries will not be enhanced'.[17] Grumbling about what might nowadays be called failure to 'pull on the green jersey' was one thing, punitive action in retaliation for critical analysis was quite another. According to a memoir by the Institute's third director, Michael Fogarty, an instance of such action occurred in the late 1960s after it had published a paper on unemployment by the retired Geary 'which could be taken as a criticism of the Fianna Fail government's policy'. In response the Minister for Finance, Charles Haughey, 'went right off the deep end, and a week before the beginning of the financial year the ESRI's budget was cut by 25 per cent' (Fogarty 1999: 124–125).

The Trinity College Library application

Although Boland had in August 1960 judged it unlikely that Trinity College would get Foundation funding for its library project this turned out to be the only successful Irish application apart from that of the ERI. The decision to build an extension had been taken in 1953 and fundraising began with the university's chancellor, Lord Iveagh, and his daughters donating £45,000 – 10 per cent of the total sum then estimated to be required. The College's hope was to tap into four potential funding sources – graduates, the wider public within and beyond Ireland, the Irish state and US foundations. A 1954 approach to the Rockefeller Foundation ended in disappointment (Grimes 2000: 185), as did an approach in the same year to the government for an allocation from the Grant Counterpart Fund. The building of a new National Library was also being mooted and it was Department of Education policy to give priority to that development. A joint project catering for Trinity and National Library needs was discussed over the following three years but 'with nothing definite emerging, Trinity decided to press ahead with its own plans' (Luce 1992: 162).

Out of these plans in October 1958 emerged the American Council for the University of Dublin, whose renewal of approaches to potential donors in the USA prompted the Irish Catholic hierarchy to circulate to US cardinals a spoiling statement 'as there is a distinct possibility that the state of Irish University Education at the present time may not be fully understood by US citizens who will be approached on behalf of the Council'.[18] Permission from the government to send parts of Trinity Library's precious early Christian manuscripts collection, including a portion of the Book of Kells, to New York for exhibition was sought but not obtained in March 1958. Agreement to an exhibition in London was, however, secured despite Department of Education opposition: 'a proposal of this kind should not be acceded to for the benefit of any particular College or University, having regard to the fact that these articles are national heirlooms'.[19]

As Trinity's fundraising revived in these and other ways, a proposal was made by the director of the National Library for a single new building to serve the needs of both libraries. This would be erected along Trinity's boundary with Nassau Street and would contain two separate libraries – the National one accessed by its readers (presumed to be mainly Catholic) from Nassau Street and a Trinity one accessed by its staff and students from within the College. The proposal was intended to eliminate wasteful duplication between the two libraries as well as to increase public access to and use of their combined resources. The political sensitivity of a National Library link with Trinity led to a slow response but, with the College's provost reacting favourably and seeking a definite decision because of the stage the planning for extending its own library had reached, a meeting between the Taoiseach and Archbishop McQuaid took place in May 1960. Here the proposal for locating the two libraries in one building was killed off (Bowman 1993). Thereafter Trinity pressed ahead with its own plans, securing by the end of 1961 a commitment from the government to supplement its Appeal Fund on a pound for pound basis up to a specified maximum sum. Early in 1964 – after more than five years of contact between the two sides – a Ford Foundation donation of £100,000 brought the Appeal Fund's final total to £815,000.

An obvious difference between the successful Trinity and the unsuccessful UCC applications was that the latter sought a grant covering the full cost of the proposed Food Technology facility (some $700,000), while the former looked for a much smaller sum that represented only a portion of the total cost. Its Catholic critics might have argued that Trinity's socially privileged position enabled it to raise more from its graduates and wider public (which the state proceeded to match pound for pound) than the NUI or its constituent colleges could hope to do. But the NUI hardly maximised its potential in this regard. Collectively it was hamstrung by tension between a large Dublin college with a leadership hostile to the federal entity and the smaller Cork and Galway ones that wished to preserve the existing structure. There was also increasing division within UCD between supporters and critics of the Tierney regime. In 1958 a Graduate Association Donation Fund, launched to mark fifty years of the NUI, was snubbed by Tierney even though Archbishop McQuaid privately 'urged for the sake of his position that Dr. Tierney allow his name to be used as Patron'.[20] The division exposed here would later lead to the petition for a Board of Visitors and that Board's verdict of illegality in relation to UCD appointments discussed in Chapter 3 above. Trinity's 'non-Catholic' character may also have worked in its favour in the US Ford Foundation context. In international affairs Stanley Gordon appears to have been uneasy about the degree of Catholic Church influence over UCC and it was he who described as 'such a good letter' Vaizey's initial intervention in support of funding for the ERI in which the Catholic clergy are held responsible for 'a terrible education system' – 'the worst in Western Europe in the opinion of OEEC officials'.[21]

IMI and the Ford Foundation

IMI had sought Ford Foundation funding in November 1958 only to be informed that 'it is not now possible to provide such assistance'. IMI's chairman, T. F. Laurie of Esso (Ireland), renewed contact while in the USA to attend an International Chamber of Commerce conference in the spring of 1959. His approach was facilitated by an oil industry friend who was a Foundation trustee.[22] A visit to IMI when a Ford Foundation representative was in Dublin was discussed, but when Shepard Stone came in February 1960 he seems only to have had contact with the two universities and government departments. Stone was later, in November 1961, the recipient of the following suggestion from John Vaizey, to which he does not appear to have responded:

> The Institute of Public Administration in Ireland has been running some very good courses and is now at the stage where it could either take off into quite a large pro- gramme of training and research or where it could jog along running one or two courses a year for senior executives. I wonder whether there is a possibility of linking the Institute of Public Administration to Geary's Institute and to the Management Association. Ireland is a small country which can hardly support three independent bodies working in much the same field, and drawing their support from much the same people. A proposal was accepted by the Institute of Public Administration to amalgamate with the Management people but rejected by the latter. It seems to me that Ford, by offering a small bait, and being a disinterested outsider, could certainly draw attention to the economies of work together.[23]

Enjoying lucrative access to the Irish state TA funding that came on stream in the adaptation to EEC industrial free-trade context during the 1960s, IMI seems to not to have further sought Ford Foundation support. This was, however, pursued by both ERI and IPA.

The Ford Foundation and 1960s Irish applications

The success of the ERI application raised high hopes within Irish official cir- cles that other projects might in the future be successfully proposed to the Ford Foundation. One approach sought the renewal for a further period of the ongo- ing ERI grant. Overtures on the subject appear to date from September 1963 when at a meeting in New York:

> Mr. Whitaker told Mr. McDaniel that he was reluctant to raise the question directly because there was a Government commitment, which the Government had every intention to honour, to support the Institute once the period of Ford Foundation aid was ended. He would not wish to suggest that the Government were not ready to do this when the initial grant was gone but did think that there would be considerable merit in prolonging the launching period of the Institute in conditions of independ- ence of Government support. The Institute would have a better chance of attracting high quality research staff if the resources of the Institute were not predominantly State-provided.

Judging Foundation officers to be receptive to such suggestions, a formal application for a further grant of $590,000 was made in July 1964, a year before the cur-
rent one was due to expire. Payment of the first grant ended without a decision
being taken on the application for a second one or the Irish government undertaking being activated, leaving the ERI to finance itself through a bank overdraft.
In April 1966 Geary wrote to McDaniel suggesting that the Irish government
would currently find it difficult to take over ERI financing as a result of problems created by British economic conditions and policies. In May Stone informed
Geary that his proposed visit to Ireland was delayed: 'We are having budgetary
problems and this inevitably holds up action on projects in Ireland.' Subsequent
correspondence in which Stone stated that 'I do not think it would serve any
useful purpose for you to visit New York' led Geary to conclude by July that 'we
now have but a remote chance of getting a grant'. Whitaker held out hope somewhat longer, but in October, after McDaniel had informed him that a further six
months would elapse before a decision could be reached by the Foundation, the
Institute's Council decided to ask for implementation of the government undertaking to provide funding once Ford ceased to do so. By this time Geary had just
retired and preparations for the ERI to become the Economic and Social Research
Institute (discussed in Chapter 5 below) were all but completed. On 7 November
Geary's successor, M. D. McCarthy, wrote that all was not yet 'plain sailing' –
pending formal government decisions 'as to the method and scale of support', he
himself had refused to retire from his directorship of the Central Statistics Office
and, as an interim measure, 'have been seconded to the Institute for a month'.[24]

Joining ERI in the search for Ford Foundation money was IPA. Initial contact
with the Foundation in relation to an Irish public administration initiative actually preceded IPA's formation:

> Prior to the establishment of the Institute an approach for support was made to the
> Ford Foundation (which has given support to corresponding Institutes elsewhere)
> but it soon became clear that assistance would only be forthcoming (if at all) if the
> Institute could point to substantial work done, and could assure the Foundation that it
> was a 'continuing' organisation with relatively substantial financial support from non-
> Foundation sources. It is significant that it is only now (after many years in existence)
> that the I.M.I. has established contact with the Ford Foundation, and that by way of
> *personal* contact which is, apparently, essential to success; the Royal Institute of Public
> Administration has had the same experience. The Institute will continue to keep this
> matter in mind but, in view of the conditions precedent to a successful application for
> Foundation support, it obviously must be left to mature.[25]

With T. J. Barrington as director, IPA was, in Vaizey's terms, actively seeking by the early 1960s to 'take off into quite a large programme of training and

research' rather than to 'jog along running one or two courses a year for senior
executives'. Two projects which it pursued were the launching of a School of
Public Administration and, through the Social Research Committee (discussed
in Chapter 5 below), creating a funding infrastructure for social research. IPA
had little success in raising funds within Ireland to build accommodation for the
School of Public Administration, which was opened in October 1964 and was
intended to cater at graduate level for both Irish students and suitably sponsored
candidates from developing countries. This deficit it sought Ford Foundation assistance to make up. However, at a June 1964 meeting in New York Matthew Cullen
told Barrington that the Foundation was disinclined to give grants for buildings
and would expect any assistance it gave to be matched by a substantial state commitment: 'he thought the pattern set by the Economic Research Institute, in
which the state contributed the buildings and the Foundation the other finance,
might be a suitable one'. Cullen also indicated at this meeting that an informal
grant quota system was in operation: 'a country as small as Ireland could not hope
to have more than one grant in a year when countries as large as Britain, France
and Germany would have no more than two or three'. This meant that there
were national queues and the recently successful Trinity College Library had been
ahead of the IPA in the Irish one. Being at the head of the Irish queue, as IPA now
was, did not guarantee success and Cullen, reiterating the difficulty of succeeding with building projects, suggested that IPA might look again at its application
before the next round of grants were approved in December.[26]

When in January 1965 word reached Dublin that both of the Irish applications –
IPA and ERI – had been set aside because of a Foundation budget shortfall, Geary
wrote a note stating that he and Whitaker 'both agreed that the IPA and ERI applications had got mixed up: in fact the fact of the IPA application was prejudicial to
ERI as we both recognised at the start'.[27] But evidence from the archives suggests
that as the 1960s went on the Ford Foundation tended to identify a useful role for
these Irish institutes in the delivery of its programmes for developing countries
rather than regarding them as priority candidates for the receipt of grant aid.

Developing countries first appeared within the relationship between Ireland
and the Ford Foundation in 1963, when the Irish government decided to respond
positively to an appeal from Kenneth Kaunda, leader of the United National
Independence Party in Northern Rhodesia, to train in Ireland African administrators for a state expected to be denuded of its existing white ones upon the
attainment of independence. This decision was taken with an explicit expectation of getting Ford or other foundation funding to defray much of the cost. The
running of the scheme by the non-governmental IPA was intended to facilitate
grant aid in a manner similar to the advancement under SSISI sponsorship of
the ERI application. Initial contact by the Washington embassy with the State

Department and with the Ford Foundation produced encouragingly positive responses. However, as the Department of External Affairs was later forced to explain to the Department of Finance, insurmountable difficulty arose in 'rationalising on general policy grounds a Foundation grant to a government or institute of a developed country for a training programme for a developing African country'. The Irish government thus ended up bearing some of the training scheme costs that it had expected to be able to recoup.[28]

Ford Foundation recognition was, however, given to IPA's credentials in this educational field early in 1965 when the Staff College set up by the Kaunda government in Lusaka received a grant to support lecturer and librarian recruitment from Ireland in conjunction with the Irish institute. Later in the decade Barrington carried out consultancy projects in Ghana for the Foundation, while its officers discussed with ESRI staff the possibility of Irish social scientists undertaking work in Nigeria and in other parts of Africa.[29] Seeking information from the Department of External Affairs on US foundations that might fund ESRI sociological studies in August 1970, Michael Fogarty was 'pretty sure' that the Ford Foundation 'would not give backing to work specially of interest to Ireland': '[W]hen I have met them they have seemed pretty pleased with the results of their pump-priming exercise in 1959/60, but have also made it clear that their interest now is in developing countries and that they would be likely to give us further support only if we were working in that area.'[30]

Irish universities and the Ford Foundation

Joseph McDaniel had, as we have seen, envisaged a role for the universities in a Ford Foundation-sponsored initiative relating to the economic future of the whole of Ireland. The obstacles to getting Irish universities working together in this way were more clearly apparent on the other side of the Atlantic. In discussion of project possibilities that might be proposed to the Ford Foundation carried on amid the optimism generated by the ERI's success, inter-university collaboration was discounted. As the Secretary of the Department of Education wrote in April 1962 to Whitaker in Finance, 'a major difficulty is, as you say, the Trinity problem vis-à-vis the other Colleges'.[31] The 1960s were, however, to see an erosion of the antagonism virulently active at the beginning of the decade. Imbibing the human capital perspective on education promoted by the OECD the Irish state became more assertive and less deferential. The Second Vatican Council opened up a space for ecumenical initiatives within the churches. By 1970 a Dublin university merger was under discussion and the ban on Catholic students attending Trinity College had been lifted.

This decade also saw a significant growth in university social science capacity both north and south of the border. When the Commission on Higher Education's long-delayed report finally appeared in 1967 social science received 'only the most general consideration' because 'social science, sociology and psychology were scarcely referred to in the evidence received' by it several years earlier, with only three submissions – from Basil Chubb (politics, TCD), Fr. Peter Dempsey (psychology, UCC) and Muintir na Tire – being made.[32] In the early 1970s the Ford Foundation was approached by a cross-border consortium of social scientists with a proposal which became the Program on Ireland in Europe and on Conflict in Ireland. Administered by the Committee for Social Science Research in Ireland, this dispensed more than £200,000 for projects and fellowships between 1974 and 1983 (Jackson 2004: 30–31). Providing specific support to conflict studies, it belatedly addressed in the context of the violent Northern Troubles the easing of tension on the island which, as reported by Lord Rosse to Frederick Boland, McDaniel had highlighted as a desirable goal for Ford Foundation involvement in Ireland back in 1959.

But, apart from the single, highly placed figure of McDaniel,[33] the foundation was little engaged with, rather than sentimentally drawn to, Ireland. Two substantial grants that injected significant resources made the social sciences an exception to this general pattern. But, as Chapter 5 will demonstrate, the Republic of Ireland's social science structures were still primarily shaped by Irish policy-makers rather than by any external agency.

Conclusion

In the late 1950s and early 1960s applied scientific research across a broad range of fields was a major beneficiary of Irish engagement with US government aid programmes and of support from US private foundations whose funding policies dovetailed with those of US government initiatives. The existing scientific infrastructure which this injection of resources expanded was very largely an inheritance from the pre-independence era of British rule. Then, as outlined in Chapter 1, Irish scientific practitioners had been predominantly Protestant and politically opposed to Home Rule. Noting the existence of this Protestant hegemony in Irish science, Yearley (1989: 314) comments that 'it is not clear that it is one consistently contrived by Protestants'. This is challenged by N. Whyte (1999), who draws on evidence from RDS and RIA committee elections to back up a charge of sustained Protestant exclusivity that gave way to a base-broadening accommodation to new politico-religious (and/or financial) realities in time to enable both institutions to survive the break-up of the United Kingdom. Whyte also acquits the Catholic Church of having discouraged scientific research, citing the absence of cases where scientists incurred the kind of censure that befell the theologian Walter McDonald. For Greta Jones (2001), on the other hand, potential conflicts between science and theology were a key factor in the pre-independence failure to create an inclusive university structure that left NUI, QUB and TCD as separate entities. Later 'all the apprehensions of the anti-home rule scientists were vindicated by the events that followed independence', with professional isolation increased, universities more distorted than ever by politico-religious division, reduced space for non-denominational institutions and sources of research funding support closed off (Jones 2001: 201).

Whyte agrees with Jones that political independence brought scientific impoverishment but attaches the blame for this not to a prevalence of fear of the modern among priests and patriots but to state parsimony. Thus he attributes the principal reduction of denominationally neutral space – the mid-1920s incorporation of the Royal College of Science into UCD (and UCC) – to a desire to avoid 'spending more money to build UCD its own science and engineering facilities' (N. Whyte 1999: 148). The divergence of views between two scholars writing at the turn of the twenty-first century about a period with ended in the 1920s is strikingly mirrored in the August 1960 exchange of letters between Fianna Fail ministers Sean MacEntee and Patrick Hillery which was quoted in Chapter 3 above. There MacEntee follows up his 'super-seminary' characterisation of the NUI with an observation that 'some important elements in the Hierarchy, perhaps even a majority ... think that scientific education is a source of danger to the Faith and they demur to provide facilities for it'. Hillery's reply contained a remarkable admission from a Minister for Education:

> I couldn't agree with you more when you say that the provision for scientific studies, whether pure, advanced or applied in the constituent Colleges of the N.U.I. is shamefully inadequate but let us put the blame squarely where it belongs, that is, on successive Governments ... [T]he income per student of the three Colleges concerned is less than a third of their counterparts in Britain. It is hardly fair to underfinance them (and indeed Trinity too) so badly and then to blame them for not doing their job properly. Like the dog that Dr. Johnson spoke of that could stand on its hind legs, the wonder is not that those Colleges are doing so much as they are doing in Science, but that they can do anything at all, with their Science staffs often working under conditions that would not be tolerated by this Department in a Secondary or Vocational school.[34]

Scientists in the direct employment of the government – Whyte's 'administration scientists' – inhabited a space less subject to denominational influences than that of the Irish universities. In relation to this administration scientist sector the key post-independence change had been the breaking up of the DATI – which had 'inaugurated a golden age for science in Ireland' (Jones 2001: 191) – between departments of Agriculture and Education. Under the Department of Education the number of science and arts institutions shrank as a result of NUI incorporations and decades of neglect was to be the fate that those whose independent existence was preserved would share with the universities. Counterpart Fund expenditure and a Ford Foundation grant saw the administration scientist sector begin to grow again, developing in new directions with industrial research and economics or trying (with limited success) to put something like the DATI's Humpty together again in the case of the Agricultural Institute. The institutional space in which scientific research operated free from denominational influence that had shrunk in the 1920s began to expand again from the late 1950s. How sociology and social research would be altered as a sector of new model administration scientists continued to grow is the subject of Chapter 5.

Notes

1   NAI, DFA 2001/3/1300, Little Review of IIRS.
2   NAI, DT S14,815/D, Proposed Agricultural and Veterinary Science Institute, Department of Agriculture Memorandum for the Government, Draft Outline of Proposed Agricultural Institute, 28/7/1955.
3   NAI, DT S15,926/B, Agriculture and Veterinary Science Institute, press cuttings, 'The Agricultural Institute', *Irish Times* clipping, 8/9/1955.
4   NAI, DT S14,815/C, Proposed Agricultural and Veterinary Science Institute, 'Agricultural Institute', 19/1/1955.
5   NAI, DT S14,815/E, Proposed Agricultural and Veterinary Science Institute, M. Moynihan, Taoiseach, to J. C. Nagle, Agriculture, 4/8/1955; for press coverage of Costello's speech to Rural Week in Navan see NAI, DT S15,926 A and B, Agriculture and Veterinary Science Institute, press cuttings.
6   NAI, DT S14,815/F, Proposed Agricultural and Veterinary Science Institute, 'Views of the Irish Hierarchy on the Draft Proposals for an Institute of Agriculture, enclosed with Bishop J. Fergus, Secretary to the hierarchy, to J. A. Costello, Taoiseach, 18/10/1955.
7   See NAI, DT S14,815/G, Proposed Agricultural and Veterinary Science Institute, for the government's detailed statement in reply enclosed with J. A. Costello, Taoiseach, to Bishop J. Fergus, Secretary to the hierarchy, 4/11/1955. A series of earlier drafts of the reply can also be found in this file.
8   NAI, DT S15,926/B, Agriculture and Veterinary Science Institute, press cuttings, 'The Agricultural Institute', *Irish Times* clipping, 8/9/1955. The 'White Paper' referred to is a statement issued by the Government Information Bureau on behalf of the Minister for Agriculture, James Dillon, on 15/8/1955.
9   DDA, McQuaid Papers, XV/15/2/24, Institute of Agriculture 1955, Bishop J. Fergus, Achonry, to Archbishop McQuaid, Dublin, 8/11/1955; NAI, DT S14,815/G, Proposed

Agricultural and Veterinary Science Institute, Bishop J. Fergus, Secretary to the hierarchy, to J. A. Costello, Taoiseach, 19/1/1956.

10   NAI, DT S14,815/H and NAI DT S14,815/I, Proposed Agricultural and Veterinary Science Institute.

11   Institute of Public Administration, Second Annual Report (year ended 30/9/1959), pp. 13–14, Third Annual Report (year ended 30/9/1960), p. 3.

12   NAI, DFA 324/339, Ford and Rockefeller Foundations, J. Conway, Consulate General New York, to C. Cremin, External Affairs, 8/4/1959.

13   NAI, DT S16,645 A, Ford Foundation and Rockefeller Foundation Aid to Ireland, F. H. Boland, Permanent Mission to United Nations, New York, to M. Moynihan, Taoiseach, 3/4/1959.

14   NAI, DFA 324/339, Ford and Rockefeller Foundations; NAI, DT S16,645 A, Ford and Rockefeller Foundation Aid to Ireland; NAI DT S16,705 A, Centre for Economic and Social Research in Ireland: Establishment.

15   FFA, Reel No. 620, Grant No. PA 60–285, memorandum, S. Gordon to W. Nielsen, 29/9/1959, memorandum, J. McDaniel to Records Center via S. Gordon, 9/12/1959, memorandum, S. Gordon to J. McDaniel, 18/12/1959; NAI DT S16705 A, Centre for Economic and Social Research in Ireland: Establishment, T. K. Whitaker note, 9/10/1959.

16   FFA, Reel No. 620, Grant No. PA 60–285, Section 4, memorandum, M. Cullen to Records, 11/6/1962.

17   NAI, DT S16,705 B/62, Centre for Economic and Social Research in Ireland: Establishment, T. K. Whitaker, Finance, to J. P. Beddy, Industrial Development Authority, 14/5/1962, N. O'Nuaillain, Taoiseach, to Taoiseach, 11/5/1962.

18   DDA, McQuaid Papers, as yet uncatalogued box UCD/UCC/NUI, 'The Irish University Question', 2/3/1959; COFLA, D'Alton Papers, ARCH 12/4/3/6–8, Education -2, Universities, Trinity College, Dublin, 2, Proposed statement – for distribution in USA to counteract Trinity propaganda, March–April 1959.

19   NAI, DT S9197 B/94, Book of Kells: Exhibition in London.

20   DDA, McQuaid Papers, as yet uncatalogued box UCD/UCC/NUI, handwritten note, 26/8/1958, on Rev. Prof. J. Horgan, UCD, to Archbishop McQuaid, 25/8/1958.

21   FFA, Reel No. 1086, Grant No. L58-787, memorandum, S. Gordon to Central Files, 23/9/1958; FFA, Reel No. 620, Grant No. PA 60-285, memorandum S. Gordon to J. McDaniel, 18/12/1959.

22   NAI, DFA 324/339, Ford and Rockefeller Foundations, copy T. F. Laurie, IMI, to Tanaiste (Lemass), 9/3/1959, enclosed with S. Lemass, Minister for Industry and Commerce, to F. Aiken, Minister for External Affairs, 14/3/1959, J. Hearne, Washington embassy, to Secretary, External Affairs, 22/4/1959, enclosing copy of T. F. Laurie to J. Hearne, 21/4/1959.

23   FFA, Reel No. 620, Grant No. PA 60-285, correspondence J. Vaizey, University of London Institute of Education, to S. Stone, Ford Foundation, 8/11/1961.

24   ESRI, box 1, History of ERI/ESRI, file 'Confidential Correspondence Ford Foundation', note marked 'Strictly Private and Confidential', New York, September 1963, file 'Ford

Foundation II', R. C. Geary, ESRI, to J. McDaniel, Ford Foundation, 22/4/1965, S. Stone, Ford Foundation, to R. C. Geary, 6/5/1965, R. C. Geary to T. K. Whitaker, Finance, 12/7/1965, file 'Dr. Henning Friis', M. D. McCarthy, Central Statistics Office, to H. Friis, Danish National Institute of Social Research, 7/11/1966.

25   NAI, DT S16,645 A, Ford Foundation and Rockefeller Foundation Aid to Ireland, 'Institute of Public Administration Application for State Support', June 1959.

26   NAI, DFA 2002/19/262, Northern Rhodesian Training Scheme (Zambia), T. J. Barrington, director, IPA, to Dr. D. O'Sullivan, External Affairs, 19/6/1964, note of meeting between External Affairs officers and IPA, 11/9/1964, T. J. Barrington, 'Ford Foundation', 11/6/1964, enclosed with T. J. Barrington, director, IPA, to Dr. D. O'Sullivan, 19/6/1964.

27   ESRI, box 1, History of ERI/ESRI, file 'Ford Foundation II', R. C. Geary, handwritten note on letter from T. J. Kiernan, New York, to T. J. Barrington, IPA, 12/1/1965.

28   NAI, DFA 2002/19/261 and 262, Northern Rhodesian Training Scheme (Zambia), especially H. McCann, External Affairs, to Secretary, Finance, 14/6/1966.

29   Eighth IPA Annual Report (1965), pp. 15–18, Tenth IPA Annual Report (1967), p. 33, Eleventh IPA Annual Report (1969), p. 24; FFA, Reel No. 620, Grant No. PA 60-285, memorandum, P. E. de Janosi, 28/4/1970.

30   NAI, DFA 2001/37/714, US Support for Projects and Institutions in Ireland, M. P. Fogarty, director, ESRI, to Hugh McCann, Secretary, External Affairs, 21/8/1970.

31   NAI, DF 2001/3/775, Proposed Pilot Study of Future Educational Needs with Organisation for Economic Co-operation and Development Assistance, T. O'Raifeartaigh, Education, to T. K. Whitaker, Finance, 4/5/1962.

32   Commission on Higher Education 1960–67, Report, vol. 1, paras 12.35 and 12.36 (Dublin: Stationery Office, 1967).

33   Informing him of the grant's approval by telephone, McDaniel told New York Consul Conway that 'you don't know how happy it makes me that we have been able to do something for the old country', NAI, DFA 324/339, Ford and Rockefeller Foundations, J. Conway, Consulate General, New York, to C. Cremin, External Affairs, 27/6/1960.

34   NAI, DT S16,803, Higher Education (1), Commission of Inquiry, 1960, (2) Commission on Higher Education Membership, S. McEntee, Minister for Health, to P. Hillery, Minister for Education, 26/8/1960, P. Hillery to S. McEntee, 1/9/1960.

5
The institutionalisation of Irish social research

Introduction

The injection of resources into Ireland's scientific research infrastructure at the end of the 1950s created two new social science research producers – the Rural Economy Division of An Foras Taluntais and the ERI. In the former rural sociology took a recognised place alongside a variety of other agriculture-relevant disciplines. In the latter, as exemplified by the letter sent by SSISI to the Ford Foundation on 20 August 1959, the distinction between the economic and the social was from the start blurred, inconsistent and indistinct.

This three-page letter begins by proposing the establishment of 'a Centre for Economic and Social Research'. It goes on to sketch the role SSISI has played since 1847 (see M. Daly 1997), quoting as the society's objective 'the promotion of the study of statistics, jurisprudence and social and economic science'. Reference is then made to Ireland's 'lack of organized research on economic and social problems' and to how 'a considerable extension in basic research work in economic and social science is essential'. The most satisfactory way to bring this about is 'the establishment of an independent body to carry out the necessary economic, social and statistical studies' enjoying 'cordial relations' with government departments and 'close links' with all the island's universities. From almost half-way through the letter, however, the social falls away and all but one of the subsequent references are to the economic on its own or to economists. The sole further appearance of the social occurs in an indicative list of research topics that includes 'a study of the factors, including social factors, affecting productivity in Irish industry and agriculture'.[1]

During the first half 1960s the unenclosed field of social research was to be the subject of a series of proposals to a variety of government departments for the creation of research centres or institutes. The chapter details these proposals, the fate they met and the context in which the Irish government moved to fill the infrastructural gap that had been left in the social research field by replacing ERI with an economic and social research institute. The chapter concludes by examining the implications of this history for the Catholic social movement, the hitherto dominant force within Irish sociology, and the manner in which approval for a central social research organisation was linked to the project of extending the scope of government programming to encompass social development as well as economic expansion.

HSC proposes an Institute of Industrial Psychology

When it was established in 1958 the HSC consisted of one third business, one third trade union and one third education representatives. The educational nominating bodies were the two Dublin universities, CWC and the City of Dublin Vocational Education Committee. UCD's Professor Feichin O'Doherty was elected chairman and an industrial psychology focus for the HSC's work quickly emerged, with a decision 'provisionally to limit consideration to problems coming under the heading "job satisfaction" which was understood to include matters such as human relations and incentives'. Towards the middle of 1960 O'Doherty sought a meeting with the Minister for Industry and Commerce, Jack Lynch, at which he informed him that the Committee 'could not fulfil its intended function unless some positive steps were taken towards the provision of research facilities'. The ideal to be aimed at, O'Doherty went on, 'would be the establishment of a research unit, either as a completely independent body or in association with one of the University colleges'. A 'less expensive alternative' was also put forward: state funding of a number of research scholarships or fellowships tenable at the Department of Psychology in UCD with a suggested value in the range of £800–1,000 each, 'which would be used to promote the study of specific problems recognised as being of particular importance in Irish industry'.

At a subsequent meeting with Industry and Commerce officials on October 7 at which O'Doherty was accompanied by the CWC nominee to the HSC, the Rev. M. J. Moloney, a proposal for a Research Institute in Industrial Psychology, with an estimated initial establishment cost of £20,000 and an annual running cost of £7,000, was put forward. The establishment costs should, the promoters argued, be entirely borne by the state, as they believed the trade unions would not contribute to its support 'and financing by management in these circumstances might prejudice labour against the scheme'. Two memoranda subsequently written by the more junior officials present called, in one case, for financial contributions to an institute from labour and management to be pursued and, in the other, for clarification of how the HSC proposal related to the overall European Research Plan envisaged by EPA. Both concluded by supporting the establishment of an institute and also the provision of some research scholar-ship/fellowship funding pending this development.

However, neither non-state financing for an institute nor the European dimen-sion of the role it might play seems to have been further explored. Nor was the institute proposal from the HSC at any stage referred upwards for discussion at a departmental conference, where the initial request for a meeting between the Minister and the HSC chairman had been considered on 30 May. Instead the only recorded action on the part of the department took the form of a letter of 3 June 1961 from the most senior civil servant who attended the 7 October meeting (an Assistant Principal) asking the HSC to 'submit detailed proposals related to a specific fellowship project' and inquiring 'if a project could be selected which could be carried out in participation with E.P.A.'.

The day before this letter was issued O'Doherty had sent his research insti-tute proposal directly to the EPA. The reply of 14 June from the head of the social factors section informed O'Doherty that EPA had no means of providing such an institute with financial assistance. The best way to proceed, it suggested, would be to select a few concrete projects dealing with issues relevant to the Irish context, such as the training of rural manpower for industrial work. EPA schemes could be used to provide suitable study placements for the researchers who would carry out these projects on their return to Ireland and also an oppor-tunity for an Irish person to acquire abroad the type of management skills that would need to be available in order to establish a research institute back home. But funding for an Irish centre pursuing the selected projects would need to be sought from Irish sources or from 'the great research foundations such as the Ford Foundation or the Rockefeller Foundation'. At the 7 October meeting Fr. Moloney had argued that while foundations such as the Ford Foundation might be prepared to fund projects carried out at the proposed institute once it was estab-lished by the state, it was not the practice of these foundations to provide finance for the setting up of research institutes. In the light of the Ford Foundation's role from 1959 in the creation of ERI, this was clearly a misconception.[2]

No HSC response to the Industry and Commerce request for details to be submitted of a specific fellowship project is on file although the Committee on 16 June 1961 approved a note that its chairman had proposed as the basis of a reply. O'Doherty also informed this meeting 'that UCD hoped to have estab-lished before the end of the year a research institute in occupational psychology'. The Department of the Taoiseach was informed in September 1962 that no such institute had yet been established at UCD but that its consideration had led to the HSC's research institute proposal being 'shelved' by Industry and Commerce.[3]

A context for this rather fractured sequence of events is provided by the HSC's first Secretary, Noel McMahon, whose involvement with the committee ended around the time of O'Doherty's meeting with Lynch. He recalls two figures within Industry and Commerce who were actively interested in HSC: Sean Lemass – who was more broadly concerned to secure business and trade union support for changes in government economic and industrial policy – and Thekla Beere:

> I was sort of briefed to make sure these [business and trade union] people were kept happy, that Lemass wanted to see this thing work. And I got this lecture from Thekla Beere who would have been subsequently the first woman Secretary, she became Secretary of the Department of Transport and Power, she was at that stage probably Assistant Secretary and her area would have included Labour ... Thekla Beere would have been interested, whether it was because of the subject matter or because she was aware of Lemass's involvement.

But, with both Lemass and Beere moving on from the department shortly after HSC had been set up, a less supportive situation emerged: 'none of my direct superiors had the slightest interest' and McMahon recollects a 'wall of cynicism'.[4] Industry and Commerce was one of the departments involved in the discussions leading up to the ERI funding application to the Ford Foundation. But its input amounted to little more than forwarding a one-page note on that Foundation's funding of programmes that Irish managers or trade unionists had participated in, which concluded by stating that 'it is understood that the Foundation have also offered to contribute towards the cost of European Productivity Projects in connection with the human sciences'. Industry and Commerce's departmental conference noted ongoing discussions with the Ford Foundation in relation to what was referred to as both 'an economic research centre' and 'a centre for economic and social research' on two occasions in late 1959, but no connection between this proposal and the work of the HSC was made.[5] Other departments seemed unaware of the existence of HSC to judge by an exchange at the luncheon in the Ford Foundation offices on 7 October 1959: '[W]e were asked to what extent research was conducted in fields other the economics. The Minister for External Affairs referred to the Institute for Advanced Studies, the Industrial Research and Standards Institute, the Agricultural Institute and medical research.'[6] Given the Foundation's backing for EPA programmes, reference to the HSC as an example of positive Irish engagement with that agency's promotion of research would surely have been advantageous to the case being put on this occasion.

Muintir proposes a Rural Sociological Research Centre

While the HSC proposal was being considered by Industry and Commerce, another government department was receiving a social research centre proposal from a different source. In January 1961 the Taoiseach, Sean Lemass, was asked to receive a deputation from Muintir. A five-page memorandum Muintir prepared for the meeting that took place on 25 January addressed a range of disparate concerns – a commemorative postage stamp for the twenty-fifth anniversary of Muintir's foundation in 1962, access for Muintir to broadcast a programme on the new national television service, the need for social surveys, a Rural Sociological Research Centre, an Emigrants' Welfare Bureau in England and a complaint that 'in the setting up of various Commissions in recent times, the Movement has been overlooked'.

In addition to this memorandum the deputation left with the Taoiseach an extract from *Sociologia Ruralis*. Running to nine pages and entitled 'Studies on Rural Sociology in Europe', this reported the replies to a questionnaire of the 'chief sociologists' of twenty European countries. No material on Ireland was included but Muintir had a proposal that might supply the state with both the studies and the chief sociologists that it currently lacked: 'a research centre on modest lines should be set up ... the Government might support it for a trial period of five years at £3,000 per annum'. Such a centre was needed because the universities lacked interest in the subject and the Agricultural and Economic Research institutes could not address it adequately. This represented a shift from the position set out by Jeremiah Newman in 1959 whereby 'the inclusion in the new Agricultural Institute of a department which deals, among other things, with Rural Sociology' was represented as a positive development supplementing the funding of the LRS, Muintir's links with the European Society for Rural Sociology and the training provided for Patrick McNabb at Wageningen: 'for the first time in this country, we have a permanent institution concerned with Rural Sociology ... this new foundation gives us every reason for hoping that Rural Sociology in Ireland has a future and a bright one' (Newman 1959: 68–69).

To Lemass Muintir now spelt out a more critical perspective whereby:

> The Economic Research Institute will carry out social research but it will be research only in the 'human elements' which impinge on economics. The Institute of Agriculture will study the 'human elements' in so far as they affect agriculture. Both will do useful research work but neither – nor both combined – could produce a School of Irish Sociology because their field must of necessity be limited to economics and agriculture and will scarcely touch upon such vital social forces as culture, the language, recreation and religion. The Institute of Rural Sociology could use the findings of the Institute of Agriculture and the Economic Research Institute, of the State Statisticians and of any other group or individuals dealing with such work. But our Institute would pool all this information, co-relate it and also carry out field work of its own. If social surveys are to be multiplied such an institute would be indispensable.

Economics and Agriculture are not sufficient for the task. An Taoiseach is giving a striking example by appealing to patriotism and community spirit, turning from military attack over to social and economic advance. He emphasises the lesson to be learned already from the Limerick Survey – the influence of non-economic causes, e.g. psychology.

Both his position and Community Development suffer from the fact that we have been thinking on conservative lines. We need the sociological study of our problems. Here is Ireland's position as regards the study of sociology … (See attached article from Sociologia Ruralis). Economics and statistics are not sufficient. An *Economic* Research Institute is insufficient without a *Social* Research Institute; if we cannot have two, let us not incur the ridicule of the world by thinking that economics includes sociology.

It remained for Muintir na Tire to make a beginning. Many people have been sent abroad in connection with agriculture; they had eyes for what they knew to be 'agriculture' and 'economics' but their curiosity was not even aroused by complete departments of Rural Sociology in Holland and Norway, and chairs of the subject in Germany, France, Belgium. The naming of the new Economic Research Institute does not suggest any preoccupation with our problems of catching up on sociology. Hence, of course, community development and anything else based on sociology have little hope of being appreciated.[7]

From the Department of the Taoiseach the Muintir memorandum was circulated to the departments of Agriculture, Education and Finance for comment. First to respond was the Department of Education, which considered that a multi-disciplinary university was the proper institutional location for rural sociology, noting that 'University College, Cork, has, through its Adult Education courses, special experience of rural problems'. Its observations then turned the *Sociologia Ruralis* extract against Muintir's proposal:

In most European countries studies and researches in rural sociology are connected with institutes of higher education – either universities or institutes of higher studies, especially institutes of agriculture. This would seem to be a more practical way of catering for the subject than the setting up of a special centre or institute to be conducted by or under the aegis of Muintir na Tire, which is a rather amorphous body, but which could, of course, be of great assistance to whatever institution might be charged with the study of the problem.

Education's observations went on to flag problems of duplication, actual (as opposed to estimated) running cost, and of a centre being set up on a 'purely experimental basis'. They concluded that it was not 'appropriate to even consider the setting up of a centre or institute pending the publication of the Report of the Commission on Higher Education' (a body to which, it suggested, Muintir might wish to make a submission).

The Department of Finance opposed state expenditure on the project. Noting that 'it is suggested that a School of Irish Sociology would eventually emerge' it echoed Education by observing that 'the establishment of such a school would be a matter for the universities and would be beyond the functions and resources of Muintir na Tire'. It raised the issue of duplication with the Agricultural Institute and the ERI before fastening on Muintir's habitual coupling of the rural with sociology: '[E]ven if such a centre could make a useful contribution to the study of sociological problems, its activities would have be to extended to urban as well as rural problems and Muintir na Tire would hardly be the appropriate body to sponsor such a development.'

The Department of Agriculture, like Finance, discerned both institutional duplication and rural limitation problems with the proposal:

> It appears that what the Organisation has in mind is the establishment of an institution whose studies would cover not only agricultural and economic aspects of rural sociology (these can be taken care of by the Rural Economy Division of the Agricultural Institute and the new Economic Research Institute respectively) but also aspects related to culture, the language, recreation, religion etc. As the latter fields of study are important to urban as well as rural population, a better case could perhaps be made for the establishment of a Social Research Institute … than for an institute confined to rural sociology.

Its observations also deployed the *Sociologia Ruralis* extract against the Muintir proposal, observing that the former 'indicates … that rural sociological problems are generally studied in the context of general sociological investigations or general rural investigations in economics or other fields' and that 'until such time as the work of the these two bodies [the Rural Economy Division of the Agricultural Institute and ERI] has got well under way it would be premature to consider the creation of a separate sociological institute or a separate institute devoted to rural sociology'. Here it added that 'having regard to the assistance and co-operation which Muintir na Tire may expect to receive from the two bodies … it is not considered that the further development of the organisation's work in the sphere of Community Development will in any way be hampered by the absence of a rural sociology research centre'.[8]

Opting to defer a decision on the research centre proposal, the Taoiseach's 20 April response to Muintir amalgamated elements of the three elicited departmental documents. It 'would be prudent to await experience with the Rural Economy Division of the Agricultural Institute and with the Economic

Research Institute before coming to any conclusions on the suggestion for making separate arrangements to study rural sociology' and it 'would also be of
advantage when considering the matter, to have the benefit of the advice of the
Commission on Higher Education'. It affirmed that 'the Taoiseach is in full sym-
pathy with the aims which Muintir na Tire had in mind in proposing the setting
up of a rural sociological research centre', continuing that 'before deciding to
suggest that the proposition be deferred for the time being, he has assured himself that the assistance and co-operation which the Movement may expect from
the Agricultural Institute and with the Economic Research Institute will be such
as to ensure that the development of their work in the sphere of Community
Development will not in any way be hampered by the absence of a rural sociology research centre'.[9] The reply from Muintir, which thanked Lemass for the
attention he had given the research centre proposal, elaborated on why Muintir
had put it forward:

> In putting forward the suggestion that a Rural Sociological Research Centre be estab-
> lished, we were aware of the time lag which will be necessary before academic circles
> in Ireland become convinced that there is a place for sociology. Our members who
> advised on this section of the memorandum submitted to An Taoiseach were taken
> aback by the apparently exclusive emphasis on economics in the shaping of the new
> Economic Research Institute. As the Statistical and Social Inquiry Society was a parent
> body, the avoidance of the word 'social' in naming the new Institute, as well as the
> announcement of the programme and the selection of the personnel, all seems to indi-
> cate a definite taking of sides in what has been recognised in other countries (e.g. the
> U.S. and Britain) as a tug-of-war between the disciplines of economics and sociology.
>
> Muintir na Tire does not claim to be an academic body, yet the carrying out of pioneer
> work in social research on rural problems was left to us and financed by a compara-
> tively small branch from Grant Counterpart funds and our own slender resources. It
> seems that the first of the Agricultural Institute's personnel to be sent for training in
> Rural Sociology was sent to Oxford, to an agricultural economics institute, in the first
> instance, and was only recently directed to Wageningen, Netherlands. We have good
> relations with An Foras Taluntais and I do not intend this as a criticism of that Institute
> but merely to illustrate the grounds for what might appear to An Taoiseach to be an
> exaggerated insistence on the importance of sociology and social research. Rather we
> wish to insist that the newer field of study should get due recognition.[10]

Muintir's criticism that sociology and social research were being neglected
prompted correspondence between the secretaries of the departments of the
Taoiseach and of Finance in the run up to the June 1961 official opening of the
ERI. This resulted in the insertion of a passage in the speech the Taoiseach delivered at this function which declared that 'the Institute's net will be cast wide ...

it does not intend to confine itself to purely economic affairs, important as these are … it is planning also to undertake research into wider social and community affairs'.[11] Concretely Muintir emerged from its 1961 approach to the government with a small amount of additional funding to extend the range of studies encompassed by the LRS.

The IPA convenes a Social Research Committee

The next organisation to take up the question of social research was the IPA, which organised an initial meeting on the subject in January 1963 – 'from the soundings we have taken we are now satisfied that we should push ahead with this project'.[12] Under its auspices a Social Research Committee (SRC) was formed with UCD economist Patrick Lynch as chairman. This committee was composed of UCD, TCD and Maynooth academics, of higher institute directors (ERI, IIRS, IPA and Foras Taluntais), of the secretaries of seven government departments and of the director of the Central Statistics Office (CSO). A document it drew up envisaged a scheme of university-based postgraduate research fellowships whose holders 'would investigate specific problems of Irish sociology, preferably of an applied nature'. The cost of such a scheme would, it was estimated, average a minimum of £10,000 a year over an initial three-year period (Friis 1965: appendix 1).

As was also the case with the IPA's School of Public Administration project, the SRC dealt with one of the departments not represented on it, Finance. From there an 'indication of how our thoughts are forming' on this proposal was provided by T. K. Whitaker in September 1963. Social research was unquestionably desirable, but so was avoidance of 'the proliferation of agencies and duplication of functions' by organisations looking to the state for funds and competing for scarce expertise. Quoting the passage that had been inserted into the speech delivered by the Taoiseach at ERI's June 1961 opening ceremony in response to Muintir na Tire's criticism that sociology was being neglected, Whitaker observed that 'the ambit of the Economic Research Institute covers social as well as economic research and there is much to be said for having both carried out by one organisation'.

At a meeting in October, Lynch and other SRC representatives accepted that in the longer term an economic and social research institute was to be desired but argued that its establishment at the outset 'would be a mistake'. Lack of trained social research workers was an immediate task to be tackled, and here 'the Economic Research Institute had no special advantage, organization or skill'. Social studies 'would at this time be wholly overwhelmed by the superior sophistication of economic studies and the standing of the Economic Research Institute would not, in any event, be enhanced by operating at two contrasting levels of sophistication'. The civil service Secretary members of SRC had, it was pointed out, been invited 'from specifically noneconomic departments': 'they were ready to co-operate in social studies; their co-operation was essential in much of the possible research, but a number of them would be likely to be highly suspicious of a preponderantly economists' approach to their problems'. The need for research-based improvement of policy-making in social spending departments was 'so urgent that those who wanted to get it started should be permitted to do this'.[13] But, hopeful at this point that a further instalment of foundation funding could be obtained, Whitaker resisted the ongoing commitment of domestic funds sought by the SRC. As an interim measure Finance agreed to the one-off inclusion of £2,500 in the Vote for the CSO. In October 1964 one student was being supported by this funding, 'Mr. Damian F. Hannan, M.A., M.Agr.Sc., who is engaged in an investigation of "Factors influencing the Occupational Choices and Life Plans of Rural Youth"'.[14]

Frustrated in its attempts to secure substantial funding at home, the SRC turned to the acquisition of expert analysis from abroad. The United Nations Technical Assistance programme had already provided support to IPA's educational programmes. Now 'to help clarify the whole situation concerning social research in Ireland, and to see what allocation of roles might be made so that the advance of knowledge, the training of research workers and the formulation of social policy might all be best developed' it offered to supply 'a very senior and experienced administrator in the social field who might draw up a report for the guidance of all the interested parties on the best allocation of roles'.[15] The consultant selected was Henning Friis, director of the Danish National Institute of Social Research, who arrived in Ireland to carry out his assignment in February 1965. Before his report was completed two further social research centre proposals had been made to government departments. One, from Muintir na Tire, was for a Canon Hayes Institute of Community Development and Rural Sociology. The other, from CWC, was for an Industrial Relations Advisory and Research Centre.

The 1964 plan for community development and rural sociology

With three appendices included, 'A Plan for Community Development in Ireland Submitted to the Government as an aid to the implementation of the Second Programme for Economic Expansion' ran to twenty-two pages in length.

It began by sketching how Muintir had embraced the concept of community development:

> The movement had little contact and derived little help from experience in countries outside Ireland and it was not really until 1958 that it began to take note of 'community development' as defined in many other countries of the world … In the years which have elapsed since the death of the Founder, Muintir na Tire has made increasing study of the community development process … Within Muintir na Tire itself the 1963 Rural Week revealed the fruition of the movement's actions in preceding years. This Rural Week clearly provided the indication that the more 'academic' study of community development must now yield way to action. It provided a convincing mandate for the movement to put before Muintir na Tire and Rural Ireland generally, a comprehensive plan for Irish Community Development.

It went on to discern a convergence between Muintir's commitment to the concept and an increasing recognition on the part of the government that community development had a vital role to play in developmental initiatives the state was undertaking such as the Pilot Area Development Programme (Scully 1968) recently launched to tackle the chronic problems facing small farmers in western counties. Community development was, therefore, 'being increasingly accepted in Ireland as a most useful instrument not only by some rural organisations but by the Government itself and by some of the service agencies (notably Bord Failte and the Agricultural Advisory Services)' and 'it would be tragic if this commitment were not supported by the most effective possible organisation to link the voluntary and public bodies'. The convergence of the movement and the government on the concept of community development was situated within a broader context of Muintir support for the fundamental shift in state strategy the Lemass government was implementing and the planning process through which change were being pushed forward:

> Muintir na Tire welcomes the new spirit abroad in Ireland – what An Taoiseach calls 'the new and positive attitude to progress' – since the advent of the First Programme for Economic Expansion. It acknowledges the stimulation and impetus given to our people by a realistic approach to our economic problems on the part of the Government. It is glad to find even more detailed programming and target-setting, especially in the field of agriculture, in the Second Programme for Economic Expansion.

> This present contribution from the National Executive of Muintir na Tire is respectfully presented as a complement to the Second Programme, a sincere endeavour from one of the oldest of Ireland's voluntary rural organisations to gear itself to a rapidly-changing rural scene and to ensure that national programming will not fail for lack of local, virile communities. To this task Muintir na Tire willingly re-dedicates the

strength of its 398 guilds throughout the country. Never before was the application of a genuine Community Development approach to rural problems a matter of such urgency.

Joint action was to be based on the creation within Muintir – an organisation that then had only a rudimentary national headquarters based in Tipperary town – of a cadre of full-time and part-time educators, administrators and community development field workers that would enable it to function as a comprehensive interface organisation linking the statutory and the voluntary sectors across the state. Forming part of an integrated plan, rather than appearing as it had in 1961 as one of a series of (at best) loosely connected concerns, one of the organisation's components was to be an Institute of Community Development and Rural Sociology. One of the plan's appendices dealt in more detail with the role of this Institute, which was to be named after Muintir's founder, Canon Hayes, and was intended to become a 'recognised Centre for research into the rural condition and the ways of its amelioration, and for the dissemination of good practice in the relevant fields of endeavour'. The three tasks on which the Institute would initially concentrate were to be leadership training for rural community leaders, 'the direction and execution of research into social processes and problems of the rural society' and, through the attraction of students from Ireland and overseas, 'the enrichment of ideas and practices through cultural cross-fertilisation':

> This institute could meet the very real need to advance the academic study of rural sociology in Ireland. This is best done outside the cities where the major institutions of higher learning and research are already established. Past neglect in this field has meant that the subject has been developed to a limited extent and on a piece-meal basis. The result has been that in spite of the opportunity which Ireland presents, this country has failed to make the contribution to knowledge and study which it very well might. There is no reason to suppose that this Institute should not develop into an International Centre for the longer-term study of this subject, possibly in some association with the United Nations and/or its agencies. Such help and support is likely to be forthcoming only if the necessary preparations are first made at home.

It was estimated that the establishment of the Institute would entail an initial capital cost of £40,000 and an annual running cost of £12,000. Government subvention would be required to meet an unspecified proportion of this cost, although it was hoped to attract financial support from 'trusts and foundations' as well as from business sources for Muintir's plans. Even without the implementation of its 'Plan for Community Development in Ireland', it was stated, Muintir was going have to look for new sources of financial support as the Marshall Aid counterpart funds it been had been drawing on since the late 1950s were now almost exhausted.[16]

Responding to the Muintir plan

On 13 August 1964 Muintir's national chairman wrote to the Taoiseach enclosing the plan and seeking a meeting to discuss it. On 17 August Lemass minuted:

> It is necessary to have them [the Muintir proposals] fully considered by the Departments concerned and comments prepared thereon with a view to a discussion with Muintir na Tire's representatives which I will arrange for a date in September. It is desirable that there should be a positive approach in all Departments to the proposals on the understanding that the Government will wish to go along with them, unless they can be shown to be impracticable or undesirable or better means of achieving the same purposes can be suggested … the meeting with the Muintir na Tire representatives should take place if possible in about a month's time.[17]

Accompanied by the Taoiseach's view on the desirability of a positive approach, the plan was circulated to seven departments – Agriculture, Finance, Lands, Gaeltacht, Local Government, Education, Industry and Commerce. Of the six that replied, two – Lands and Gaeltacht – made no comment on the proposed Canon Hayes Institute. Three of the four departments that did comment had also done so on Muintir's 1961 research centre idea. Finance and Agriculture responded to the new proposal much as they had to its predecessor. For Finance economics and sociology were matters for the universities, the ERI ('which also has social research within its ambit') and the Agricultural Institute. The existence of a committee examining how Irish needs in the field should be met (the SRC) provided a further argument against piecemeal institute creation. Finance also considered both capital costs and running costs to be greatly underestimated. Agriculture's comments on the Canon Hayes Institute proposal were framed by its wider observation that:

> It has been the experience of the Department of Agriculture that Muintir na Tire is disappointing as an organisation in the promotion of agriculture. Theoretically it covers a very wide field of activities but in practice there is very little effective work done by the organisation and in many types of activity in the field of agriculture it tends to be outshone by other rural organisations e.g. Macra na Feirme, Macra na Tuaithe, I.C.A., N.F.A.

The proposed institute would overlap with the Agricultural Institute, the ERI and the universities. Macra na Feirme, with departmental and advisory service help, was already providing leadership courses. Muintir could do likewise without the necessity for creating a new institute. The institute's costs were again considered to have been underestimated and its creation 'would create jealousy amongst other rural organisations and give rise to demands for other prestige making projects'.

By contrast, the Department of Education was more positively disposed than it had been in 1961 – 'the Institute of Management, and the Institute of Public Administration, have both done very good work and are continuing to do so. There would seem to be room for an Institute for Community Development and Social Administration in our national economy' – although for the present it favoured deferral. The Department of Local Government, which had not been consulted in 1961, also looked favourably on the proposal: 'the Institute could play an important part in research and training in the wide area of common ground between rural community development and physical planning with benefit to local planning authorities'.

In addition to the individual departmental responses there was also a composite memorandum drawn up within the Department of Agriculture following a meeting it had hosted of all the departments invited to respond to the plan. This stated as a shared view that consideration should be deferred until the consultant the SRC proposed to secure had reported.[18] Reacting to these responses on 25 September, Lemass minuted that:

> It seems to me that the Muintir na Tire proposals are approached in the Departmental Memorandum on the basis that Muintir na Tire is just another rural organisation trying to cut in on work now being done by other similar organisations in the agricultural field. I do not think this is quite fair to Muintir na Tire, which is concerned with social activities of various kinds, and not merely agricultural problems, and which has, notwithstanding its weakness in organisation, already done something significant in creating community consciousness and self confidence, as well as in promoting understanding of, and respect for, the social teachings of the church.

On the specific issue of the Canon Hayes Institute, his view was that:

> I think we need an Institute of Rural Sociology. Research into rural social processes and problems is almost non-existent. Whether this Institute should be linked with Muintir na Tire is another question but I see advantages in so doing, although it could not be left entirely to their administration, in view of the amount of money involved, their own organisational inadequacies, and the need to associate the universities or other bodies with them. In this respect, I suppose we must await the report of the enquiry now in progress, but it can hardly result in anything else but a recognition of the need for such an Institute, however it may be organised.[19]

The views of ministers on the lines along which Lemass proposed to respond at his meeting with the Muintir delegation, as set out in the minute, were then sought. Again, however, the appeal for a positive approach fell on deaf ears. From Agriculture came a reiteration of the previously expressed view that Muintir was ineffective. The initial response from Lands had made no comment on the Canon

Hayes Institute proposal but in a second expression of its views 'the Minister profoundly disagrees with the proposition that it is either necessary or desirable to set up an Institute of Rural Sociology. In his view there are more than enough institutions and organisations capable of supplying information about rural Ireland or carrying out any research work which might be needed from time to time.'[20]

The report of the meeting between Lemass and a nine-person Muintir deputation on 29 October indicates that – while Muintir continued to criticise the existing research bodies and wanted to continue its own involvement in social research – the proposal for a separate rural sociology institute had by then been both ruled out by the government and dropped by the movement. While Lemass referred to the SRC's ongoing work he stated that 'it was unlikely … that a new body would be set up to handle [social research]; we already had institutions like the Economic Research Institute, An Foras Taluntais and the Universities doing a certain amount of social research and it would seem wasteful to create a new Institute'. On Muintir's side:

> Dr. Newman appeared to have reservations about both the Economic Research Institute and an Foras Taluntais. Both he and [Muintir chairman] Fr. Browne stressed that a special new Institute of Rural Sociology was not now being advocated by Muintir na Tire. What they envisaged was the inclusion of rural social research in the general work of the organisation that would be aided by the Government grant; it was important that Muintir na Tire should carry out social research, rather than that members should rely on official sources or the work of other groups for the statistical etc. material necessary for cultivating forward-looking attitudes in rural communities.

The 'Government grant' referred to here had been suggested in the composite cross-departmental memorandum and affirmed by the Lemass minute of 25 September:

> It is not contested that the Muintir na Tire organisation in rural areas requires to be improved and strengthened, that this would be advantageous, and that there is a case for Government financial help in this respect, sufficient to provide it with a National Director and some subsidiary staff. I think a subvention of about £5,000 per annum should with their own resources meet their requirements in this respect. There is something to be said in favour of providing this subvention through the Department of Education rather than through the Department of Agriculture.

As recorded by the report of the meeting, this 'something to be said' was put in the following terms by the Muintir deputation when it met Lemass on 29 October;

> The deputation was anxious to have it established and understood that Muintir na Tire had wider interests than agriculture; if getting the grant from a source other than the Department of Agriculture would help towards getting this across they would favour it. If there was any aspect of their work they wanted to stress it was education in the broad sense. This would suggest the Vote for the Department of Education.[21]

The effect of this arrangement was to end to the grouping of Muintir with Macra and the ICA that had existed during the period of anticipation or availability of Marshall Aid Grant Counterpart money from about 1950 onwards. On the Education Vote the movement would join institutional expressions of the Catholic social movement like the CWC and the DICS, although, as we will see below, Macra na Feirme's youth wing – Macra na Tuaithe – also appeared among Education's clientele.

CWC proposes an Industrial Relations Advisory and Research Centre

While the work of the SRC was an important background factor in the official consideration given to the Canon Hayes Institute proposal, the work of the consultant it secured was almost completed by the time Fr. Edmond Kent of the CWC circulated a memorandum entitled 'Proposal to Establish an Industrial Relations Advisory and Research Centre' in May 1965. As noted in Chapter 2 above, CWC felt threatened with marginalisation in the changed context shaped by economic programming and EEC entry adaptation. Its response was to lay claim to the specific field of industrial relations, to change its name to reflect this concentration of focus and to propose an advisory and research initiative complementary to its teaching role. Identified as critical factors relating to the 'very real and urgent need' for improved industrial relations were:

(a) The expansion of industry has increased the extent and variety of industrial relations problems. New factories, new industries mean new industrial relations problems.
(b) The pressures in all industry, old and new, are increasing because of the new kinds of problem arising from rationalization, re-training etc.
(c) The effect of the changing social climate – increased prosperity does not necessarily bring increased social harmony: the opposite may be the case cf. especially with young workers, the crisis of authority etc.
(d) the Second Programme for Economic Expansion may be retarded in the absence of good industrial relations.

The memorandum presented industrial relations as one of a range of functions whose integration within the firm was essential. But such integration 'cannot be successful without a joint commitment by employers and trade unions to a common set of supra-monetary values ... such as the College is capable of providing'.[22]

The initial response of Industry and Commerce's departmental conference on 21 June was that 'there was a need for greater attention to be given to industrial relations but it was questioned whether Fr. Kent's proposal would meet that need'. Moreover, 'during the discussion on the matter it was suggested that close association of the proposed centre with a religious community might be inhibiting'.[23] Nonetheless, prompted by Lemass, the minister, Patrick Hillery, met Fr. Kent and the proposal was subsequently discussed in detail between department officials and CWC representatives. One aspect clarified in this discussion was the financial basis upon which the centre would be launched – a government grant of £20,000 a year for three years. Over this period the centre hoped to generate fee income and secure endowments sufficient 'to make further state subsidy unnecessary and possibly enable the centre to repay past State subsidies over a number of years'. Other aspects upon which light was shed were the proposal's main promoter and its source of social scientific inspiration. The Department's report of the second meeting, which took place on 27 July, concluded with a note stating that:

> Most of the running on the visitors' side was made by Mr. Eoin McCarthy who lectures at the Workers College. It is understood that he was at one time an officer of the Federation of Irish Industries and is at present a Deputy General Manager in C.I.E., having been in charge of labour relations at C.I.E. for a period.[24]

McCarthy, who was – according to this report – willing to fill the post of director of the new centre for the first two years on secondment from his present job, might have embarked on an Irish social research career a decade earlier. He was then the candidate Professor Feichin O'Doherty had in mind for the post of director of the emigration study to be jointly carried out by Liverpool University and UCD with Ford Foundation funding. As noted in Chapter 2 above, the qualities required in the study director were that he be a layman, 'be fully trained in Catholic Philosophy and social principles, be a good mixer with a gift of leadership and a high intelligence'. O'Doherty's choice was endorsed by both Professor Simey and Archbishop McQuaid but the emigration study never got off the ground. After the 27 July 1965 meeting McCarthy had drawn up his own *aide-mémoire*, sending a copy to the department on 3 August. This strongly emphasised the importance of a commitment to shared values and argued that the kind of work it was envisaged that the centre would do was distinct both from mainstream scholarly research and from the activities of the Labour Court. Reference was also made to the Tavistock Institute, 'which itself recognises the importance of a prior commitment and of an indigenous organisation and has expressed its unwillingness to set up its own organisation here'.[25]

The Tavistock Institute of Human Relations had been created after the Second World War 'to carry forward the wartime applications of sociological, anthropological, psychological and psychiatric expertise to the problems of peacetime social life' (Miller and Rose 1988: 182). By the early 1960s studies in work situations as diverse as British coal mines and Indian textile mills formed the basis of its distinctive synthesised set of socio-technical systems principles which centred on reconciling enterprise efficiency and worker well-being through the creation of semi-autonomous work groups which gave workers an increased degree of control over their work situations (Trist and Murray 1990; Miller 1999). Based in London and enjoying an international reputation, Tavistock Institute staff members were frequently invited speakers at INPC conferences and HSC seminars once these got under way. Local academic connections were also established when the Institute enlisted the help of UCD psychologists to collect Irish data for a consumer research project carried out for Guinness (Miller and Rose 1996).

Then in 1963 the Tavistock Institute was commissioned to carry out a study of Dublin bus crews. The study was backed by company management and unions and sponsored by the HSC. The bus crew formed part of the more than 20,000 employees of Coras Iompair Eireann (CIE) – the state-owned bus, railway and road freight company – at the start of the 1960s. This workforce made it the largest single employer in the Republic of Ireland. Under the terms of the Transport Act 1958 the company was to receive an annual subvention of £1.75 million for a five-year period, after which it would be expected to pay its own way. Provided with a large measure of commercial freedom, the new chairman of the CIE, C.S. Andrews, set about a programme of massive railway line closures and organisational change in pursuit of this goal. In Dublin buses were operated by a driver and a conductor. When the company moved to introduce vehicles designed for driver-only operation in 1962 a series of strikes, both official and unofficial, ensued. The commissioning of the Tavistock study was a response to this conflict.

A two-phase study was planned. The first was to be a survey of the existing situation, the second a joint examination of the survey results and the agreement of a series of joint measures to effect improvements The first phase, carried out by a team of five researchers directed by Hans van Beinum, got under way in September 1963 and was largely concluded by the summer of 1964. Against the backdrop of the emergence of a militant breakaway union and badly deteriorating relations between the company and all of its bus-crew unions, the second phase never proceeded (Peter Murray 2005). The key issues investigated in the first phase were the socio-technical characteristics of the jobs the crews had to carry out; the management the crews experienced, directly and indirectly; the relationship between the crews and their unions and the shared attitudes of crews towards these matters and towards their position in general. The data collection ranged across semi-structured group interviews with drivers and conductors, observation of a sample of different types of bus 'run' and extended interviews with the observed crews together with interviews with management at different levels and interviews with trade union officials and representatives. A report of the phase one findings was eventually published in 1967 (van Beinum 1967).

At the time the CWC proposed its Industrial Relations Advisory and Research Centre this report was in early draft stage. Recollecting forty years later the time he spent conducting the research in Dublin, van Beinum stated his impression that the Archbishop of Dublin – whom he did not meet – was not in favour of the project at all and was suspicious of democratisation of work ideas. However, members of the Jesuit order were interested and supportive and he recalls having dinner with them. Within CIE he remembers having got on well on the management side with Eoin McCarthy and on the union side with the ITGWU's John Carroll.[26] Through these personal contacts, as well as through more structured project steering committee discussions, Tavistock concepts and ideas entered the mix of social science perspectives prompting proposals for the creation of new Irish social research infrastructure.

The fleshing out of the CWC proposal through discussion and additional documentation left Industry and Commerce unconvinced, however, and a recommendation 'against getting involved in setting up this centre' went to its Secretary. Fr. Kent was informed by Hillery that, because of an ongoing review of the whole field of industrial relations that might lead to the introduction of new legislation, 'it would be premature for me to come to a decision on your proposal'. Enclosing a copy of his letter to Fr. Kent, Hillery told Lemass that 'while it might be possible to provide financial support for a centre established at the instance of employers and workers what Father Kent has in mind is for the centre to be established by the Government who would be responsible for it financially for an indefinite period'.[27] Correspondence in the Irish Jesuit Archive indicates that Eoin McCarthy continued to pursue the creation of the new centre for a number of years, seeking financial support from Catholic Church sources in Europe and the USA.[28]

The Friis report and its implementation

Having studied the Irish situation Henning Friis wrote that 'while the growing interest in social research is impressive, the actual difficulties in implementation of social research are not less impressive' (Friis 1965: 12). These difficulties he enumerated as the availability of a small number of social scientists, limited technical facilities (particularly in relation to survey research), absence of research planning and coordination as well as the absence – outside Foras Taluntais – of collaboration across disciplinary boundaries. Another problem he identified as being 'of increasing importance in Ireland' was 'the inclination of "consumers" of research to look upon research activities mainly from the "consumer's" end i.e. from the point of view of those particularly interested in rural problems, industrial relations, manpower, health or physical planning etc.', stimulating demands that a special research organisation be established for each particular area of interest (Friis 1965: 12–13).

Such demand had already been recently acceded to by the government through the 1964 creation of an Foras Forbartha (the National Institute for Physical Planning and Construction Research) and that of the Medico-Social Research Board (MSRB) in 1966. But, according to Friis, the scale upon which each of a range of special organisations would have to operate in order to become effective producers of research would be prohibitively expensive for a state of Ireland's size and level of development. The most effective solution from the research production viewpoint was to establish a single multi-purpose institute. This could employ a permanent staff working on a programme that was both long-range and responsive to societal research demands, could bring different disciplines together to work on the same problem, could balance policy relevance with scholarly freedom of inquiry and could justify the maintenance of a specialised organisation for carrying out and processing social surveys. In Ireland such an institute could most effectively be formed by reorganising the ERI as an Economic and Social Research Institute (ESRI).

This recommendation was also informed by the public policy-centred manner in which Friis conceived of social research: 'empirical scientific investigation of social conditions, social programmes and social factors affecting economic development, in particular with aim of being of assistance to policy formation' (Friis 1965: 9). Flanking this recommended multi-purpose research institute should be 'a central programming unit' within each government department 'able to pose relevant questions for further research and use the research results in their programming work'. Relations between the Institute and the universities should also be 'very close'. In this context Friis noted that university research was restricted by the combination of heavy teaching loads with 'very limited funds' and pointed out that 'most other countries have a publicly sponsored science foundation or council to which researchers from various disciplines can apply for research funds, and part of the problem of financing

university research is thereby solved'. He concluded by hoping that this problem would be 'studied in the context of the Irish science and technology survey'
(Friis 1965: 29–31).

This was a reference to an ongoing study being carried under OECD sponsorship by a team headed by Patrick Lynch (see Peter Murray 2009: 160–162).
But, while critically noting that the policy-orientated Friis 'gave little space
to observations on the need for more basic research in the fundamental social
sciences', when it reported the Lynch team took government approval of the
Danish adviser's recommendation to create a central multi-purpose research
institute as a *fait accompli* and did not specifically advance proposals to give additional structural support to social science research (Department of Industry and
Commerce 1966: 141–143). Speaking at an OECD meeting in Paris in January
1966, the Minister for Education put support for Irish university social science
research on what would prove to be a very long finger – while 'we would hope
that research in the Social Sciences will develop in Ireland and that we may in
the not too distant future reach the stage where it will be desirable formally to
establish a National Social Science Council in our country', such an initiative
would at present be 'premature'.[29]

In advocating a permanent organisation for social research outside the universities the Friis recommendations converged with the position taken in the
autumn of 1963 by T. K. Whitaker rather than with that of the SRC. The Dane's
hostility to 'a mushrooming of minor institutes' and insistence on centralisation
also closed the door on the type of proposal from HSC, Muintir and CWC that
government ministers and their civil servants had been receiving since the beginning of the decade. The Friis report contained only two references to Muintir –
the first at the outset when the LRS featured in an enumeration of social research
exercises carried out to date in Ireland and the second in an appendix listing the
individuals and organisations with whom Friis had held meetings while preparing his report. No ongoing relationship between an ESRI and Muintir was envisaged by Friis. This was remarkably short shrift for a movement that could claim
to have played a pioneering role in initiating Irish social research, had made two
proposals to the government for the creation of social research bodies linked
with itself and had received the Taoiseach's assurance of a level of assistance and
co-operation from both the ERI and the Agricultural Institute that would leave
its community development work unhampered by the deferral of official action
on the first of these proposals.

It also stands in noteworthy contrast with the treatment by Friis of the HSC,
which by this time had been absorbed into a reorganised INPC (Peter Murray
2009: 172–175). Friis was positive in his assessment of the job HSC had done
and wanted to see its structure preserved within the new ESRI. 'To develop

programmes for particular areas of research', his report suggested that 'the Council [of ESRI] might set up committees with experts in the particular field', supplying the example that 'the existing Human Sciences Committee of the Irish National Productivity Committee might be re-organized so as function as the committee on labour market research and human relations in industry' (Friis 1965: 24). Why did Friis not propose a similar association with the new integrated institute for Muintir? The only clue provided by the text of a report that strongly prioritised social research with a public policy orientation is the characterisation of Muintir (where Friis makes reference to its LRS initiative) as 'a private organization' (Friis 1965: 11).

There is no documentary evidence of any protest being made against this treatment of Muintir by the figure whose presence on the SRC was presumed by civil servants to provide the movement with an input into that body's discussions, Jeremiah Newman. The minutes of SRC meetings are admittedly uninformative about the detail of these discussions. They give no indication of Muintir's future role within the social research field being raised at any point by Newman or by any other member.[30] Leaving Newman aside, no protest, either private or public, appears to have been made by any Muintir figure about the manner in which Friis treated the movement in his report. By October 1964, several months prior to the arrival of Friis in Ireland, Muintir, as we have seen, was no longer pressing for government funding of a separate social research institute operating under its own aegis. But it still remained actively committed to carrying out its own social research. In February 1966 Muintir's monthly magazine *The Landmark* reproduced a newspaper report of the Paris OECD meeting speech by the Minister for Education which outlined the government's intentions regarding social research structures. It accompanied this piece with a commentary headed 'Muintir Leads the Way':

> The Limerick Rural Survey was the first piece of social research to be carried out on a large scale by the native Irish. At the time of the formation of the Economic Research Institute, regret was expressed in Muintir circles that a body which derived its lineage from a society for 'statistical and social' research should in the nineteen sixties be blind in one eye from birth. The defect is now happily being remedied and the scope of university training in social skills can now be enlarged.[31]

But if Muintir seemed to accept without demur the government's new social research regime, its own plans for a Canon Hayes Institute were to be obstructed by government departments mainly because social research featured (or was suspected of featuring) among the range of activities envisaged for this body.

The later history of Muintir's Canon Hayes Institute proposal

During the summer of 1965 Muintir's chairman and public relations officer visited the USA, where they had meetings with Kellogg and Ford Foundation officials and at the UN. In August Muintir circulated an application for UN Technical Assistance which stated that 'Muintir na Tire proposes to establish an Institute of Community Development which will promote training courses at different levels and also initiate survey and research work' and that 'this Institute would be available to the United Nations for courses or for giving experience to personnel'.[32] In October a representative of the Kellogg Foundation met Muintir representatives in Dublin and 'made a number of suggestions which he intimated would give the application a greater chance of success'. Evidence that Muintir's proposals enjoyed the support of the government and of other Irish rural organisations featured prominently among these suggestions and in November a Muintir deputation went to the Department of Agriculture to discuss their latest effort to establish 'a permanent Institute of Rural Community Development'. In December Agriculture circulated a draft Memorandum for the Government on the matter. This stated that:

> The proposal which Muintir na Tire have put before the Kellogg Foundation is basically the same as that described in the 'Plan for Community Development'. More emphasis is, however, placed on the development of community leadership and the provision of facilities for overseas students, and less on social research. The Organisation has in fact made it clear that the Institute would not be involved in basic research but would be confined in the main to the investigation of community problems and the application of community development processes. Assisting the field work of groups of students from abroad, and assembling data which would be made available to those concerned with community development, within and outside the country.

For Agriculture, 'although the previous objections as to the proposed Institute's involvement in social research would appear to have been largely met', the concern previously expressed about overlapping between the proposed institute and other bodies in the leadership training area remained valid while 'the establishment of an Institute as proposed might well involve the Exchequer in a heavy and continuing financial commitment'. The minister (Charles Haughey) considered that he could supply the specific forms of assistance Muintir had sought from him 'but as the offer of such assistance could be construed as official endorsement of the proposal to establish an Institute he would be glad to have the decision of the Government in the matter'.[33]

Both the departments known to have responded (Finance and Education) took the contrary view that earlier objections to Muintir's involvement in social research remained unmet. From Finance the memorandum was then sent to M. D. McCarthy, the CSO director, who has assumed responsibility for organising the transition from the ERI to the ESRI, for his views. In relation to Muintir social research involvement he concluded that 'the new formulation [of the Kellogg application] can, I think, be interpreted exactly as the old one [of the 1964 plan]'. Widening the focus, he wrote:

> A number of steps have been taken to implement the decision in principle by the Government that it would accept the Friis report in connection with the Economic Research Institute. The legal and organizational of changes needed [sic] are in process of being carried out but no final decisions have yet been taken as to the scale or the financing of the new organization. I think that I can say that it is envisaged that it will endeavour to act as a co-ordinating agency for all empirical social research in this country. In fact consultations are already taking place with the relevant university faculties and with the Human Sciences Committee of the Irish National Productivity Agency with a view to avoiding overlapping. Relations have also been established with the new Medico-Social Research Board which has been set up by the Minister for Health with the same objective in view. With the great shortage of technical manpower capable of carrying out social research in this country it is eminently desirable that there should not be too much fragmentation and certainly no overlapping of effort.

Referring to the ERI experience, he also emphasised that Foundation funding would not last indefinitely and that therefore 'it is essential that the Government should have a very clear, realistic idea of what implicit financial commitments it would be entering into before it gave any official endorsement to the proposal'. To McCarthy, the costs estimated by Muintir seemed 'quite unrealistic'.[34]

The Finance response sent to Agriculture enclosed a copy of McCarthy's letter and spelt out its own four grounds of objection to Muintir's proposal – overlapping activities, scarce personnel, underestimated costs and lack of clear objectives warranting substantial state subsidisation. Muintir should concentrate on improving its organisation and 'expanding the area served by it which at present represents only a small portion of the country', while 'no indication of Government support should be given to Muintir na Tire regarding the suggested Training and Research Centre'.[35]

In the case of Education – the department into whose sphere of operation Muintir's financial relations with the government had been shifted – the late 1964 acceptance that there was 'room for an Institute for Community Development and Social Administration in our national economy' had by early 1966 been replaced by a set of objections that were very similar to those being expressed by Finance:

> While the Minister notes that the proposed Institute's involvement in social research has not been stressed in the organisation's proposal to the Kellogg Foundation, he considers that, pending further development of the arrangements now being made to further the promotion of research in the social sciences generally, no action should be taken which might encourage the establishment of an Institute of Rural Community Development with functions (even limited functions) in this field. The Minister also agrees that the establishment of such an Institute with support from the Kellogg Foundation would be likely to involve the Exchequer in a heavy and continuing financial commitment. In this connection he recalls that the Kellogg Foundation's support of a scheme of organizational development for Macra na Tuaithe led eventually to the provision of grants-in-aid of that organization from this Department's Vote … [T]he Minister for Education is not convinced that it is in the best interests of Muintir na Tire to embark on enquiries of the type proposed or that doing so would be in accordance with the aims and ideals of its founders. He also finds it difficult to accept that the costs appertaining to an Institute as contemplated would be within the estimated amounts stated.[36]

This opposition – which the conclusion to the Agriculture draft memorandum positively invited – seems to have effectively killed off the Kellogg Foundation application. A similar fate seems to have befallen support for Muintir in the form of UN Technical Assistance shortly afterwards. When External Affairs sought the views of other departments on the matter in May 1966, Education replied that 'the application to the United Nations does not appear to this Department to differ fundamentally in its conception from that to the Kellogg Foundation and in this Department's view the same general criteria should apply in relation to consideration of official support for it'.[37]

Despite this succession of rebuffs suffered by Muintir the 'inclusion of rural social research in the general work of the organization' did continue for several years. By the mid-1960s, however, the movement's strong identification with rural sociology does appear to have been waning. In August 1966, the conference of the European Society for Rural Sociology was held in Maynooth without any marked interest or involvement by Muintir in evidence, although Newman and Morris played a prominent part in the proceedings.[38] Eclipsing rural sociology as the main concern of Muintir's top echelon by this time was community leadership training. The Department of Education report of its minister's discussion of the new government grant-in-aid with Muintir representatives on 10 December 1964 quotes Newman as stating that 'the thing they needed most … was a Training Centre … Muintir na Tire was concerned mainly with community leadership'[39] and it was with this focus that the Canon Hayes Institute project was also kept alive amidst the setbacks documented above. Under the headline 'Buiochas le Dia', *The Landmark* announced in September 1966 that 'after years of frustration ... the Institute is to be established in Foynes, Co. Limerick, immediately'.[40] Such references caused alarm in the Department of Education, where a senior inspector in the Vocational Education Branch reported the results of the inquiries he had made on 17 November:

> I understand that the Institute would be a centre for Leadership Training courses, refresher courses of various kinds – particularly those dealing with Community Development – the type of work now being carried on in temporary accommodation at Foynes. I have been informed that it is *not* to be an Institute of Rural Sociology, about which we have grave reservations.[41]

The Foynes initiative appears to have been an ill-fated and short-lived experiment that – along with a financially unsuccessful Community Organisation Officers scheme – drained Muintir's coffers. By the end of the 1960s its second national director, Tomas Roseingrave, was desperately seeking to shore up its finances through a mixture of internal income generation and appeals to government for an increased grant-in-aid. Around this time as sympathetic an observer as Charles McCarthy (1968: 50) could write that 'there is no one connected with Muintir na Tire that does not feel that it has reached a crisis in its life. It is in serious danger of becoming irrelevant'. Searching for renewed relevance the movement turned to 'a committee of distinguished people' drawn from outside its ranks and chaired by Agricultural Institute director Dr. Tom Walsh to formulate the basis of a five-year plan for its development. Published in August 1971, the Review Committee Report on Muintir na Tire advocated the creation (by the Minister for Local Government) of a national council for community development. Muintir, it envisaged, 'would act as an agent of this council' as well as having a specific responsibility for establishing and servicing local community councils. Such a servicing role would require the establishment of a development unit within Muintir receiving financial support from both central government and local authorities.[42] Just over a year before this report was completed, a Department of Education official prepared 'Notes on Muintir na Tire' in advance of a deputation's meeting with his minister. This document contains an epitaph of sorts for Muintir's endeavours over the previous decade: 'the big project during the early 1960s was to found a School of Rural Sociology, in memory of Canon Hayes. This was a grandiose scheme that never got "off the ground". The Department was opposed to it since it would impinge on the work of the Universities which were then starting faculties of Sociology.'[43] In other departments the grounds differed but the opposition was shared.

Conclusion

This chapter has chronicled the fate of four proposals for the creation of social research centres made to Irish government departments in the early 1960s. All could be said to emanate from Catholic social movement sources. While it failed to meet Archbishop McQuaid's exacting standards, Muintir is generally regarded as a core component of that movement in the middle decades of the twentieth century. The proposals with an industrial rather than a rural focus may be said to be hybrids with mixed European productivity drive and Irish Catholic social movement parentage. This is more apparent in the case of the CWC's embrace of a version of the Tavistock socio-technical systems approach. It is at first sight less so in the case of the HSC, with its membership drawn mainly from business organisations and the trade unions. In practice, however, these elements deferred to the educational sector representation from which the committee's chair was initially filled. It was the two priest members of the HSC – UCD's Professor O'Doherty and CWC's Fr. Maloney – who met the Minister for Industry and Commerce and his civil servants in 1960 to discuss the Institute of Industrial Psychology proposal. More broadly, O'Doherty is described by HSC's first Secretary, Noel McMahon, as having been the driving force of the Committee – 'an affable, enthusiastic man, very articulate, spoke ... like a machine gun, you know, but a very nice, decent kind of guy, full of ideas, bubbling with ideas'.[44]

According to John Whyte (1980: 337), the early 1960s 'saw the end of the tension between bureaucratic and vocational outlooks which had so bedeviled Church–State relations in the forties and fifties'. This stemmed from changes occurring on both sides of the divide. In the case of the Church 'instead of promoting a ready-formed corpus of doctrine, the Catholic social movement appeared increasingly concerned with empirical investigation of the actual needs of the Irish people' and, as this concern grew, 'denunciations of excessive state intervention died away. For in many ways investigation showed that the state in Ireland stepped in not too much but too little' (J. H. Whyte 1980: 332–333). This view is echoed by Don O'Leary (2000: 166–167): 'the Catholic social movement in the 1960s was less dogmatic in its response to complex social issues ... more effort was spent on obtaining and assessing factual information in order to attend to the actual needs of the Irish people. As Catholic clergymen became more familiar with sociological research studies they perceived that the Irish state was not doing enough for some of its citizens. Ironically, priests and bishops began to advocate more state intervention.'

As this chapter has shown, actors within the Catholic social movement sought to move beyond concern with empirical social investigation and familiarity with its findings to become institutionalised producers of sociological research. But to do this they required access to substantial resources, in search of which they primarily turned to the state. Here they met with consistent refusal – empirical social research in Ireland was to be funded and organised in a manner that effectively excluded the participation of any Catholic social movement actor without a university base. By the end of the 1960s the non-university elements of the Catholic social movement that had embraced sociology were either disbanding, like the Christus Rex Society, or turning away to seek survival elsewhere, like Muintir with its new community council focus.

Within the government departments a variety of attitudes to social research is discernible. After the departure of Lemass, Industry and Commerce was largely indifferent and unreceptive to the proposals it received. Through the grant-in-aid it made to INPC, its Vote was the source of HSC grants to researchers after 1964 and the department also began the funding of manpower surveys in an economy where adaptation to free-trade conditions was being promoted. This was relocated within the Department of Labour when it was created in 1966. As Taoiseach, Sean Lemass displayed a strikingly – and, perhaps, surprisingly – positive attitude towards Muintir's social research institute proposals. Anti-urbanism had been a central component of Muintir's ideology (Devereux 1991), while Lemass, according to a close political associate of longstanding, had 'little real rapport with rural Ireland and, considering the amount of travelling he did when building up the Fianna Fail organization, he had surprisingly little intimate knowledge of the countryside and its people. He was essentially the Dublin Jackeen with the ready wit and derisive humour so common in the city' (Andrews 2001: 247). Before becoming Taoiseach in 1959 Lemass had spent almost all of his ministerial career in Industry and Commerce, a department upon whose responsibilities Muintir's activities impinged only slightly. As two of its officers told colleagues from Finance's Economic Development Branch in December 1960, 'while representations have been received from time to time from this organisation and while they will assist where possible in endeavours to attract an industry to a locality, on the whole, their contacts with Industry and Commerce are infrequent'.[45] Industry and Commerce was the only department to which Muintir's 1964 community development plan was circulated not to respond with comments.

During the Second World War, however, Lemass had headed an improvised Department of Supplies and Muintir had been to the fore in organising shortage-alleviating local initiatives in growing food and cutting turf (O'Leary 2004: 237–240). While documentary evidence is lacking, it may be plausibly suggested that the high regard in which Lemass held Muintir during the 1960s dated back to this Emergency period. Why this evidently positive disposition failed to translate into substantive resourcing benefits for Muintir may be related to the role played at this time by the Department of the Taoiseach within the Irish government system. This department has dramatically expanded in size over the past half century. A recent study attributes this growth to EU membership after 1973, orchestration of social partnership arrangements after 1987 and the manner in which 'the Department may be used by different Taoisigh to "incubate" favoured policy areas and pet projects associated with the different governmental pro-grammes' (Adshead and Tonge 2009: 27). The Taoisigh referred to here are those who have held the office since the retirement of Jack Lynch in 1979. Prior to the operation of such expansionary influences, the Department of the Taoiseach, while it was 'responsible for the administration of such of the Public Services as are not assigned to any other department', was very small and played a role that was construed in minimalist terms. In September 1964 the attachment of the Muintir grant to the Department of the Taoiseach's Vote had been suggested by the Department of Education 'since the aims of Muintir na Tire and the scope of its activities have a bearing on the work of many Government Departments and since their new programme lays particular stress on Community and Economic Development'. But this was opposed within the Department of the Taoiseach itself and Education subsequently agreed to carry the subvention on its Vote.[46] Such a minimalist assumption of direct responsibility by his department left measures favoured by a Taoiseach vulnerable to the indifference or worse of those administering them. At the end of the Second World War, for example, de Valera had sought to initiate a 'positive and liberal' policy on the admission of refugees but the Department of Justice and other agencies exercising day-to-day control over entry frustrated this by adhering to existing highly restrictive prac-tices (O'Halpin 1999: 293–295).

The case of Muintir's plans differed from this scenario in that a Taoiseach's view that it was 'desirable that there should be a positive approach in all Departments to the proposals on the understanding that the Government will wish to go along with them, unless they can be shown to be impracticable or undesirable or better means of achieving the same purposes can be suggested' was openly countered by departmental responses characterising the propos-als as impracticable, undesirable or sub-optimal. Duplication loomed largest among the objections to the proposed sociological research centre or institute. As a latecomer Muintir faced the problem that, even if it were accepted that sociology was being neglected with significant deleterious consequences, the problem could be addressed by restructuring existing institutes rather than cre-ating a dedicated new one. In this context it is noteworthy that the duplication argument was also deployed against the ERI when it was first proposed. The source of the objection then was the Agricultural Institute's director, Dr. Tom Walsh, who contended that inevitable duplication between his existing institute and the proposed ERI made the provision of state aid to the latter inappropriate and requested the Minister for Agriculture to seek clarification on the issue from the government. When he was told that the 'Minister feels that the necessity does not arise of raising the matter with the Government' and that 'the Taoiseach is in general accord', Walsh persisted until closure on the matter came from the top: '[T]he Taoiseach has instructed me to inform you that it is his view that no further clarification of the matter is necessary or, indeed, practicable at this stage.'[47] Possessing a broad base of powerful backers was plainly advantageous when duplication charges had to be seen off. In the case of Muintir this breadth was evidently and fatally absent.

The government department that possessed both the inclination and the capacity to shape an infrastructure for social research was Finance. From as early as 1961 its position had been that any state funding should be channelled through existing institute structures and particularly through that of the ERI, which it had played the major role in bringing into being. After the completion of the Friis report the conversion of the ERI into the ESRI was brought before the government in August 1965 by a memorandum from Finance entitled 'Social Development Programme'. This sought, and obtained, approval for two proposals. One was that the Friis recommendation to create an integrated economic and social research institute with a survey unit attached be accepted in principle. The other was that M. D. McCarthy, the CSO director, be asked 'to formulate a preliminary programme for the organisation and integration of the studies and inquiries on which the official aspects of a social development programme should be based'. The two were linked by the expectation that, when the ERI's director, Roy Geary, retired in the following year, McCarthy would succeed him. The CSO director was a close associate of T. K. Whitaker, whom he had assisted in the drafting of *Economic Development* (R. Fanning 1978: 516). McCarthy had subsequently carried out much of the detailed work involved in setting up the ERI, was actively involved in the SRC and then took in hand the minutiae of the ERI's conversion into the ESRI (Kennedy 1993: 226 and 239–241). In his new social research role he would, by his own account, be much more than just an Irish executor of a foreign expert's conception: 'I had very close contact with Dr. Friis when he was preparing his report and found that he was able to take account of all the views which I gave him while drafting his document.'[48] The Social Development Programme he was now being asked to prepare the ground for represented a substantial enlargement of the scope of the economic planning through which Finance had established control over the Irish policy-making agenda since the late 1950s. The context for its creation, and the shape it would assume, are the subject matter of Chapter 6.

Notes

1   NAI, DT S16705, A Centre for Economic and Social Research in Ireland: Establishment, copy W. A. Honohan, SSISI, to J. McDaniel, Ford Foundation, 20/8/1959.

2   See NAI, DIC TIW/1280/2, National Joint Committee on the Human Sciences and Their Application to Industry, Research Institute and Fellowships for correspondence, reports of meetings and memoranda; NAI, DIC MIS/1/12, G. Schretzmary, head of Social Factors Section, EPA, to Fr. O'Doherty, UCD, 14/6/1961.

3   NAI, DET&E 2000/12/913, National Joint Committee on the Human Sciences and Their Application to Industry, Minutes, Meeting no. 15, 16/6/1961; NAI, DT S15,453/G62, European Productivity Agency and Irish National Productivity Agency: Industrial Productivity, St. J. Connolly, Industry and Commerce, to T. O'Cearbhaill, Taoiseach, 24/9/1962.

4   Noel McMahon interview with Peter Murray, 14/6/2006.

5   NAI, DFA 324/339, Ford and Rockefeller Foundations, 'Approach of Irish Management Institute to Ford Foundation for Financial Support', 12 Marta 1959, enclosed with J. C. B. McCarthy, Industry and Commerce, to C. Cremin, External Affairs, 14/5/1959; NAI, DET&E 2000/13/21, Minutes of Departmental Conference no. 590, 28/9/1959, item Request to Ford Foundation for Assistance in Establishment of a Centre for Economic and Social Research, Minutes of Departmental Conference no. 593 19/10/1959, item Possibility of Support from Ford Foundation for an Economic Research Centre.

6   NAI, DT S16705, A Centre for Economic and Social Research in Ireland: Establishment, by T. K. Whitaker, note on luncheon meeting with Ford Foundation officers in New York, 9/10/1959.

7   NAI, DT S10,816 Muintir na Tire general file, 'Deputation from Muintir na Tire to an Taoiseach, Wednesday, 25th January, 1961 Memorandum submitted to an Taoiseach'.

8   NAI, DT S10,816, Muintir na Tire general file, Department of Education to Department of the Taoiseach, 8/3/1961, enclosing 'Memorandum Presented by Muintir na Tire to the Taoiseach', Observations of the Department of Education, Observations on Section (4) of the memorandum headed 'Rural Sociological Research Centre', Taoiseach's Private Secretary to Frank Lyddy, 8/3/1961, passes on the Department of Education's suggestion that Muintir na Tire make a submission on the matter to the Commission on Higher Education. For the Commission's treatment of the submission see Commission on Higher Education 1960–67, Report, vol. 1, paras 12.35 and 12.36, Department of Finance to Department of the Taoiseach, 15/4/1961, Department of Agriculture to Department of the Taoiseach, 19/4/1961.

9   NAI, DT S10,816, Muintir na Tire general file, Taoiseach's Private Secretary to F. Lyddy, Honorary Secretary, Muintir na Tire, 20/4/1961.

10 NAI, DT S10,816, Muintir na Tire general file, F. Lyddy, Honorary Secretary, Muintir na Tire, to Taoiseach's Private Secretary, 25/4/1961.

11 NAI, DT S16,705 B/61, Centre for Economic and Social Research in Ireland: Establishment, N. O'Nuallain, Department of the Taoiseach, to T. K. Whitaker,

Department of Finance, 5/5/1961, T. K. Whitaker to N. O'Nuallain, 8/5/1961, text of speech delivered by an Taoiseach.

12   ESRI, box 1, History of ERI/ESRI, file 'Social Research Council', T. J. Barrington, IPA, to R. C. Geary, ERI, 11/1/1963.

13   ESRI, box 1, History of ERI/ESRI, file 'Institute of Public Administration, 59 Lansdowne Road, Dublin 4, Social Research Council', T. K. Whitaker, Finance, to C. S. Andrews, chairman, IPA, 12/9/1963, 'Social Research', 21/10/1963.

14   ESRI, box 1, History of ERI/ESRI, file 'Institute of Public Administration, 59 Lansdowne Road, Dublin 4, Social Research Council', M. D. McCarthy, CSO, to Secretary, Department of Education, 18/10/1964.

15   ESRI, box 1, History of ERI/ESRI, file 'Institute of Public Administration, 59 Lansdowne Road, Dublin 4, Social Research Council', 'Social Research Committee', 7/7/1964.

16   NAI, DT S17,138 B/95, Community Development: Federation of Local Development Associations, General, 'A Plan for Community Development in Ireland Submitted to the Government as an aid to the implementation of the Second Programme for Economic Expansion'.

17   NAI, DT S17,138 B/95, Community Development: Federation of Local Development Associations, General, S. Lemass, Taoiseach, to Assistant Secretary, Department of the Taoiseach, 17/8/1964.

18   NAI, DT S17,138 B/95, Community Development: Federation of Local Development Associations; 'General Observations of the Department of Finance on "A Plan for Community Development in Ireland", prepared by Muintir na Tire', Department of Agriculture, 'Muintir na Tire Plan for Community Development in Ireland', Department of Education, 'A Plan for Community Development in Ireland. Muintir na Tire Document, Published August, 1964', 'Department of Local Government observations on Muintir na Tire document entitled A Plan for Community Development in Ireland', composite memorandum prepared after representatives of seven departments met in Agriculture on 8/9/1964, entitled 'Muintir na Tire Plan for Community Development'.

19   NAI, DT S17,138 B/95, Community Development: Federation of Local Development Associations; General Minute, S. Lemass, Taoiseach, to Assistant Secretary, Department of the Taoiseach, 25/9/1964.

20   NAI, DT S17,138 B/95, Community Development: Federation of Local Development Associations, General, Private Secretary to Minister for Lands to Secretary, Department of the Taoiseach, 9/10/1964.

21   NAI, DT S17,138 B/95, Community Development: Federation of Local Development Associations, General Report of Meeting, 29/10/64, Muintir na Tire, Plan for Community Development, August 1964.

22   NAI, DET&E 2001/50/57, The Catholic Workers' College, College of Industrial Relations, 'Proposal to Establish an Industrial Relations Advisory and Research Centre, Memorandum, 15/5/1965, Edmund Kent SJ, Superior and Director of Studies'.

23   NAI, DET&E 2001/50/57, The Catholic Workers' College, College of Industrial Relations, extract from Report of Departmental Conference no. 817, 21/6/1965,

S. Lemass, Taoiseach, to P. Hillery, Minister for Industry and Commerce, 25/5/ 1965.

24 NAI, DET&E 2001/50/57, The Catholic Workers' College, College of Industrial Relations, Report of Meeting, Proposal by the Catholic Workers' College that a 'National Centre of Industrial Relations' be established, 27/7/1965.

25 NAI, DET&E 2001/50/57, The Catholic Workers' College, College of Industrial Relations, *aide-mémoire* enclosed with E. McCarthy, deputy general manager, CIE, to W. Kelly, Industry and Commerce, 3/8/1965; DDA, McQuaid Papers, as yet uncatalogued box UCD/UCC/NUI, memorandum on 'Research-Project "Emigration"', enclosed with Rev. Prof. E. F. O'Doherty, UCD, to Fr. C. Mangan, Archbishop's House, 30/8/1955, Archbishop McQuaid to E. F. O'Doherty, 1/9/55.

26 Hans van Beinum interview with Peter Murray, 17/8/2005.

27 NAI, DET&E 2001/50/57, The Catholic Workers' College, College of Industrial Relations, P. Hillery, Minister for Industry and Commerce, to Fr. E. Kent, College of Industrial Relations, 2/9/1965, P. Hillery to S. Lemass, Taoiseach, 3/9/1965.

28 Irish Jesuit Archive, CIR/57, file of documents relating to the proposal to establish an industrial relations advisory and research centre in the College of Industrial Relations, E. McCarthy, CIE, to Provincial, 13/3/1968, 21/5/1968; copy of E. McCarthy to Fr. Swain, 21/5/1968.

29 ESRI, box 1, History of ERI/ESRI, file 'No. 1 Closed', Statement by Minister for Education at the OECD Ministerial Meeting on Science – Paris, 13 January 1966.

30 These minutes are in ESRI, box 1, History of ERI/ESRI, file 'Institute of Public Administration, 59 Lansdowne Road, Dublin 4, Social Research Council'.

31 'Muintir Leads the Way', *The Landmark*, February 1966.

32 NAI, DET&E 2002/67/25, Muintir na Tire, 'Adviser in Community Development. A Request from Ireland under the United Nations Technical Assistance Regular Programme towards the salary of an Adviser in Community Development for a period of two years'.

33 NAI, DET&E 2002/67/25, Department of Agriculture, Draft Memorandum for the Government, 'Application of Muintir na Tire for financial assistance from W. H. Kellogg Foundation'.

34 NAI, DF 2001/3/1000, Plan for Community Development in Ireland, M. D. McCarthy, CSO, to L. D. O'Neill, Finance, 11/3/1966.

35 NAI, DF 2001/3/1000, L. D. O'Neill to Runai, Agriculture and Fisheries, 25/4/ 1966.

36 NAI, DET&E 2002/67/25, Muintir na Tire, Department of Education to Department of Agriculture, 24/2/1966.

37 NAI, DET&E 2002/67/25, Muintir na Tire, Department of Education to Department of External Affairs, 8/6/1966.

38 While Newman – a member of the European Society for Rural Sociology Council – was still expressing reservations about the Agricultural Institute in October 1964, the Institute's extensive sponsorship and support for the holding of the Society's conference in Ireland is acknowledged in the foreword to vol. 6, nos. 3–4 of *Sociologia Ruralis*. An editorial note also states that 'with the kind help of An Foras Taluntais (The Agricultural

Institute), Ireland, we have been able to present to our readers in this double issue the Proceedings of the Fifth Congress of our Society, which was held in Maynooth College, August, 1966'. No reference is made to Muintir na Tire in either the foreword or the editorial note.

39   NAI, DET&E 2002/67/25, Muintir na Tire, 'Minister's Discussion with Representatives of Muintir na Tire on 10/12/64'.

40   'Buiochas le Dia', *The Landmark*, September 1966 (English translation: 'Thanks be to God').

41   NAI, DET&E 2002/67/25, Muintir na Tire, Note from M. MacEachmharcaigh to B. O'Foghlu, 17/11/1966.

42   NAI, DT 2003/16/89, Muintir na Tire general file, Review Committee Report on Muintir na Tire, August 1971.

43   NAI, DET&E 2002/67/25, M. MacEachmharcaigh, 'Notes on Muintir na Tire', undated (adjacent material in file indicates a mid-1970 composition date).

44   Noel McMahon interview with Peter Murray, 14/6/2006.

45   NAI, DF 2001/3/166, Community Development, 'Community development role of local development associations'. 5/12/1960.

46   NAI, DET&E 2002/67/25, Muintir na Tire, Department of Education to Department of Agriculture, 17/9/1964, enclosing desired amendment to memorandum drafted after the meeting in the Department of Agriculture on 8 September 1964; NAI, DT S 17,138 B/95, Community Development: Federation of Local Development Associations, General, note from Assistant Secretary, Department of the Taoiseach, to Taoiseach, 22/9/1964, states that 'the Department of Education's idea that provision of a grant to Muintir na Tire should be included in this Department's Vote, because several Departments are concerned, would be unacceptable'; NAI, DET&E 2002/67/25, Muintir na Tire, Secretary, Department of Education, to Secretary, Department of the Taoiseach, 20/10/1964.

47   NAI, DT S16,705, A Centre for Economic and Social Research in Ireland: Establishment, T. Walsh, director, Agriculture Institute, to M. D. McCarthy, Honorary Secretary, Statistical and Social Inquiry Society of Ireland, September 1959 and 21/9/1959, M. D. McCarthy to T. Walsh, 16/9/1959, T. Walsh to J. J. Nagle, Secretary, Department of Agriculture, September 1959 and 2/10/1959, J. J. Nagle to T. Walsh, 26/9/1959, M. O'Muineachain, Secretary, Department of the Taoiseach, to T. Walsh, 12/10/1959.

48   NAI, DT 97/6/209, Programme for Social Development, J. Lynch, Minister for Finance, to S. Lemass, Taoiseach, 26/5/1965, Department of Finance, Memorandum for the Government, 'Social Development Programme', 24/8/1965, M. D. McCarthy, Central Statistics Office, to N. O'Nuallain, Department of the Taoiseach, 25/8/1965.

6

Social research and state planning

Introduction

The First Programme for Economic Expansion was launched in 1958. By the early 1960s the scope of programming was widening as the stagnation prevailing for most of the 1950s gave way to a period of continuous economic growth. Initial crisis conditions had enabled increased social spending to be left off the programmers' agenda. The changed politics of increasing prosperity, as well as their own expanding ambitions, meant that this could no longer be sustained. This chapter begins by sketching Ireland's social security provision and the manner in which it became an object of both political debate and social scientific analysis in the early 1960s. The official response to this ferment was a Social Development Programme to which the ESRI was seen as a provider of vital inputs. During the 1960s a Save the West movement challenged both programmers and governing politicians. The official response to this challenge involved new structures for rural development with which the social sciences interacted as well as expanded social welfare provision to a class of smallholders whose resilience would later become a significant object of sociological study.

Economics, sociology and social security in Ireland

In January 1965 the Minister for Social Welfare characterised the system for which he had responsibility in the following terms:

> Hitherto we, being largely an agricultural community with a high level of self-employed persons and family labour, have leaned towards non-contributory schemes and the bulk of Exchequer expenditure on Social Welfare arises on such schemes as Children's Allowances (over £10 million per annum) and non-contributory Old Age Pensions (also over £10 million per annum). It is not unnatural therefore that the bulk of expenditure in this country should be met out of general taxation. Great Britain, on the other hand, being a highly industrialised country, has opted for comprehensive compulsory social insurance.[1]

Total central state expenditure on social welfare in 1964–65 was close to £34 million. The cost to the state of the social insurance fund to which employers and employees also contributed came to almost another £10 million and two other non-contributory schemes (unemployment assistance, widows and orphans pensions) accounted for almost all of the remainder of the total. Two of the three major components of this social welfare expenditure had been in place when the independent Irish state was created. Between 1906 and 1914 Liberal governments enacted a series of measures to which the beginnings of the United Kingdom's 'welfare state' are usually traced. These included the introduction of old age pensions and (albeit with limited coverage) compulsory unemployment and health insurance schemes (Hay 1975). The effect on financial relations between Britain and Ireland was dramatic. At the time of the second (1893) Home Rule Bill Irish revenue comfortably exceeded Irish local expenditure: by the time the third was introduced in 1912 Irish local expenditure was greater than Irish revenue and this deficit was projected to increase in the future. Between 1896 and 1911 Irish revenue increased by 28 per cent but Irish local expenditure rose by 91 per cent. Old age pensions accounted for half this total increase and for one third of all Irish local expenditure in 1911.[2]

In June 1911 the Catholic hierarchy came out in opposition to the National Insurance Bill's application to Ireland 'as only a mere fraction' of its working population were wage earners and 'the immense majority' were not. In fact 800,000 people in the Irish labour force stood to benefit from the proposals. During the Act's passage one significant departure from United Kingdom uniformity was made. Against the backdrop of Church and press hostility, in response to pressure from the Irish medical profession, and in spite of trade union protests, the Irish Party moved amendments to exclude Ireland from a medical benefit that in Britain enabled insured workers to visit a general practitioner (GP) and receive prescribed medicines free of charge. Northern Ireland workers would have this exclusion reversed during the 1920s: their southern counterparts were not to be so fortunate (Barrington 1987: 39–66 and 106–108). By the late 1930s half of the British adult population attended a GP free of charge under National Insurance entitlements (Digby and Bosanquet, 1988). South of the Irish border free GP attendance sustained by state-channelled funding was still available only on a means-tested basis through a dispensary service from which the Poor Law's name was removed after independence without the Poor Law's underlying realities being altered.

After independence the Cumann na Gaedhael government moved to reduce welfare expenditure, famously cutting the rate at which the old age pension was paid in 1924 and introducing a much more restrictive regime of means testing prior to the granting of claims. By the late 1920s 'the old age pension became something of a defining issue between Fianna Fail and Cumann na Gaedhael' (O'Grada 2002: 155), with the former attacking the latter's policy in opposition and effectively reversing it on assuming office in 1932. O'Grada (2002: 161) notes that Fianna Fail's 'more populist stance on this issue, and on social policy generally, did more than hurt Cumann na Gaedhael: its appeal to the disadvantaged also helps explain the weakness of social democracy or labourism in Ireland'. While, as discussed in Chapters 2 and 4 above, other factors were also at work, the Labour Party certainly suffered a reverse following the passage in 1944 of legislation providing for children's allowances (to be paid universally without a means test to families with three or more children), when 'in the surprise 1944 election campaign, in contrast to the 1943 campaign, Fianna Fail heavily emphasised social policy measures' (Cousins 2003: 120; see also McCashin 2004: 34).

When the second stage of British welfare state construction occurred after 1945, the development produced highly divergent Irish reactions. Irish exponents of Catholic social teaching deployed the principle of subsidiarity against interventionist state projects. The first inter-party government having been thrown into crisis by the Mother and Child Scheme and having lost office before its White Paper on Social Security could be translated into legislation, the reshaping of Irish health care and social insurance was undertaken by the 1951–54 Fianna Fail government. What Ireland acquired in the 1952 Social Welfare Act was what Sophia Carey has termed a 'hybrid and truncated Beveridgean model'. Then an attempt to design a system whereby 'workers could pay contributions for schemes they alone needed' while 'farmers and workers together could be covered by non-contributory tax-financed schemes for common risks' had foundered. Instead 'policy legacies from 1911 and subsequent legislation meant proposals to abandon contributory schemes for widows and orphans presented serious problems in the area of acquired rights, and the finance minister was extremely hostile to the increased expenditure involved at a time when extremely negative financial realities were becoming clear' (Carey 2005: 308). The extended insurance scheme devised in 1952 excluded the self-employed, contained special contribution and benefit arrangements for public sector workers and for agricultural labourers and at the same time distinguished in a convoluted way between manual and non-manual employees. Once the earnings of the latter exceeded a specified threshold they were effectively pushed out of the scheme unless they opted to remain voluntarily insured for a restricted range of benefits at a substantially higher contribution cost.

In the health field opposition from the Catholic hierarchy and the medical profession meant that 'the original departmental goal of a gradual move towards a universal and first class health service without charge for the whole population, in which most doctors would be employed by salary, was severely modified'

(Barrington 1987: 247). Instead the 1953 Health Act defined three categories of service users with entitlements to receive free services shrinking as level of income rose. A stratification which put about 35 per cent of the population into a low income category, about 50 per cent into a middle income one and about 15 per cent into a higher income one (for which the state was later to sponsor and subsidise a voluntary health insurance scheme) came into being. The thresholds dividing the different categories were defined by either annual income or the rateable valuation of farms. For the dividing line between the upper and middle groups the income level was initially set at that which took a non-manual employee out of compulsory social insurance and this linkage was maintained in the subsequent revision of eligibility conditions.

From the late 1950s a developmental strategy shift aimed at making the 'extremely negative financial realities' that had stymied social security reform in 1952 a thing of the past was embodied in the first of a series of programmes for economic expansion. The programme's rationale derived from the analysis and prescriptions of *Economic Development*, the 'Grey Book' published over T. K. Whitaker's name in November 1958. A key tenet of the new approach held that high taxation was 'one of the greatest impediments to economic progress because of its adverse effects on saving and enterprise'. 'Steady growth in real national income' would, when well established, allow improved social services to be provided alongside stabilised or reduced taxation. For the present, available resources needed to be devoted to providing productive employment rather than making improvements in social welfare: 'the national candle cannot be burned at both ends' (Department of Finance 1958: 24).

Programming was, however, a joint venture between civil servants and politicians, with divergences between the two apparent from the outset (Bew and Patterson 1982). Whitaker was later to single out the second inter-party government's Minister for Finance, Gerard Sweetman, as a politician who, had he remained in office, would have 'had both the energy and the capacity the carry a thing like *Economic Development* through' (quoted in J. F. McCarthy 1990: 43). But Sweetman had by the time he left office 'fallen out with most, if not all, of his Fine Gael colleagues and … was universally hated within Labour' (Puirseil 2007: 203). Sean Lemass, who was Taoiseach for the greater part of the programming period, immediately on assuming that office in 1959 began to press his Minister for Social Welfare, Sean MacEntee, to bring forward a contributory retirement pension scheme. Included in the inter-party government's White Paper of 1949 but omitted from the 1952 Act, the absence of such a scheme meant that 'at age 70, insured workers would often move directly from higher contributory benefits to the lower means tested old age pension' (Carey 2007: 213). This, the 'possibly most important but certainly most expensive'

(Kaim-Caudle 1967: 38) of the additions made to the range of social insurance benefits since the 1920s, was introduced during the lifetime of the First Programme in 1961. Carey (2007: 215) observes that 'although Lemass left no record of his motivations, it seems unproblematic to assert that he recognised that an [old age contributory pension] would help in the process of co-opting the trade union movement into the emerging internationalised economy' – a calculation similar to that which had earlier led him to support the initiation of industry-orientated research in the human sciences.

Nonetheless overall social spending did fall as the First Programme got under way, a trend facilitated by both the Health and Social Welfare portfolios being held until after the 1961 general election by Sean MacEntee, a former Minister for Finance who had in that role resisted the more permissive old age pension regime of the 1930s and limited the scope of the Social Welfare Act in 1952, the year in which he also introduced a famously austere budget. In these years the economy consistently grew at a higher rate than the target one that the programme had set. This performance ensured that the allocation of a sizeable share in the new prosperity to higher social spending was being actively canvassed by the early 1960s. An important social scientific contributor to this discussion was Peter Kaim-Caudle. A visiting scholar in the ERI, he challenged the 'low tax, low welfare' orthodoxy by arguing that 'in Ireland a crusade against poverty, a determination to improve the welfare of the poorest citizens of the state could possibly generate social and moral forces which would do more, or quite as much, to further economic expansion and discourage emigration as economic planning per se' (Kaim-Caudle 1964: 31).

Ministers, civil servants and social welfare in the mid-1960s

By this time, with the Second Programme under way, the programmers themselves were beginning to consider how social development might be grafted on to economic expansion. In July 1964 Finance Assistant Secretary Charles Murray sent Whitaker a note arguing that 'it would be well to get some work going now on the forms which improved and extended social services might take according as the Second Programme's targets are achieved'. One possible form was at this stage ruled out as 'undesirable': 'more or less uniform across-the-board increases'. The model for carrying out the work was supplied by the preparatory study of the fuel and transport sectors done for the Second Programme: 'a high level interdepartmental committee supplemented by some qualified outsiders'. Social Welfare, Health and Education were identified as departments to be approached on the matter.[3]

In September attention was drawn to social welfare provision by the publication of Kaim-Caudle's ERI paper, *Social Security in Ireland and Western Europe*. This prompted the production of a Department of the Taoiseach document dated 11 September and entitled 'Some Notes on Department of Social Welfare'. These notes began by referring to the way in which this department had been envisaged at the time of its creation in the late 1940s as a policy-making agency but now operated merely as a scheme administrator. From ministerial discussion that had taken place in 1962 the conclusions were drawn 'that policy decisions on social welfare are taken by the Government in the context of the Budget, and that the voice of the promoting department carries inadequate weight'. The notes went on to make reference to Kaim-Caudle's paper and to a variety of other manifestations of 'the growing interest in social, as opposed to economic, research', suggesting that 'as the Minister for Social Welfare may have to contend with the results of much of this sociological study work, there may be a case for giving him the responsibility for [social research]'. Apparently in response to this document, Lemass indicated on 14 September that he wanted the idea of a programme for social development – covering social welfare, housing and other social amenities but not education – discussed informally.[4] Two days later the Taoiseach received a (possibly solicited)[5] memorandum from his Minister for Social Welfare, Kevin Boland, commenting in detail on Kaim-Caudle's paper. This was accompanied by a covering letter that belittled the work: 'the author wrote this paper during a three month's stay in Dublin during which he made a study, more or less on paper, of the Irish scheme without doing any real research'. Lemass replied that 'in view of the favourable notices which this paper has been getting – an article in yesterday's *Irish Times*, for instance, refers to it as "a remarkable paper providing something close to a blue-print for the reform and improvement of our system of social welfare" – I wonder should you take some opportunity to correct any wrong impressions caused by the publication of the paper'. The reply also indicated that the memorandum had gone too far in dismissing as 'far-fetched' Kaim-Caudle's proposal for a UK–Ireland Social Insurance Equalisation Fund as consideration was being given to raising this issue in forthcoming Anglo-Irish negotiations.[6]

By the end of September the Finance and Taoiseach social development initiatives had been aligned with one another through the acceptance by Lemass of Whitaker's suggestion for 'an internal confidential study focused on rational evolution of policy rather than a published programme'.[7] Unwilling to proceed in this manner were most of the 'social' departments. Local Government wanted its services (principally housing) left out of any review, while Social Welfare insisted on proceeding departmentally rather than inter-departmentally. With Lemass unable to prevail upon Boland to change his stance, the idea of a Social

Development Programme was – for the time being – abandoned before the end of the year.[8]

Appointed Minister for Defence on his first day in the Dail in 1957, Kevin Boland followed in the ministerial footsteps of his father Gerald and became one of the first of the post-revolutionary generation in Fianna Fail to attain Cabinet rank. He held the Social Welfare portfolio from 1961 until 1966 and was a member of the Cabinet until 1970, when he resigned in the midst of the Arms Crisis. Having left Fianna Fail, in 1971 he founded a new party, Aontacht Eireann, whose electoral failure ended his career in parliamentary politics. During the 1970s and 1980s he published a number of books and pamphlets (principally Boland 1971, 1977 and 1982) whose recurrent theme was the abandonment of republican principles by Fianna Fail as the Northern Ireland Troubles exploded from the late 1960s. The roots of this betrayal he traced to an earlier date, recording the 'uneasiness' and 'disillusion' he had felt from the time he had become a minister in relation to a number of policy areas. One of these was social policy, where 'in the post-coalition depression of 1957–58 a really progressive social welfare policy was out of the question but economic growth did little to lessen resistance to social progress' (Boland 1971: 26). Yet, although he considered doing so (Boland 1977: 117), he never fully discussed this issue in print. Here Boland's ministerial correspondence will be used to examine the nature of the social policy debate carried on within the Fianna Fail governments of the early and mid-1960s.

After his move from Defence in 1961, Boland quickly raised the shortcomings of existing social welfare arrangements at government level. While he argued that a fundamental reform of basically inadequate rates needed to be undertaken, he succeeded only in securing approval for the 'preparation of an improved Social Welfare Scheme within the limits set by the Minister for Finance in his Financial Statement, 1962' and for an invitation to the Federated Union of Employers and ICTU to submit observations on 'the allocation of the additional funds to the different types and rates of benefit and on the question of increasing the contribution rates'. From the latter exercise Boland informed Lemass on 30 May 1962 that 'no worthwhile suggestions have emerged', while the Taoiseach was 'very disappointed at the unconstructive responses'.[9] In the following year Boland's efforts focused on the income limit for the insurability of non-manual employees. Since 1958 this had stood at £800 per annum and Social Welfare sought an upward adjustment calculated to bring back into the scheme those who had been covered by it in 1958 but had been taken over the limit by two subsequent pay rounds. Opposition to this came from not only Finance but from Health, whose response quoted an Irish Medical Association warning that the knock-on effect on health service eligibility would be 'to reduce still further the already small pool of private practice with consequent considerable financial loss to the medical profession'. Writing personally to Boland, Sean McEntee warned that:

> Much has been done in the recent past to re-establish reasonable relations with the medical profession. Some matters remain to be settled and I have no doubt that, if the present atmosphere of good will continues, the outstanding difficulties can be resolved; but if the classes eligible for the services I have mentioned are now extended, we can expect a very strong reaction and open opposition to the Government.

Boland's rejoinder pointed out that, in terms of political consequences, not raising the limit at the behest of the medical profession 'would certainly involve open conflict with the Trade Unions, and widespread discontent and agitation might be expected among the rank and file of our own party'. With differences unresolved, the ongoing deliberations of a Dail Select Committee on the Health Services provided a pretext for deferring a government decision on the issue.[10] Boland was thus three years into his term as Social Welfare Minister with nothing to show for his efforts to reform the system when the Social Development Programme initiative was broached. His December rebuff of this idea was combined with a letter-writing offensive of his own by which Minister for Finance James Ryan declared himself to be 'completely taken aback'. Boland responded that:

> My suggestion that after eight years spent in promoting economic expansion something reasonably substantial should now be done for Social Welfare is not an effort to wreck the Second Programme for Economic Expansion. On the contrary, it is put forward because I am convinced it is necessary, and necessary this year, if this Government is to remain in a position to implement the programme. I maintain that it is not only justifiable but also politically expedient that Social Welfare recipients should be given something approaching their due share of the increase in National Income (bearing in mind that the rates have always been basically inadequate) if necessary by withdrawing in whole or in part the tax concessions given since 1957 to induce the economic expansion that is now under way.

The 'politically expedient' part of this argument Boland supported with references to by-election defeats of Fianna Fail candidates. East Galway was not lost 'because we were opposed by a footballer' but primarily because of 'a general feeling that we have not paid sufficient attention to the weaker section of the community and that there has not been an equitable distribution of the increased prosperity to which we point as an achievement'.[11] A Tuam Fianna Fail supporter who wrote to Lemass endorsed this analysis, though hardly in a way that would have gratified Boland: 'you have some brilliant men among your ministers, men

such as Mr. Jack Lynch and Dr. Hillery but sad to say you have a couple of pas-
sengers ... [I]t was Mr. McEntee Minister for Health and Mr. Boland Minister
for Social Welfare who was directly responsible for losing the By Election in
East Galway.' This correspondent went on to provide a 'glaring example' of what
was going wrong, describing a visit he and a priest had made to a man suffering
from cancer who had recently come home from hospital. Living on his own and
depending on a disabled person's allowance, all of this man's meals consisted of
'bare bread and black tea' and he had no fuel for a fire. The letter concluded:

> I will now tell you what the priest said to me when we came out. There is money in
> this country for Industrialists (foreign and native) for farmers for sending troops to
> the Congo and Cyprus, for the building of luxury hotels and if a war started tomor-
> row morning he said there would be hundreds of thousands of pounds spent on arma-
> ments and the question would never be asked where is the money to come from. That
> question only arise[s] when someone ask[s] the Minister for Health or the Minister
> for Social Welfare to grant an increase to the disabled[,] the old age pensioners or
> the people getting unemployment assistance[. O]f course Fine Gael went to all those
> people and got their votes and also the votes of those people[']s friends and relatives.[12]

Fianna Fail could have been vulnerable when a general election was held on 7
April 1965 at which both Fine Gael and Labour presented the electorate with
programmes calling for greatly improved social welfare provision. But two factors undermined this challenge to the outgoing government. First, a leftward
policy lurch by a Fine Gael party with a very conservative leadership profile
suffered from a major credibility problem (Meehan 2013). Second, 'the election
became one where Fine Gael and Labour stood on remarkably similar platforms
but were precluded from forming a government together afterwards, leaving
Fianna Fail to run on its record – "Let Lemass Lead on!" – and its promise that
it was the only party capable of forming a government' (Puirseil 2007: 234).
Labour, whose refusal to countenance entering a coalition had brought this situation about, had the consolation of having at last regained the Dail representation
it had held at the time of its 1944 split.

Electoral vulnerability thus impinged to a very limited extent on the debate
about social welfare within the Fianna Fail government. Instead of discussing how they might save their ministerial skins, Boland and Ryan traded
well-established departmental positions while the general election came and
went. Finance asserted that excessively high social insurance scheme costs
were falling on the state because of Social Welfare's mismanagement. Social
Welfare retorted that costs to the state were high because the scheme was
being distorted to subsidise agriculture and because the remuneration limit

disproportionately depleted the insured pool of its 'good risks'. Ryan was, however, prepared to offer a deal. Insurance benefits might be increased provided the long-established tripartite principle was set aside and the full cost was borne by higher employee and employer contributions. With western smallholders about to be hived off into a separate scheme of their own, he proposed that unemployment assistance in future be paid out of social insurance funds, thus shifting most of the cost burden away from the state. With savings accruing to the Exchequer in this manner, it would be possible 'to contemplate some improvements on the social assistance side'. Writing to the Taoiseach on 22 March, he 'frankly' confessed himself 'disappointed' at the rejection of these proposals.[13]

While this correspondence was in progress, Lemass became engaged with the remuneration limit issue after a Cork shop assistant's complaint caught his attention. Writing to Boland on 28 January, he was 'surprised' that shop assistants were regarded as non-manual employees. Referring to previous discussion of raising the remuneration limit, he suggested that it might be 'worthwhile to consider the classification of occupations so as to extend the definition of manual worker to all occupations to which it might, even by stretching the definition, be made to apply'. Boland in reply detailed the legal difficulties surrounding ad hoc redesignation to cater for certain occupations falling foul of the remuneration limit, such as shop assistant and barman, concluding that potentially complex legislation would be required. Lemass then threw his weight behind the raising of the limit.[14] With £1,200 replacing £800, this took place only after the election was over and after rearguard actions by Finance and Health had been worn down. Health circulated a letter from the Irish Medical Association objecting to any rise in the limit as an annex to its memorandum. Including an argument to the effect that compulsory social insurance was being progressively rendered redundant by the ever-expanding benevolence of the Irish employer, the observations Finance put forward on this narrow issue exhibited the Mr. Hyde side of an entity that had been professing a Dr. Jekyll-like interest in social development. Social Welfare accurately characterised these observations as 'an attempt to justify permitting the social insurance scheme to run down'.[15]

The general election did, however, prompt Lemass to refer in campaign speeches to the possibility that a Social Development Programme might be devised and, safely back in office, he made a more extensive statement on the subject in May when the budget was debated:

> This country is facing problems of social adjustment, facing the need to think about social policy, but it would be very inadvisable if ideas on these matters were limited

to changes in the State's social services ... [A] social development programme, as I understand it, would be a much wider conception than a review of social welfare arrangements although, of course, adequate social services would be an important part of it. In the fullest form, it could no doubt extend to attempting to sketch the type of society we desire to build here, recognising that this would not solely or even mainly be a function of the Government or of expanding the function of Government or of the enactment of legislation by the Dail but of developing a social attitude in, and defining the social obligations of, business concerns and trade unions and arising in other similar activities so as to place the improvement of relations within our society and the general welfare of the country in at least equal importance with the particular aims of individual concerns and organisations, leading perhaps eventually to the setting up of arrangements and procedures which would reflect these new attitudes.[16]

Social development and social research

Finance interest in the Social Development Programme idea had not been extinguished by Boland's adamant opposition to interdepartmental deliberation. In late January 1965 Murray sent Whitaker a note that made reference to two recent *Irish Times* articles by Garret FitzGerald and continued that 'in view of the continued public criticism on this score, I think it would be well to bring some mild pressure on Social Welfare'. A draft letter to Social Welfare Secretary W. A. Honohan accompanied the note, but Whitaker replied that 'I wd. prefer to inquire orally & will take an early opportunity of doing this'. In mid-April Murray sent Whitaker clippings of a number of critical press pieces, commenting that 'we are certainly being "beaten over the head". When the budget is introduced I hope that Social Welfare will come up with the fruits of their study.' To this Whitaker replied that 'I have been talking to Honohan & was promised sight (personally) of a document recently sent to the [Taoiseach]. So far it hasn't come!'[17] Headed 'A preliminary bird's eye review of the Social Welfare Services with some indications of the Minister's tentative ideas on reform', a 'rough memorandum' running to twenty-five pages in length had been sent by Boland to Lemass on 22 February. It referred to the interdepartmental action proposed in the previous autumn as having 'quickly lost its way by narrowing the field down to a study of income-maintenance services only with, in effect, Finance supervision'. In this context it observed that 'it is also unfortunate that we should have to fight so hard for increases from year to year which do no more than keep parity with wage or cost-of-living increases; the relatively large sums that have to go out in this way give a false idea that much more is "being done" for the necessitous than is, in fact, the case'. Moreover 'while our benefit levels remain too low, it seems, we must, as a first priority, keep plugging this point to the exclusion of other major reforms, at least until reasonable levels are achieved' so that 'what will come from my Department will be a plan for the income-maintenance services but nothing more than this, nothing which could be labelled a plan for "social" development'.[18]

Such a plan was put back on the agenda by Finance before the end of May, when it linked what Lemass had said in the Dail budget debate to the work Henning Friis had just completed: 'a social development programme will call for much empirical social research, and it is timely that we have now available a report on how this might be organised'.[19] The three propositions that an ESRI would replace the ERI, that McCarthy would succeed Geary as its director and that McCarthy would be asked 'to formulate a preliminary programme for the organisation and integration of the studies and inquiries on which the official aspects of a social development programme should be based' were then advanced. By the end of August all had secured government approval.[20] On September 9 Murray suggested to Whitaker that Finance officers should provide McCarthy with staff assistance: 'this would be good training for our people and would help to introduce them to this field, which will be no stranger to us in coming years'. At a meeting held on 26 November McCarthy 'thought his report might be made to the Taoiseach but Mr. Murray pointed out that the approach to the Government had been made by the Minister for Finance and it was to that Minister that Dr. McCarthy's findings should be submitted'.[21]

By the end of the year, however, it was clear that there was divergence between the expectations within Finance as to what McCarthy in his various roles might accomplish and what he considered would be feasible. On 24 December Whitaker acknowledged that 'it appears that any action by an expanded Economic and Social Research Institute will have little effect on the formulation of official policy in the social field for quite a number of years ahead'. Nonetheless he hoped that it would be possible for McCarthy to produce 'a preliminary and tentative framework' within which reconciliation of the supply of and demand for resources in social fields might be attempted. Discussions with Health and with Social Welfare were held by McCarthy and his Finance assistant, Brian Kissane, in December 1965 and January 1966 but thereafter the 'preliminary programme' initiative stalled.[22]

What McCarthy did push forward during 1966 was the process of converting the ERI into an ESRI. On 14 October he sent Whitaker a list of names of those who might represent the social side on the Institute's Council that corresponded exactly with the eventual outcome. The list was drawn up in the light of George O'Brien's concern that 'any vacancies might lead to somebody being "foisted" on us at the General Meeting'. Concerned to balance different disciplines and different institutions he had been 'forced to ignore [J. J.] McElligott's point of view about the clergy since they predominate in the Social Sciences in the N.U.I.' Here:

> I cannot see us excluding Kavanagh, O'Doherty and Newman. I would prefer not to have Dempsey from U.C.C. but I do not think the Sociology people in Cork are possible and would prefer Dempsey to them. I do not feel that I should include O'hEideain from Galway. He 'pretends' to teach Sociology but his post is in Philosophy and there is nobody else I would think possible in U.C.G.

Higher institutes would be represented by the directors of Foras Taluntais, Foras Forbartha, IPA and IMI. The HSC and the Medico-Social Research Board would be represented by their chairmen, Charles McCarthy and Patrick Lynch. Lynch's UCD affiliation would enable both Louden Ryan and Basil Chubb to be included from TCD. From the civil service would come Tadgh O'Cearbhaill, Secretary of the Department of Labour, while McCarthy favoured the inclusion as an Education representative of Fr. Cregan, the president of St. Patrick's College, Drumcondra – 'they have an Educational Research Unit there' – although 'I recognise that this further increases the number of clergy'. The Jesuit College of Industrial Relations was not to be represented 'both because the role of that institution does not seem to relate directly to empirical research and because of the number of clergy already suggested'.[23]

What the clerical teachers of social science in the NUI thought of the creation of the ESRI is also recorded in correspondence either with McCarthy or with HSC. In UCD Kavanagh initially drafted a document which he marked '1st Edition – Not Circulated or Shown to Anyone', arguing that 'the suggestion to set up an Institute of Social Research is premature ... Some bodies (e.g. U.C.D.) in recent years have been giving increasing attention to Social Research. I think they should be given an opportunity of "proving themselves" over the next few years ... [W]e must not stifle what is already developing.' However another document – on which '2nd Edition – given to Mr. Friis' is written – expresses 'general agreement with the central conclusion of Mr. Friis's report', while listing a number of reservations. The emphasis placed on economics and statistics by Friis is questioned: 'the impression received is of little importance being attached to sociological and other studies in depth'. Friis is considered to be 'not, perhaps, sufficiently optimistic about the trained personnel who will be available in the very near future'. His emphasis on 'the need for increased staff and facilities in university departments of social science should not be misinterpreted as implying that the present standards, methods and products are not satisfactory. Our standards in the Department of Social Science, U.C.D., for example, are those of the best British universities.' Finally, the need for social research interviewers to be academically trained in sociology is argued.[24] Writing to the HSC Secretary, O'Doherty expressed his 'uneasiness' about the creation of an ESRI. His letter did not elaborate on the reasons for this, although a postscript states 'there is a great deal more to be said and perhaps we can discuss it at Committee level some day'.[25] But if O'Doherty did contribute to such a HSC discussion, it appears not to have been minuted.

From UCC McCarthy had received comments from the two sociologists whom he considered 'not possible' as ESRI Council members. The veteran Fr. Jerome O'Leary welcomed the stress being placed on interdisciplinary co-operation: 'you remember Alfred made a start in that direction here a long time ago. Since then instead of co-operation we are having cold war and demarcation disputes.' The young Fr. Liam Ryan wondered whether the Institute's proposed Council was too large, questioned the optimism of Friis regarding collaboration between the Institute and the universities while hoping that no monopolisation of social research was implied by the proposals.[26] From UCG the disparaged Fr. Eustas O'hEideain, writing to the HSC, attached substantial reservations to his general welcome for the Friis report. The view of Friis that the universities' departmental structure made them unsuited to interdisciplinary work was challenged, 'especially in a small university college like ours': 'some of the staff in the Sociology, Economics and Geography departments are at present co-operating in an inter-disciplinary survey in Mayo'. The advocacy by Friis of both a central social research institute and strengthened university capacities was viewed with scepticism: 'in practice … if money is spent on establishing a central research institute, it will become increasingly difficult – especially for Galway – to get the money essential for the development of the university sociology departments'. The suggested building of links through ESRI staff teaching in the universities might be practical in the case of Dublin colleges but was irrelevant to UCG. More generally:

> The area in which social research has been most neglected is the West of Ireland, and yet it is among the areas that most need it. We fear that a central Dublin-based institute will be under too much pressure from other directions to give proper attention to the West of Ireland. Besides, it is our experience that the problems of the West are in large measure unreal to most Dublin-based organisations. One has to live in the West to understand the human problems and to have the incentive to set about measuring them. We feel therefore that social research in the West of Ireland must be based in Galway, if not in U.C.G. (where we feel it should be based) then at least in a special western branch of the Research Institute.[27]

Up until his death in 1957 sociology in UCG had been associated with the Franciscan professor of philosophy Feilim O'Briain, who 'gave up the teaching of speculative philosophy and devoted himself to the social sciences, lecturing widely throughout the province of Connacht' (Foley and Bateman 1999: 418). Appointed a lecturer in philosophy in 1959, the Dominican O'hEidean sustained the subject – although not to McCarthy's satisfaction – until in 1968 he was appointed Professor of Education at the same time that another Franciscan, Edmond Dougan, became UCG's first Professor of Political Science and Sociology. O'hEidean's November 1965 comments on the proposed ESRI were made 'after discussion with some of my colleagues here', and, with no western branch of the ESRI in prospect, economics, geography, political science and sociology came together the following month to create their own UCG Social Sciences Research Centre (UCG SSRC). O'hEidean was the first director, and was succeeded in the position by Dougan. With geographer Breandán MacAodha as its most prolific contributor, the UCG SSRC published a series of research papers on agriculture, migration, urban planning and industrial relations. In 1971 its role in a Galway Gaeltacht survey embroiled the UCG SSRC in a controversy with George Colley, who, in the wake of the Arms Crisis, held ministerial responsibility for both Finance and the Gaeltacht. The centre was involved as a sub-contractor to Daithi Hanly, the architect and planning consultant, from whom a report was commissioned by Foras Forbartha. Lengthy negotiation preceded the granting of permission for the SSRC to publish its own report and recommendations alongside those of Hanly. These Colley dismissed in a radio interview as not being 'a professional report on which Government policy could be based'.[28]

While McCarthy made progress towards the replacement of the ERI by the ESRI, the funding of increased social expenditure continued to preoccupy the government. In May 1966 an exchange took place between Boland and Lemass in which the former argued for a broader tax base while the latter took up Finance proposals from the previous year to shift the burden from taxation to higher social insurance contributions.[29] By the end of 1966 – when Lemass retired and was succeeded as Taoiseach by Jack Lynch – the government had set up an interdepartmental group to examine the financing of social welfare, health and education 'on the tripartite insurance principle'. However, when it reported in February 1967, the group preferred a social development tax to insurance contributions.

Militating against the latter option in its view were, first, fears about higher inflation and reduced export market competitiveness. Second, it was considered that an insurance scheme would generate demands for expensive further extension of services, particularly in the health field. Here pressure was anticipated for the extension of free health services to the whole insured population – bringing about in effect a restoration of the medical benefit denied to covered Irish workers in 1911. With an earmarked social development tax, on the other hand, the group believed that a generalised appeal to social solidarity could be made which would counter resistance to an increased level of taxation without creating the sense of automatic entitlement to benefits that insurance contributors were thought likely to acquire. The group leaned towards a direct, and possibly a graduated, tax but – noting the conflict between this and the Second Programme's statement that 'reliance will continue to be placed on indirect rather than direct taxation' – it concluded that 'whether or not a tax of this nature would be preferable to, say, an increase in the Turnover Tax or other indirect taxes would need to be examined fully by qualified economists and tax experts'.[30]

During the summer of 1967 the programming process was to be thrown into disarray not only with regard to its attempts to add in a social development component but also in relation to its core pursuit of economic expansion. In August, with the actual performance of the economy substantially adrift of its targets, the Second Programme was abandoned about mid-way through its projected lifespan. In the previous month, after about eight months in the post of ESRI director, McCarthy had been appointed president of UCC. McCarthy's ESRI successor, announced in December, was to be Michael Fogarty, the English Catholic social scientist previously encountered in Chapter 3 above as a source of serious vexation to the Archbishop of Dublin.

Fogarty was born in 1916 in Burma, where his father worked in the Indian civil service. His mother died of septicaemia shortly after Michael was born and the baby was sent to his father's relatives in Galway. Thereafter he experienced what he later described as 'the classic problems of children of the Empire, long separations and early resort to boarding schools: I started at Ampleforth just before my eighth birthday' (Fogarty 1999: 16). From his Benedictine schooling he went first to Oxford, next to the army evacuated from France in 1940 (where he was seriously wounded), then back to Oxford to work on post-war social reconstruction research before becoming Professor of Industrial Relations in Cardiff. In the early 1960s he left Cardiff for a lucrative contract post with the London-based think tank Political and Economic Planning. In Britain he was a defender of the welfare state against its proto-Thatcherite detractors within the Catholic Social Guild (Keating 1998). A longtime Labour activist, his particular brand of progressive politics eventually took him into a Liberal Party revitalised under Jo Grimond's leadership. He stood unsuccessfully for parliament as both a Labour and a Liberal candidate. A leading authority on the emergence of European Christian Democracy, his academic and political interests beyond Britain had mainly drawn him eastwards to the continent rather than westwards to Ireland. However, residual family ties, the role of the Catholic Social Guild as a point of intersection between English and Irish Social Catholicism and the speaking engagements at Irish Catholic social study gatherings which his public prominence attracted kept his Irish connections alive.

In 1958 Whitaker emphasised the gloom pervading Irish society: 'the common talk amongst the parent in towns, as in rural Ireland, is of their children having to emigrate as soon as their education is completed in order to be sure of a reasonable livelihood'. But Fogarty, in a *tour d'horizon* written for a US Catholic periodical, was considerably more upbeat. A generational change of leadership was inevitably imminent, already 'our Angry Young Men are taking over' and 'there are in Ireland today all the signs of a new age'. Among these signs were the vitality of Muintir and of adult education initiatives, the emergence of new movements such as IMI and NFA as well as, within a 'patchy' university system, the intellectual liveliness of Maynooth: 'five learned journals are published from it, and ideas are whirling around in it in history or philosophy or social affairs, including religious sociology'. For Fogarty 'the most encouraging sign is the way that Ireland is beginning to open onto the world'. Instanced here were positive responses to emergent movements towards European unification, the vigour of worldwide missionary endeavour and the way in which the evils of emigration were counterbalanced by possibilities of leadership open to the Irish professional man 'who is free to come and go in the Commonwealth ... yet is not tarred with the brush of British colonialism'.[31]

Fogarty's appointment as ESRI director broke the successional link between the directorship of the CSO and that of the ESRI that could – once a precedent, twice a custom – have become institutionalised as a humbler version of the progression of retiring Finance Secretary to Central Bank Governor. As an expatriate outsider in Ireland as in Wales, Fogarty was hardly equipped to fill the mediating insider role that had been envisaged for McCarthy in the devising of a Social Development Programme. Instead his social science expertise found its main Irish outlet in conducting inquiries set up by the Department of Labour, whose subject matter included major industrial disputes affecting electricity supply and banking. He was also a member of the Commission on the Status of Women. During his period as director of the ESRI the proportion of Irish staff markedly increased, with figures such as Brendan Walsh, Dermot McAleese and Damian Hannan becoming prominent (Fogarty 1999: 121). Back in March 1961 a Seanad motion had regretted 'to note that all the senior staff of the Economic Research Institute (with the sole exception of the Director) have been recruited everywhere except in Ireland'.[32]

To replace the Second Programme, a successor that was to be sub-titled *Economic and Social Development 1969–72* was prepared. As the transition began, the death of the approach Finance had devised in mid-1965 for evolving a Social Development Programme was acknowledged in a note to a colleague from Charles Murray: 'at one stage it was hoped that Dr. M. D. McCarthy would act as a catalyst in this matter. Pressure of other duties has prevented him doing much in this area and, while he is still hopeful, I think that we will have to go it alone.'[33] This meant that 'the new programme will have to be a simpler and in many ways a less ambitious undertaking than we would have wished for in relation to social development ... [W]hat can be done in connection with the Third Programme must necessarily be limited and must, indeed, be regarded as a *first* step in the evolution of a comprehensive social development programme.' Once such evolution had taken place, 'an attempt can be made to balance one need against another so that expenditure will reflect a conscious decision regarding the relative importance of each'. But 'this approach calls for information which is not at present fully available, and which only widespread research can provide; research is under way in the Departments concerned and in the Economic and Social Research Institute but it will be some time before results become available'.[34]

The information base for the 'first step' was to be departmental projections of expenditure 'distinguishing between existing policies, policies announced but not fully effective and other likely changes'. These were to be jointly examined by officials from Finance and from the departments involved. At the ESRI Peter Kaim-Caudle, now back in a senior staff role, was in charge of research 'into the pattern of social investment in other countries'. Divergence between Finance and Social Welfare continued to be evident while the Third Programme was being drawn up. Boland had departed, but, reflecting no doubt the strong influence of Social Welfare's Secretary W. A. Honohan, continuity with his predecessor was the watchword of the new minister, Joseph Brennan.[35] Plugging of the point that payment levels were too low continued through a succession of circulated memoranda, while the kind of interdepartmental approach Finance favoured was kept at arm's length. In a March 1968 note to Charles Murray, Brian Kissane discerned echoes of statements made to McCarthy and himself in December 1965 in recent communications from Social Welfare in which 'it seems clear that they are opposed to the idea of co-ordinating their plans with those of other departments and of examining the over-all plans in relation to the financial position'.[36] Nonetheless, by the time the programme was being finalised in early 1969, Honohan appeared to be reasonably satisfied with the provision for his department's schemes and future plans that the programme had made.[37]

An analysis of the published Third Programme by Garret FitzGerald noted that 'at least it is clear that social welfare is now being taken seriously'.[38] Two years later he highlighted the divergence between actual and planned social expenditure that had occurred. Education and Housing had undershot by 5 and 8 per cent respectively, Health was fractionally above its target but income maintenance spending had overshot by 13 per cent. On this outcome he commented that 'it would be interesting to know why the Government's priorities between these different types of social expenditure have changed so radically in the short period since the Third Programme was prepared'.[39] In late 1965, between his two periods working in Ireland, Kaim-Caudle completed a monograph on *Social Policy in the Irish Republic*. Here he had concluded that 'it seems more probable that the next few years will see major reforms in social insurance and assistance rather than in either health or education'. Three considerations formed the basis of this forecast. First, 'social security cash payments affect a large portion of the electorate'. Second, 'quantitative differences in pension rates between countries are more obvious than qualitative differences in health services and education'. Third, changes in social security cash payments 'do not create quite the same danger of friction as may arise with the Church about education or the doctors about health services' (Kaim-Caudle 1967: 106).

If rate of increase in spending is taken as its measure, this forecast turned out to be accurate. But, more than forty years on, it is still not possible to ascertain whether this was a case of Kaim-Caudle being right for the right reasons or right for the wrong reasons. Government department files that ought under the thirty-year transfer rule of the National Archives Act to be available to researchers are not, and this non-compliance with the legislation is particularly acute in the case of social spending departments such as Education, Health and Social Welfare. In 1964, when he numbered among the critics by whom Charles Murray would shortly afterwards feel 'beaten over the head', Garret FitzGerald (1964a: 246) had dubbed income maintenance schemes 'the Cinderella of [the Second] Programme'. A decade later this Cinderella got to go to the public spending ball in some style. The team that pulled her carriage along the way comprised social science radicalism and party political realignment.

The social sciences, party politics and Irish welfare state expansion in the 1970s

Like the Catholic bishops in their dealings with the NDS, programme-devising civil servants approached empirical social science from the standpoint of institutional utility while, as was also the case with NDS, social scientists were inclined to play the role of independent critical analysts and advocates. In relation to social policy an independent stance was articulated at the conference on poverty held in Kilkenny in November 1971. With the conference being held under the auspices of the Council on Social Welfare, the post-conciliar Catholic Church structures whose emergence was noted in Chapter 3 above were central to the initiative. Of the four main papers at the conference, two were delivered by clerics – one by Dr. Peter Birch, Bishop of Ossory and an episcopal member of the Council on Social Welfare, and the other by James Kavanagh. The other two main papers were by members of the growing Irish academic social science community. Seamus O'Cinneide was then a Research Officer in the IPA and a part-time lecturer in social administration in UCC. Eileen Kane was a professor of anthropology in Pittsburgh University who was in Ireland attached to the MSRB and lectured in anthropology in Maynooth. The proceedings of the conference comprised one of the 1972 issues of *Social Studies*, the title that *Christus Rex* had adopted the year before. In an introduction, Kavanagh assured readers that 'the Kilkenny Conference will not be allowed to remain a mere talking-shop, no matter how interesting that was in itself'.

Meanwhile, after three general elections in which facing a divided opposition had greatly facilitated the return of outgoing Fianna Fail governments, Fine Gael and Labour re-embraced coalition. Faced with a surprise dissolution of the Dail in February 1973, the two parties jointly issued a fourteen-point Statement of Intent that included a pledge that money saved from EEC entry would be channelled into pensions and welfare benefits and reduction of the pensionable age, as well as a commitment to legislation which would end discrimination against women. As the campaign got under way, 'the main concentration [of the National Coalition parties] was on rising prices, rates, the housing shortage, and the poor welfare system which allowed almost 600,000 people to live below subsistence level'. Fianna Fail initially ridiculed the idea that the opposition proposals could be implemented without huge tax rises, but then, in an about-turn, 'also announced that the government proposed to channel into the Social Welfare fund the £30 million made available by EEC entry' (Knight and Baxter-Moore 1973: 18–20).

In the new government the Labour Party leader and Tanaiste Brendan Corish was Minister for Social Welfare, with another Labour TD, Frank Cluskey, as his Parliamentary Secretary. Over the lifetime of the government major welfare expansion took place, some of which – pay-related benefits, payments to deserted wives – built upon initiatives of the preceding Lynch administration. In his 1967 monograph Kaim-Caudle judged the Irish social insurance system to be as comprehensive in covering contingencies as most European systems but to be notably lacking in universality. With taxation of farming profits one of the decade's thorniest political issues, the self-employed were not brought into the social insurance scheme by the National Coalition but the 1975 abolition of the non-manual employee remuneration limit at a stroke increased the insured population by 20 per cent. For Kaim-Caudle (1967: 106–107) one reform deserved absolute priority: 'the extension of social assistance to cover all contingencies and needs'. Unified national provision should absorb local authority-administered schemes of last resort that suffered from fragmentation, administrative duplication, arbitrary variation and the taint of pauperism. Here the introduction of the supplementary welfare allowance in 1975 is generally regarded as a landmark change. Another area of unmet need Kaim-Caudle highlighted was 'Family Assistance for women having care of children not supported by their fathers' – a set of issues examined in much greater detail by the Commission on the Status of Women, which reported in 1972 (McCashin 2004: 172–178), and addressed during the early 1970s by the introduction of a succession of schemes making provision for deserted wives, prisoners' wives and unmarried mothers.

Social welfare spending doubled during the National Coalition's first year in office. With high inflation already affecting the Irish economy before EEC entry and the first oil price shock, some of this and of rises in subsequent years fell into Boland's category of 'increases from year to year which do no more than keep parity with wage or cost-of-living increases'. For both sides in the 1973 election campaign, as we have seen, extended social welfare was to be funded without the necessity for increased taxation by EEC-derived funds. But, following the election, an option eschewed in pre-EEC entry days – government borrowing for current expenditure – would bridge the gap between rising social spending and a domestic tax base which governments continued to shy away from broadening other than at the expense of the wage or salary earner subject to Pay-As-You-Earn (PAYE) deduction (Sweeney 1983; Wilson 1989; Girvin 2010).

The programming state and the plight of the west

Having defined a new role for itself with *Economic Development* and the First Programme, Finance soon afterwards undertook an internal reorganisation with the creation of an Economic Development Branch (EDB) headed by Charles Murray. While the increasing complexity of programming would eventually absorb its energies, EDB initially undertook a series of examinations that ranged widely and encompassed topics such as community development, management education and the attraction of investment from the US electronics industry. In March 1961 Lemass referred to EDB the consideration of 'the main, if not indeed the only question arising in national economic policy to which we have not yet found a satisfactory answer'. This was 'how to deal with the small (mainly western) farms and to ensure reasonable standards of income for those who live on them'. As was later to be the case with the Social Development Programme,

Finance was already moving on the issue and its suggested line of approach was the one that was subsequently adopted.[40]

In October 1960 T. K. Whitaker in a letter to his Agriculture counterpart, J. C. Nagle, referred to a holiday he had recently spent in West Cork and observed that 'the economic forces have almost spent themselves there in the sense that enough land of sorts seems now to be available to provide those who have stayed behind with viable holdings but these people are naturally dispirited by the departure of so many of their neighbours and relations and they need to have their morale and sense of community restored'. There was 'a great field here for a well-trained organiser who could rally all the help needed – psychological, social and economic – from the various bodies equipped to provide it: the local clergy and teachers, your Department and its advisory staff, An Foras Taluntais, the Banks, the Agricultural Credit Corporation, Muintir na Tire, Macra na Feirme, the creameries etc.' Fearful of renewed division of within advisory service provision, Agriculture argued that County Committees of Agriculture should be central to mobilising initiatives. Moreover these should be undertaken across the country and not just in underdeveloped areas (a category into which West Cork was not seen as really fitting). While reiterating his view that it was 'important for psychological and other reasons to make a beginning with the *underdeveloped* areas', Whitaker was willing to fall in with Agriculture's approach to the organisational side of 'the active pushing of existing schemes and services of all kinds'. Out of these exchanges emerged agreement that an interdepartmental committee on the problems of small western farms should be set up. This Lemass subsequently accepted to be 'the only immediately practicable arrangement'.[41]

Published in March 1962, and actively followed up by Lemass,[42] the Report of the Inter-Departmental Committee on the Problems of Small Western Farms set in motion a policy shift that had by the end of the decade installed non-farm sources of employment in industry, tourism, forestry and fishing alongside 'more intensive farming in economic units' as the key components of rural development. County Development Teams (CDTs) had been established in thirteen western counties that operated in tandem with the Finance-chaired Central Development Committee (CDC), whose role was to co-ordinate the activities of all the economic departments and state agencies concerned in the development of the west. From 1967 the CDTs and the CDC could draw upon a Special Regional Development Fund (SRDF) for project finance. Initially through its Small Industries Programme, and subsequently through its Regional Plans and network of Regional Offices, the IDA loomed ever larger on this scene as industrial decentralisation accompanied the decimation of the previously protected manufacturing base and a greatly increased inflow of foreign direct investment (O'Malley 1989: 95–96). Against this backdrop, land consolidation was 'minimal' with 'small-scale landholders, by and large, holding on to their land'. Over time three small-farm sub-groups were to emerge – a minority generating a viable household income from farming, 'pluriactive' households with different sources of earnings spread across different household members and impoverished households dependent on social welfare payments, though with some farm income (Hannan and Commins 1992).

During the period immediately following the report's appearance a movement in opposition to government policy emerged in the west in the form of the Charlestown Committee. Centred in Mayo, this movement derived its inspiration from community efforts to regenerate the Glencolumbkille area of west Donegal led by its parish priest, Fr. James McDyer (Tucker 1989 and 1999). To save the west in Fr. McDyer's view two things were essential: 'local cooperation and adequate capital for development'. The government was in favour of local co-operation provided it was subject to official direction of a kind Fr. McDyer and his followers viewed with great suspicion. As the Inter-Departmental Committee was being set up, James Ryan, Minister for Finance, deprecated 'any "solution" which involved heavier subsidisation of uneconomic production and a consequent increase in taxation adversely affecting the real growing points of the economy'. It was Fr. McDyer's view that 'if you are a foreign industrialist and you are looking for adequate capital, you will get it without any trouble but if you are a small farmer it's a different matter'.[43]

The relationship between state officialdom and voluntary organisations was raised soon after the CDTs were set up. Membership of the teams was confined to officials whose position, it was argued (especially by Agriculture), would be invidious were representation to be broadened. A 'right of audience' for voluntary organisations was the extent of the concession made to Muintir and other advocates of their full inclusion. The issue emerged again at the level of the CDC during the summer of 1964 following government acceptance of a Charlestown Committee proposal that pilot areas be chosen for intensive support in order to generate a wider demonstration effect throughout the west of Ireland.[44] The Charlestown Committee was rebuffed when it sought direct involvement in running the pilot area programme as 'Officials are no better equipped in matters concerning Community Development than ourselves and we also feel that these good Officials might either be subjected to undesirable pressures by the respective County Committees in the choice of areas, or on the other hand might follow the line of least resistance and choose areas where the land would be good and the effort involved in promotion would be simple.'[45] As with the Parish Plan, official implementation of the pilot areas proposal was accompanied by the dissociation from the initiative of the voluntary group with which it had originated.[46]

In the autumn of 1964 the Charlestown Committee mounted a broader attack on government policy by publishing *Broadsheet No. 1* which, highlighting some of the Second Programme's projections, alleged that a policy of land clearances was under way: 'the truth is industry, banking, big business have taken over the State. They speak through policy-making civil service cadres, who preserve the appearance of democratic government by using Ministers as their public relations officers.' A series of handwritten notes preserve the reaction to this *Broadsheet* among the indicted civil servants. First, within Finance Whitaker wrote to Murray that 'this shows how reasonable & fair the Charlestown Committee are'. Murray responded:

> This wd. be laughable (because it is so infantile) were it not so serious. These are the people who want to decide policy in conjunction with the Central Development Ctee. We should insist that they adopt a reasonable attitude. We don't ask them to agree with official policy – but there are ways of disagreeing. I suggest that this be shown to the Minister and the Taoiseach in view of the pressures exerted by the Charlestown Ctee to have a voice in policy formation.

From the Taoiseach's Department Assistant Secretary Tadgh O'Cearbhaill confirmed that 'the Taoiseach has seen – and asked M/Social Welfare to hasten submission to Government of proposals for amending the Unemployment Assistance Acts'. In response Boland wrote that 'recent outbreaks of propaganda in connection with this problem have increased my concern to have this submitted to the Government at the earliest possible date'.[47]

Social Welfare featured in consideration of policy relating to small western farms in two main ways. First, in conjunction with the 1965 Land Act, the manner in which means testing for the old age pension was carried out changed to encourage the transfer of land from the inactive old to the active young. But, as Hannan and Commins (1992: 98) note, 'special pension schemes to induce elderly farmers to retire, and release the use or ownership of their land to other farmers, did not prove attractive to the targeted population'. Second, the Report of the Inter-Departmental Committee suggested that 'the basis of qualification for unemployment assistance should be reviewed in so far as smallholders are concerned to remove the present disincentive effect' whilst also appreciating 'the difficulties of devising a system which would not have unfortunate side effects'. Lemass was initially inclined to dwell on the difficulties inherent in such a change. When he met a deputation from the Charlestown Committee in July 1963 the most he could offer was the possibility of 'suspending means assessments for, say, three years so that a small farmer at present qualifying for Unemployment Assistance would be assured of a continuation of payments for a certain number

of years despite increases in income from vegetable growing or other productive activity'.[48] But the new assistance scheme for western smallholders enacted
in 1965 went a great deal further than this and ran along the lines advocated in
many speeches from Charlestown Committee platforms. Means were henceforth to be calculated by reference to the rateable valuation of the land with £20
per annum of income imputed for each £1 valuation of the land exclusive of the
valuation of the buildings. As the Department of Social Welfare (1968: 23) put it,
'under the liberalising effects of the new method' small farmers should now 'be
able to take full advantage of the many schemes that have been devised for the
benefit of the Western areas' without imperilling their unemployment assistance
payments. The following year the Employment Period Orders that had since the
1930s been used to restrict payment of unemployment assistance to small farmers to certain months of the year were abolished and it became a year-round
source of smallholder income (Cousins 2003: 63–64; McCashin 2004: 201).

Such a shift suggests that the ruling party was nervous about the effect of
the Charlestown Committee's campaign on its electoral support. In June 1964
Sean Flanagan, who had captained Mayo to All-Ireland football success before a
political career that had brought him to the verge of Cabinet rank, was 'deeply
concerned about the present situation':

> Since some of the more important men in the Charlestown Committee have been
> our best supporters in the past, they can do a great deal of damage merely by being
> lukewarm now. As for the others – and this has been Fr. McDyer's approach right
> through – they will spread discontent with all politics and politicians.[49]

Laying the blame for depopulation and developmental failure at the door of
party politics had long been a strand of Irish Catholic social thought, with Joseph
Hanly's National Action group as its most single-minded exponent. Fr. McDyer
echoed this in calls 'to soar above the splintering and stultifying effects of party
politics … [A]ll those who are committed to parties are good Irishmen, but they
will be better Irishmen if they sink their differences and unite in defence of the
West.'[50] National Action did on one occasion contest an election but, thanks to
a combination of priestly and personal considerations, Fr. McDyer would not
countenance a similar move. He would later regret not having agreed to organise
a march on Dublin from the West of Ireland: 'at least it would have drawn attention to the pressure building up behind the proposal to form a Western political
party'. He then derived consolation from the reflection that 'it is almost certain
that the intensity of this campaign in the West did highlight the neglected condition of the more remote counties and certainly galvanised the government into
making a greater effort on their behalf' (McDyer 1984: 85).

The central focus of the Charlestown movement – and inevitably coupled with Mayo's own Michael Davitt – Fr. McDyer derived a prestige which made him publicly unassailable from his regeneration project in Glencolumbkille and his position was further strengthened by the Church hierarchy's facilitation of his wider western campaigning. Both factors, however, operated to constrain his radicalism. The people might be called on to take back their state from the interests that would clear the west in *Broadsheet No. 1* but various Glencolumbkille enterprises were dependent on Fr. McDyer's ongoing ability to work the system on their behalf. The western bishops wrote to the Taoiseach expressing support for the Charlestown Committee in June 1964, but compared with other interventions – such as that on the Agricultural Institute issue discussed in Chapter 4 above with its specific demands in relation to the NUI and to Trinity College – this was a limp epistle that combined lamentation over the state of the west with advocacy of 'a combined effort of Government and people' to ameliorate it. As Patrick Smith, Minister for Agriculture, commented, 'it is too general to help even as a guide to their thinking on the kind of solutions we should look for'.[51] Illustrative of the twin constraints is a letter from Fr. McDyer to CDC chairman J. H. Harman written in November 1966 while NFA protestors were camped outside the Department of Agriculture. In it Fr. McDyer when next in Dublin proposes phoning Harman from Bord Failte's offices to make arrangements to meet. Harman's Finance office isn't a suitable venue because 'if I appear in Merrion Sq. I will be expected to be photographed with Mr. Deasy and his colleagues. This would incur ecclesiastical displeasure here.'[52]

A division between militants and moderates existed within the Save the West movement which, after the replacement of Smith by Charles Haughey as Minister for Agriculture in October 1964, the government would skilfully exploit by multiple consultation exercises and the cultivation of clerical goodwill by the CDC and CDTs through a series of special seminars held in a variety of western locations.[53] 'Physically unable to bear the pressure but also because there was a danger that the momentum would be lost in Glencolumbkille', Fr. McDyer stepped back from his Save the West campaigning in 1968, a loss that triggered the movement's disintegration (McDyer 1984: 86; Varley and Curtin 1999: 74).

The social sciences and the salvation of the west

What social science input was there into the official package of initiatives designed to address western small farm problems? Foras Taluntais was represented on the Inter-Departmental Committee and publications by two of its Rural Economy Division staff, E. A. Attwood (1962) and Rosemary Fennell (1962), joined a variety of departmental memoranda in the documentation for a meeting of ministers Lemass convened in June 1962 to press for follow-up on the recommendations of that committee's report. Lemass also had a series of complaints recorded in Fennell's survey of grant-aided industries in the Congested Districts followed up with the relevant departments.[54] In the case of the IDA 'one of the effective nudges towards a small industries programme was the publication of the Limerick Rural Survey', where Newman's contribution had drawn attention to similar initiatives in other countries.[55] As the CDC prepared to hold meetings for western clergy, one of its members, Dr. Henry Spain of Agriculture, in December 1967 suggested that these 'could be organised in the context of the Christus Rex organisation in which the best of the diocesan priests were active'. Similarly, in February 1969, it was suggested in the context of ongoing contacts with the clergy at another CDC meeting 'that it might be a good idea to have a Priest or Minister as speaker at future seminars – possibly a sociologist who would be briefed beforehand'.[56] Neither suggestion seems to have been followed up.

When the development officers themselves met in Athlone in May 1969 one of the speakers who addressed them was Fr. Harry Bohan. Ordained in 1963 for the diocese of Killaloe, Fr. Bohan subsequently embarked on postgraduate study in Cardiff under George Thomason, an admirer of Muintir who from the early 1960s contributed to its adoption of international community development theory (Thomason 1961, 1962a and 1962b). On his return to Ireland, Fr. Bohan was in 1968 seconded by his diocese to work with Muintir as its first (and only) community organisation officer. Muintir had envisaged that the salaries and expenses of these officers would be funded by 'industrial, commercial and professional interests, on the general argument that as long as local communities remain viable purchasing power and manpower will continue'. However, the movement found itself having to support its officer out of its own funds 'because of the failure to raise the necessary money from the local industrial, commercial and professional people in the counties of Galway and Clare'.[57]

A grant from the SRDF subsequently supported a community leadership course conducted by Thomason and Fr. Bohan in Lahinch in September 1969. This was attended by groups from the counties of Clare, Galway, Mayo and Roscommon within which clergy and laity were equally represented. Supporting a proposal to provide funding for the course, CDC chairman J. H. Harman wrote to the Secretary of Finance that 'Fr. Bohan is very active and progressive and is already making a big impression on the clergy inside and outside his home diocese.'[58] Discussion of the course proposal reveals Muintir to have been viewed in a much less positive light in official rural development circles. Complaints were aired of its being 'more active in some areas than in others', it was said to be 'dominated by the clergy at Committee level' while its' 'practical efforts' were described as having 'left something to be desired'. Regarding Muintir as inter-denominational, Archbishop McQuaid had denied the movement access to his archdiocese; however, in a newly ecumenical climate, it was regarded by some as being insufficiently inter-denominational.[59] But, whatever its intrinsic merits, 1960s religious ecumenism was not necessarily an aid to official development efforts. Of a meeting held in Ballybofey in February 1969 with substantial Protestant participation it was observed that 'the Clergy were slightly overawed by the ecumenism of the occasion in that while all the speakers made reference to cooperation by the clergy in the work of development, no questions were asked as to how this could be achieved. The Development Officer felt that the meeting had lacked bite.'[60]

Another speaker addressing the May 1969 meeting of development officers was John Raven of the ESRI. Raven had earlier sent J. H. Harman a subsequently published paper (Raven 1971) which argued that the rate of economic development in a society was greater the more a specified set of (eleven) attitudes was diffused within it. Moreover 'people can be explicitly encouraged to develop these characteristics and ... society can be modified so that people who have a spontaneous tendency to behave in this way can be more effective'. Indeed 'these changes can be brought about relatively quickly, not only in children but in adults as well. You *can* teach an old dog new tricks.' With an input of American expertise, such teaching could in Ireland make an impact not only on potential business entrepreneurs but also on community development and on education more generally. Raven was keen to discuss these ideas with the county development officers and got an opportunity to do so at the Athlone meeting. The meeting's minutes indicate considerable interest in his ideas, with IDA programmes looming ever larger in CDT work and a perceived need 'to evolve a pattern or standard of judgement by which to measure applicants applying for grants'.[61]

As well as funding the Lahinch community leadership course, SRDF money was also to play a central role in a revitalisation of UCG's adult education programme at the end of the 1960s. Under the successive direction of two Franciscan professors, Feilim O'Briain and Edwin Rabbitte, UCG had since 1949 run an extra-mural diploma course in social and economic studies in Connacht and Clare 'on a limited scale due to financial stringencies'. Anticipating the national initiative of the following year, the UCG governing body in 1968 commissioned a review of its extra-mural activities by Con Murphy. In 1969 with Padraig MacDiarmada taking over from Rabbitte and the SRDF injecting funds, expansion got under way, with a social action diploma course focused on community leadership being offered at a larger number of centres. In one centre a conflict arose between a new and an old course:

Sligo Town had an old Social Diploma Course started at the behest of the then Bishop of Elphin. University College Galway made a value judgement on it and decided to replace it with the leadership-orientated course. I need hardly explain why Sligo town ended up having two courses – while Mayo and Galway went without. The Bishop was right and Galway University was right – except the bishop's course turned out to be more right than the other. It is true that the people of Sligo Town had a democratic choice of courses: the Bishop's course or the other one. The faithful were given the message from the pulpit quite publicly. And then out around the catchment area the words was quietly spread that 'the other course' did not have the official blessing because you had to be careful of the Communistic tinges of some of the lecturers. Slightly pink. Guess which course was stuffed? Guess which course had room to spare when – at every other centre – the punters had to be turned away and denied, some for a second time, a chance from society to get a few crumbs of the educational cake?

This May 1971 account from the Backbencher column in the *Irish Times* written by John Healy (a Charlestown native and prominent commentator on the problems besetting the west)[62] recalled the tactics successfully used against Labour by Jack Lynch's Fianna Fail in the 1969 general election (Puirseil 2007: 268) and drew attention to a western educational juxtaposition of famine and feast that was not confined to university extra-mural courses (see McGahern 2005: 168). Education was not one of the departments represented on the Inter-Departmental Committee but the 1962 report contained two suggestions relating to its field. These were, first, that 'a rural bias should be given to the general education of pupils in rural schools' and, second, that 'the facilities available at the Vocational Schools should be brought within reach of all children in remote areas by organising transport or extending scholarship schemes'. The push for follow-up on the report by Lemass was to provide a context within which a much further-reaching initiative was shaped, one that responded to wider internal and external forces pushing for educational change in Ireland (Walsh 2009; Peter Murray 2009).

On the grounds that, whether it was embodied in religious congregations or lay people, private enterprise had failed to supply adequate secondary schooling in remote locations and that families with children would not stay in places without educational opportunities, a proposal for a 'Comprehensive Post-Primary Education Pilot Scheme related to Small Farm areas' was brought forward in January 1963. Despite considerable watering down in the course of discussions with bishops (Clarke 2010), state-established schools would for the first time provide academic secondary education, breaking out of the confines of an understanding with the Catholic Church dating back to the establishment of the vocational education system in the early 1930s.

Ironically the remoteness factor does not seem to have unduly depressed western educational participation. As Education pointed out in December 1965 when asked for input into the preparation of replies to parliamentary questions on western disadvantage, 'a higher proportion of the population is at secondary or vocational school in Connaught than is the case in Dublin County Borough or in Leinster as a whole'.[63] Yet John Healy (1968: 74–75) contrasted deep frustration among small farmers in Mayo at the failure of the 1965 Land Act to produce substantial redistribution with the secondary education initiatives pushed through by Donogh O'Malley, where 'they have been able to see the actuality of mini-buses bringing their children into school "for free" and you get one spark of hope'. Twenty-five years later, Hannan and Commins (1992: 92–95) would highlight how 'not only have smallholders as a class succeeded in retaining their property and their relative income position' but had also used the expanded education system very effectively to gain access for their children to a high proportion of the available off-farm employment opportunities. More recent studies have built on this work to explore the agrarian dimension of welfare state development through Irish case studies (Fahey 2002: Carey 2007).

Conclusion

With the creation of the ESRI and the preceding denial of support to the various research institute or centre proposals discussed in Chapter 5, empirical sociology was moved out of the ambit of its original champion, the Catholic social movement, and into that of the state's policy-making. There it was connected to Finance's project of a Social Development Programme which was envisaged as a framework within which social spending would rise in a controlled and prioritised way in line with the generation of additional resources by economic growth. In fact such planning for social development as took place for the Third Programme did so in the absence of major input from ESRI research and the pattern of social spending under that programme was at variance with the target rates that it specified for different areas. An unrealistic conception of what and when social science research could deliver to the programming process was one key weakness of this Finance project. Compounding this was the legacy of the decades in which Finance had played the role of the political system's 'abominable no man'. This had deeply ingrained suspicion of its proposals and meant that the concept of a Social Development Programme was not endorsed by other departments whose support it required.

   In the comprehensive schools specifically rural and western development planning produced a nationally important educational initiative. Support structures for 'pluriactive' households that were to be boosted in the 1970s by the higher farm incomes that accompanied EEC membership and the more dispersed industrialisation pattern over which the revamped IDA presided were also created. Cultivation of community leadership was strongly emphasised in this planning context. As we have seen, John Raven at the ESRI explicitly aligned the community leader's role with that of business entrepreneur, and entrepreneurship study was also taken up by Fr. Harry Bohan as he pursued his work on rural development outside the ambit of Muintir during the 1970s. Focusing on entrepreneurs 'who were all Irish and local, either by birth or adoption' and on the state and other support services available to people like them, Fr. Bohan concluded that 'if we are to develop native industry then more fundamental changes will have to be made' and that 'a system that promotes foreign industry can be almost irrelevant to native industry' (Bohan 1979: 64 and 73). The overwhelming emphasis the IDA placed on attracting foreign investment meant that, while national industrial policy shifted radically away from protectionism, politics of the clientelistic and localistic variety continued to be a feature of its implementation, with the IDA replacing Industry and Commerce in the patron's role.

In 'Laketown', a south Mayo locality whose development association was the subject of a case study by Curtin and Varley (1986), 'the consensus was that, given the competition for outside industry, the Association's only hope was to strike up a special relationship with the state so that Laketown would get favoured treatment in the allocation of industry'. More specifically, 'the problem, as [Development Association] members saw it was that Laketown, lacking its own politician, was disadvantaged *vis-à-vis* other towns who could use their representatives to help them in competition for industry' (Curtin and Varley 1986: 182). Others drew similar conclusions. A decade after the collapse of the Charlestown Committee's campaign, Fr. McDyer's mantle as priest-champion for western investment would be taken up by Fr. James Horan, who eventually succeeded in overcoming hostility or indifference to his Knock airport project on the part of Dublin-based civil servants and ministers. In Knock Fr. Horan adopted a distinctly locality-centred approach to electoral politics. He believed that 'people who vote according to family tradition vote with their feet and not with their heads' and he advocated voting for candidates 'who were capable and willing to work for the development of the area' (Horan 1992: 173).

In 1961 the future of the 'small (mainly western) farms' had been characterised by Sean Lemass as 'the main, if not indeed the only question arising in national economic policy to which we have not yet found a satisfactory answer'. In a more modest vein, T. K. Whitaker in 1967 pointed, as the best indication of what planning could achieve, to the performance of the economy between 1958 and 1963, when 'we achieved a steady growth rate, a fairly stable price level, rising employment and a reasonable balance in our external payments'. But the external environment for this performance began to take a distinct turn for the worse when severe balance of payments difficulties prompted Britain's new Labour government to impose a hefty surcharge on a wide range of imports in late 1964. A sterling devaluation would follow in 1967, with further measures to curb imports being resorted to in 1968. The appearance of a large Irish balance of payments deficit in 1965 prompted the introduction in 1966 of restrictions on credit and two budgets which increased taxation on incomes, private motor vehicles, petrol and tobacco as well as introducing a 'selective' (but wide-ranging) wholesale tax. The incidence of strikes rose after 1965 and the NFA pursued a campaign of street protests that embroiled it in bitter conflict with the government in 1966–67.

All of this proved fatal to the ambitious planning concept that had been embodied in the Second Programme for Economic Expansion: 'disconcerted by a relatively minor recession in 1966, as a result of which the Government feared the plan targets for 1970 would not be met, it dropped the Second Programme in 1967 and substituted a far less detailed Third Programme, designed to fudge all the key issues as a preliminary to dropping altogether the concept of quantified targets at the end of the decade' (FitzGerald 1991: 59). As the 1970s began, the fairly stable price level of the early 1960s was a distant memory. Serious inflation preceded both the first oil price shock and entry into the EEC's relatively high food price regime. The beginning of this chronic inflation is traced by Kieran Kennedy and Brendan Dowling (1975: 263–268) to the knock-on effects of the 1967 sterling devaluation. Into this fed further increases in the cost of food as Irish cattle prices rose against the backdrop of a world shortage of beef. Conflict between farmers and government unsurprisingly subsided, while strike activity remained high as the purchasing power of wages and salaries fell. Further fuel was added by the governmental predilection for indirect taxation, with rates rising particularly steeply in the 1969 and 1970 budgets. This was reflected in consumer price index changes and thereafter in higher pay demands. Overall economic growth continued but the vulnerability of indigenous industries officially supposed to be undergoing adaptation to freer trade conditions increased. Just as the economy began to be seriously opened up to competing manufactured imports, inflation critically weakened the competitive position of manufacturing production for the home market.

By the time the Irish state joined the EEC in 1973 both its old parsimony and its new-fangled planning had effectively fallen by the wayside. But, as this played out, the pace of economic and social change was continuing to quicken. In the final chapter we turn to look at how relations between Church and state altered during and after the rise and fall of planning.

Notes

1   NAI, DT 97/6/312, copy of K. Boland, Minister for Social Welfare, to J. Ryan, Minister for Finance, 15/1/1965.

2   Report of the Committee on Irish Finance (Primrose Committee), *Parliamentary Papers 1912–13*, vol. XXIV.

3   NAI, DF 2001/3/952, CHM to Secretary, 6/7/1964, T. K. Whitaker, Finance, to W. A. Honohan, Social Welfare, 27/8/64.

4   NAI, DT S17,685/95, 'Some Notes on Department of Social Welfare', 11/9/1964, Taoiseach to Assistant Secretary, 14/9/1964.

5   For an example of Lemass prodding one of his ministers into responding to critical press comments see NAI, DT S12,891 D/2/62, S. Lemass, Taoiseach, to P. Hillery, Minister for Education, 23/11/1962.

6   NAI, DT S17,474 D/95, K. Boland, Minister for Social Welfare, to S. Lemass, Taoiseach, 16/9/1964, enclosing "Social Security in Ireland and Western Europe by P.R. Kaim-Caudle", S. Lemass, Taoiseach, to K. Boland, Minister for Social Welfare, 17/9/1964.

7   NAI, DF 2001/3/952, N. O'Nuallain, Taoiseach, to T. K. Whitaker, Finance, 17/9/1964; NAI, DT S17,685/95, T. K. Whitaker, Finance, to N. O'Nuallain, Taoiseach, 23/9/1964, N. O'Nuallain, Taoiseach, to T. K. Whitaker, Finance, 23/9/1964.

8   NAI, DT S17,678/95, J. Garvin, Local Government, to N. O'Nuallain, Taoiseach, 29/9/1964, 'Pattern of Social Development – Note of Interdepartmental discussion', 8/10/1964, Social Welfare to Taoiseach, 9/11/1964, S. Lemass to K. Boland, 1/12/1964, K. Boland to S. Lemass, 16/12/1964.

9   NAI, DT S13,384 K/62, Memorandum for the Government, 9 Feabhra 1962, 'The General Level of Social Welfare Payments', S. Lemass, Taoiseach, to K. Boland, Minister for Social Welfare, 10/2/1962, K. Boland to S. Lemass, 12/2/1962; NAI, DT S13,384 L/62, copy of government decision, 1/5/1962, K. Boland to S. Lemass, 30/5/1962, S. Lemass to K. Boland, 31/5/1962.

10 NAI, DT S17,474 B/63, Secretary, Health, to Secretary, Social Welfare, 11/12/1963, S. MacEntee, Minister for Health, to K. Boland, Minister for Social Welfare, 18/12/1963; NAI, DT S17,474 B/95, K. Boland to S. MacEntee, 8/1/1964.

11 NAI, DT 97/6/312, K. Boland, Minister for Social Welfare, to S. Lemass, Taoiseach, 31/12/1964, enclosing copy of K. Boland to J. Ryan, Minister for Finance, 31/12/64, J. Ryan to S. Lemass, 7/1/1965, enclosing copy of J. Ryan to K. Boland, 7/1/1965; NAI, DT 97/6/85, K. Boland to S. Lemass, 15/1/1965, enclosing copy of K. Boland to J. Ryan, 15/1/65.

12 NAI, DT 97/9/173, P. Garvey, Tuam, to S. Lemass, Taoiseach, 15/12/1964.

13 NAI, DT 97/6/85, K. Boland, Minister for Social Welfare, to S. Lemass, Taoiseach, 4/2/1965, enclosing K. Boland to J. Ryan, Minister for Finance, 4/2/1965; NAI, DT 97/6/312, J. Ryan to S. Lemass, 22/3/1965, enclosing copies of K. Boland to J. Ryan, 15/1/65, J. Ryan to K. Boland, 22/2/19665 and K. Boland to J. Ryan, 5/3/1965.

14 NAI, DT 97/6/312, S. Lemass, Taoiseach, to K. Boland, Minister for Social Welfare, 28/1/65, K. Boland to S. Lemass, 2/2/1965, S. Lemass to K. Boland, 3/2/1965.

15   NAI, DT 97/6/312, letter from Irish Medical Association is appended to Department
     of Health memorandum, 25/3/1965, copy of Breathnach, Finance, to Secretary,
     Social Welfare, 22/3/1965, Department of Social Welfare, Memorandum for the
     Government, 24/3/1965, 'Proposal to raise the remuneration limit for social
     insurance', p. 11.
16   Dail Debates, 13/5/1965, cols 1301 and 1302.
17   For notes and press clippings see NAI, DF 2001/3/952.
18   NAI, DT 97/6/209, 'A preliminary bird's eye review of the Social Welfare Services
     with some indications of the Minister's tentative ideas on reform' is enclosed with
     K. Boland, Minister for Social Welfare, to S. Lemass, Taoiseach, 22/2/1965.
19   NAI, DT 97/6/209, J. Lynch, Minister for Finance, to S. Lemass, Taoiseach, 26/5/
     1965.
20   NAI, DF 2001/3/952, Department of Finance, Memorandum for the Government,
     'Social Development Programme', 24/8/1965, Secretary, Taoiseach, to Secretary,
     Finance, 31/8/1965.
21   NAI, DF 2001/3/952, CHM to Secretary, 9/11/65, note of discussion between M. D.
     McCarthy, director, Central Statistics Office, and Finance officers, 26/11/1965.
22   NAI, DF 2001/3/952, M. D. McCarthy, director, Central Statistics Office, to T. K.
     Whitaker, Finance, 21/12/1965, T. K. Whitaker to M. D. McCarthy 24/12/65, note
     on meeting of M. D. McCarthy and Brian Kissane with Social Welfare officers, 21/12/
     1965, note on meeting of M. D. McCarthy and Brian Kissane with Health officers, 5/
     1/1966.
23   ESRI, box 1, History of ERI/ESRI, file 'No. 1 Closed', M. D. McCarthy, director,
     Central Statistics Office, to T. K. Whitaker, Finance, 14/10/1966.
24   ESRI, box 1, History of ERI/ESRI, file 'Institute of Public Administration, 59
     Lansdowne Road, Dublin 4, Social Research Council', 'Report on Development of
     Social Research in Ireland Comments from James Kavanagh, Lecturer in Social Science,
     U.C.D.', 'Report on Development of Social Research in Ireland Comments from the
     Department of Social Science, U.C.D.'.
25   NAI DFA 2001/3/952, copy of Rev. Professor E. F. O'Doherty, UCD, to D. Walsh,
     Secretary, Human Sciences Committee, 11/11/1965.
26   ESRI, box 1, History of ERI/ESRI, file 'Institute of Public Administration, 59
     Lansdowne Road, Dublin 4, Social Research Council', Fr. J. O'Leary, UCC, to M. D.
     McCarthy, director, Central Statistics Office, 1/2/1966, Fr. L. Ryan, UCC, to M. D.
     McCarthy, 8/2/1966.
27   NAI, DFA 2001/3/952, copy of Fr. E. O'hEideain, UCG, to D. Walsh, Secretary,
     Human Sciences Committee, 19/11/1965.
28   'Resentment at Minister's Criticism', Irish Times, 10/6/1971.
29   NAI, DT 97/6/85, K. Boland, Minister for Social Welfare, to S. Lemass, Taoiseach, 25/
     5/1966, S. Lemass to K. Boland, 27/5/1966.
30   NAI, DT 98/6/689, 'Financing Social Services by Insurance. Report of
     Interdepartmental Group on the question of financing Social Welfare, Health and
     Education on the tripartite insurance principle', February 1967.

31 M. Fogarty, 'Our Angry Young Men Are Taking Over', *Irish Digest*, July 1958, pp. 3–6, 'condensed from the *Commonweal* (New York)'.

32 NAI, DT S16,705 B/61, Seanad Eireann Notice of Motion, 13/3/1961, 'That Seanad Eireann regrets to note that all the senior staff of the Economic Research Institute (with the sole exception of the Director) have been recruited everywhere except in Ireland' (Senator John O'Donovan).

33 NAI, DFA 2001/3/1468, memorandum from C. H. Murray to M. Breathnach, 25/8/1967.

34 NAI, DT S18,149, C. H. Murray, Finance, to N. O'Nuallain, Taoiseach, 27/2/1968, *Third Programme: Economic and Social Development 1969–72*, p. 19.

35 NAI, DT 99/1/394, J. Brennan, Minister for Social Welfare, to J. Lynch, Taoiseach, 29/9/1967.

36 NAI, DFA 2001/3/1468, memorandum from BK to Mr. Murray, 6/3/1968.

37 NAI, DT 2000/6/399, copy of W. A. Honohan to Aire [i.e. Minister for Social Welfare], 7/2/69.

38 NAI, DT 2000/6/399, G. FitzGerald, 'Defects – But Programme Has Its Merits, Too', *Irish Times*, 7/3/1969, clipping.

39 NAI, DT 2004/21/385, G. FitzGerald, 'Progress with Third Programme', *Irish Times*, 6/5/1971, clipping.

40 NAI, DT S17,032 A/61, S. Lemass, Taoiseach, to J. Ryan, Minister for Finance, 6/3/1961, J. Ryan to S. Lemass, 9/3/1961.

41 NAI, DT S17,032 A/61, copy of T. K. Whitaker, Finance, to J. J. Nagle, Agriculture, 27/10/1960, copy of Nagle to Whitaker, 17/2/1961, copy of T. K. Whitaker to J. J. Nagle, 22/2/1961, S. Lemass, Taoiseach, to J. Ryan, Minister for Finance, 11/3/1961.

42 See correspondence, memoranda, etc. in the succession of files NAI DT S17,032 A/61 to NAI DT S17,032 F/63.

43 NAI, DT S17,032 I/95, 'Committee in Defence of the West', *Western People*, 5/12/1965, clipping, J. Ryan, Minister for Finance, to S. Lemass, Taoiseach, 9/3/1961.

44 NAI, DT S17,032 I/95, especially P. Smith, Minister for Agriculture, to S. Lemass, Taoiseach, 25/6/1964, J. Ryan, Minister for Finance, to Lemass, 1/7/1964.

45 NAI, DT S17,032 I/95, Fr. J. McDyer, Glencolumbkille, to S. Lemass, Taoiseach, 15/5/1964.

46 NAI, DT S17,032 I/95, 'Government Rebuffs Small Farmer Deputation', *Irish Independent*, 21/5/1964, clipping, 'Charlestown Committee Will Go It Alone, *Western People*, 23/5/1964, clipping.

47 NAI, DET&E 2002/67/48, *Penny Broadsheet No. 1*, sheet with handwritten comments by Whitaker and Murray, 29/10/1964, TOC to Whitaker, 29/10/1964; NAI, DT S17,474 D/95, S. Lemass, Taoiseach, to K. Boland, Minister for Social Welfare, 23/10/1964, K. Boland to S. Lemass, 26/10/1964.

48 NAI, DT S17,032 G/63, report of meeting, Economic Development in Western Areas, 25/7/1963.

49 NAI, DT S17,032 I/95, S. Flanagan TD to S. Lemass, Taoiseach, 13/6/1964.

50   NAI, DT S17,032 I/95, 'The West Will Not Accept Depopulation', *Western People*, 19/12/1964, clipping.

51   NAI, DT S17,032 I/95, J. Fergus, Bishop of Achonry, to S. Lemass, Taoiseach, 27/6/1964, conveying letter over names of six western bishops, 24/6/1964, P. Smith, Minister for Agriculture, to S. Lemass, Taoiseach, 1/7/1964.

52   NAI, DET&E 2002/67/48, Fr. J. McDyer, Glencolumbkille, to J. H. Harman, Finance, 3/11/1966.

53   NAI, DET&E 2002/67/48; NAI, DT 96/6/269; NAI, DET&E 2002/67/217.

54   See NAI, DT S17,032 B/62; NAI, DT S17,032 C/62; NAI, DT S17,032 D/62.

55   Michael Viney, 'The I.D.A. Learns to Think Small', *Irish Times*, 28/5/1968.

56   NAI, DET&E 2002/67/217, extract from minutes of CDC meeting, 8/12/1967, extract from minutes of CDC meeting, 12/2/1969.

57   NAI, DET&E 2002/67/25 Part I, T. Roseingrave, Muintir na Tire, to Secretary, Education, 21/6/1968, T. Roseingrave to B. O'Foghlu, Education, 1/8/1968; NAI, DET&E 2002/67/25 Part II, T. Roseingrave to B. O'Foghlu, 16/6/1969.

58   NAI, DET&E 2002/67/25 Part II, JH to Secretary [of Finance], 17/7/1969.

59   NAI, DET&E 2002/67/415, extract from minutes of CDC meeting, 16/5/1969.

60   NAI DET&E 2002/67/217, extract from minutes of CDC meeting, 12/2/1969.

61   NAI DET&E 2002/67/217, J. Raven, ESRI, to J. H. Harman, Finance, 15/4/1969, extract from minutes of meeting of Development Officers, Athlone, 13 and 14 May, 1969.

62   NAI DET&E 2002/67/217, Backbencher column, *Irish Times*, 29/5/1971, clipping.

63   NAI, DT 96/6/269, S. MacGearailt, Education, to Secretary, Taoiseach, 9/12/1965.

7

Conclusion

Introduction

Sketching a wider context for the survey data on vocations they were presenting to the hierarchy in 1971, Frs. Newman, Ward and Ryan produced a highly ambivalent appraisal of the changes wrought by 'Whitakerism' or 'Lemassism'. The successful redefinition of life 'in such a manner that hope, opportunity, promise, success, and all that made life meaningful were seen in purely economic terms' had produced 'a stabilisation and an overcoming of alienation' whose disappearing symptoms included 'late marriages, no marriages, emigration, banning the literature of the contemporary world' and the superabundance of religious vocations. But a 'second stage alienation' was now becoming evident which 'finds an outlet in drugs, in strikes and protests, in cries against bureaucracy and demands for involvement and participation. And students and intellectuals and others are beginning to say that something has gone wrong and society must be changed.' These symptoms were appearing 'precisely where the new philosophy of life has been most successful – in the cities'. The new philosophy created 'its own forms of alienation' because 'it is, in the last analysis, a pseudo-definition of life'. Yet, in spite of this characterisation, they conclude that 'the redefinition of life in purely economic terms is not entirely wrong': 'in many ways, it offers the first real hope of a solution to Ireland's problems for fifty, perhaps even for one hundred and fifty, years' (Newman, Ward and Ryan 1971: 49).

Orchestrating the production of *Economic Development*, Whitaker had been at pains to avoid being seen as operating within 'purely economic terms'. Its introduction concludes with an acknowledgement of the inspiration that Whitaker derived while 'pressing on with this study despite the claims of ordinary office work' from Dr. William Philbin's observation that since achieving self-government 'we have shown little initiative or organisational ability in agriculture and industry and commerce' and the accompanying suggestion that 'there is here the widest and most varied field for the play of the vital force that our religion contains'. Whitaker's study was thus presented as being 'a contribution, in the spirit advocated by the Bishop of Clonfert, towards the working out of the national good in the economic sphere' (Department of Finance 1958: 9). But discord between churchmen and economic planning enthusiasts soon put in an appearance. When Patrick Lynch spoke at a Tuairim seminar in April 1959 he referred to Bishop Philbin as being 'a distinguished source of Mr. Whitaker's inspiration'. But he was also quoted by the *Irish Times* as saying that 'we shall welcome the day when churchmen generally courageously address themselves to public affairs and indicate, by the circumstances and settings of their statements, and perhaps by their conflicting views, that their statements are personal ones, deriving their support not from faith and/or morals, but from technical knowledge, experience, intelligence and good sense'.[1] In a letter to the newspaper Jeremiah Newman, having quoted at length from Pope Pius XII, concluded that 'we feel sure that Mr. Lynch would not want his statement to give the impression that the knowledge necessary for adequate analysis of public affairs is always limited exclusively to politics and economics and that churchmen cannot sometimes teach, not merely with competence but with authority, concerning the moral aspect of public affairs'.[2]

On this occasion the controversy was brought to an end by Lynch's response that 'it was clear, I think, to my Tuairim audience, if not to Professor Newman' that he had been commenting on a specific remark by Bishop Browne of Galway denigrating 'all those highly-paid officials of the Department of External Affairs, Coras Trachtala and an Bord Failte, who have been tripping over one another in New York without obvious benefit to Ireland'. Pronouncements of this sort, Lynch concluded, were hardly what the pope had had in mind when making the statement that Newman had quoted.[3] Six years later, however, Lynch would move from specific to general criticism and, in the company of his fellow economist Garret FitzGerald, cast a cold eye over Irish Catholic sociology. Then his *Studies* respondent would be Fr. James Kavanagh rather than Newman.

The exchange in *Studies* was prompted by its editor's posing of the question: 'what sort of Ireland do we want to see here in ten years' time?' Responding in its winter 1964 issue, Garret FitzGerald – then a UCD economics lecturer whose circumstances (FitzGerald 1991: 51–52) lent support to John Vaizey's 1959 observation that Irish academic economists had salaries 'so low that they have to hold innumerable jobs' – identified the 'urgent need to develop an agreed philosophy for social action'. Such a development required the qualified acceptance, rather than the exclusion, of English liberal ideas and socialist thought:

> If we can successfully graft these liberal and socialist ideas, themselves largely Christian in their origin and inspiration, on to the particular form in which the

Christian tradition displays itself in our country in this generation, we may succeed in developing an internally consistent philosophy of our own, appropriate to the needs of the times in which we live, and clearly superior to the excessive conservatism sometimes found in Catholic attitudes, as well as to the wishy-washy liberalism common in Britain, and the doctrinaire socialism of other countries.

Sociology is given a central role in this process of national philosophical development:

> A fostering of sociological studies may at first sight appear an odd approach to the problem of creating a valid and specifically Irish philosophy of life, but the fact is that it is in this area that we are at present most inadequate, while at the same time having the greatest potentialities. If we fail through studies of this kind, among others, to synthesize the Christian, liberal and socialist traditions into a system of thought that is internally consistent and suited to the needs of our society, this society may flounder under the pressure of the contradictions within itself flowing from the pressure of these different ideas. (FitzGerald 1964b: 344)

Here an anomic state in which the 'liberal Irish Catholic' might eventually lose faith in himself as well as in Christianity is envisaged by the author, who then proceeds to critique Catholic social teaching in Ireland. The Church is credited with leaning towards the worker and small farmer rather than the employer or large landowner and with having contributed, through its acceptance of the 1937 Constitution, to developing an advanced type of Church–state relationship. In its thinking on social welfare, however, 'in the 1930's and 1940's the Irish Church took a wrong turning'. Yet a substantial portion of the laity have reached an accommodation between 'the traditional anti-socialist views of many of their clergy and what they have instinctively felt to be valid aspects of modern liberalism and socialism'. Upon this base the 'inspired pragmatism' of 'politicians, administrators and men of affairs' is building. Some progress has been made in state provision of social security and, within a predominantly private enterprise economy, a sector of productive state companies has been created. Consultative mechanisms concerned with adapting the economy and increasing its efficiency levels now involve civil servants, employers and trade unions although further progress is threatened by class tension for which an acquisitive bourgeoisie with an appetite for conspicuous consumption is held to be primarily responsible. The modern Irish society that FitzGerald hopes to see emerge would be 'profoundly Christian, idealistic, liberal, proudly Irish but antipathetical to traditional nationalism, outward-looking and reconciled to the better manifestations of the modern world' – although even with these aspirations the author is strikingly slow to contemplate denominational desegregation within the education system.

The next issue of *Studies* carried Lynch's contribution, in which FitzGerald's criticism of Irish Catholic sociologists and his lionisation of state planners is echoed:

> Mr FitzGerald is, indeed, right in criticizing the timidity and negative approach in the past of the conventional wisdom of much Irish sociology towards government intervention. The sociologists were afraid of the State, because the State for them raised visions of authoritarian rule. They looked to Germany and the Soviet Union and they rightly rejected what they saw. They failed, however, to urge that the role of the State could be directed not towards depriving the individual of his liberties but in enlarging these liberties by raising his economic status in society … Events since the publication of *Economic Development* have shown how fruitful the inspiration of some Irish civil servants has been. If, however, the then prevailing attitudes of formal Irish sociology towards government intervention had decisively influenced public policy in the 1960's the economic revival that followed Mr Whitaker's publication might not have taken place. (Lynch 1965: 32–33)

In the new, more affluent, Ireland a new role was required of sociologists. Embracing the virtues of state intervention in the field of social planning, they should become promoters of public welfare over private consumption through the advocacy of increased taxation and wealth redistribution. In taking part in 'the formulation of a broad, practical social policy suited to Irish requirements' their contribution could complement that of other experts: 'the economist can act alone in advising about the quantitative aspects of economic growth. He needs the help of the sociologist to advise on the quality of that growth [so that] economically and socially the environment is designed to encourage personal initiative and public service.'

Responding to the two economists, James Kavanagh generally preferred to engage with the policy-related specifics of Lynch than the philosophical generalities of FitzGerald. 'A concentration on airy principles without a scientific awareness of facts' was, he admitted, 'a charge that might be levelled with some truth at sociology in Ireland up to recently.' Empirical studies 'helping to determine priorities of social policy' were undoubtedly needed but these should be carried out by properly trained professionals rather than enthusiastic but ill-prepared amateurs. Historically, against charges of excessive conservatism and hostility to state intervention on the Church's part, Kavanagh claimed that the episode of the Mother and Child Scheme was widely misunderstood and that the Church's progressive social concern was demonstrated by the Dignan health insurance plan which Kaim-Caudle's work had just then rescued from two decades of obscurity. A conservative Church had not, he points out, attempted to block the extensive development of state-owned enterprises, although he adds the comment that 'one of the fears of sociologists (conservatism again, no doubt!) is the too-ready acceptance in this country of the proliferation of State enterprises and Institutes'. In contrast to the broadly positive view of this sector held by FitzGerald and Lynch, Kavanagh suggests that 'a suitable empirical research project would involve a cool hard look at this network of State enterprises. Some of these are highly successful but there are many geese, one suspects, among the swans.' He goes on to make an observation that the Catholic social movement actors whose social research projects were consistently rejected by government departments might have echoed: 'The cynics among us say that it is easier to get a million or half-a-million pounds than fifty from the State nowadays provided the requirement is remotely associated with economic development.'

Whitaker's *Economic Development* had, he claimed, received a favourable reception from most sociologists and sociology was, in his view, entitled to a substantial share of the credit for its success:

> This plan was much more than a call for increased State activity. It appealed for a total, all-out effort by everybody in the community. I would consider that the psychological impact alone was responsible for much of the success of the programme. And I believe also that part of the infra-structure so necessary for this success was the number of adults who had participated in sociological courses for at least a decade before the emergence of the plan. Mr Whitaker's ideas had a ready response because so many people were able to understand and appreciate the significance of what he was trying to accomplish. (J. Kavanagh 1965: 166–167)

Echoing the discussions of the NUI college presidents and the bishops of the early 1950s, Kavanagh concludes his article by emphasising the importance of philosophy to social innovation: 'Am I being "airy-fairy" in suggesting that Seminars on productivity and management and trade unionism should include always a lecture on some philosophical aspect?' He also advocates greater lay access to the study of theology at university level: 'In the years that lie ahead, with the growing preponderance of technology, the study of theology by the laity may be a necessary safeguard in the preservation of our values.' There should, he re-emphasises, be 'more empirical studies of our social problems' provided these are undertaken by 'trained specialists': 'I am alarmed at the number of groups who are going "to engage in research", as if this were a new form of recreation.' Turbulent industrial relations are his final port of call: 'The greatest desideratum in our community at present is an awareness on all sides of the dignity of work.' An attribution of materialistic moral irresponsibility to both employers and employee follows, one which sits oddly with an earlier observation that 'Mr FitzGerald is on surer ground when he is worried about the materialistic preoccupations of some of our fellow-citizens and especially "the devotion of the merchant families of many Irish towns to the accumulation of wealth" – and, I might add, an accumulation often achieved by the payment of miserable wages to their employees in country towns.' But in relation to this instance of social injustice Kavanagh considered that 'we don't need the sociologist specifically for the task of arousing the consciences and sensibilities of our people. Our leaders in the community – graduates of our universities particularly – should already be equipped with a system of values.'

Recalling his late 1964 *Studies* piece in his autobiography, FitzGerald (1991: 65) presents it as a milestone passed on a personal journey whereby 'the conservatism and indeed clericalism of my youth had given way gradually to a much more liberal and progressive outlook', stating that 'part of my motivation in publishing this article was a feeling that I ought before entering politics to give notice to my future colleagues of my basic political stance'. The son of a Cumann na Gaedhael Cabinet minister, FitzGerald was part of a group assisting Declan Costello in developing the Just Society policy documents that Fine Gael would ambivalently present as its 1965 general election programme (Meehan 2013). He then declined an opportunity to stand as a candidate for the Dail but subsequently ran successfully in the Seanad election. FitzGerald (1991: 68) recalls that when he told his 'mentor' Whitaker of his intentions, 'he was shocked and markedly hostile' towards the idea: 'He said that if I entered politics I would lose the considerable power to influence events that I had acquired through my writings and my involvement with public affairs.'

In a collection of readings that celebrates and documents Irish economic planning of the later 1950s and 1960s, Basil Chubb and Patrick Lynch (1969: 118) describe FitzGerald as 'an economic commentator of rigorous intellectual detachment' who 'could interpret and criticise with skill and dexterity the writings of specialists for readers who were not trained in economic analysis'. The 1958 *Administration* article by FitzGerald they republish is remarkable for the two criticisms it incorporates into its very positive overall appraisal of *Economic Development* and of the First Programme for Economic Expansion – their failure to address education system deficits which the author identifies as 'a matter of growing concern at every level throughout the community' and the absence of 'sufficient emphasis on the urgency of reducing taxation'.

By late 1962 the groundswell of public criticism of the education system was such that Lemass would write to his Minister of Education, Patrick Hillery, about the 'present tendency, among speakers at certain types of public functions, commentators in the press and others, towards criticism, amounting in some cases to disparagement and derision, of various features of educational policy' and suggesting that 'the publicity given to this criticism could possibly lead to erroneous notions at home and abroad, unless steps are taken to deal with it, including the suggestions of outdated methods, hide-bound administration, etc., which appear to be getting prominence recently'.[4] But in 1958 FitzGerald's contrasting of the 'almost passionate interest in our educational problems' he characterised as being common to both urban and rural areas with 'what appears to the public to be complacency in official circles' marked him out as a very early public critic of the system upon which the Church exercised its grip of unique strength. Criticism of both educational defects and a high level of taxation also feature in John Vaizey's 1959 letter to a Ford Foundation officer quoted at length in Chapter 1, above. By 1965, however, Peter Kaim-Caudle had challenged Irish policy orthodoxy with the argument that a higher tax, higher welfare crusade against poverty 'could possibly generate social and moral forces which would do more, or quite as much, to further economic expansion and discourage emigration as economic planning'. Contributing to the *Studies* exchange early in a year when the work of the SRC he chaired would come to fruition in the Friis report and the *Investment in Education* team he headed would complete its study (Department of Education 1965), Vaizey's friend and co-author Patrick Lynch was then prepared to argue for higher taxation at the expense of morally dubious forms of private consumption and, as we have seen, to cast the sociologist in the role of leading advocate for such a policy shift:

> Increased taxation will be necessary in Ireland to restrain private affluence and redress the balance in favour of public welfare over the next decade. The total of government and local expenditure from taxation as a proportion of national income is still almost certainly lower than in many other European countries. In 1961, of European countries for which figures were available, only Denmark and Portugal had lower proportions than Ireland had. To the economist, taxation, as such, is neither good nor bad; it must be judged by its effect on the gross national product. One looks to the sociologists, therefore, not merely to support this particular re-distribution of wealth but, in addition, to help towards the formulation of a broad, practical social policy suited to Irish requirements. (Lynch 1965: 35)

A willingness to increase taxation was less apparent in government circles as exemplified by the setting up in 1966 of the interdepartmental group to examine the financing of social welfare, health and education 'on the tripartite insurance principle'. The Finance approach to a Social Development Programme was, as Chapter 6 has shown, one which sought to establish an order of priority among social spending demands which would be responded to as economic growth made more resources available without radically altering the taxation take from the existing quantum of resources or changing the existing bias towards regressive rather than progressive tax measures.

From the Catholic sociology viewpoint, James Kavanagh's contribution is a largely defensive one from which references to educational or taxation changes are absent. The economists are complacent in attributing all the advances of the present to their planning expertise and all the faults of the past to conservative sociologists. Through the public receptiveness fostered by their adult education efforts, sociologists have contributed substantially to the planners' success and through the development of technically proficient, policy-orientated empirical studies they can contribute more. The 'too-ready acceptance in this country of the proliferation of State enterprises and Institutes' he detects would shortly confront him in relation to empirical sociology when the Friis report recommended the creation of the ESRI. In this instance, as Chapter 6 showed, he did not follow through his initial inclination to oppose the recommendation but confined himself to qualifying comments.

Yet, like FitzGerald's 1958 comments on educational dissatisfaction, Kavanagh's detection of complacency among the economic planners in 1965 was prescient. The confident tone pervading the 1964–65 *Studies* articles departed from social commentary as the success which had attended planning up to that point came to be surrounded by the new instability and uncertainty sketched in the conclusion to Chapter 6 above. Both a trade union leader deeply involved in the consultative bodies that grew up around the planning project and a Catholic social movement activist – he was a long-time voluntary lay lecturer at CWC – Charles McCarthy reflected this change in his 1968 book *The Distasteful Challenge*. Here a gulf is discerned between the economic planning elite and the mass of the people. In contrast to Kavanagh's depiction of adult sociological education as part of the social infrastructure of state planning's success, there is an emphasis here on a widespread malaise with a more negative, cynical tinge than the second-stage alienation later discerned by Frs. Newman, Ward and Ryan. In another contrast, for McCarthy it is in the rural areas rather than the cities that the malaise is at its most acute, although it envelops both. Developing the theme of 'a certain second-rateness throughout our society', he anticipates the emphasis John Whyte (1980: 21–23) would place on 'the authoritarian strain in Irish culture' a few years later, drawing a comparison with Eastern European Communist states that discerned the shared cultural traits 'of intellectual rigidity, of strong social pressures to conform to certain basic beliefs and modes of behaviour, in a manner greater and more oppressive than was either healthy or desirable' (C. McCarthy 1968: 106).

The Catholic sociologist as social planner

Empirical sociology had been judged by the state planners to be a valuable source of inputs into their project as that project's scope extended beyond economic expansion to encompass social development. Institutionally the planning process shaped empirical sociology in a way that would long outlast its own disintegration. But empirical sociology was not merely a creature of economic planning. It had an independent existence that preceded the inauguration of economic planning by a number of years and, as shown in Chapter 3 above, it derived considerable initial impetus from Newman's proposal to save rural Ireland by deploying empirical social science techniques to underpin planned social change – the 'rurbanisation' of his 1958 Canon Hayes Memorial Lecture or the 'rural centrality' of his 1963 contribution to the Limerick Rural Survey.

How did the salvation of rural Ireland fit into the worldview of Irish economic planning? As Hannan and Commins (1992: 101) have noted, the independent Irish state inherited 'powerful strains of rural fundamentalist ideology' which they define as 'a set of values and beliefs which stressed (i) the advantages of family-owned, family-operated farms and of a numerous class of landholders, (ii) the healthy nature of farming as an occupation and open country farming communities as ideal settlement models and (iii) agriculture as a basis of national prosperity'. Such rural fundamentalism was, they go on to note, both inscribed in the 1937 Constitution and congruent with Catholic social thought. They judged it to remain alive and well in the early 1990s, commenting that 'despite the increasing deterioration of the conditions of the lower working class in Dublin over the past two decades, it is almost inconceivable that an equivalent Episcopal response would arise to that of the recent Western Bishops' Conference on the problem of the small farm Communities of the West'.

Back in the mid-1960s top Finance officials were, as we saw in Chapter 6, nettled by a Charlestown Committee *Broadsheet* charge that they were lackeys of 'industry, banking and big business' engineering a clearance of the small-farm west. When he launched the Limerick Rural Survey volume edited by Newman in Limerick the following month (November 1964) Lemass, with specific reference to the assumption of a much-reduced agricultural workforce in the Second Programme, dwelt on the inevitability of change and on how adopting a realistic attitude towards its extent and likely future course did not imply approval of its character (Murray and Feeney 2011: 128–129). Enumerating the achievements of planning to a trade union audience in 1967, Whitaker was to be less circumspect. Admitting that to date planning had not increased the quantity of employment to the extent projected, he emphasised its improved quality. A decrease in the number employed in agriculture was, he claimed, 'almost balanced' by the creation of new jobs in industry and services. But those who left farming 'had not been employed, except in an artificial statistical sense, in agriculture; they left the land, in fact, because they had no acceptable income from it and production has not suffered in consequence'. Numbers employed had stayed much the same but, he argued, there had been 'a change for the better in the character of employment' – a change from low-income under-employment to worthwhile, self-sustaining employment (Whitaker 1969: 300).

In calling on sociologists to assist in 'the formulation of a broad, practical social policy' in *Studies* Lynch in 1965 specified that 'structural changes in agriculture will have to be promoted if incomes on the land are to be raised', spelling out that 'this means that there must be an end to the "sociology" that suggests that agricultural occupations are in a particular sense the recipients of divine esteem and that, while other occupations may not deserve censure, there should nevertheless be a withholding of praise'. Kavanagh's response demurred, noting that 'the Pope praises the life of the farmer precisely because he is still the master of his own decisions – his work remains essentially "personal"'. In Ireland 'economically it may be true that many must continue to leave the land, but nevertheless we should not too readily dismiss the appeal of farming as a way of life in planning for the future of the national economy'.

Had he been the representative of sociology in this exchange, Newman might have fallen into line with Lynch's demand more readily. After 1958 this advocate of planned rural regeneration was increasingly drawn into the workings of state economic planning. In 1962 he was appointed a member of the Steering Committee flanking the research team that produced the *Investment in Education* report. Further appointment or election to Board or consultative Council positions in Foras Forbartha (1964), the Medico-Social Research Board and the ESRI (both 1966) followed. It was as chairman of the Physical Planning and Development Committee of Foras Forbartha that Newman wrote his 1967 monograph *New Dimensions in Regional Planning*. Effectively the last book he wrote as a working sociologist – he was succeeded as sociology professor by Fr. Liam Ryan after he became president of his college in 1968 – this extends and revises his earlier work advocating planned social change within the new and more complex context created by the coming into operation of a state physical planning system under the Local Government (Planning and Development) Act, 1963. For some functions, the relevant planning authority was an existing borough or county council, but during 1964 a grouping of these units into nine larger planning regions was also instituted. This was quickly followed by the commissioning of British consultants to prepare plans for the Dublin and Limerick regions. For plan implementation, the issue was whether investment should be concentrated on the building up of large centres (with Waterford and Galway to be added to Dublin, Cork and Limerick/Shannon/Ennis) or whether resources should be spread more widely, with medium-sized 'secondary' centres also benefiting. Economists, such as Garret FitzGerald and Louden Ryan, favoured the former; Newman championed the latter. With 'its accompanying socio-cultural changes', industrialisation and urbanisation in Ireland might reproduce the pattern of Britain's industrial revolution, 'i.e. within a pattern of relatively few large urban complexes, with a predominantly city-type culture'. Alternatively it could 'crystallise around a pattern of some larger and some smaller urban centres, of a kind that will ensure the continued survival of a rural culture in Ireland side by side with and properly integrated with a city culture'. If the second option were pursued, Newman believed that 'a new Irish culture that will be urban without entirely ceasing to be rural' could be created (Newman 1967: 36).

Such an outcome was possible because 'rural culture is to be found not only in the purely rural milieux of scattered farmsteads and traditional small villages but also in the semi-rural milieux of city fringes (at least at the outer edge), industrialised country towns and satellite villages, with their new pattern of commutation to work and leisure activity'. Here it was admitted that 'these two types of rural milieu and rural culture are not at all identical' but it was also claimed that 'they have the common characteristic of differing from urban in the sense of city-type culture' (Newman 1967: 37). An exclusively city-type culture was, Newman proclaimed, a danger to society. Here he took the example of the USA and quoted in support Jefferson, Emerson, Thoreau, Veblen and Lloyd Wright before citing Tonnies's distinction between *Gesellschaft* and *Gemeinschaft*. Even more briefly he identified the advantages of small-scale society, with an absence of the alienation typified by urban teenage gangs or 'the way of life of the beatnicks, the protest generation or angry young men'. On what the rural was, as opposed to what it was not, Newman was vague but elastic. Before the Maynooth European Society for Rural Sociology congress in 1966 he told a press conference that 'we should develop good centres that would be in culture rural and to find out what rural culture was the social psychologists must get to work', adding that 'in France rural culture is conserved in good new towns of up to 100,000 people, not in miserable, worn-out, little villages'.[5]

Newman's regional planning intervention was noteworthy for its claim to be based on European (particularly British and Dutch) 'scientific rural sociological research' and for the virtually complete absence of arguments explicitly related to the welfare of religion or the interests of the Church. Writing on vocations and on others aspects of 'sociological ecclesiology' (Newman 1965), he did clearly link the rural with the religious and here he was doing little more than repeating the common sense of his Church. Thus nationality and religiosity combined to underpin the regionally specific statement of Irish rural fundamentalism six western bishops sent to Lemass in June 1964:

> The people of the small western farms area are in a special way representative of the nation inasmuch as they have clung longer than people in other parts of the country to the traditions which are characteristic of the Irish way of life and of Irish culture including the native language ... Moreover, their homes have always been nurseries of religious vocations, thus contributing to the building up of Ireland's spiritual empire. We believe that it would be an irreparable loss to the nation and to the Church if they were left to thin themselves out under the merciless operation of economic laws.[6]

Newman's particular contribution was to challenge economics not by invoking a religious virtue such as mercy but on grounds of scientific overreach. Thus 'to the sociologist it is not only frustrating but painful to witness situations in which economic experts dictate policies in the social domain to the exclusion of relevant data available from the human sciences' (Newman 1967: 112). Here the advent of the physical planner may help to right the balance, as he claims it has done in France: 'called in simply to put the plans of the economists into effect, they immediately raise problems about "man" and "society" that go well beyond the limits of economics' (Newman 1967: 45). Fluently speaking the language of planning and engaging easily with the concepts of an emerging technocracy, Newman is therefore at first sight a surprising incumbent of the role of 'principal spokesman ... of the right wing of the hierarchy' (J. H. Whyte 1980: 387) at the end of the 1970s. Later, in 1983, one of his political adversaries, Conor Cruise O'Brien, would dub him 'the Mullah of Limerick'.[7]

However the lengthy and insightful piece which appeared in the *Irish Times* after Newman's death at the age of sixty-nine in April 1995 was inaccurate when it stated that 'he was unable to rise above the narrow Catholic social thinking of the 1940s and 1950s which demanded that the rights of the religious majority should be enshrined in the Republic's civil laws'.[8] The conception of the state's duty to the Church underlying this demand was substantially distinct from and long pre-dated Leonine Social Catholicism. Within the field of social thought, Newman was, as earlier chapters have shown, an innovator who was chiefly responsible for the empirical turn that Irish Catholic sociology took during the 1950s. In doing so he loosened the grip on sociology of the conventional natural law thinking that tended to reduce the discipline to a fairly sterile exercise in ethical exposition. While he was not notably to the fore in highlighting issues of poverty and social disadvantage, he certainly contributed to a more flexible and sophisticated understanding of the concept of subsidiarity that legitimated state intervention to address such issues. Thus he told a social study conference in Limerick in August 1966 that while voluntary welfare agencies were generally preferable to state welfare agencies, 'it must be emphasised that as far as Catholic social thinking is concerned, there is no limit to the amount of State welfare which is acceptable and in fact, desirable if the circumstances are such that this is the only practicable way of providing social services. This is something which has not been sufficiently realised in the past.'[9]

The observation of a character in Di Lampedusa's novel *The Leopard* that 'if we want things to stay as they are, things will have to change' reasonably encapsulates Newman's approach to rural sociology. But, given the 'continuing dominance of traditional interests and attitudes' producing 'change without modernisation' that Brian Girvin (2010: 349) discerns in Ireland between 1959 and 1989, this hardly involved straying from the centre ground of Irish politics and policy-making. What did justify placing Newman on the right wing was his stance on Church–state relations. In 1973 the hierarchy – whose ranks Newman would join in the middle of the following year – was prompted by the introduction in the Seanad of a Private Member's Bill that would allow the importation and sale of contraceptives to issue a statement in which for the first time it was 'officially and publicly stated that what is considered wrong by the church need not be prohibited by the state'. This, Liam Ryan argued, constituted the adoption of a wholly new 'conscience of society' position by the hierarchy: '[T]he bishops have listed the evils likely to result from the sale of contraceptives and they have said to legislators and people "this is the situation, what are you going to do about it?"' (Ryan 1979: 13 and 17). As a bishop, Newman was soon embroiled in a controversy with two Coalition Cabinet ministers – Garret Fitzgerald of Fine Gael and Conor Cruise O'Brien of Labour – in the course of which he declared that 'the Catholic people of our state have a right – a political right – to have the provision of the kind of framework that supports them in the living out of their moral and religious principles' (quoted in J. H. Whyte 1980: 412). To Whyte (1980: 416), while 'the hierarchy as a whole, in its collective statements since 1973, seems to have stuck closely to the "conscience-of-society" model', Newman appeared 'to be using a different set of assumptions'. These involved insistence on an undiluted theological traditionalism in the sphere of Church–state relations.

When Newman began writing about the relationship between Church and state in the mid-1950s he did so within a context shaped by concern about the implications of the growing influence of the Catholic community in the USA for the separation of Church from state enshrined in the US constitution. Anti-Catholic prejudice had long been a feature of right-wing US 'nativism', but a novel feature of post-1945 debate was a stress by political liberals on the incompatibility of the fundamental intolerance they attributed to Catholic Church teaching with core democratic values. The issue came to a head when the Democratic Party in 1960 chose John F. Kennedy as its presidential candidate, the first Catholic to run for the office since New York Governor Al Smith's heavy defeat in 1928 (T. Carty 2004). In the decade prior to this landmark election prominent US Catholics, most notably the Jesuit theologian John Courtney Murray, sought both to rebuff the American attacks the Catholic Church was coming under and to develop a Catholic theological case for changing the stance of their Church on Church–state relations, which they regarded as being both outdated and a product of purely European circumstances. As they did so, the biggest stick with which they found themselves being beaten was Spain, where the Franco dictatorship concluded a concordat with the Vatican in 1953. Here Catholicism was installed as the state religion and manifestations of a distinctly intolerant attitude towards non-Catholics abounded (Blanshard 1973: 233–236). But, when a leading US critic imagined the Constitution the USA might find itself with were Catholics to come to form a majority in its population, a Jesuit reviewer responded that 'although he can describe the American hierarchy … as entirely Irish, he does not advert to the fact that in recent years Ireland has produced a Constitution which might be expected to serve as a pilot model for any American Catholic lawmaker of the end of this century who might be in the position he describes and who would certainly not be more anxious to follow Spanish than Irish prec-edents, seeing that Ireland and the USA are Common Law countries, while Spain is not' (Crehan 1951: 159). The author, Paul Blanshard, accepted this suggestion and spent about six months in Ireland in 1952 and 1953 producing a further book, *The Irish and Catholic Power*.

While this for the most part conjured up for US readers what its author termed a 'woeful vision in the Irish crystal ball', its concluding comments envis-aged the possibility of progressive developments. Here Blanshard refers to the ongoing engagement of Irish-American clerics in a 'great doctrinal war for and against the Spanish (and Papal) theory that freedom may be denied to non-Catholics in a predominantly Catholic state'. For Blanshard, Cardinal Ottaviani's March 1953 address constitutes a significant reactionary offensive in this wider conflict. In relation to its American participants, he writes that 'it is probably not too optimistic to say that there are two Irish Catholicisms emerging in the toler-ant atmosphere of America: the medieval, Spanish and old-Ireland type in which the priests are all-powerful and the people are moral serfs; and a new Irish-American Catholicism which seeks to apply to the Church the militant spirit of the Irish revolutionists who believed in genuine self-determination'. While the Irish ambassador to the Holy See lent his support to US critics of Ottaviani, and Archbishop McQuaid referred to 'the correction made by the Holy Father, after Cardinal Ottaviani had spoken', adding that 'the Cardinal's words, I have learned, caused great worry in the United States',[10] a *Christus Rex* commentary by Newman declared that while 'some have been inclined to think the Papal Address was by way of being corrective of Cardinal Ottaviani ... careful examination shows that there is absolutely no point on which the two documents contradict one another'. He went on to conclude that 'the Papal allocution, like the manuals of Public Ecclesiastical Law, speaks in such a way that we can infer that the separation of Church and State is opposed to the Natural Law if not to the Divine law itself. Catholic teaching on it is, therefore, something which can never be changed' (Newman 1955: 84–85).

The *Studies in Political Morality* Newman published in 1962 devoted more than half of its 450 pages to aspects of Church–state relations and showed that the changes of the intervening period – Kennedy was in the White House, the Second Vatican Council opened in October – had not altered the author's previous position. As a *Studies* reviewer noted: 'the hope that he had provided for the present age of renewal and reform in the Church a frank and radical treatment of theological topics that, more than most, have been encrusted with tortuous speculation ... has been disappointed ... [T]hesis and hypothesis (in connexion with the topic of toleration) are examined at immense length and Father John Courtney Murray is declared unsound ... broadly speaking, his position is traditionalist' (Cameron 1963: 97–102). With specific reference to the Irish Constitution of 1937 Newman argued that a juridical privilege had been created by Article 44's special position formula: 'what the Catholic Church enjoys, as her exclusive right, concerns the influence of religious and moral ideas on civil legislation. When a choice has to be made between measures that have the support of the religious majority and minority respectively, there is only one way for the government to act' (Newman 1962b: 443).

But, under the influence of the Second Vatican Council, the Taoiseach of the day was soon begging to differ. In September 1965 Lemass wrote to his Minister for Justice, Brian Lenihan, asking 'whether the Vatican Council Decree on Religious Liberty calls for any action by the Government', continuing that 'I have in mind particularly our divorce laws. Do the provisions of the Council Decree oblige or permit us to change this law so as to allow divorce and remarriage for those of our citizens whose religion tolerates it?' (quoted in Girvin 2013: 408). By contrast with the dropping of the new library proposal (Chapter 4 above), early in his tenure as Taoiseach, Lemass was not now deterred by a negative ecclesiastical response and moved on to initiate in the following year a wider review of the Constitution. This was carried out by an all-party informal committee of which Lemass became an active backbench member when he retired as Taoiseach late in 1966. What was intended as an interim, but was in fact the Committee's only, report in December 1967 contained recommendations for a reformulation of Article 41's blanket prohibition of divorce so that 'in the case of a person who was married in accordance with the rites of religions, no law shall be enacted providing for the grant of a dissolution of that marriage on grounds other than those acceptable to that religion'. It also recommended the deletion of Article 44 in its entirety, taking the view that it was merely a statement of statistical fact with no judicial effect. Here, as Brian Girvin (2013:418) notes, not only were recent Council declarations cited but 'the involvement by Jesuit John Courtney Murray in preparing the Declaration on Religious Freedom was highlighted and it was noted that Murray's writings on religious liberty "were at one time censored by the Vatican"'. The Lynch government's decision to (unsuccessfully) bring forward in 1968 what were widely perceived as partisan constitutional amendments relating to electoral arrangements fatally undermined the all-party committee approach to broader issues of constitutional reform. After 1968 the Northern Ireland Troubles created a new context in which southern constitutional reform was debated with renewed urgency but liberalisation was long-delayed by the strength of conservative forces.

With co-operation on economic development issues having by the mid-1960s replaced strident anti-partition rhetoric as the principal feature of the southern state's attitude towards Northern Ireland, the informal committee on the constitution had proposed to tone down the territorial irredentism commonly associated with the wording of Article 3. Aspiration to consensual thirty-two county unity also provided a ground for removing the constitutional prohibition on divorce, although 'the committee decided not to include a suggestion that any change be postponed until a united Ireland was achieved'. Removing Article 44 would, in the committee's unanimous view, 'dispel any doubts and suspicions which may linger in the minds of non-Catholics, north and south of the border, and remove an unnecessary source of mischievous and specious criticism' (quoted in Girvin 2013: 416–418). The later 1960s emergence of a civil rights critique of the Stormont Unionist record saw some of that regime's defenders dust off the contrast – endorsed by Paul Blanshard among others – between the progressive British features of the North and the reactionary repressive ones of the South with which the southern state-sponsored anti-partition propaganda of the 1940s and 1950s had been countered. From the radical wing of the civil rights movement fire was directed at the sectarian 'Green Tories' ruling in Dublin as well as the Orange ones ensconced in Stormont.

In response to escalating northern violence, southern elite acceptance that pluralist constitutional and legislative changes formed a necessary part of any reconciliatory political settlement increased. But although an inter-departmental unit on Northern Ireland established in 1970 made recommendations along these lines, the Lynch government was disinclined to take the initiative and only under strong opposition pressure did it hold the December 1972 referendum that rescinded the now friendless Article 44. Thereafter deep conservative–liberal divisions emerged in the south around the issues of contraception, abortion and divorce which to the present day remain unresolved in some respects. Northern violence had been ongoing for some twenty-five years and the foundations of a peace process were being laid by the time the constitutional prohibition of divorce was removed in 1995 at the second attempt and by a very narrow major-ity. For much of this period, and particularly in referendum results, an effect-ive conservative coalition comprising the Catholic hierarchy, a Fianna Fail Party which after the retirement of Lemass exhibited an aversion to change at both leadership and grassroots levels together with a newly mobilised constituency of Catholic lay activists whose principal achievement was the 1983 insertion of a 'pro-life' amendment into the constitution demonstrated its strength (Girvin 2008a, 2008b and 2010).

The hierarchy's presence within this coalition was a consequence of the con-cession by its 'conscience of society' position of a general freedom of action to the state that was combined with a duty of legislators and voters to appraise spe-cific measures proposed in terms of their contribution to the common good. The 1973 statement that unveiled the 'conscience of society' position contained what Whyte terms 'a bleak picture' of the effects that would flow from relaxing the law on the sale and importation of contraceptives. But it was more than a decade later that a referendum to remove the constitution's prohibition of divorce 'presented for the first time in history an opportunity for the Irish people to vote in favour of legislation that was contrary to Church teaching' (Dillon 1993: 94–95). On this occasion the decisive defeat of a measure for which opinion polls indicated majority support when Garret FitzGerald's government brought it forward 'saw the hierarchy's most extensive use to date of selective sociological evidence … [T]he bishops argued that the divorce amendment should be assessed in terms of its societal consequences.' Illustrative of this was an interview given during the campaign by Bishop Joseph Cassidy in which he invited his listeners to '*take a look at the evidence … take a look at the evidence. Take a look at the evidence in any country in the world*' (Dillon 1993: 105–106, with her added emphasis retained). In defend-ing 'traditional Christian teaching' against FitzGerald's divorce initiative in the mid-1980s the hierarchy played off a selective assemblage of empirical evidence against liberal arguments without calling upon the aid of natural law precepts, raising the spectre of a diminution of the quality of Irish life rather than that of a violation of Catholic moral principles.

In Liam Ryan's formulation of the hierarchy's 'conscience of society' stance the question 'what are you going to do about' a specific set of empirical facts was addressed to the legislators and to the people by whom they were elected. But the

review powers the 1937 Constitution conferred on the higher courts has made
the judiciary a third significant actor. As David Gwynn Morgan (1999: 8) puts
it: 'if in its central political organs Ireland is a daughter of the mother of parlia-
ments in Westminster, the impact of her higher judiciary on the political process
makes her a sister of Washington'. The emergence of judicial activism is usually
dated from the 1960s but the constitution's first three decades were not without
significant court rulings. The striking down of trade union legislation in the late
1940s was discussed in Chapter 2 above and, in relation to marital breakdown,
the established common law rule that a father was entitled to determine the
religion of his children was in 1951 held to have been superseded by Article 42
of the Constitution's vesting in both parents' of the right to provide, according
to their means, for the education of their children. This ruling in the Tilson case
was surrounded by public controversy because the marriage concerned was religiously mixed as well as broken and especially because of the judgment that had
been delivered by the president of the High Court, George Gavan Duffy, before
the case was considered on appeal in the Supreme Court. Gavan Duffy had in
the High Court supported a different constitutionally grounded change in the
existing law – that the promises with regard to the upbringing of any children
as Catholics required of the non-Catholic party in order to secure a Catholic
Church dispensation for a mixed marriage to take place should, because of that
Church's acknowledged special position, be enforceable through the courts.

As he died in 1951, Gavan Duffy's Tilson case judgment represented the cli-
max of the career of 'one of the most important judicial innovators that Ireland
has had', whose policy, where religious issues arose in the cases he heard, 'was
to use the provisions of the constitution to override precedents built up by
English and Protestant judges, and thus give Irish law a more distinctly Catholic
cast' (J. H. Whyte 1980: 167). Before Whyte, Gavan Duffy's project had been
highlighted by Jean Blanchard, a French diplomat encouraged by Archbishop
McQuaid's friend Professor Gabriel Le Bras to undertake a doctoral thesis on
the Irish Catholic Church in the course of a Dublin embassy posting. Blanchard's
book was published in French in 1958 and – as *The Church in Contemporary
Ireland* – in a 1963 English translation. In the previous year Newman had written
that 'given a judiciary composed of men like Gavan Duffy, the Catholic Church
in Ireland could rest assured of receiving treatment, at least at common law, of a
kind that would fully measure up to the requirements that Public Ecclesiastical
Law lays down, while non-Catholics conversely, would be assured that their religious rights and liberties would be respected'. The late judge is also invoked for
(qualified) support of Newman's interpretation of Article 44: 'there can be little
doubt that it was Mr. Justice Gavan Duffy's personal view that this juridical position might be acknowledged, although, in the absence of full investigation of the

subject, he had to base his decisions on other grounds. His appeal to the special position of the Catholic Church was always secondary' (Newman 1962b: 444).

Shortly before these books were published, key judicial appointments ensured that 'a judiciary composed of men like Gavan Duffy' would not preside in the Irish courts. In making these appointments, Lemass possibly did more to stimulate effective constitutional change than he achieved through setting up and contributing to the all-party committee on the constitution. He also took the opportunity to convey to the appointees his views on the role the court should fulfil. Brian Walsh later recalled that at the time of his appointment as a Supreme Court judge in 1961 Lemass 'very briefly but quite clearly' indicated that he would like the Irish Supreme Court to become more like its US counterpart by developing an active interpretative role: 'I am not saying that that influenced me in any particular way, but I think the horse was chosen for the course. He probably felt he was talking to someone who had very much the same views' (Sturgess and Chubb 1988: 418–419).

During the 1960s the judiciary began to discover within the 1937 Constitution a range of 'unenumerated personal rights'. A key case in the process concerned the last cause for which a documentary link exists to Maria Duce / Firinne activity – opposition to fluoridation of the public water supply. In 1973 one such unenumerated right – marital privacy – was the basis upon which the legislation forbidding the importation of contraceptives was declared unconstitutional in the McGee case. Hogan (1987: 69) argues that 'McGee was to prove to be a watershed in the annals of Church / State relations. To put it crudely, it was the first time the Hierarchy had "lost" on a sensitive issue pertaining to faith and morals.' He goes on to draw a direct line between this judgment and the campaign for a 'Pro-Life' amendment to the constitution. A US judgment on privacy (Griswold v. Connecticut) formed the basis for both the Irish McGee case outcome and the landmark US decision on abortion in Roe v. Wade: 'who was to say that the Irish Supreme Court would not follow the example of the U.S. Supreme Court and hold that the right to privacy guaranteed by Article 40.3 of the Constitution encompassed the right to abortion?' (Hogan 1987: 75).

An amendment was duly secured but it subsequently proved unable to withstand judicial interpretation, which held that a constitutional right to have an abortion existed where the life of a woman was threatened by suicidal tendencies arising from her pregnancy. Transatlantic influences were not notably to the fore in this instance and American-influenced jurisprudence (Boss 2002) was not the only legal threat to Irish moral conservatism. EEC entry increased the extent to which Irish actions came under the purview of European courts. After the 1983 passage of the 'Pro-Life' amendment Girvin (2008a: 88) notes that 'the first challenge came from Europe with significant judgements from the

European Court of Justice (ECJ) and the European Commission on Human Rights (ECHR) weakening what had been achieved'. The ECJ controversially concluded that abortion was 'a service within the meaning of the Treaty of Rome and that restrictions on those with a commercial interest in the service' – such as Irish non-directive counselling agencies that facilitated women to have abortions carried out in Britain – 'contravened the treaty'. The ECHR also found against Victorian legislation criminalising male homosexual acts that had previously survived constitutional challenge in the Irish courts.

Non-judicial international influences on policy development in the education and health fields also came under Irish conservative fire in the 1970s and 1980s with book titles asking *Have the Snakes Come Back?* (Walsh 2008) and *Is the School Around the Corner Just the Same?* (McCarroll 1987). The latter, with its argument that the value orientation and methodology of Lifeskills programmes for school children were incompatible with the Catholic religious and family ethos, revived one of the objections made to the state provision of health education by the hierarchy during the clash over the Mother and Child Scheme at the beginning of the 1950s. Fr. Fahey's admirers had at this time attacked the Marshall Plan in *Fiat*, characterising it as part of 'the Judaeo-Masonic forces of the Western Hemisphere'.[11] In the 1970s and 1980s UNESCO, the World Bank and the 'American project' of 'substituting psychotherapy and secular humanist indoctrination for moral formation' (McCarroll 1987: 157) were all portrayed as baleful influences by militant Irish conservatives. More recently a critique of international influences on developments in Irish family law discerns 'a deeper shift from classical Thomist to Enlightenment-inspired understandings as the basis for moral reasoning' as in discourses emanating from the EU and the UN 'human rights are used to overreach the democratic process and marginalize Ireland's constitutional protections' (Holmes 2009: 307 and 314).

Against such vulnerability to erosion from external sources Irish moral conservatism has principally relied upon a set of attitudes and values predominating on an island whose two polities 'have long stood out in Europe as places where religion and churches matter' (Fahey, Hayes and Sinnott 2006: 30). But the enduring relative strength of this set of attitudes sits alongside a trend of significant absolute decline, as these authors show by drawing on data from a variety of datasets created at different points in time. The core resource for this exercise is the three rounds of the European Values Survey (EVS) carried out in 1981, 1990 and 1999–2000. One particularly striking finding is the fall in Catholic regular church attenders expressing 'a great deal of confidence' in their Church. In 1981 57 per cent of this group had such a high level of confidence, but by 1990 the figure was down to 44 per cent and by 1999–2000 it stood at just 29 per cent (Fahey, Hayes and Sinnott 2006: 48). Such a fall had crucial implications for the viability of the hierarchy's 'conscience of society' position. Here the hierarchy retained control over the definition of the situation so long as its listing of the undesirable consequences associated with a particular innovation was treated as being an accurate and authoritative statement to be first accepted and then applied by the generality of legislators and voters. In a situation characterised by very high regular church attendance and 'a great deal of confidence' in their Church being expressed by most regular attenders, voices articulating virtues associated with a disparaged innovation or sceptically interrogating the reliability of the account of the matter provided to legislators and voters by the bishops were unlikely to prevail. But such voices were growing louder over time and, as regular church attendance declined – as it did from over 90 per cent in the early 1970s to 50 per cent in 2003 (Fahey, Hayes and Sinnott 2006: 44) – and confidence in the Church plummeted even among regular attenders, they could critically address secular empirical arguments about societal consequences in an increasingly effective manner.

In the early 1960s the pioneering American Jesuit collector of Irish survey data Fr. Bruce Biever (1976: 519–522) discerned the existence among his respondents of 'a new breed': 'an articulate though pronounced minority of Irish Catholics who in key areas have manifested unqualified disagreement with the majority attitudes … [T]hey are young; they are educated; they are laymen.' Frustrated and isolated in many ways as those who comprised it were, for Biever the new breed represented 'the greatest challenge which traditional Irish Catholicism will have to face in the next decade' as 'new factors are arriving in Ireland with staggering force and power'. From the late 1960s a number of studies of UCD students (Gallagher 1974; O'Doherty 1969; Power, 1969) reflected and in some respects confirmed concern about deviation and disengagement among better-educated young Catholics. Analysing the 1990 EVS data Hornsby-Smith and Whelan (1994:27) found that 'while on average only two-thirds of those with third-level education attended [Mass] weekly compared with over four-fifths of those with lower levels of education, the effect is almost entirely to be found among those born since the early 1950s … [I]t is apparent that significant cultural shifts can be dated from around the 1960s.' As Chapter 1 noted, the latter decade was a period when the Church's 'grip of unique strength' on Irish education began to loosen as participation levels rose and the system's priorities were reorientated away from religious instruction and language revival and towards the mathematics, science, technology and modern languages capabilities that were marketed to foreign investors.

But over time it was not only towards the top of the social scale that new factors weakened church attendance. Shifting strategy to escape one type of economic and social crisis from the late 1950s, the Ireland that entered the brave

new world of European integration and foreign investment reliance found itself
plunged into a deep trough of unemployment and emigration through most of
the 1980s. Liam Ryan had entitled his path-breaking 1960s study of early school
leavers *Social Dynamite*. But when this low-skilled stratum bore the brunt of per-
sistently high unemployment in the 1980s the predominant effect was one of
psychologically distressed implosion (Whelan, Hannan and Creighton 1991)
rather than socially destabilising explosion. Showing up in the 1990 EVS data,
the negative religious impact was nonetheless substantial as 'unemployment
and deprivation affect church attendance through the impact they have on an
individual's self-esteem rather than through the estrangement of significant sec-
tions of the working class from Catholicism per se' (Hornsby-Smith and Whelan
1994: 26–27).

Back in the early 1960s Biever had commented on how a combination of
'external influences plus internal inadequacies … pose real problems for the
future church in Ireland'. Internal inadequacies were laid bare in a manner
he could hardly have foreseen from the early 1990s as a stream of revelations
emerged about prominent clerics with flouted celibacy vows, about sex crimes
against children in parishes, schools and other institutions and about a multiplicity of forms of abuse of children and adult women perpetrated over decades
in Church-run industrial schools and Magdalene laundries. While public confidence could hardly fail to be dented in Church leaders who were shown to have
concealed crimes against children from the civil authorities and to have adopted
the management practice of moving subordinates suspected of perpetrating sexual abuse from one place to another where similar offences were then often
committed, assessments of the magnitude of the effect differ. Fahey, Hayes and
Sinnott (2006: 33 and 48–49) argue that, as a cause of loss of confidence in the
Church, the sex scandals are less important than the 'more relevant' contraception, divorce and abortion issues.

However, a different emphasis emerged when Betty Hilliard re-interviewed
in 2000 the traceable members of a sample of Cork mothers she had first inter-
viewed in the mid-1970s. She found that in the wake of the scandals that had
by then come to light 'these mothers no longer accorded the Church the automatic legitimacy it had previously enjoyed' and that in some cases 'the legitimacy
of their own positions as defenders and transmitters of the faith was irrepar-
ably undermined' (Hilliard 2003: 45). Evidence drawn from in-depth qualitative interviewing with a small localised sample is obviously difficult to compare
with that drawn from standardised questionnaires administered to large national
samples. It can, however, be noted that, originally selected in the mid-1970s as
'mothers of intact families who had at least one school-going child, and who
lived in settled working class areas of Cork City', Hilliard's respondents in 2000

possessed all but one (rural location) of the characteristics that analysis of survey data has consistently identified as protective against detachment from the Church – female sex, older age and (in all likelihood) lack of third-level education. Focusing on extremes in presenting their multivariate analysis of the 1990 EVS data, Hornsby-Smith and Whelan (1994:28) note that 'a 65-year-old woman in full-time unpaid home duties has a 0.98 probability of attending church weekly or more often, while for a twenty-year-old urban unemployed male the probability falls to 0.32'. Hitherto a source of bedrock support to clerical power, regular attenders with similar characteristics to Hilliard's sample may have contributed a lot more to the downward momentum of confidence in the Church recorded after the era of scandals began then they had previously done.

The succession of scandals links most directly with the present study through the early 1970s appointments as bishops of the two longstanding leading figures of academic Catholic sociology in Ireland, James Kavanagh and Jeremiah Newman. Kavanagh left UCD to become an auxiliary bishop in the Dublin archdiocese in 1972; Newman's appointment as bishop of his native Limerick followed in 1974. Despite its size, the Dublin archdiocese had only two auxiliary bishops at the time of Archbishop McQuaid's retirement in 1972. The number of auxiliaries increased substantially after Kavanagh's fellow UCD academic, Dermot Ryan, succeeded McQuaid and the former professor of social science is one of thirteen holders of the position whose actions in relations to alleged clerical sex abuse cases were reviewed in 2009 by the Report of the Commission of Investigation into the Catholic Archdiocese of Dublin (the Murphy report). Retiring in 1998, Kavanagh was the longest-serving of these auxiliary bishops. He died in 2002, four years before the establishment of a Commission that concluded that he was one of two Dublin auxiliary bishops that had handled clerical sex abuse complaints 'particularly badly'. The Commission's specific adverse findings are that Bishop Kavanagh 'failed to deal properly with Fr. William Carney even when he had pleaded guilty to child sex abuse', that 'he tried to influence the Garda handling of the criminal complaints against Fr. Carney' and that 'he persuaded a family to drop a complaint they made to the Gardai' in relation to another priest whose name is redacted in the report. Most of the material relating to Bishop Kavanagh in the Murphy report is to be found in the chapter devoted to Fr. Carney's case. The report describes Fr. Carney as 'a serial sexual abuser of children, male and female' and describes the handling by the archdiocese of the 'large number of allegations and suspicions' concerning him as 'nothing short of catastrophic ... inept, self-serving' (Commission of Investigation into the Catholic Archdiocese of Dublin 2009: 13–14 and 414–454).

Criticism of their actions in the Murphy report prompted a number of resignations by bishops who had served as auxiliaries in Dublin before appointment to other dioceses. One of those who resigned was the Bishop of Limerick, Donal Murray, who had been a Dublin auxiliary from 1982 to 1996 and then moved to Limerick to fill the vacancy caused by Jeremiah Newman's death. Most Irish dioceses have not been the subject of the kind of detailed inquiries concerning the handling of clerical sex abuse allegations that were carried out in Dublin, Ferns (Crowe 2008) and Cloyne but the Church's own watchdog body, the National Board for Safeguarding Children in the Catholic Church in Ireland (NBSCCCI), is in the process of completing a series of Safeguarding Review Reports covering the whole country and taking in religious orders. The report for Limerick was published in September 2012. This commended the departed Donal Murray for the procedures he had put in place after his arrival in the diocese. In relation to a look-back at files starting in 1975, it commented that 'prior to Bishop Murray, practice was very poor and in our view, in one case potentially dangerous. There is documentary evidence relating to a former bishop, whilst apparently having knowledge of a priest's abusive behaviour in England, giving faculties to him to minister in Limerick, where it is believed he may have gone on to abuse again' (NBSCCCI 2012: 13). The only bishop Limerick had between 1975 and the advent of Donal Murray was Jeremiah Newman.

Aside from such posthumous reputational damage to prominent former practitioners, the Church scandals also connect with the social sciences through the revisitation of an old issue and the advent of new social forces. The old issue is the relationship in Ireland between civil law and canon law. A key context for the withholding from the Gardai and the Health Boards of information about clerical sexual abuse by Church leaders was that 'the church deemed canon law to take precedence over national statute law and did not formally acknowledge its proper obligations to the latter until 1996' (Crowe 2008: 55; see also FitzGerald 2003: 134–147). The broader underlying issue had been broached in the 1950s by Jean Blanchard (1963: 75–77), who wrote that Irish relations between Church and state are 'not codified and no one feels that they need to be'. Maria Duce – 'where zeal outstripped discretion' – had in its idiosyncratic way stood apart from this consensus but this had set it at variance with the 'practical attitude of the church'. The realisation of a programme of the Maria Duce type might have resulted 'in making more "official" a civil order which the church wishes to ignore to some extent in law, though she recognises it in practice'. In a 1958 preface to Blanchard's French original, his academic mentor Gabriel Le Bras wrote that 'perhaps a commendable discretion has controlled his pen on the fringe of some delicate problems' (Blanchard 1963: ix). Four decades later, mounting pressure on elite norms infused by such discretion was evident (Inglis 1998: 203–242): a further decade on, the considerable extent to which elite accommodation had succeeded in surviving admissions of responsibility to abuse victims could be emphasised (Arnold 2009: 79–295).

From below, abuse survivor movements emerged in the 1990s to challenge the elites of Church and state. Key advocates for and allies of these abuse survivor movements have been drawn from the ranks of academics, media professionals and artists. Personal testimonies have provided the raw material for a succession of powerful factual, 'docudrama' and fictionalised representations of survivor experiences in a variety of media (Kenny 2009). For those who had suffered abuse in industrial schools the 1999 *States of Fear* television documentary series preceded a Taoiseach's apology, a redress scheme and a commission of inquiry. In-depth, diocese-wide studies of the handling by the Church of clerical sexual abuse allegations in Ferns and Dublin followed in the wake of the 2002 television screenings of investigative reports entitled *Suing the Pope* and *Cardinal Secrets*. In the case of Magdalene laundry inmates a 2002 film, *The Magdalene Sisters*, played a key role in building the momentum of a campaign that – via the McAleese report – in 2013 secured another Taoiseach's apology and the initiation of another redress scheme.

As these advances were made, personal testimony came to be supplemented by institutional documentation. The combination was present in *Suffer the Little Children*, the 1999 book that complemented the *States of Fear* television series, where it was found that 'many of the Department of Education's industrial school files are completely missing and others contain gaps spanning several decades with no documentation available' (Raftery and O'Sullivan 1999: 330–331). Following Taoiseach Bertie Ahern's apology to victims in May 1999, a Commission to Inquire into Child Abuse (CICA) was established with extensive powers of discovery covering public and private bodies. By 2004 discovery of Department of Education documents had proven sufficiently problematical for a separate special inquiry into the issue to be held. The account of this special inquiry's findings contained in CICA's final report is a catalogue of the missing, the incomplete and the non-existent. Calls for an apology to and the provision of redress for Magdalene women continued to be resisted by governments until the McAleese committee was established in July 2011. It too was in a position to combine information from private Church and – subject to huge gaps particularly, as CICA had already reported, in the Department of Education – public state records to create a database of information on former laundry inmates. Deplorably incomplete as it was, documentary evidence thus played a significant role in propelling forward and vindicating the cause of abuse survivors.

This is somewhat ironical in the light of the methodological stance adopted by John Whyte in 1971. Covering a period that came up to the then present day, unpublished documents played a very minor part in his research, with reliance being placed instead on an wide-ranging trawl through published sources and an extensive programme of interviewing. This was a necessity out of which he proceeded to try and make a virtue. He was inclined to minimise the possibility that he had missed out any significant episode of the period covered as 'my experience, when comparing interview evidence with published evidence, is that nearly all the events which participants in Church–State negotiations remember left some trace in the public record at the time. This makes me hopeful that, even when an episode was *not* recalled by my informants in interview, I shall none the less have picked up some traces of its existence from published sources.' While admitting that a definitive study would have to await access to archives, he also proceeded to play down the likely significance of their contents: 'for people do not put everything they think onto paper. It is possible that some of my informants have revealed more to me in conversation – about their attitudes, more likely, than about the actual course of event – than would ever be evident to a scholar working solely from documents in the future' (J. H. Whyte 1980: ix).

In fact, subsequent research in opened archives has brought to light a series of 'significant encounters' between Church and state that were not part of the public record and were not referred to by Whyte's interviewees. The Agricultural Institute and new National Library proposals discussed in Chapter 4 above provide two examples and more can be cited. Whyte's expectation that 'some day this book will be superseded by a more definitive study based on archives' finds a specific point of application when in his concluding discussion he identifies four key circumstantial variables[12] that affect the power the hierarchy possesses – that body's degree of internal unity, the party composition of the government, the time period and the area of intervention. Noting how knowledge that the bishops' opinions were divided influenced the policy pursued by mid-nineteenth-century British governments in relation to establishing the Queen's Colleges, he points out that in the post-1923 period covered by his book 'the importance of internal divisions within the hierarchy is a factor which can only be guessed at ... [I]t will have to be left to future researchers, with access to the archives, to assess how important divisions within the hierarchy have been.' Ongoing failure to observe the thirty-year rule laid down for public records by the National Archives Act (see Chapter 6 above) and the variable practices of the private archives that hold Church records means that researchers have yet to attain the requisite level of access for a definitive assessment of the extent and significance of such divisions in the period Whyte covered. But public and private archival access has advanced sufficiently to suggest that the conclusions Whyte reached in relation to his other three circumstantial variables require significant modification.

With regard to party composition of the government, Whyte himself in the second edition of his book (1980: 417–418) revised his earlier view that Fianna

Fail was 'somewhat more independent of the hierarchy than were other parties' to one where during the 1970s 'a traditional gap between the parties has closed'. Further realignment in the 1980s pushed Fianna Fail closer to, and its rivals further away from, the hierarchy on abortion, contraception or divorce issues before that party repositioned itself with less conservative stances in the follow-ing decade (Girvin 2008a, 2008b and 2010). Had he had fuller information on the interaction between the hierarchy and the second inter-party government in relation to the Agricultural Institute (see Chapter 4 above), Whyte might have been less inclined to discern a significant difference in the first place although, given the emphasis he places on the importance of Dr. Browne's isolation within the first inter-party government's Cabinet as the Mother and Child Scheme crisis unfolded in 1950–51, the more robust response of the Cabinet to opposition from the hierarchy in 1955 would probably not have surprised him.

In relation to area of intervention, Whyte contrasts long-established and long-unchallenged Church power in the education field with issues 'where public opin-ion was not accustomed to hear [the hierarchy] speak' and where Church–state clashes could consequently occur. Health policy, to which four out of the twelve chapters of his book's first edition are devoted, provides the principal example of the latter. But the Church had substantial and long-standing institutional interests as a health service provider (Barrington 1987), while its endorsement of graduates of approved institutions being given preference in public medical appointments dated back to the turn-of-the-century democratisation of local government under British rule. Continuation of this practice after independence helped to prompt a 'back me or sack me' communication from W. T. Cosgrave to Cardinal MacRory in 1931 (Keogh 1995: 205–207). In the light of the succession of recent abuse reports referred to above, Whyte's (1980: 21) contrast between the world as a whole where 'education has caused more trouble between Church and State than any other single topic' and self-governing Ireland where 'it has only rarely been an issue' can hardly now be seen as anything other than the identification of a defective feature of the Irish polity. At the same time the emer-gence of 'significant encounters' between Church and state that were not part of the public record and were not referred to by Whyte's interviewees substantially changes the view of the education field as having been conflict-free. Because they derived in large part from the hierarchy's commitment to championing NUI interests and its desire to marginalise the anathematised Trinity College, both the new National Library and the Agricultural Institute episodes discussed above are effectively Church–state conflicts over education issues. A list of things Irish pub-lic opinion has not been and is not yet accustomed to would include full access to documentation and information, either contemporaneously or subject to a delayed-release rule. In the health field Dr. Noel Browne sensationally provided full contemporaneous access with the material he handed over to the *Irish Times* after his resignation from the Cabinet in April 1951 (J. H. Whyte 1980: 419–448). This was an action without precedent and arguably still without parallel in any field of Irish public policy.

Finally, Whyte distinguishes three distinct time periods. During the first – from the foundation of the state to the late 1930s, when maintenance of traditional standards of morality was an overriding common concern of bishops and all parties in government – there was 'little need for bishops to intervene' and 'episcopal influence on State policy was not obtrusive' (J. H. Whyte 1980: 373). But, as Patrick Murray (2000) has shown, the fact that during this period many of the bishops and the clergy subordinate to them remained active political partisans was a key element in a much more complex relationship between Church and state than Whyte allows for. During the second, covering the 1940s and 1950s, Whyte (1980: 373–374) argues that 'many' churchmen 'believed that in the concept of "vocationalism" they had a solution to the ills of Ireland and they pushed it with naïve energy'. Here the vagueness of 'many' underlines the problem acknowledged earlier of assessing internal divisions and, with growing access to archives, subsequent researchers have tended to the view that for the Church leadership in this period Catholic social movement enthusiasm was trumped by both ongoing moral standard concerns and an appreciation of how well the status quo protected the generality of Catholic institutional interests. Finally, there was the period from the end of the 1950s, in which Church and state responded to rapid social change with 'adjustment by consent' (J. H. Whyte 1980: 380). The theme of post-1950s consensus rather than conflict was strongly reaffirmed by the epilogue covering 1970s developments included in the book's second edition. Here he noted that legislation on contraceptive availability had been passed in the wake of the McGee case judgment, while abortion and divorce had yet to feature on the political agenda. But the McGee case judgment had sparked a conservative reaction which would very shortly turn abortion into a battleground, while, as Taoiseach, Garret FitzGerald would bring the divorce issue to the fore.

Sociology and the Catholic social movement by which it was encompassed feature in Whyte's account initially as disruptive forces creating serious conflict between Church and state in the 1940s and 1950s. They are depicted as subsequently evolving and maturing to become supportive of an overarching consensus that reduced such conflict to a low level. In this transition the emergence of a cadre of priests sent abroad by their superiors for further study before being appointed to academic social science teaching posts is seen as playing an important role. The academic institutionalisation of sociology in Ireland has been the focus of a considerable amount of scholarly attention in recent years (B. Conway 2006 and 2011; L'Estrange 2007a and 2007b; B. Fanning 2008 114–136 and

2015: 169–186; Fanning and Hess 2014). With these analyses our account shares a set of emphases – the identification of natural law as an overarching discursive framework for Catholic sociology, the significance of that sociology's 1950s turn from ethical exposition to empirical investigation and the complexity of the role played by Jeremiah Newman with its combination of social science innovation with implacable opposition to revision of established Catholic conceptions of the proper relationship between Church and state.

Writing at greater length, we have been able to flesh these themes out with concrete historical detail to a much greater extent. We have also, perhaps, been able to more systematically relate the academic discipline to its two enveloping contexts – the somewhat amorphous Catholic social movement with its key Christus Rex Society and Muintir na Tire later stage embodiments and the hierarchical structures of the institutional Church, where appearances of unified command and control were not necessarily matched by the ways in which things actually worked. In the case of Christus Rex, for instance, Bryan Fanning and Andreas Hess (2014: 32–35) single out the society's eponymous journal, which they subject to content analysis and critical comparison, while Sean L'Estrange (2007b: 241) focuses on the overall project of the society, which for him makes it 'a veritable "First Estate" reincarnate'. Both assume that a society of priests that has received the formal endorsement of the hierarchy can for analytical purposes be treated as a unitary national entity. But the surprisingly sparse material on the society available in his papers shows that Archbishop McQuaid's attitude to Christus Rex was at best an ambivalent one. Admittedly he donated £1,000 to the society's Jubilee fund in 1966 but the length of his 1950 delay in nominating one of his priests as a diocesan representative prompted Dr. Cahal Daly to appeal anxiously to one of his secretaries for 'your advice and help in my difficulty about interpreting His Grace The Archbishop's silence regarding my request'. When Fr. James Kavanagh sought his guidance regarding an approach from Dr. Daly to join the General Purposes Committee of Christus Rex in 1959, the archbishop replied that 'you have ample work to do, if you do it, without Christus Rex complexities'. Formally Christus Rex had a recognised status that Muintir did not have but the informal factor of 'clerical etiquette' discussed with remarkable frankness by Stephen Rynne (1960: 169–171) in his biography of Canon Hayes was not rendered irrelevant or insignificant by such recognition. Etiquette was in this context a velvet glove covering an institutional iron fist whose career-damaging descent most clerics were understandably anxious to avoid.

But if the complex specificities of the Church context have to be taken into account in charting the discipline's emergence, it is possible on occasion to give too much weight to the Catholic and not enough to the sociology. Bryan Fanning's (2015: 169) argument that 'a keen sense of the impending decline

of Irish Catholicism' loomed over Jeremiah Newman's work on rural society
and religious vocations is a case in point. As we noted above, Newman in the
late 1950s and 1960s approached issues of rural sociology in a scientific and
socially comparative manner rather than from a religious point of view. Drawing
on Dutch and other examples, he then argued that it was possible to stabilise
rural society and preserve rural culture by utilising social and economic planning techniques to these ends. A balanced pattern of growth may not have been
achieved in the Irish context but this has not deterred Newman's secular suc-
cessors from continuing to advocate and pursue such an outcome through an
ongoing series of unimplemented spatial strategies. On vocations, as we saw in
Chapter 3 above, the research group he led advised the hierarchy in 1971 that it
was too soon to conclude that a trend of consistent decline had been established.
In any case more was not, in his view, necessarily better. Carried out while vocations remained abundant, his earlier studies, discussed in the same chapter, had
drawn attention to issues of poor Irish clerical manpower deployment and the
problematical consequences for the Church that might flow from such a situation
of oversupply.

Irish Catholic sociology had scarcely attained healthy maturity in Whyte's
terms before its demise occurred. This demise Whyte does not record. Like
Whyte, Fanning and Hess see Irish Catholic sociology as having 'flourished briefly
in the 1960s' after taking its empirical turn. This, however, was 'too little too
late', as 'the new Irish modernisation project demanded better and more reli-
able sociological analysis' and by the 1970s Irish Catholic sociology was 'unable
to come up with viable alternatives for the future' (Fanning and Hess 2014: 39–
45). Our research has shown how a marginalisation process began much earlier
as a succession of proposals emanating from the Catholic social movement for
state funding to assist the creation of research centres or institutes were turned
down. Expansion of the education system subsequently hastened the end but
the Catholic monopoly in social science was decisively broken by a pattern of
investment in an infrastructure of applied scientific research institutes outside
that system. Coming from the Marshall Aid Grant Counterpart Fund and from
private foundation grants, the money invested in this infrastructure either came
from US sources or was subject to US approval of its use.

The interaction between external and internal forces was crucial to the changing of Irish ideas, institutions and policies between Marshall Aid and EEC entry.
What Fanning and Hess term the Irish 'technocratic developmental nation-
building project' exemplified by Sean Lemass in politics, T. K. Whitaker in the
civil service and Patrick Lynch in academia took shape within a wider context
of the pervasive Atlanticist projection of US 'soft power'. The afterlife which its
Counterpart Funds bestowed on the Marshall Plan (Whelan 2000), the OEEC

that provided an umbrella for the European Productivity Agency and the Office for Scientific and Technical Personnel before transforming itself into the OECD (Peter Murray 2009), the European Youth Campaign (McKenzie 2015) and the US foundations discussed in Chapter 4 above were all sources from which this power emanated. Around their operation formed personal and professional networks that, for instance, linked Patrick Lynch with his Cambridge friend John Vaizey, Danish social scientist Henning Friis and Shephard Stone of the Ford Foundation. Taking a liberty with Matthew the Evangelist when discussing film censorship in 1925, a contributor to the *Irish Times* noted how 'the people whose ideal is a Gaelicised and isolated Ireland … strain violently at the gnat of "Anglicisation" but swallow the caramel of Americanisation without a murmur' (quoted in Morash 2010: 155). Relations between Church and state in Ireland also featured such a gnat and such a caramel. The gnat was welfare state development along British lines, which the Church and the Irish medical profession combined to successfully oppose. The caramel was the Atlanticist conception of human capital formation as a key factor in the economic growth process. Once swallowed, this would shake loose the Catholic Church's grip of unique strength on education within a state where, as Fanning and Hess (2014: 43) put it, 'OECD reports came to replace the papal encyclicals'.

Notes

1   'No Place for Old-Fashioned Dogmas in Irish Economy – Tuairim Speaker', *Irish Times*, 13/4/1959.
2   Letter to the editor, *Irish Times*, 15/4/1959.
3   Letter to the editor, *Irish Times*, 17/4/1959.
4   NAI, DT S12,891 D/62, S. Lemass, Taoiseach, to P. Hillery, Minister for Education, 23/11/1962.
5   'Lay Congress to be Held at Maynooth', *Irish Times*, 30/7/1964.
6   NAI, DT S17,032 I/95, J. Walsh (Archbishop of Tuam), M. Browne (Bishop of Galway), J. Fergus (Bishop of Achonry), V. Hanly (Bishop of Elphin), P. O'Boyle (Bishop of Killala) and T. Ryan (Bishop of Clonfert) to S. Lemass, Taoiseach, 27/6/1964.
7   'The Mullah of Limerick', *Irish Times*, 4/10/1983.
8   'Bishop Who Kept On "Fighting the battles of long ago"', *Irish Times*, 4/4/1995.
9   'Christians Lag in Social Security', *Irish Times*, 4/8/1966.
10   NAI, DFA P256, J. Walshe, ambassador to the Holy See, to S. Nunan, Secretary, External Affairs, 30/11/1953; DDA, McQuaid Papers XXI/80/6A/2, Archbishop McQuaid to Mgr. Arthur Ryan, QUB, 19/3/1954.
11   NAI, DFA A55/1, F. Boland, Secretary, External Affairs, to Col. D. Bryan, G2 [Army Intelligence], 1/10/1948.

12   The context for the discussion of these circumstantial variables is provided by Whyte's
      (1980: 376) answer to the question 'how much influence does the [Catholic Church]
      hierarchy possess on Irish politics?' Observing that 'the theocratic-State model on the
      one hand, and the Church-as-just-another-interest-group model on the other, can both
      be ruled out as over-simplified but it is by no means easy to present a satisfactory model
      intermediate between these two', he concludes that 'it depends on circumstances'.

References

Adshead, M. and J. Tonge (2009) *Politics in Ireland: Convergence and Divergence on a Two-Polity Island* Basingstoke: Palgrave Macmillan

Akenson, D. H. (1975) *A Mirror to Kathleen's Face: Education in Independent Ireland, 1922–1960* London: McGill-Queen's University Press

Andrews, C. S. (2001) *Man of No Property* Dublin: Lilliput Press

Ashley, D. and Orenstein, D. H. (1990) *Sociological Theory: Classical Statements* London: Alleyn and Bacon

Arnold, B. (2009) *The Irish Gulag: How the State Betrayed Its Innocent Children* Dublin: Gill and Macmillan

Aspden, K. (2002) *Fortress Church: The English Roman Catholic Bishops and Politics, 1903–63* Leominster: Gracewing

Athans, M. C. (1991) *The Coughlin–Fahey Connection: Father Charles E. Coughlin, Father Denis Fahey, C. S. Sp., and Religious Anti-Semitism in the United States, 1938–1954* New York: Peter Lang

Attwood, E. A. (1962) 'Agriculture and Economic Growth in Western Ireland' *Journal of the Statistical and Social Inquiry Society of Ireland* 20, 5: 172–195

Barr, C. (2003) 'University Education, History and the Hierarchy' pp. 67–79 in L. MacBride (ed.) *Reading Irish Histories: Texts, Contexts and Memory in Modern Ireland* Dublin: Four Courts Press

Barrington, R. (1987) *Health, Medicine and Politics in Ireland, 1900–1970* Dublin: Institute of Public Administration

Beames, M. (1982) 'The Ribbon Societies: Lower Class Nationalism in Pre-Famine Ireland' *Past and Present* 97: 128–143

Berghahn, V. (2001) *America and the Intellectual Cold Wars in Europe: Shepard Stone between Philanthropy, Academy and Diplomacy* Princeton: Princeton University Press

Bew, P. and H. Patterson (1982) *Sean Lemass and the Making of Modern Ireland, 1945–66* Dublin: Gill and Macmillan

Biever, B. (1976) *Religion, Culture and Values: a Cross-Cultural Analysis of Motivational Factors in Native Irish and American Irish Catholicism* New York: Arno Press

Blanchard, J. (1963) *The Church in Contemporary Ireland* Dublin: Clonmore and Reynolds

Blanshard, P. (1954) *The Irish and Catholic Power: An American Interpretation* London: D. Verschoyle

Blanshard, P. (1973) *Personal and Controversial: An Autobiography* Boston: Beacon Press

Boel, B. (2003) *The European Productivity Agency and Transatlantic Relations, 1953–1961* Copenhagen: Museum Tusculanum Press

Bohan, H. (1979) *Ireland Green: Social Planning and Rural Development* Dublin: Veritas

Bohlen, J. M. and T. Breathnach (1968) *Study on Adoption of Farm Practices in Ireland* Dublin: An Foras Taluntais

Bohlen, J. M. and T. Breathnach (1970) 'Irish Farmers' Uses of Information Sources' *Irish Journal of Agricultural Economics and Rural Sociology* 3, 1: 1–28

Boland, K. (1971) *We Won't Stand (Idly) By* Dublin: Kelly Kane

Boland, K. (1977) *Up Dev!* Rathcoole: K. Boland

Boland, K. (1982) *The Rise and Decline of Fianna Fail* Dublin: Mercier Press

Bolster, E. (1979) *The Knights of Saint Columbanus* Dublin: Gill and Macmillan

Boss, M. (2002) 'Constitutional and Legal Reform in Ireland, 1937–1998: The American Context: An Essay in Culture and Law' *Nordic Irish Studies* 1: 121–146

Bowen, K. (1983) *Protestants in a Catholic State: Ireland's Privileged Minority* Dublin: Gill and Macmillan

Bowman, J. (1993) ' "The Wolf in Sheep's Clothing": Richard Hayes's Proposal for a New National Library of Ireland, 1959–60' pp. 44–61 in R. Hill and M. Marsh (eds) *Modern Irish Democracy: Essays in Honour of Basil Chubb* Dublin: Irish Academic Press

Boylan, T. (1999) 'The Founding of the Queen's Colleges: Context and Origins' pp. 1–15 in J. Davis (ed.) *Rural Change in Ireland* Belfast: Queen's University Belfast Institute of Irish Studies

Brown, M. (2005) 'Darwin at Church: John Tyndall's Belfast Address' pp. 235–246 in J. H. Murphy (ed.) *Evangelicals and Catholics in Nineteenth-Century Ireland* Dublin: Four Courts Press

Burke, A. (1990) 'Trinity College and the Religious Problem in Irish Education' pp. 95–126 in J. Kelly and U. MacGearailt (eds) *Dublin and Dubliners* Dublin: Helicon

Byrne, A., R. Edmondson and T. Varley (2001) 'Introduction to the Third Edition' pp. I-CI in C. M. Arensberg and S. T. Kimball *Family and Community in Ireland*, 3rd edn, Ennis: CLASP Press

Cahill, E. (1932) *The Framework of a Christian State: An Introduction to Social Science* Dublin: M. H. Gill

Cameron, J. M. (1963) 'Review of *Studies in Political Morality* by Jeremiah Newman' *Studies* 52, 205: 97–101

Carew, A. (1987) *Labour under the Marshall Plan: The Politics of Productivity and the Marketing of Management Science* Manchester: Manchester University Press

Carey, S. (2005) 'Land, Labour and Politics: Social Security in Post-War Ireland' *Social Policy and Society* 4: 303–311

Carey, S. (2007) *Social Security in Ireland, 1939–52: The Limits to Solidarity* Dublin: Irish Academic Press

Carty, F. X. (2007) *Hold Firm: John Charles McQuaid and the Second Vatican Council* Dublin: Columba Press

Carty, F. X. (2010) *The Impact of the Second Vatican Council on the Archdiocese of Dublin: Issue and Relationship Management in Turbulent Times* Saarbrucken: Lambert Academic Publishing

Carty, T. (2004) *A Catholic in the White House? Religion, Politics and John F. Kennedy's Presidential Campaign* Basingstoke: Palgrave Macmillan

Catholic Association (1903) *The Handbook of the Catholic Association* Dublin: Catholic Association

Chubb, B. and P. Lynch (eds) (1969) *Economic Development and Planning* Dublin: Institute of Public Administration

Clarke, M. (2010) 'Educational Reform in the 1960s: The Introduction of Comprehensive Schools in the Republic of Ireland' *History of Education* 39, 3: 383–399

Cody, S. (1979) 'May Day in Dublin, 1890 to the Present' *Saothar* 5: 73–79

Commission of Investigation into the Catholic Archdiocese of Dublin (2009) *Report* Dublin: Stationery Office [Murphy report]

Commission to Inquire into Child Abuse (2009) *Report* Dublin: Stationery Office

Conway, B. (2006) 'Foreigners, Faith and Fatherland: The Historical Origins and Present Status of Irish Sociology' *Sociological Origins*, Special Supplement to 5, 1: 1–36

Conway, B. (2011) 'Catholic Sociology in Ireland in Comparative Perspective' *American Sociologist* 42, 1: 34–55

Conway, M. (1996) 'Introduction' pp. 1–33 in T. Buchanan, T and M. Conway (eds) *Political Catholicism in Europe, 1918–1965* Oxford: Clarendon Press

Coolahan, J. (1981) *Irish Education: History and Structure* Dublin: Institute of Public Administration

Coolahan, J. with P. O'Donovan (2009) *A History of Ireland's School Inspectorate, 1831–2008* Dublin: Four Courts Press

Cooney, J. (1999) *John Charles McQuaid: Ruler of Catholic Ireland* Dublin: O'Brien Press

Corish, P. (1995) *Maynooth College, 1795–1995* Dublin: Gill and Macmillan

Coser, L. (1977) *Masters of Sociological Thought: Ideas in Historical and Social Context*, 2nd edn, New York: Harcourt Brace Jovanovich

Cousins, M. (2003) *The Birth of Social Welfare in Ireland, 1922–52* Dublin: Four Courts Press

Crehan, J. (1951) 'Mr. Blanshard: Freedom and Catholic Power' *Studies* 40, 158: 158–166

Crofts, A. (1935) *Workers of Ireland Which Way?* Waterford: Aquinas Study Circle

Crofts, A. (1960) *Catholic Sociology: A Text Book for Beginners* Dublin: M. H. Gill

Cronin, M. (1924) *Primer of the Principles of Social Science* Dublin: M. H. Gill

Crowe, C. (2008) 'The Ferns Report: Vindicating the Abused Child' *Eire-Ireland* 43, 1–2: 50–73

Curran, C. E. (2002) *Catholic Social Teaching, 1891–Present: A Historical, Theological and Ethical Analysis* Washington, DC: Georgetown University Press

Curtin, C. and T. Varley (1986) Bringing Industry to a Small Town in the West of Ireland *Sociologia Ruralis* 26: 170–185

Curtis, M. (2010) *Challenge to Democracy: Militant Catholicism in Modern Ireland* Dublin: History Press Ireland

Daly, C. (1967) *Christus Rex: The First Twenty-Five Years* Belfast: P. Quinn

Daly, C. (2009) 'Preface' pp. 7–11 in J. McEvoy and M. Dunne (eds.) *The Irish Contribution to European Scholastic Thought* Dublin: Four Courts Press

Daly, M. (1984) 'An Irish Ireland for Business? The Control of Manufactures Acts, 1932 and 1934' *Irish Historical Studies* 24, 94: 246–272

Daly, M. (1992) *Industrial Development and Irish National Identity, 1922–1939* Syracuse, NY: Syracuse University Press

Daly, M. (1997) *The Spirit of Earnest Inquiry: The Statistical and Social Inquiry Society of Ireland 1847–1997* Dublin: The Statistical and Social Inquiry Society of Ireland

Daly, M. (2002) *The First Department: A History of the Department of Agriculture* Dublin: Institute of Public Administration

Daly, M. (2006) *The Slow Failure: Population Decline and Independent Ireland, 1920–1973* Madison, WI: University of Wisconsin Press

Delaney, E. (2001) 'Political Catholicism in Post-War Ireland: Revd Denis Fahey and Maria Duce, 1945–54' *Journal of Ecclesiastical History* 52, 3: 487–511

Delaney, E. (2007) *The Irish in Post-War Britain* Oxford: Oxford University Press

Delap, C. and T. Kelleher (2005) 'Local Authority Social Work in Ireland: Origins, Issues and Developments' pp. 51–76 in N. Kearney and C. Skehill (eds) *Social Work in Ireland: Historical Perspectives* Dublin: Institute of Public Administration

Department of Education (1965) *Investment in Education* Dublin: Stationery Office

Department of Finance (1958) *Economic Development* Dublin: Stationery Office

Department of Industry and Commerce (1966) *Science and Irish Economic Development* Dublin: Stationery Office

Department of Social Welfare (1968) *Report 1963–66* Dublin: Stationery Office

Devereux, E. (1991) 'Saving Rural Ireland – Muintir na Tire and Anti-Urbanism, 1931–1958' *Canadian Journal of Irish Studies* 17, 2: 23–30

Devereux, E. (1992) 'Community Development – Problems in Practice: The Muintir na Tire Experience, 1931–1958' *Administration* 39, 4: 351–370

Digby, A. and N. Bosanquet (1988) 'Doctors and Patients in an Era of National Health Insurance and Private Practice, 1913–1938' *Economic History Review* 41: 74–94

Dillon, M. (1993) *Debating Divorce: Moral Conflict in Ireland* Lexington, KY: University Press of Kentucky

Dorril, S, (2000) *MI6: Fifty Years of Special Operations* London: Fourth Estate

Dublin Archdiocese Commission of Investigation (2009) *Report into the Catholic Archdiocese of Dublin, July 2009* Dublin: Stationery Office

Earner-Byrne, L. (2007) *Mother and Child: Maternity and Child Welfare in Dublin, 1922–60* Manchester: Manchester University Press

Fahey, T. (2002) 'The Family Economy in the Development of Welfare Regimes: A Case Study' *European Sociological Review* 18, pp. 51–64

Fahey, T., B. Hayes and R. Sinnott (2006) *Conflict and Consensus: A Study of Values and Attitudes in the Republic of Ireland and Northern Ireland* Dublin: Institute of Public Administration

Fanning, B. (2008) *The Quest for Modern Ireland: The Battle of Ideas 1912–1986* Dublin: Irish Academic Press

Fanning, B. (2015) *Histories of the Irish Future* London: Bloomsbury

Fanning, B. and A. Hess (2014) *Sociology in Ireland: A Short History* Basingstoke: Palgrave Macmillan

Fanning, R. (1978) *The Irish Department of Finance 1922–1958* Dublin: Institute of Public Administration

Faughnan, S. (1988) 'The Jesuits and the Drafting of the Irish Constitution of 1937' *Irish Historical Studies* 26, 101: 79–102

Fennell, R. (1962) *Industrialisation and Agricultural Development in the Congested Districts* Dublin: An Foras Tauntais Rural Economy Division

Ferriter, D. (2004) *The Transformation of Ireland, 1900–2000* London: Profile

Finnegan, D. and J. Wright (2015) 'Catholics, Science and Civic Culture in Victorian Belfast' *British Journal for the History of Science* 48, 2: 261–287

FitzGerald, G. (1964a) 'The Second Programme: Reflections' *Studies* 53, 211: 233–251

FitzGerald, G. (1964b) 'Seeking a National Purpose' *Studies* 53, 212: 337–351

FitzGerald, G. (1991) *All in a Life: An Autobiography* Dublin: Gill and Macmillan

FitzGerald, G. (2003) *Reflections on the Irish State* Dublin: Irish Academic Press

Fleming, T. (2012) 'Cinderella or Princess? History and Other Narratives of Adult Education in a University' at www.tedfleming.net/doc/Cinderella_or_princess.pdf on 12/6/2014 (accessed 6 May 2016)

Fogarty, M. (1999) *My Life and Ours* Oxford: Thornton

Foley, T. and F. Bateman (1999) 'English, History and Philosophy' pp. 384–420 in T. Foley (ed.) *From Queen's College to National University: Essays on the Academic History of QCG/UCG/NUI Galway* Dublin: Four Courts Press

Foy, M. (1976) 'The A.O.H.: An Irish Political-Religious Pressure Group 1884–1975' MA thesis, Queen's University Belfast

Friis, H. (1965) *Development of Social Research in Ireland* Dublin: Institute of Public Administration

Fuller, L. (2002) *Irish Catholicism since 1950: The Undoing of a Culture* Dublin: Gill and Macmillan

Gallagher, M. P. (1974) 'Atheism, Irish Style' *The Furrow* 25, 4: 183–192

Garvin, T. (1998) 'The Strange Death of Clerical Politics in University College, Dublin' *Irish University Review* 28, 2: 308–314

Gaughan, J. A. (1986) *Alfred O'Rahilly 1: Academic* Dublin: Kingdom Books

Gaughan, J. A. (1989) *Alfred O'Rahilly 2: Public Figure* Dublin: Kingdom Books

Gaughan, J. A. (1992) *Alfred O'Rahilly 3: Controversialist Part 1, Social Reformer* Dublin: Kingdom Books

Gaughan, J. A. (1993) *Alfred O'Rahilly 3: Controversialist Part 2, Catholic Apologist* Dublin: Kingdom Books

Gemelli, G. (1998) 'American Influence on European Management Education: The Role of the Ford Foundation' pp. 36–68 in R.P. Amdam (ed.) *Management Education and Competitiveness: Europe, Japan and the United States* London: Routledge

Girvin, B. (2006) *The Emergency: Neutral Ireland 1939–45* Basingstoke: Macmillan

Girvin, B. (2008a) 'Church, State and Society in Ireland since 1960' *Eire-Ireland* 43, 1–2: 74–98

Girvin, B. (2008b) 'Contraception, Moral Panic and Social Change in Ireland, 1969–1979' *Irish Political Studies* 23: 555–576

Girvin, B. (2010) 'Before the Celtic Tiger: Change without Modernisation in Ireland 1959–1989' *Economic and Social Review* 41, 3: 349–365

Girvin, B. (2013) '"Lemass's Brainchild": The 1966 Informal Committee on the Constitution and Change in Ireland, 1965–73' *Irish Historical Studies* 38, 151: 406–421

Grimes, B. (2000) 'The Library Buildings up to 1970' pp. 72–90 in V. Kinane and A. Walsh (eds) *Essays in the History of Trinity College Library Dublin* Dublin: Four Courts Press

Gwynn, D. (1967) 'Biographical Memoir' pp. 7–54 in D. Gwynn (ed.) *Reminiscences of a Maynooth Professor* Cork: Mercier Press

Hannan, D. and P. Commins (1992) 'The Significance of Small-Scale Landholders in Ireland's Socio-Economic Transformation' pp. 79–104 in J. Goldthorpe and C. Whelan (eds) *The Development of Industrial Society in Ireland* Oxford: Oxford University Press

Hannigan, K. (1981) 'British Based Unions in Ireland: Building Workers and the Split in Congress' *Saothar* 7: 40–49

Hay, J. R. (1975) *The Origins of the Liberal Welfare Reforms 1906–1914* London: Macmillan

Healy, J. (1968) *The Death of an Irish Town* Cork: Mercier Press

Hilliard, B. (2003) 'The Catholic Church and Married Women's Sexuality: Habitus Change in Late 20th Century Ireland' *Irish Journal of Sociology* 12, 2: 28–49

Hogan, G. (1987) 'Law and Religion: Church–State Relations in Ireland from Independence to the Present Day' *American Journal of Comparative Law* 35: 47–96

Holland, J. (2003) *Modern Catholic Social Teaching: The Popes Confront the Industrial Age, 1740–1958* New York: Paulist Press

Holmes, E. (2009) 'Reforming Ireland? An Inquiry from the Standpoint Afforded by Rival Traditions' *Catholic Social Science Review* 14: 305–320

Horan, J. (1992) *Memoirs 1911–1986* Dingle: Brandon Books

Horgan, J. (1997) *Sean Lemass: The Enigmatic Patriot* Dublin: Gill and Macmillan

Hornsby-Smith, P. and C. T. Whelan (1994) 'Religious and Moral Values' pp. 7–44 in C.T. Whelan (ed.) *Values and Social Change in Ireland* Dublin: Gill and Macmillan

Humphreys, A. J. (1955) 'Migration to Dublin: Its Social Effects' *Christus Rex* 9, 3: 192–199

Humphreys, A. J. (1966) *New Dubliners: Urbanisation and the Irish Family* London: Routledge and Kegan Paul

Inglis, T. (1998) *Moral Monopoly: The Rise and Fall of the Catholic Church in Modern Ireland* Dublin: UCD Press

Inter-Departmental Committee to Establish the Facts of State Involvement in the Magdalen Laundries (2013) *Report* Dublin: Stationery Office [McAleese report]

Jackson, J. A. (2004) 'Research Policy and Practice in Ireland: A Historical Perspective' pp. 23–40 in M. MacLachlan and M. Caball (eds) *Social Science in the Knowledge Society: Research Policy in Ireland* Dublin: Liffey Press

Jacobson, D. (1978)'The Political Economy of Industrial Location: The Ford Motor Company at Cork 1912–1926' *Irish Economic and Social History* 4: 36–55

Jennings, G. (2009) 'Peter Coffey (1876–1943), from Neo-Scholastic Scholar to Social Theorist' pp. 231–253 in J. McEvoy and M. Dunne (eds) *The Irish Contribution to European Scholastic Thought* Dublin: Four Courts Press

Jones, G. (2001) 'Scientists against Home Rule' pp. 188–208 in A. O'Day and D. G. Boyce (eds) *Defenders of the Union: A Survey of British and Irish Unionism since 1801* London: Routledge

Kaim-Caudle, P. (1964) *Social Security in Ireland and Western Europe* Dublin: Economic Research Institute

Kaim-Caudle, P. (1967) *Social Policy in the Irish Republic* London: Routledge and Kegan Paul

Kavanagh, J. (1954) *Manual of Social Ethics* Dublin: M. H. Gill

Kavanagh, J. (1965) 'Are Irish Economists Too Complacent?' *Studies* 54, 214: 162–171

Kavanagh, J. B. (1886) *The Study of Mental Philosophy by Catholic Students in the Royal University Ireland* Dublin: Browne and Nolan

Kearney, H. (2007) *Ireland: Contested Ideas of Nationalism and History* Cork: Cork University Press

Kearney, N. (2005) 'Social Work Education: Its Origin and Growth' pp. 13–32 in N. Kearney and C. Skehill (eds) *Social Work in Ireland: Historical Perspectives* Dublin: Institute of Public Administration

Keating, J. (1998) 'Faith and Community Threatened? Roman Catholic Responses to the Welfare State, Materialism and Social Mobility, 1945–62' *Twentieth Century British History* 9, 1: 86–108

Kennedy, K. A. (1993) 'R. C. Geary and the ESRI' *Economic and Social Review* 24, 3: 225–245

Kennedy, K. A. and B. Dowling (1975) *Economic Growth in Ireland: The Experience since 1947* Dublin: Gill and Macmillan

Kenny, C. (2009) 'Significant Television: Journalism, Sex Abuse and the Catholic Church in Ireland' *Irish Communications Review* 11: 63–76

Keogh, D. (1986) *The Vatican, The Bishops and Irish Politics, 1919–1939* Cambridge: Cambridge University Press

Keogh, D. (1995) *Ireland and the Vatican: The Politics and Diplomacy of Church-State Relations, 1922–1960* Cork: Cork University Press

Keogh, D. (1996) 'The Role of the Catholic Church in the Republic of Ireland 1922–1995' pp. 85–213 in Forum for Peace and Reconciliation, *Building Trust in Ireland: Studies Commissioned by the Forum for Peace and Reconciliation* Belfast: Blackstaff Press

Keogh, D. (1997) 'The Catholic Church and the 'Godless Colleges', 1845–1995' pp. 54–102 in P. Corkery and F. Long (eds) *Theology in the University: The Irish Context* Dublin: Dominican Publications

Kernan, M. (2005) 'Developing Citizenship through Supervised Play: The Civics Institute of Ireland Playgrounds, 1933–75' *History of Education* 34, 6: 675–687

Kerr, J. (1916) *A Catechism of Catholic Social Principles for Employers, Workmen, Social Workers, Study Circles, etc.* Dublin: Browne and Nolan

Kilmurray, E. (1988) 'Joe Deasy: The Evolution of an Irish Marxist, 1941–1950' *Saothar* 13: 112–119

Kissane, B. (2003) 'The Illusion of State Neutrality in a Secularising Ireland' *West European Politics* 26: 73–94

Knight, J. and N. Baxter-Moore (1973) *Republic of Ireland: The General Elections of 1969 and 1973* London: Arthur McDougall Fund

Kochavi, A. J. (1995) 'Britain, the United States and Irish Neutrality, 1944–5' *European History Quarterly* 25: 93–115

Larkin, P. (1917) *Marxian Socialism* Cork: Purcell

Larragy, J. (2014) *Asymmetric Engagement: The Community and Voluntary Pillar in Irish Social Partnership* Manchester: Manchester University Press

Lee, J. J. (1989) *Ireland 1912–1985: Politics and Society* Cambridge: Cambridge University Press

L'Estrange, S. (2007a) 'A Community of Communities – Catholic Communitarianism and Societal Crises in Ireland, 1890s–1950s' *Journal of Historical Sociology* 20, 4: 555–578

L'Estrange, S. (2007b) 'Religious Authority, Religious Rule: The Priesthood, Politics and the Promotion of the "Reign of Christ" in Mid-Twentieth Century Ireland' *European Journal of Sociology* 48, 2: 239–261

Loftus, P. (2010) 'An Exercise in Mutual Cooperation: The Second Inter-Party Government, the American Embassy and the Establishment of the Agricultural Institute, 1954–7' *Irish Studies in International Affairs* 21: 105–121

Luce, J. V. (1992) *Trinity College Dublin: The First Four Hundred Years* Dublin Trinity College Dublin

Lynch, P. (1965) 'The Sociologist in a Planned Economy' *Studies* 54, 213: 31–40

Lynch, P. and J. Vaizey (1960) *Guinness's Brewery in the Irish Economy 1759–1876* Cambridge: Cambridge University Press

McCarroll, J. (1987) *Is the School Around the Corner Just the Same?* Dublin: Brandsma Books

McCarthy, C. (1968) *The Distasteful Challenge* Dublin: Institute of Public Administration

McCarthy, C. (1977) *Trade Unions in Ireland 1894–1960* Dublin: Institute of Public Administration

McCarthy, J. F. (1990) 'Ireland's Turnaround: Whitaker and the 1958 Plan for Economic Development' pp. 11–71 in J. F. McCarthy (ed.) *Planning Ireland's Future – The Legacy of T. K. Whitaker* Dublin: Glendale Press

McCartney, D. (1999) *UCD: A National Idea: The History of University College Dublin* Dublin: Gill and Macmillan

McCashin, A. (2004) *Social Security in Ireland* Dublin: Gill and Macmillan

McCullagh, D. (2010) *The Reluctant Taoiseach: A Biography of John A. Costello* Dublin: Gill and Macmillan

McDiarmid, L. (2000) 'The Man Who Died for the Language: The Reverend Dr. O'Hickey and the "Essential Irish" Controversy of 1909' *Eire-Ireland* 35, 1–2: 188–218

McDonald, D. (1989) *The Ford Foundation: The Men and the Millions* New Brunswick, NJ: Transaction Publishers

McDonald, W. (1925) *Reminiscences of a Maynooth Professor* London: Jonathan Cape

McDyer, J. (1984) *Father McDyer of Glencolumbkille: An Autobiography* Dingle: Brandon Books

McGahern, J. (2005) *Memoir* London: Faber

McGarry, F. (1999) *Irish Politics and the Spanish Civil War* Cork: Cork University Press

McGarry, F. (2000) ' "Catholics First and Politicians Afterwards": The Labour Party and the Workers' Republic, 1936–39' *Saothar* 25: 57–65

Mac Giolla Phadraig, M. (1995) 'The Power of the Catholic Church in the Republic of Ireland' pp. 593–619 in P. Clancy, S. Drudy, K. Lynch and L. O'Dowd (eds) *Irish Society: Sociological Profiles* Dublin: Institute of Public Administration

MacGreil, M. (2014) *The Ongoing Present – A Critical Look at the Society and World in Which I Grew Up* Dublin: Messenger Publications

McKenzie, B. (2015) 'The European Youth Campaign in Ireland: Neutrality, Americanization and the Cold War 1950 to 1959' *Diplomatic History* doi: 10.1093/dh/dhv0101 (accessed 2 October 2015)

McKevitt, P (1944) *The Plan of Society* Dublin: Catholic Truth Society of Ireland

McMahon, J. A. (1981) 'The Catholic Clergy and the Social Question in Ireland, 1891–1916' *Studies* 70, 280: 263–288

McManus, R. (2002) *Dublin, 1910–1940: Shaping the City and Suburbs* Dublin: Four Courts Press

McNabb, P. (1964) 'Social Structure' pp. 193–247 in J. Newman (ed.) *The Limerick Rural Survey* Tipperary: Muintir na Tire Publications

MacSweeney, A. M. (1917) *Poverty in Cork* Cork: Purcell

McSweeney, B. (1980) *Roman Catholicism: The Search for Relevance* Oxford: Blackwell

Magrath, T. (1885) *Catholic Philosophy and the Royal University Programme* Dublin: M. H. Gill

Meehan, C. (2013) *A Just Society for Ireland? 1964–1987* Basingstoke: Palgrave Macmillan

Meghen, P. J. (1961) 'Community Studies in America and Ireland' *Rural Ireland* 1961: 48–67

Meghen, P. J. (1963) 'Sociological Survey-Work on Ireland' pp. 177–201 of J. Newman (ed.) *Organising the Community: Report and Papers of European Study Group on Organising Resources for Community Development, Gormanstown, Ireland 30th June–7th July 1962* Tipperary: Muintir na Tire

Miller, E. (ed.) (1999) *The Tavistock Institute Contribution to Job and Organizational Design* Aldershot: Ashgate

Miller, P. and N. Rose (1988) 'The Tavistock Programme: The Government of Subjectivity and Social Life' *Sociology* 22: 171–192

Miller, P. and N. Rose (1996) 'Mobilising the Consumer: Assembling the Subject of Consumption' *Theory, Culture and Society* 14, 1: 19–23

Moody, T. W. and J. C. Beckett (1959) *Queen's Belfast, 1845–1949*, vol. 1, London: Faber and Faber

Morash, C. (2010) *A History of the Media in Ireland* Cambridge: Cambridge University Press

Morgan, D. G. (1999) 'The Future of the Irish Constitution' pp. 1–19, in N. Collins (ed.) *Political Issues in Ireland Today*, 2nd edn, Manchester: Manchester University Press

Morrissey, T. A. (2010) *Edward J. Byrne, 1872–1941: The Forgotten Archbishop of Dublin* Dublin: Columba Press

Muintir na Tire (1975) *Parish and Community (A Social Inventory of Three Tipperary Parishes)* Tipperary: Muintir na Tire

Murray, Patrick (2000) *Oracles of God: The Roman Catholic Church and Irish Politics, 1922–37* Dublin: UCD Press

Murray, Peter (2005) 'The Pitfalls of Pioneering Sociological Research: The Case of the Tavistock Institute on the Dublin Buses in the Early 1960s' National Institute for Regional and Spatial Analysis (NIRSA) Working Paper No. 25

Murray, Peter (2009) *Facilitating the Future? US Aid, European Integration and Irish Industrial Viability, 1948–73* Dublin: UCD Press

Murray, Peter (2012a) '"Can I Write to You about Ireland?" John Vaizey, the Ford Foundation and Irish Educational Policy Change, 1959–62' *Irish Educational Studies* 31, 1: 67–75

Murray, Peter (2012b) '"Much Leeway Needs to be Made Up in Our Equipment": Muintir na Tire and US Scholarships for Irish Sociology Students, 1958–59' *Irish Journal of Sociology* 20, 1: 65–83

Murray, Peter and M. Feeney (2011) 'The Market for Sociological Ideas in Early 1960s Ireland: Civil Service Departments and the Limerick Rural Survey, 1961–64' *Administration* 59, 1: 111–131

Murray, Peter and J. Wickham (1982) 'Technocratic Ideology and the Reproduction of Inequality: The Case of the Electronics Industry in the Republic of Ireland' pp. 179–210 in G. Day *et al.* (eds) *Diversity and Decomposition in the Labour Market* Aldershot: Gower Press

National Board for Safeguarding Children in the Catholic Church in Ireland (2012) *Review of Safeguarding Practice in the Diocese of Limerick* Dublin: National Board for Safeguarding Children in the Catholic Church in Ireland

Newman, J. (1955) 'On Church–State Relations' *Christus Rex* 9, 1: 76–85

Newman, J. (1957) 'The Sociology of Rural Ireland' *Rural Ireland* 1957: 75–80

Newman, J. (1958a) 'The Future of Rural Ireland' *Studies* 47, 188: 388–402

Newman, J. (1958b) 'Priestly Vocations in Ireland' *The Furrow* 9, 11: 710–721

Newman, J. (1959) 'The Future of Rural Sociology in Ireland' *Rural Ireland* 1959: 67–72

Newman, J. (1962a) 'The Priests of Ireland' *Irish Ecclesiastical Record* 98, 2: 65–91

Newman, J. (1962b) *Studies in Political Morality* Dublin: Scepter

Newman, J. (1964a) 'Preface' pp. vii–ix in J. Newman (ed.) *The Limerick Rural Survey* Tipperary: Muintir na Tire Publications

Newman, J. (1964b) 'Social Provision and Rural Centrality' pp. 248–306 in J. Newman (ed.) *The Limerick Rural Survey* Tipperary: Muintir na Tire Publications

Newman, J. (1965) *Change and the Catholic Church* Baltimore, MD: Helicon

Newman, J. (1967) *New Dimensions in Regional Planning: A Case Study of Ireland* Dublin: An Foras Forbartha

Newman, J., C. Ward and L. Ryan (1971) *A Survey of Vocations in Ireland, 1971: Report Submitted to the Irish Hierarchy June 1971* Dublin: Catholic Communications Institute

Nyhan, M. (2007) *'Are You Still Below?' The Ford Marina Plant Cork 1917–1984* Cork: Collins Press

O'Broin, N. and G. Farren (1978) *The Working and Living Conditions of Civil Service Typists* Dublin: Economic and Social Research Institute.

O'Buachalla, S. (1985) 'Church and State in Irish Education in This Century' *European Journal of Education* 20, 4: 351–359

O'Connor, E. (2005) 'Labour and Politics, 1830–1945: Colonisation and Mental Colonisation' pp. 27–43 in F. Lane and D. O'Drisceoil (eds) *Politics and the Irish Working Class, 1830–1945* Basingstoke: Palgrave Macmillan

O'Doherty, K. (1969) 'Where Have All the Faithful Gone? A Survey of Religion in the University' *The Furrow* 20, 11: 575–591.

O'Drisceoil, D. (1996) *Censorship in Ireland, 1939–1945: Neutrality, Politics and Society* Cork: Cork University Press

O'Drisceoil, D. (2005) '"Whose Emergency Is It?" Wartime Politics and the Irish Working Class, 1939–45' pp. 262–280 in F. Lane and D. O'Drisceoil (eds) *Politics and the Irish Working Class, 1830–1945* Basingstoke: Palgrave Macmillan

O'Driscoll, F. (2000) 'Social Catholicism and the Social Question in Independent Ireland: The Challenge to the Fiscal System' pp. 121–143 in M. Cronin and J.M. Ryan (eds) *Ireland: The Politics of Independence, 1922–49* Basingstoke: Macmillan

O'Flynn, P. (2012) *A Question of Identity: The Great Trinity and UCD Merger Plan of the 1960s* Dublin: A. & A. Farmar

O'Grada, C. (2002) '"The Greatest Blessing of All": The Old Age Pension in Ireland' *Past and Present* 175: 124–161

O'Halpin, E. (1999) *Defending Ireland: The Irish State and Its Enemies since 1922* Oxford: Oxford University Press

O'Halpin, E. (2002) 'Irish Neutrality in the Second World War' pp. 283–303 in N. Wylie (ed.) *European Neutrals and Non-Belligerents during the Second World War* Cambridge: Cambridge University Press

O'Leary, D. (2000) *Vocationalism and Social Catholicism in Twentieth Century Ireland: The Search for a Christian Social Order* Dublin: Irish Academic Press

O'Leary, D. (2004) 'Vocationalism in Emergency Ireland' pp. 230–243 in D. Keogh and M. O'Driscoll (eds) *Ireland in World War Two: Diplomacy and Survival* Cork: Mercier Press

O'Leary, D. (2012) *Irish Catholicism and Science: From 'Godless Colleges' to the Celtic Tiger* Cork: Cork University Press

O'Malley, E. (1989) *Industry and Economic Development* Dublin: Gill and Macmillan

O'Rahilly, A. (1916) *A Guide to Books for Social Students and Workers* Dublin: Educational Company of Ireland

Ottaviani, A. (1954) *Duties of the Catholic State in regard to Religion* Thurles and Dublin: 'The Tipperary Star' and Regina Publications

Papadopoulos, G. (1994) *Education 1960–1990: The OECD Perspective* Paris: Organisation for Economic Cooperation and Development

Power, B. (1969) 'Opinions and Attitudes of Irish University Students' at http://brianpowerswriting.com/media/cd06d71e7f431cecffff8016ffea400a.pdf (accessed 2 October 2015)

Privilege, J. (2009) *Michael Logue and the Catholic Church in Ireland, 1879–1925* Manchester: Manchester University Press

Puirseil, N. (2007) *The Irish Labour Party, 1922–73* Dublin: UCD Press

Raftery, M. and E. O'Sullivan (1999) *Suffer the Little Children: The Inside Story of Ireland's Industrial Schools* Dublin: New Island Books

Raven, J. (1971) 'Social and Economic Development' *Social Studies* 0, 0: 49–55

Raymond, R.J. (1985) 'The Marshall Plan and Ireland, 1947–52' pp. 295–328 in P. J. Drudy (ed.) *The Irish in America: Emigration Assimilation and Impact* Cambridge: Cambridge University Press

Robins, J. (1993) *Custom House People* Dublin: Institute of Public Administration

Rogers, E. M. (2003) *Diffusion of Innovations*, 5th edn, New York: Simon and Schuster

Rouse, P. (2000) *Ireland's Own Soil: Government and Agriculture in Ireland, 1945 to 1965* Dublin: Irish Farmers' Journal

Rosenberg, J. L. (1980) 'The 1941 Mission of Frank Aiken to the United States: An American Perspective' *Irish Historical Studies* 22, 86: 162–177

Ryan, L. (1979) 'Church and Politics: The Last Twenty-Five Years' *The Furrow* 30, 1: 3–18

Rynne, S. (1960) *Canon John Hayes, Founder of Muintir na Tire, The People of the Land* Dublin: Clonmore and Reynolds

Saunders, F. S. (1999) *Who Paid the Piper? The CIA and the Cultural Cold War* London: Granta

Scully, J. (1968) 'The Pilot Area Development Programme' *Journal of the Statistical and Social Inquiry Society of Ireland* 21, 6: 51–71

Sheehan, J. (1987) 'Higher Education: The Case for Selective Measures' University College Dublin Centre for Economic Research Policy Paper No. 25

Simey, T. S. and M. B. Simey (1960) *Charles Booth: Social Scientist* Oxford: Oxford University Press

Smith, L. and S. Healy (1996) *Farm Organisations in Ireland: A Century of Progress* Dublin: Four Courts Press

Spencer, A. E. C. W. (1964) 'The Newman Demographic Survey 1953–64: Reflection on the Birth, Life and Death of a Catholic Institute for Socio-Religious Research' *Social Compass* 11, 3–4: 31–40

Spencer, A. E. C. W. (2012) *Arrangements for the Integration of Irish Immigrants in England and Wales* Dublin: Irish Manuscripts Commission

Streib, G. F. (1968) 'Old Age in Ireland: Demographic and Sociological Aspect' *Gerontologist* 8: 227–235

Streib, G. F. (1970a) 'Farmers and Urbanites: Attitudes towards Intergenerational Relations in Ireland' *Rural Sociology* 35, 1: 26–39

Streib, G. F. (1970b) 'Migration and Filial Bonds: Attitudes of Cork Farmers and Dublin Men' *Irish Journal of Agricultural Economics and Rural Sociology* 3, 1: 61–73

Streib, G. F. (1973a) 'Attitudes of the Irish towards Changes in the Catholic Church' *Social Compass* 20, 1: 49–68

Streib, G. F. (1973b) 'Social Stratification on the Republic of Ireland: The Horizontal and Vertical Mosaic' *Ethnology* 12, 3: 341–357

Streib, G. F. (1974) 'The Restoration of the Irish Language: Behavioural and Symbolic Aspects' *Ethnicity* 1: 73–89

Sturgess, G. and P. Chubb (1988) *Judging the World: Law and Politics in the World's Leading Courts* London: Butterworths

Sutton, F. X. (1987) 'The Ford Foundation: The Early Years' *Daedalus* 116, 1: 41–91

Sweeney, P. (1983) 'The PAYE Sector's Perspective of Taxation and Trade Union Demand for Reform' *Journal of the Statistical and Social Inquiry Society of Ireland* 25, 1: 27–35

Thomason, G. (1961) *Community Development in Ireland* Tipperary: Muintir na Tire

Thomason, G. (1962a) *Rural Community Development: Aspects of the U.S. Approach to Rural Community Development* Tipperary: Muintir na Tire

Thomason, G. (1962b) *The Community's Industry* Tipperary: Muintir na Tire

Tierney, M. (2004) *The Story of Muintir na Tire 1931–2001: The First Seventy Years* Tipperary: Muintir na Tire

Tiratsoo, N. and J. Tomlinson (1998) *Industrial Efficiency and Conservatism, 1951–1964: Thirteen Wasted Years?* London: Routledge

Trist, E. and H. Murray (eds) (1990) *The Social Engagement of the Social Sciences: A Tavistock Anthology* Philadelphia: University of Pennsylvania Press

Tucker, V. (1989) 'State and Community: A Case Study of Glencolumbkille' pp. 283–300 in C. Curtin and T. M. Wilson (eds) *Ireland from Below: Social Change and Local Communities* Galway: Galway University Press

Tucker, V. (1999) 'Images of Development and Under-Development in Glencolumbkille, Co. Donegal, 1830–1970' pp. 84–115 in J. Davis (ed.) *Rural Change in Ireland* Belfast: Queen's University Belfast Institute of Irish Studies

Vaizey, J. (1986) *Scenes from Institutional Life and Other Writings* London: Weidenfeld and Nicholson

van Beinum, H. (1967) *The Morale of the Dublin Busmen: A Socio-Diagnostic Study of the Dublin City Services of Coras Iompair Eireann* Dublin: Irish National Productivity Committee

Varley, T. and C. Curtin (1999) 'Defending Rural Interests against Nationalists in 20th-Century Ireland: A Tale of Three Movements' pp. 58–83 in J. Davis (ed.) *Rural Change in Ireland* Belfast: Queen's University Belfast Institute of Irish Studies

Vercruissje, E. (n.d.) *The Shannon Hinterland Survey 1961: Preliminary Report* Leyden: Leyden University

Walsh, J. (2008) 'Have the Snakes Come Back? The Family and the Defence of Catholic Educational Structures in Ireland (1957–75)' *History of the Family* 13: 416–425

Walsh, J. (2009) *The Politics of Expansion: The Transformation of Educational in the Republic of Ireland* Manchester: Manchester University Press

Walsh, J. (2014) '"The Problem of Trinity College Dublin": A Historical Perspective on Rationalisation in Higher Education in Ireland' *Irish Educational Studies* 33, 1: 5–19

Ward, C. (1964) 'Socio-Religious Research in Ireland' *Social Compass* 11, 3: 25–29

Whelan, B. (1992) 'Ireland and the Marshall Plan' *Irish Economic and Social History* 19: 49–70

Whelan, B. (2000) *Ireland and the Marshall Plan, 1947–57* Dublin: Four Courts Press

Whelan, C. T., D. F. Hannan and S. Creighton (1991) *Unemployment, Poverty and Psychological Distress* Dublin: Economic and Social Research Institute

Whitaker, T. K. (1969) 'Economic Planning in Ireland' pp. 291–301 in B. Chubb and P. Lynch (eds) *Economic Development and Planning* Dublin Institute of Public Administration

Whitaker, T. K. (2006) *Protection or Free Trade – The Final Battle* Dublin Institute of Public Administration

White, T. (2002) *Investing in People: Higher Education in Ireland from 1960 to 2000* Dublin Institute of Public Administration

Whyte, J. H. (1971) *Church and State in Modern Ireland, 1923–1970* Dublin: Gill and Macmillan

Whyte, J. H. (1980) *Church and State in Modern Ireland, 1923–1979*, 2nd edn, Dublin: Gill and Macmillan

Whyte, J. H. (1981) *Catholics in Western Democracies: A Study in Political Behaviour* Dublin: Gill and Macmillan

Whyte, N. (1999) *Science, Colonialism and Ireland* Cork: Cork University Press

Wilks-Heeg, S. (2005) 'The Appliance of Social Science: A Hundred Years of Sociological
    Teaching and research at the University of Liverpool' *BSA Network*, summer, at www.liv.
    ac.uk/sspw/conference/100_years_of_sociology__at_the_University_of_Liverpool.
    pdf (accessed 26 November 2011)

Wilson, T. M. (1989) 'Large Farms, Local Politics and the International Arena: The Irish Tax
    Dispute of 1979' *Human Organization* 4: 60–70

Yearley, S. (1989) 'Colonial Science and Dependent Development: The Case of the Irish
    Experience' *Sociological Review* 37, 2: 308–331

Yearley, S. (1995) 'From One Dependency to Another: The Political Economy of Science
    Policy in the Irish Republic in the Second Half of the Twentieth Century' *Science, Technology
    and Human Values* 20, 2: 171–196

Index